NO PARTY NOW

NO PARTY NOW

Politics in the Civil War North

Adam I. P. Smith

OXFORD
UNIVERSITY PRESS

2006

OXFORD
UNIVERSITY PRESS

Oxford University Press, Inc., publishes works that further
Oxford University's objective of excellence
in research, scholarship, and education.

Oxford   New York
Auckland   Cape Town   Dar es Salaam   Hong Kong   Karachi
Kuala Lumpur   Madrid   Melbourne   Mexico City   Nairobi
New Delhi   Shanghai   Taipei   Toronto

With offices in
Argentina   Austria   Brazil   Chile   Czech Republic   France   Greece
Guatemala   Hungary   Italy   Japan   Poland   Portugal   Singapore
South Korea   Switzerland   Thailand   Turkey   Ukraine   Vietnam

Copyright © 2006 by Oxford University Press, Inc.

Published by Oxford University Press, Inc.
198 Madison Avenue, New York, New York 10016

www.oup.com

Oxford is a registered trademark of Oxford University Press

Library of Congress Cataloging-in-Publication Data
Smith, Adam I. P.
No party now : politics in the Civil War North / Adam I. P. Smith.
p. cm.
Includes bibliographical references and index.

ISBN-13 978-0-19-518865-3

1. Political parties—United States. 2. United States—History—
Civil War, 1861–1865. I. Title.
JK2265.S615 2006
973.7′1—dc22   2005057729

3 5 7 9 8 6 4 2

Printed in the United States of America
on acid-free paper

For my parents

Preface

I began the research for this book with a relatively simple question in mind: how did the Civil War affect politics in the North? I knew that there were contested elections throughout the war and that, according to most historians, party politics was a stabilizing influence. Historians agreed that by channeling antiwar dissent into the familiar framework of party competition, elections aided the Union war effort.[1] This rather counter-intuitive thesis intrigued me. I wanted to know more about how elections were conducted under the pressure of war and what they might reveal about the northern wartime experience. Did this unique crisis change the way in which politicians appealed for votes, did it alter the substance and structure of party competition, or the meaning of popular political engagement?

Unlike their southern counterparts, most northerners on the home front experienced the Civil War at arms' length: through newspaper reports, letters from loved ones in the field, and the "vacant chair" at the family table. On the surface at least, life somehow continued: the harvests were gathered, the factories and workshops were busy, and the school-rooms were full. So too, with the regularity of the seasons, elections carried on as well. Yet, I came to the conclusion that the continuity in the wartime political experience of northerners was more apparent than real. In some parts of the Union, especially but not exclusively in the Border States, a military presence of some kind added an entirely novel element to politics. Everywhere the language of politics was altered, sometimes subtly, sometimes dramatically. Even where the outward form of political activity was unchanged, the exceptional context altered its meanings. As Abraham Lincoln observed, "the dogmas of the quiet past" proved "inadequate to the stormy present."[2]

The story of how northerners managed to fight a civil war while also engaging in fierce electoral combat on the home front has been oddly neglected by historians. The lack of attention to this issue is all the more surprising given the central role that the political process played in the re-imagining of the American nation in wartime. I argue in this book that only by appreciating the tension created by "normal" partisan conflict amid a yearning for consensus can we understand the way in which the critical questions of wartime politics played out. Foremost among these was the fundamental debate about what kind of a nation northerners were going to war to preserve, or to create. And bound up with that discussion, of course, were the issues of slavery and race. What I have tried to do in this book is to place the familiar story of the debate about emancipation and the nature of the Union into a solid political framework, one that tries to recapture, so far as it is possible to do so, the assumptions and calculations made by politicians and other players in the political process.

This is a study of American politics at a moment of national crisis, the greatest crisis, in fact, that the country has ever faced. But American politics is rarely entirely crisis-free. Whether it was the Great Depression that justified exceptional measures, or the threat of Soviet Communism, or more recently, the "war on terror," there has usually been a reason for those in power to urge unity in the face of danger. It also true that "partisanship" has usually been a derogatory term in American politics, even though it is difficult to imagine how the system would work without parties. For these reasons, this book, although it is intended as a contribution to an understanding of the Civil War, reflects some of the long-term problems and paradoxes of American political culture.

Among the many pleasures of finishing a book, especially one that has taken as long to write as this, is the opportunity to thank the people and institutions who have helped me along the way. My research has been funded by the Arts and Humanities Research Council; the British Academy; the Prince Consort Studentship at Cambridge University; the Mellon Fund for American History at Cambridge University; the Royal Historical Society; the Gilder Lehrman Institute; Sidney Sussex College, Cambridge; the UCL Graduate School and the UCL History Department.

The two people who have had the greatest influence on my development as a historian in general, and on this book in particular, not least because of their infectious affection for Abraham Lincoln, are Peter Parish and Richard Carwardine. Peter, who died in May 2002, was a great historian, and a friend and mentor to me and many others. As I worked on this book over the last three years, I sorely missed his shrewd advice and good company, not to mention his encyclopedic knowledge of the American Civil War. Like Peter, Richard is a wonderful historian, an enviably elegant writer, and a generous friend. And in their different ways, Peter and Richard demonstrate the truth that great historians are also great dramatists.

My happy years in Cambridge as a graduate student and a junior research fellow at Sidney Sussex were enriched by many people, but I am especially grateful for the (continuing) support that I have received from John Thompson and Tony Badger. Heather Cox Richardson, Martin Crawford, Michael F. Holt, Michael S. Green, the late Mark Kaplanoff, and the late William E. Gienapp all read my work at various stages and gave stimulating feedback. Even when I have chosen to disregard their advice, every page has been improved by their input. Heather Richardson has cheerfully been subjected to my writing on more than one occasion, and to her I owe particular thanks for her tireless encouragement. My ideas have also been shaped by conversations about politics and the American Civil War with other fine scholars whose own work has served as a model for me to emulate. In particular I would like to thank, in no particular order, Daniel Walker Howe, Lawrence Goldman, Robert Cook, Brian Holden Reid, Silvana R. Siddali, Clive Webb, Graham Peck, David Brown, and Jon Bell.

Most of the people I've named so far have been leading figures in BrANCH—the association for British American Nineteenth Century Historians—and the convivial annual conferences of that organization, which I have attended since I was a graduate student, always serve to remind me what a good choice I made when I decided on my field of study. I am also fortunate to have wonderful colleagues in London in the UCL history department, at my former college, Queen Mary, and at the seminar in United States history hosted by the Institute for the Study of the Americas. Susan Ferber, my editor at Oxford University Press, has been unfailingly efficient and helpful. The two readers were generous and constructive in their criticism.

What I value most about my job is that it combines the solitary life of the library-bound scholar with the theatricality and sociability of teaching. I owe a great debt of thanks to my students at Cambridge, Queen Mary and now at UCL for their insights and enthusiasm. I would particularly like to thank the students who took my "Crisis of the American Republic" course at UCL in 2003–2004 and 2004–2005.

One of the pleasures of researching a book of this kind is that it has provided an excuse to travel across the United States, or at least that portion of it that remained loyal to the Union back in the 1860s. State historical societies are fabulous, welcoming places, treasure-troves of under-used archives with unfailingly generous and friendly librarians. At the New York Public Library and the Library Congress, I was also helped along the way by incredibly knowledgeable members of staff. Much of my research was done at Harvard, where I was a Visiting Fellow, using the greatest, most user-friendly library in the world. Over the years, my friends in the United States have made it hard to distinguish between research trips and holidays. For their generous hospitality I want to thank especially Ian Cooper, Emma Prunty, Sanjay Ruparelia, Tanni Mukhopadhyay, Mike Ebeid, Kira Gould, Paul and Karen Smith, and Larisa Mendez-Penâte. I am sure there are others who I have forgotten to thank and I must apologize in advance to them for being so remiss.

I have known my beloved Caroline Brooke for as long as I have been working on this book. She has helped me in countless ways to finish it, not only by reading drafts of chapters, but also by tolerating with good humor my soliloquies on antipartisanship and even agreeing to play Civil War electioneering songs on the piano.

The last word should go to my parents. They have supported me through long years of student-hood and beyond, and this book is dedicated to them with love and thanks.

Contents

NO PARTY NOW

Introduction

The Rebels thought we would divide,
And Democrats would take their side;
They, then, would let the Union slide. . . .
But, when the war had once begun,
All party feeling soon was gone;
We join'd as brothers, ev'ry one!
—Union Party election campaign song, 1864[1]

When the Civil War began, Northerners—like their southern foes—called for the suspension of party politics. Newspapers warned that unity was imperative and party politicking destructive. "Every man feels that this is no time for the old party slogans," pronounced a Connecticut newspaper editor in the fall of 1861. "Politicians may harp upon the old strings, but the people will not dance to that music."[2] Encapsulating this vision of a politics of unity was the title of a pamphlet written by the German-American intellectual Francis Lieber in 1863: *No Party Now But All For Our Country*.[3]

A year later, on a cold, damp October evening in 1864, a crowd gathered in the streets of Cleveland, Ohio, to watch a parade in support of the re-election of Abraham Lincoln. The route was brightly lit by young men clad in protective oil-skin capes carrying kerosene torches. At the head of the parade was a splendid live eagle tethered to a flag-festooned perch and a brass band playing patriotic airs. Then came a horse-drawn wagon bearing "thirty-five beautiful young ladies, representing the States, with Columbia in the center." Behind them, marchers held aloft images of George Washington and Thomas Jefferson, and carried home-made "transparencies"—canvases illuminated by oil lamps or candles—displaying patriotic slogans such as "the three Ps we propose: Patriotism, Perseverance and Pluck." The highlight of the parade, though, was undoubtedly a column of Union soldiers, guns at their shoulders, marching behind their regimental flags and drums. These men had been furloughed home from the battle front by sympathetic officers who wanted to help the President's re-election campaign.

As the parade ended, the night sky was lit up by blazing bonfires and rockets that exploded in showers of golden and crimson fire. The bright lights were intended to symbolize national purification, an image emphasized by clergymen who spoke to the meeting earlier in the day. The crowd, many of whom had spent the afternoon listening to speeches and enjoying the free beer and hog roast provided by the organizing committee, remained into the early hours "lustily" singing patriotic and sentimental songs such as "The Union Forever" and "Just Before the Battle Mother." One song that may well have entertained the Cleveland crowd that September night was entitled simply "Lines to a Copperhead." Echoing the message of Lieber's "No Party Now" pamphlet in more colorful language, the song denounced the "fetid filth and nauseous dust of Party."[4]

This parade, with its potent mix of patriotic imagery, denunciations of partisanship, and manifest partisan purpose, was typical of many hundreds of similar events that occurred throughout the North during the war. It illustrated the importance of the political process in the re-construction of American nationalism: concepts of party and nation were deeply interconnected in Civil War America. If Northerners sometimes seemed to fight each other with almost as much venom as they reserved for the Southern rebels, perhaps a party battle that revolved around fundamental questions of loyalty and patriotism exacerbated the problem.

One of the distinctive features of American political culture from the Revolution onwards was that nationalist rites, while ostensibly a reflection of patriotic unity and ideological consensus, had always been rooted in political conflict.[5] In the midst of a civil war, this conflation of party and nation had more momentous consequences than in times of peace. The tension between the habits and patterns of antebellum partisanship and the pressures of an utterly new situation created an instability that was never fully resolved.[6] If, as many historians have argued, participation in nineteenth-century American elections was a signifier of citizenship and an expression of community identity—in other words, if on some level, it was always about nationhood—then the Civil War raised the stakes even higher: electoral politics in wartime became more than ever a battle over who constituted the legitimate nation.

Whatever Francis Lieber may have advocated, it was difficult—not to say impossible—for Civil War Northerners to organize politically in anything other than a partisan way. No one of prominence ever suggested that the wartime emergency justified suspending elections. Elections were, after all, the symbol of the great American experiment with an egalitarian democracy. Nineteenth-century Americans were proud that their republic was the first nation in the modern world in which white men could participate equally in the process of choosing their rulers. But if there were to be elections, and if people were to become deeply divided over basic questions about what kind of nation they were fighting for, then the partisan form was unavoidable. Partisanship provided the organizing basis for

Congress and state legislatures, guided policy-making, and provided the indignation and moral outrage that was the stock in trade of many antebellum newspapers. Party appointees staffed the federal and state governments, and ran the post office and the customs houses. Parties controlled the electoral process itself: they printed and distributed the ballot papers and even counted the votes.[7] In America, parties served functions in society and the state that elsewhere were performed by nonpartisan institutions such as a monarchy, a professional civil service, local magistrates, or a standing army. In such circumstances, administration supporters like Lieber, or the crowds marching in Cleveland, could only call for an abandonment of partisanship because they did not consider the administration to be a party at all. As one Republican explained the situation in 1862, "the Administration party . . . really becomes the nation."[8] He could equally well have reversed the proposition.

In refuting their own partisanship—insisting that they did "not deserve to be called a party"—Republicans wanted not just to win elections but to delegitimize and destroy their partisan opponents.[9] Convinced that partisan opposition could never be respectable or constructive, that even organizing a Democratic public meeting carried the serious implication of treason, administration supporters fought the war against their internal enemies in the North as fiercely as they did against their Southern foes. "Factions in the North will co-operate by contrary measures with factions in the South," warned Lincoln's Secretary of State, William H. Seward, in 1862, "but we shall survive the combination."[10] When Peace Democrats, or Copperheads as they were known, ran in elections calling for an armistice and savaging the Lincoln administration not just for its emancipation policy but as a tyrannous usurper of republican government, administration supporters were quick to connect partisanship with treason. Drawing on a nonpartisan patriotic ideal dating back to the founders, Lincoln supporters presented a vision of patriotic loyalty and unity that was intended to stand in opposition to the "divisive" partisanship that they associated with Democrats, demagoguery and disloyalty.

In order to act politically, many Civil War Northerners denied their own partisanship and the legitimacy—or patriotism—of their opponents. In the week of the 1864 presidential election, an editorial in *Harper's Weekly* warned its readers that the contest would decide "the most important question in history," whether the American republic would succumb to the fate of all previous republics and allow "party spirit" to "overpower patriotism."[11] "Factionalism," warned another newspaper editor, has "sapped our national will."[12] Meanwhile, protestant ministers told their flocks that the cause at stake was no less than a "holy crusade," one that was "higher than party."[13] The word *Tory*—used to curse loyalists in the Revolution and long associated with the royalist cause in England—was a particularly emotive epithet employed liberally by administration supporters to describe partisan opponents.[14]

This wartime political language arising out of the tension between "normal" party conflict and the pressure for unity in the face of the enemy provides a lens through which to interpret the political and ideological shifts that took place during the war. This book will trace the subtle but determined way in which administration supporters connected a powerful nationalist ideology to antislavery arguments and will argue that an antiparty discourse was critical to the process. Through the mechanism of purportedly nonpartisan organizations like the Loyal Publication Society, elite Republicans tried to construct an ideal relationship between citizens and government by inculcating a proper patriotic spirit in the people while also asserting the elites' own claims to moral and political leadership. They did this because to many Republicans, slavery was only the most virulent symptom of a larger national malaise. Yankee Protestant elites, with their allies in the evangelical churches and with the moral idealism of rank and file Republicans behind them, saw the war as the great test of the discipline and virtue of the republic. Historians have long recognized the importance of the war to the formation of a new upper class identity. What has been less noticed is that antipartisanship was intrinsic to this elite-influenced Yankee conception of patriotism.[15]

The book also explores the impact of the war on the way in which Northerners understood the meaning of elections. "Politics never much interested me before . . . but they seem to matter now," wrote Mattie Blanchard, the wife of a Connecticut soldier, in 1863.[16] A sentiment common in Civil War letters and diaries, politics mattered for Northerners like Blanchard because it raised questions about race, slavery and national identity. Such profound questions intensified the significance of electoral battles, which frequently spilled over into violence or the threat of violence. At the same time, the creation of a mass citizen army added a new element to the political process. The army was a community that could politicize men on an unprecedented scale in a context that exemplified the theoretical and practical difficulties of reconciling free elections with partisan organization. It also became an active agent in the electoral process in some parts of the North and the Border States, demonstrating clearly the association of loyalty with support for the Lincoln administration.

This book contends that politicians' attempts to mobilize voters and to build new alliances in shifting sands, took place in a climate in which "old parties" had been discredited. Clearly, in such circumstances, party identities and alignments were fluid not fixed.[17] Quite simply, the two-party system of Republicans and Democrats that characterized Gilded Age politics was not yet securely in place during the war.[18] For much of the 1850s the party system had been in flux, and the coming of war did nothing to dampen the ubiquitous assumption of politicians that important groups of voters—particularly former Whigs and Know-Nothings—were, in Michael Holt's phrase, "up for grabs."[19] As many historians have noted, although initially most Democrats and conservative former Whigs could

unite with all wings of the Republican Party in support of a war to preserve the Union, beneath that superficial unity lay profound differences
about the implications of the war for the kind of nation that the United
States was to become.[20] This book argues that the initial patriotic consensus splintered in a complex way. Different groups laid claim to the mantle
of patriotism, battling to define loyalty. A large number of Northerners,
describing themselves as Unionists and conservatives, fiercely opposed
secession but argued that abolitionists had to share some of the blame
for the crisis. Conservatives were the swing voters of the Civil War. Some
became fervent supporters of emancipation on the grounds that it was
the only way to win the war; others retreated into increasingly despairing
attacks on the radicalism of the administration that shaded into sympathy
for the rebel cause; many more vacillated between these two extremes.
Only in the climactic election of 1864 did the exigencies of a presidential
race polarize political opinion into two clear-cut camps. Once it became
likely that slavery would be destroyed by the war, many even wondered
if the electorally successful Republican Party had a future. "The mission
of the Republican Party was ended when its work was accomplished,"
claimed radical Republican Senator Samuel Pomeroy of Kansas in 1864.
"That work was to stay the progress of slavery and preserve the public
domain to freedom. It never pretended to aim at more. But it made two
splendid campaigns and died in its last triumph!"[21]

The approach taken in this book, emphasizing the fluidity and the
tensions within the Northern party system and stressing the importance
of a discourse of antiparty patriotism, makes it easy to explain the most
distinctive institutional development of Northern wartime politics: the
creation of the Union Party.[22] Union parties were not always initiated by
Republicans, and they were usually supported enthusiastically by non-
Democrat conservatives. Initially, radicals in the Republican Party opposed
the Union Party strategy, correctly fearing that it was a plot to marginalize
the revolutionary agenda of many radicals who saw the war as a chance
to destroy the Southern slave system and the social and cultural system
that sustained it. However, by 1863, the radical aims of emancipation, and
a new conception of nationality based on equal rights had itself harnessed
the themes of "Union."

On one level the malleability of party labels and the use of antiparty
rhetoric were an extension of the process of Republican party–building;
this populist rhetorical style was suited to a nationalist appeal driven by the
moral power inherent in the wartime themes of emancipation and national
redemption. On another level, though, something of the complexity of
wartime political culture is lost if we depict the antiparty discourse that
suffused wartime politics simply as a cynical Republican electoral ploy.
The Union Party label was not only an indication of the continual process
of renegotiation of the identity and purpose of the Republican Party that
took place in wartime, but also the most striking embodiment of the cen-

tral dynamic of wartime politics: the search for a way to fuse party political mobilization with patriotism and the perceived need for social and political unity.

Wartime politicians had to negotiate the balance between a discourse of preservation and a discourse of redemption and renewal. Before secession, Constitutional Unionism had offered faith in a stable, unchanging constitutional order as the antidote to sectional extremism. Shorn of this context, calls to "preserve the Union" lost their stable meaning. In wartime, a language of Union could be harnessed by some speakers to a radical agenda. The Union Party strategy offered a rhetorical strategy for embedding the fruits of a changed world, most obviously emancipation of the slaves, within a reassuring nationalist discourse.

Chapter one sets the scene by reviewing the development of the party system before the war. It argues that the founding fathers' fastidious republican disapproval of party organization was augmented in the antebellum period by a widespread popular disdain for the practices of partisan "wire-pullers." Given this background, it was unsurprising that Americans in both sections were apt to lay the blame for the coming of war on the excesses of partisanship. Chapters two and three deal with the early period of the war, stressing the sense of uncertainty about party identity, the widespread and genuine desire to avoid partisan conflict so far as possible, and the shifting and diverse contours of electoral competition that resulted. The slow fuse of tensions over the future of slavery exploded with the publication of the Preliminary Emancipation Proclamation in September 1862, with politicians on all sides laying claim to the mantle of Unionism. Chapters four and five focus on new organizations and sites of political action—the Loyal Leagues and the army—that complicated and gave new meaning to electoral battles. Chapters six and seven explain the process by which two-party politics was reconstituted in time for the 1864 presidential election and how the Union Party's "anti-party nationalism" finally achieved the feat of making antislavery politics seem conservative and nationalist. Rallying support in the name of the nation and the "loyal, earnest, patriotic" public was the means by which an increasingly divisive war could be presented by the Union Party as a truly national cause.[23] It was the construction of an image of consensus where none existed.

I

Concepts of Party and Nation
before the Civil War

In July 1861, the *New York Times* issued a premature obituary: "The party has failed us. Party organization is dead." No tears were to be shed for this particular casualty of war. Partisanship, it claimed, had exacerbated rather than resolved fundamental conflicts, and as a result had "brought the nation to this state of Armageddon."[1] This line of analysis was strikingly similar to the strong antiparty political culture in the Confederacy, which celebrated the ideal of consensus and national harmony.[2] From the new Confederate capital, the *Richmond Whig* voiced widely held views when it announced that it had a "very great aversion to anything like party in a crisis such as this" and argued that "the old system [of parties] has failed, and we should profit by the failure for our future guidance."[3] Historians have conventionally argued that party political competition contributed to political stability and aided the development of the United States in the nineteenth century.[4] Civil War Americans were much less sanguine. While declarations that party conflict should cease obviously have to be understood in the context of the unprecedented crisis of civil war, they were also shaped, inevitably, by assumptions about politics that pre-dated the firing on Fort Sumter.

Civil War Americans on both sides of the conflict, and in all parties, had been schooled to see parties as potentially dangerous, even though the realities of organizing a mass electorate and effectively wielding power meant that parties arose almost inevitably as the means through which representatives and public officials could be selected. To many Americans in 1861, the fact that war had broken out seemed in itself to indicate that something had gone very badly wrong with their body politic. Party politics should certainly be suspended for the duration of the war, many Northerners felt, but there was to be no return to "politics as usual" when peace returned. Parties must be *purged and purified* in new forms when the crucial test is over," argued the *New York Times,* explaining that "one of the great providential ends secured by this terrible strife [is] that the old party corruptions shall in some good measure cease; that the public soul, in its renewed patriotism, shall realize, as it has not before, what deadly agencies they are and no more tolerate them."[5]

Two strands of antebellum political discourse were particularly important in shaping the political behavior and perceptions of Civil War Northerners. First was the persistent, if limited, popular culture of antipartyism,
which was a populist reaction against established party politicians and partisan practices, and an effort to create nonpartisan means of organizing
public life. Second was a tradition of vehement partisan rhetoric that made
every election seem like a battle for the survival of the republic. Many
nineteenth-century Americans worried about the way in which what
they often called "blind partisanship"—which usually meant the partisanship of one's opponents—led to a polemical, distorted public discourse
that obscured rational discussion. These two impulses—a yearning for a
nonpartisan alternative and overheated partisan rhetoric—which at first
appear to be rooted in very different mindsets, were both characteristic of
a political community that had not yet fully developed a modern, plural-
ist conception of politics. Both inculcated genuine suspicions about the
legitimacy of partisan opposition; both reified the idea of the unmediated
will of the people.

In the antebellum period, the boisterous and communal act of voting was far removed from the discreet and decorous business that it was
to become in the twentieth century. Rather than simply the expression
of multiple individual choices, the very public and physical act of voting
meant that mid-nineteenth century elections were social rituals that created and reinforced community and national identity.[6] Much more was at
stake than contrasting public policy programs (although, especially for the
active partisans who attended the party conventions and ran for office, policy mattered greatly). A persistent tension in antebellum American politics,
therefore, arose out of the conflict between the belief in free and fair elections and the conviction that the right side should win.[7] The war massively
intensified pre-existing fissures in the political culture. Both the strength of
parties and a culture of resistance to them undermined any possibility that
the Union could have conducted the war with a smoothly functioning and
generally accepted two-party system.

Antipartisanship and Political Culture

Parties appeared to be so dominant in public life that the decades from the
late 1820s to the 1890s have been characterized as the "party period" in
American history.[8] Alongside the judicial system, parties were the primary
national networks that facilitated the transmission of ideas and information.[9] They were also one of the most significant forces for social integra-
tion operating in what was otherwise a fragmented national community.
By interpreting national politics in terms of local group identities and
conflicts, by providing a ready-made set of heroes and villains, and by
creating a community of believers that sustained itself from election to

election, parties played a key role in helping to integrate a fragmented and mobile society.[10] Partisan affiliation was seemingly a key component of the identity of many white Americans in the middle years of the nineteenth century.[11]

As party organizations were established, a new generation of political leaders—dedicated party men like Martin Van Buren, Thurlow Weed and William L. Marcy—began to celebrate parties as "the natural consequences of a Republican and Representative government," arguing that "their regular formation shows the political body to be in the healthy action."[12] Intellectuals sounded similar notes, providing the first, modern-sounding analyses of the benefits of a party system. Frederick Grimké, brother of the more famous abolitionist Grimké sisters, produced a detailed and thoughtful account of the American political system in 1848 in which he argued that "popular parties [are] not only the natural result of elective government but, what is of much more consequence, they are absolutely essential to uphold and preserve it."[13] Similarly, Francis Lieber, professor of political science at South Carolina College in Charleston was among those who, in a long treatise on government, his *Manual of Political Ethics* (1838–39), saw a party system as a natural and healthy mechanism for translating the theory of popular sovereignty into reality.[14] "I know of no instance of a free state without parties," he observed, explaining that "political liberty" and "freedom of action" would lead naturally to the formation of parties.[15] Indeed no state is safe "which excludes lawful opposition, and treats all disagreement from the opinion of those in power, as sedition or treason."[16]

Not all citizens at all times succumbed to the partisan embrace. Recent scholarship has suggested that the "party period" paradigm overstates the depth of popular partisanship and overlooks important dimensions of public life in which partisanship seemed less relevant.[17] According to Mark Voss-Hubbard, antipartyism was a persistent element in the political discourse of antebellum America. Grounded in an ideal of nonpartisanship in local politics and in community activism, and in the grievances of particular social groups at particular times, antipartisanship was a populist means of expressing frustration with political leaders.[18] Antiparty rhetoric provided a set of rhetorical tools to those who wanted to resist established practices or to tap a suspicion of "politics as usual."[19] The Know-Nothing lodges are the classic case of a populist antiparty movement.[20] Beginning as a secret fraternal order devoted to limiting the influence of immigrants, especially Catholics, in public life, Know-Nothingism spread rapidly through the Northern states in 1853–1854 and increasingly supplanted the Whig Party in the South as well. Its nonparty origins enabled its self-projection as an "alternative antiparty movement" that would sweep away the corruption of existing parties and restore a sense of virtue and honor to public life.[21] The effect on the political system was explosive. By 1854, the Know-Nothings were the largest anti-Democratic political force in the North. Stephen Miller, one of the leaders of the movement explained that its purpose was to "take from the professional politicians the government of States and cities." Whig and Democratic leaders alike, Know-Nothings charged, had treated "this country as the mere skittle ground of gambling politicians."[22]

Antiparty discourse also indicated a more general malaise about the standards of public life. No reader of late antebellum or Civil War newspapers or personal diaries and memoirs can fail to be struck by the frequency with which party machines and politicians were disparaged as corruptors of the republican independence of citizens and as the cause of a decline in the rationality and seriousness of political debate. Examples abound, even in the most unlikely places. Abraham Lincoln's old law partner, William Herndon, for example, condemned politicians as "corrupt-fish—dollar-power seekers—mud hunters—scoundrels."[23] The "spoils system" (the term was coined by William Marcy when he cheerfully acknowledged that "to the victor belong the spoils") had grown rapidly since the 1830s. Government printing contracts were handed to supportive newspapers; jobs in the Post Office were prizes for hard-working party activists. The Washington correspondents of supportive newspapers were given undemanding extra jobs as clerks and secretaries of congressional committees.[24] The standard means of amassing a campaign "war chest" was by demanding money from party-appointed office-holders in proportion to their annual income. Yet such practices were never fully accepted and in the 1850s, the collapse of the second party system was accompanied by a widespread reaction against political organization and politicians in general.[25]

The idea that corruption was pervasive in public life, especially in the 1850s, and that parties had something to do with the problem, gained emotive power from the republican tradition.[26] Republican ideological formulations were everywhere evident in antiparty thought. In San Francisco in 1849 the editor of the *Daily Alta California* was concerned that there was a "disposition on the part of scheming factionists in this place and elsewhere, to attempt the basis of party structure; to mark the lines of distinctions, raise the necessary hue and cry, and thus early sow the seeds of division and political discord."[27] As that city on the frontier of American settlement was being transformed by the dramatic rush of speculators hoping to make their fortunes from the discovery of gold, partisan division was regarded as a threat to the republican polity.

With deep roots in English political culture, the association of party with *faction* was a major influence on the founding fathers of the American Constitution who sought, in the words of Richard Hofstadter, to create a "constitution against parties."[28] Partisan conflict appeared to be a corrosive, antirepublican force that led naturally to demagoguery and the erosion of republican independence.[29] George Washington protested in a letter to Jefferson in 1796 that "I was of no party myself and the first wish of my heart was, if parties did exist, to reconcile them."[30] Washington's famous Farewell Address, written in 1796, in which he warned of the danger of faction instantly became a sacred text of the antiparty tradition. Describing parties as "often a small but artful and enterprising minority of the community," he warned that "they are likely, in the course of time and things, to become potent engines, by which cunning, ambitious and unprincipled men will be enabled to subvert the Power of the People, & to usurp for themselves the reins of Government." This sweeping condemnation reflected a conservative preoccupation with authority and order, and a fear of demagoguery, which was to recur in the language of Republican Party spokesmen in the Civil War. Partisanship would not only "render alien to each other those who ought to be bound together by fraternal affection," it threatened to subvert the constitution itself. The first president carefully explained that although "the basis of our political System is the right of the people to make and to alter their Constitutions of Government," the constitution "which at any time exists" was "sacredly obligatory upon all." Only "an explicit and authentic act of the whole People" could alter the government, he insisted. Parties, in contrast, put their own sectional, selfish interests ahead of the "delegated Will of the Nation."[31] Washington's Farewell Address, with its rousing call for unity, was read from the platform of countless Fourth of July celebrations in the antebellum period and, during the Civil War, it was republished as a pamphlet and continuously quoted by politicians.

The popularity of the first president's nonparty ideal was not necessarily an indication that antebellum and Civil War Americans still thought of parties as inherently disloyal, although it does indicate that there was still an emotional appeal to a call for a patriotism that transcended party. More important, Washington's warning, soaked in classical republican assumptions about "cunning, ambitious and unprincipled men," chimed with the mid-nineteenth century variant of the antiparty theme, which was concerned less with the evils of party per se and more with the conduct of politicians and the unscrupulousness of partisan practices. Crucially, even Francis Lieber, who valued a party system, stressed a vital caveat: parties must uphold a certain standard of behavior or they would slip back into the status of *faction*. "By a party," Lieber explained, "we understand a number of citizens, who, for some period and not momentarily, act in unison respecting some principles, interest or measure, by careful means, keeping therefore within the bounds of the fundamental law and for the real or sincerely supported common good of the whole commonwealth." A faction, on the other hand, was either "selfish or sordid" in its aims or it sought a change in the fundamental law.[32] Even if parties remained within the bounds of the Constitution, he warned, there was always the possibility that "they might foment the spirit of dissension, while it is the duty of every citizen to assuage discord, and allay civil strife as much as possible." Party must not become "the end and object," but should be given "sense and meaning" only by "the community, the commonwealth, the country."[33] At no time, Lieber warned, was the danger of party becoming factious more pressing than in time of war. "If an opposition feels really and conscientiously convinced that the war is inexpedient, let them follow the old Roman rule: treat after victory but fight till then."[34] Anticipating twentieth-century political scientists who judged the "health" of a political system according to how closely parties conform to a model of "responsible behavior," Lieber was establishing a powerful normative standard against which parties could be measured. In this case, the measure was patriotism and loyalty to the government.[35]

Some historians have suggested that antiparty discourse also drew on the visibility and power of evangelicalism.[36] Evangelicals prized individual conscience and self-control; to them any institution or social practice that undermined those values by making men dependent, or which removed their capacity for moral growth was a social evil that had to be confronted. The temperance movement and abolitionism were both given moral power by the evangelical community, which saw in drunkards a similar loss of self-control that was most drastically evident in the institution of human bondage. The deep Protestant animus against the Catholic church was also fuelled by this impulse, as was the fear of Freemasonry, which was seen as a sinister controlling force that corrupted men's free will, similar to the Catholic layman's submission to the dictates of the parish priest. The construction of "partisanship" as inherently subversive of individual autonomy echoed some of these concerns. Evangelicals were also suspicious, especially in the early years of the Second Party System, of the new spectacular style of electioneering, which they saw as contributing to a corruption of public morals.[37] To evangelicals, millennial progress required social unanimity. The "foul spirit of party" was creating artificial division in a naturally harmonious community. "Invidious distinctions are made and the parties excited against each other," purely for the selfish advantage of the partisans rather than because there was any "natural and irreconcilable" enmity between them, complained a Presbyterian minister in 1839.[38]

On a more abstract level, the conception of parties in wartime political discourse reflected a theoretical ambivalence about conflict in a culture that prized rationality as the basis for political action. As Kimberly K. Smith has cogently argued, "partisanship implied prejudice and passion, rather than a manly and honorable rational independence."[39] One newspaper editor argued that "strong party feeling, vehement and interested zeal, are apt to weaken the force of conscience; to counteract the sense of honor; or at least to pervert the judgment."[40] If the truth could be discerned by all right-thinking people, then all that was needed was to state the facts. Hence, when a local party committee in Connecticut was searching for people to address their public meeting, they defined a "good speaker" as one who "cracked no jokes."[41] Antebellum newspaper editors encouraged their readers to "hear [political arguments] with patience, and impartially to weigh what they hear, in order that they may be the better judge."[42] In 1831, the *Mechanics Free Press* implored its readers to ask themselves "have you been discussing the subject dispassionately—each endeavoring to promote in himself, a willingness to perceive more truth in the views of the other than he had been accustomed to do? And to impute to them pure motives for holding those views to be correct?—if you have not, and instead of cherishing a desire to arrive at truth, you have each been laboring to obtain a victory—in other words, to perplex and defeat each other, it is not wonderful that you have not agreed."[43]

When nineteenth-century Americans imagined the act of voting, they saw it as the sort of cheery but serious-minded democratic deliberation depicted by painters like George Caleb Bingham. In his wildly successful series of paintings of a Missouri election, Bingham self-consciously contrasted the American democracy with the ribald, cynical, anarchic world of Hogarth's paintings of an election in eighteenth-century England.[44] The characters that populate Bingham's paintings (all of them men) are hardy frontier souls. Even if some of them are a touch rascally, it is the process itself—dignified, respectful, and forever bathed in bright sunshine—that is truly important. That the election series was so popular as to be mass-produced as prints suggests that Bingham struck a chord with his comforting celebration of the idea that the "will of the people" was put into practice through the masculine, communal, deliberative model of election.

How did parties fit into this model? In practice, parties answered the question of how the people should engage in democratic politics: they were a disciplined, ordered alternative to mobs. But in theory, their practices catalyzed anxieties about the gap between the ideal and the reality of democracy. Open to the allegation that partisanship was a form of deference, a party man could be perceived as lacking true independence. Bingham himself was a sometime Whig Party politician, but his art expressed a yearning to see politics as the product of Lincoln's "better angels of our nature" rather than the "base" art of party struggles. Partisanship, then, was, in the words of Kimberly Smith, "a slippery matter that had to be negotiated very carefully."[45] In this as in so many other respects, the exceptional circumstances of war explain much but not everything about the attitudes and behavior of Civil War Northerners.

Partisan Antipartisanship

Antiparty language was everywhere in nineteenth century America, but that very ubiquity can make it hard to evaluate. In a straightforward sense, antiparty political culture was only "authentic" when, as in the case of the Know-Nothing movement, it rejected all established parties and advanced the idea that there was a genuine nonpartisan alternative to party organization. But in other contexts, similar rhetoric could be used by party politicians to claim that their party was not a party as such, but the embodiment of the political will of the "whole people" or the "real nation." There is, in other words, a larger issue here about the way in which a tendency to denigrate partisanship colored political discourse more generally, including the way in which mainstream party politicians defined their relationship to the public.

What David Waldstreicher, in his work on the early republic, has characterized as "partisan antipartisanship," reflected the persistence of an ideal of consensus in a world in which party organization was practically necessary in order to act politically.[46] Federalists and Antifederalists who fundamentally disagreed about the future direction of the young republic could unite behind a rejection of the language of party, while each was quick to identify partyist tendencies in their opponents. As Waldstreicher puts it, in the early years of the nineteenth century, "partisanship remained mostly an accusation, not a widely legitimized (much less theorized) practice."[47] The paradox of early national politics, it appears, was that, although party organization was inescapable, politicians denied their own partisanship and impugned the legitimacy of their opponents. Washington's famous 1797 Farewell Address is a good illustration of this. Despite its warnings against the curse of faction, it was itself a partisan document in the sense that it was intended to delegitimize the opposition from the Jeffersonians. Much of the address was drafted by Alexander Hamilton, a man who well understood the value of antipartisanship as a tool against political opponents.[48]

The discourse of partisan antipartisanship combined a disdain for partisan practices with the claim that the only issue of consequence was the survival of the republic. When, in 1800, a determined Connecticut Jeffersonian, Abraham Bishop, made a well-publicized speech attacking the Federalist establishment in the nation and the state, his angry opponents denounced him for engaging in "the base art of electioneering" which "tended to destroy the purity of elections."[49] Bishop's response was that he had been forced to take to the stump precisely because the insidious influence of the Federalists meant that elections were already tainted. His point was that the people needed to be roused in order to save the practice of election—and for that matter the spirit of patriotic festivals like the Fourth of July—from subversion.[50] To Republicans like Bishop, the decisive election of 1800 enabled American nationalism and the entire republican Revolutionary legacy to be appropriated by his party, just as in the 1790s the Federalists had laid claim to the symbols of the nation and claimed to be the inheritors of the Revolution. As ever, there was much in a name. In Worcester, Massachusetts, the Fourth of March celebration in 1803 marking the second anniversary of the day Jefferson took office, was, according to a Jeffersonian newspaper, "welcomed by *all* true republicans."[51] Their opponents were condemned sometimes as aristocrats, but more often simply as "anti-republicans," suggesting that they were opposed to the very principle of republican government and thus enemies of the entire national project. Those drawn into the political sphere in the Early Republic thus acted out roles that were simultaneously partisan and nationalist. Rival political leaders in Jefferson and Madison's time presented themselves to the public in much the same way as the supporters of Lincoln would do in the Civil War: as the patriotic saviors of the nation against the factionalism and anti-republicanism of their opponents.

Even in the "party period" itself, a discourse celebrating the healthy benefits of a two-party system did not entirely displace older "partisan anti-party" ideas. As Marc Kruman, Ronald Formisano, and Gerald Leonard have shown, the partisan form of organization was inescapable in the hey-day of the second party system yet the mass of active partisans and their supporters in the electorate embraced the practices and ideology of partisanship without rejecting key components of the antiparty ideal.[52] Both parties conceived of themselves as the true protectors of the inheritance of the Revolution, the only legitimate expression of the "real people" or, in Andrew Jackson's words, "the bone and sinew of the country."[53] From Jeffersonian rhetoric, Jacksonians borrowed the idea that the "great body of the people" could not be a faction. Party nominating conventions, for example, became "meetings where the power of the people [was] made manifest."[54] The premise—in practice an implausible one—was that the county, state, and presidential conventions that became such a visible element in the party machinery in the antebellum period, re-legitimized the party as an embodiment of the people each time they met. In party discourse, nominations happened when, spontaneously seeking the common good, virtuous citizens came together to select their candidates.[55]

Jacksonian party builders thus challenged the notion that parties were inherently antagonistic to the interests of the many, but they did so in a way that avoided them having to recognize the legitimacy of their opponents. The self-righteous vituperation that partisan politicians would pour on their partisan opponents, with each side accusing the other of ignoble, purely selfish pursuit of office—of being, in other words, essentially factious—reinforced the underlying assumption that politics should be conducted according to nonpartisan, patriotic principles.[56] Leonard has emphasized that the antebellum American discourse had its roots in eighteenth century England, where parties emerged as representatives of the different orders of society. In nineteenth-century America, the only legitimate "order" was "the people" and Jacksonians argued that, since their party was the defender of the democratic constitution, passionate commitment to it was legitimate. This, then, was a very different conception of party from the functionalist idea of parties as vehicles for organizing political debate that was visible at times in the work of Lieber and Grimké, and which became dominant in the twentieth century. As Marc Kruman has concisely put it, the party innovators of the 1830s invented "the idea of party but not of a party system."[57]

In a similar way, the defense of the partisan press as serving the cause of human freedom by pursuing the truth could only work if the editor was motivated solely by a conviction that the party in question was the repository of all truth (rather than, for example, the product of patronage). Partisan editors were quick to condemn their opponents for being the recipients of party or government patronage. As the editor of the *National Gazette* pointed out "there can be no real independence of the press where patronage is . . . indiscriminately bestowed, or given, preferably to mere party prejudices and designs." Although this editor produced a paper that generally supported Andrew Jackson he insisted that he had "neither sought nor received any benefit from the President;—no attempts have been made upon the independence of this gazette."[58] The ideal of disinterested, independent journalism in the modern sense was not developed until after the Civil War, but most editors adhered to the notion of a *free* press—free, that is, from party interests as well as money interests. The penny press that emerged in the 1830s claimed to be politically neutral. The *Baltimore Sun* proclaimed that "our object will be the common good without regard to that of sects, factions, or parties; and for this object we shall labor without fear or partiality."[59] This rhetoric did not mean that newspapers, especially by the 1850s, had no political opinions, merely that they felt it was important to declare that they had none. Although he was active in the local Democratic Party, Thomas Kinsella, editor of the *Brooklyn Daily Eagle*, wrote in 1861 that he had "long ago found that mere party journalism is a losing business" and that his newspaper was now "entirely independent of party support."[60] In defining the stance of the *New York Tribune*, Horace Greeley made clear that he would be political and opinionated but that his opinions—eccentric as they were often to be—would be entirely his own. Declaring that he would not be in hock to a party machine he announced that his newspaper would avoid "servile partisanship" without succumbing to "gagged, mincing neutrality."[61]

The character of the candidates for public office became an issue of prime importance to political debate in this context. The key to Andrew Jackson's political appeal, for example, was that, as a soldier and as a farmer, he seemed to be a man who embodied the enduring spirit of republican simplicity and therefore above the party fray. Jackson's campaign biographers portrayed him as a "private citizen, committed to no party, pledged to no system, allied to no intrigue, free of all prejudices, but coming directly from the people."[62] The standard of public morals was widely supposed to be falling in the Jacksonian era, now that the new democratic political system chose candidates for their devotion to party rather than their honesty, virtue, or competence. By emphasizing the republican simplicity of their candidates, party propaganda implicitly refuted the allegation that party organization led to a loss of republican independence. The ideal candidate was a man whose life story was as far removed from the grubby world of partisan politics as possible. In the idiom of the day, candidates were introduced to the public as being "fresh from the loins of the people."[63]

Figure 1.1. *The Seven Stages of the Office Seeker.* This print by Currier and Ives satirizes the corruption of party politics in the early 1850s. Based on the theme of the "seven ages of man" it is a cynical portrayal of the life of a political hack: plying voters with liquor in a saloon, begging for office, ignoring the common people when he gets in office, losing office, and hanging himself in despair. Politicians, especially anti-Democrats, sought to harness the suspicion of partisan practices by representing themselves as "above party" (Library of Congress, Prints and Photographs Division. Reproduction no. LC-USZ62-9638).

Committed partisans prized their own consistency—their steadfast adherence to party principles—on the basis that the party was the repository of truth. Equally though, it was possible to argue that lack of partisan consistency was a sign of commitment to an unchanging truth. This was precisely the justification given by the many politicians in the 1850s who abandoned old party identities in favor of new ones. Such a willingness to change parties indicated that one was not bound by "mere party doctrine." The *Philadelphia Evening Bulletin* concluded a discussion about the likely partisan orientation of Zachary Taylor that he "has frequently voted for both parties, now for the Whigs, now for the Democrats, as he considers either right. An honest patriot considers it difficult always to go with the party to which he nominally belongs. To be a partisan, in the usual sense of that term, requires more pliability of conscience than high-minded citizens usually possess."[64]

Anti-Democrats, Antislavery, and Antiparty Discourse

Jacksonian Democrats developed a discourse that moved beyond the denunciation of party-as-faction and defended their own party organization as the necessary means of defending the republic and giving voice to the people. This was a long way from a vigorous defense of a party system. But their opponents—Whigs, Free Soilers, and later Republicans—were even more likely to use antiparty rhetoric. For third parties, a denunciation of the major parties carried obvious political value. Free Soil campaigners in 1848—supporting, of all people, that old Jacksonian party-builder Martin Van Buren for president—sang "Too long we've dwelt in party strife/ 'Tis time to pour on oil/ So here's a dose for Uncle Sam/ Of freedom and Free Soil."[65] Echoing Whig and Free Soil language in earlier years, Republican campaign songs in the 1856 and 1860 elections almost always included an obligatory attack on the "party knaves who rule the land" and criticism of their Democratic opponents as unthinking tools of party machines ("And if the party told him to, would vow that round was square" ran one insult aimed at James Buchanan.)[66] Years of Whig and Republican attacks on the corrosive effects of their partyism made the Democrats especially vulnerable to charges of disloyalty during the Civil War.

Many Whigs turned to nonpartisan means of effecting political and social change like temperance associations and abolitionist societies, which provided powerful networks in which citizens—often including nonvoting women—could have a political voice. While Democrats identified the antirepublican enemies in banking corporations and the Whiggish "aristocrats," Whigs utilized the antipartisan tradition to condemn the professional politicians and "spoilsmen" of the Democratic Party.[67] A campaign song for William Henry Harrison during the 1840 election captured this Whig antipartyism with the lines, "We know indeed that men must rule/ But we spurn the party tool."[68] Another warned of a land "where party men vie in the art of deceiving" and where money was "pilfer'd and spent through the vigilant care of collectors and agents whom party put there."[69] A third boasted that "no party chains" shall bind Harrison.[70] Whigs proclaimed themselves "too independent to wear the collar of party discipline" and were contemptuous of the creation of political machines by the Democrats. To them, Martin Van Buren, the creator of the New York state party machine known as the Albany Regency, personified the threat posed by partyism to the virtue of citizens whose independence was being sacrificed to party discipline.[71] Whigs were particularly prone to argue that moral standards in public life had sunk as politicians put the claims of party before those of country and individual conscience. If Van Buren won the 1836 election, Whigs warned, "the necks of the American people are forever subjected to the yoke of a system of party discipline subversive of personal independence, destructive to freedom of opinion, and fatal to our free institutions."[72] Immediately after the closely contested election of 1840, in which Whigs had triumphed with the warning that the election would determine "whether we are to live as SLAVES or as FREEMEN," an underlying ambivalence about the implications of party organization were spelled out by the victorious candidate, William Henry Harrison.[73] "If parties in a republic are necessary to secure the vigilance sufficient to keep the public functionaries within the bounds of law and duty, at that point their usefulness ends," the first Whig president declared in his inaugural address, but "beyond that they become destructive of public virtue."[74] After Harrison's untimely death just weeks later, ministers told evangelical congregations across the nation that God was punishing the republic for having descended into party strife.[75]

In part because antipartyism was bound into the political culture of their party, Whigs were more susceptible than the Democrats to party decay. Whigs, many of whom understood their mission as being no less than to redeem the republic through what Paul Kleppner has referred to as their "anti-party crusade for righteousness," had never fully accepted the trappings of party discipline and hence the challenge of preventing splits and of getting out the vote had always been greater for them than for Democrats.[76] The issues that came to the fore in the 1850s were those that, to Whigs, influenced as so many of them were by protestant evangelicalism, went to the heart of their millennialist vision for the transformation of society. Not only the increasingly dominant question of slavery but also the apparent challenge to Yankee Protestant values from the waves of Catholic Irish immigrants demanded more urgent political action than could be provided within the framework of the existing party system. By the 1850s these people were unwilling to make the compromises necessary for Whig Party unity.

Antipartyism provided the discursive frame for the Fremont campaign in 1856. Supporters pledged themselves to "sunder all party ties, forget old party names, and unite as one man in opposition to the administration."[77] The back-room deals and factional tension within the Fremont coalition were hidden by an appeal that described the candidate as having been "singled out by the people themselves to retrieve the government from maladministration and restore it again to the cause of liberty, justice, and humanity."[78] In part as a means of binding together so many different factions, the leaders of the Republican–Know-Nothing fusion tickets claimed that the organization was not the result of "party leaders, but of the *people* themselves breaking away from all party connections." One Fremont campaign club declared that "we are not operated upon by party names or party influence."[79]

Republicans offered their leadership as a solution to the mounting crisis. Republican candidates presented themselves as firm, respectable men who had been dragged from their normal business by the exigencies of the time. Shrewdly capitalizing on antagonism to established parties and to "spoilsmen" and "wirepullers," and deliberately drawing on republican rhetoric, Civil War Republicans characterized themselves as independent men, above politics, and removed from the encrusted partisan political practices that they associated with their Democratic opponents. Competing to be the second party in a system that—because of the winner-takes all electoral system and the one-man executive that favored no more than two dominant parties—Republicans used antiparty language in the service of party building.

The new Republican Party's political style was suited to its message. In (partisan) antiparty discourse, images of slavery featured prominently; partisan opponents were said to have surrendered their rational independence to their party "masters." Republicans had denounced Democrats for their "slavish devotion to party" and connected the discipline of the Democratic organization with the ability of the "slave Power aristocrats" in the South to control their lackeys in the free states.[80] Bolstered, in the Republican imagination, by the unthinking masses of Democratic voters, a deadly conspiracy between national Democratic leaders and the "Slaveocracy" threatened the very existence of the republic.[81]

Republicans argued that national regeneration could only be realized through the unification of the North behind their antiparty crusade. This conflation of a virulent defense of sectional interest with the language of national redemption was only effective given the specific political context of the late 1850s in which anxiety was rising about the growing crisis over the expansion of slavery and the profound questions it raised about the character of the American republic.[82] Patriotism as defined by Republicans demanded a defense of sectional interest.

As the Republican Party set about building an anti-Democratic majority in the Northern states based on a nationalist vision that was implicitly antislavery and antipartisan, Democrats responded by emphasizing that they were now the only truly national party. By turning American symbols—the Eagle, the flag, the ritual of July Fourth—into objects of partisan devotion, the rituals of electioneering simultaneously reinforced Democratic partisanship and nationalism.[83] Democrats offered a contractual vision of citizenship, which contrasted with the anti-immigration rhetoric to which their opponents often succumbed. This association between "the Democracy," as it was still commonly known, and the nation may therefore have been an important factor in fixing the Democratic loyalties of new immigrants. As one Irish immigrant in 1850s New York recalled, "I cast my ballot for the Democracy and became an American."[84] Democratic nationalism was based on a theory of states rights. For Democrats, the federal government was not the object of loyalty. The increasingly confident Republican assertion of the power and authority of the government—which was to reach its apogee during the Civil War—was a challenging alternative to this traditional Democratic conception of the nation. While Republicans saw the Slave Power as threatening republican liberty, Democrats saw the moralism and sectional extremism of the Republicans as a dire threat to the Union. Even after the catastrophic schism in the Democratic Party in 1860, the presidential candidate and leader of the Northern Democrats, Stephen A. Douglas, insisted on touring the South, emphasizing his national credentials at a time when all the talk was of secession and war. To campaign in person in this way was unprecedented for a major presidential candidate. That Douglas undertook this punishing schedule reveals how seriously he, at least, took the threats of secession and disunion.

It was not only Democrats who remained resistant to the antislavery nationalism of the Republican Party. Those conservative Northerners who had supported Millard Fillmore in 1856—mainly Know-Nothings and former Whigs—continued to hope for the restoration of a national non-Democratic alternative.[85] In 1860, some of these Old Line Whigs combined to form a Constitutional Union Party that placed national harmony above all else and nominated John Bell of Tennessee and Edward Everett of Massachusetts for president and vice-president. These conservative Unionists were a small but influential bloc of voters in the North who had been marooned by the political realignments of the 1850s and remained especially susceptible to nonpartisan appeals to unity. As the nation collapsed into Civil War, they were left searching for a political home. One old admirer of Henry Clay, Senator John J. Crittenden of Kentucky, concluded on the eve of war that if parties were the product of independent thought, they could also stifle it. "We have listened to the voice of our parties, and on occasions have obeyed the summons of party rather than considered, as we ought to do, what our own sense of duty was," he reflected. Parties would multiply as the differences between men multiplied. But, though "parties may be numberless, we have but one country."[86]

The larger worldview that can be detected in political rhetoric is always, as the historian Robert Kelley once put it, "a special kind of dramatic vision."[87] And the drama lies in the acute consciousness of conflict, the creation of a Manichean conception of the choice confronting the nation. In the imagination of Northerners, parties could be great engines of moral re-birth, defenders of basic values, conveyors of identity, even, for some, the agents of God's will; but whatever else they were, parties were a means of serving the larger cause of nationhood. The political-cultural context in which the theory and practice of partisan politics developed only served, therefore, to reinforce the momentous significance of each election and to bestow, for the most zealous partisans, a righteousness on their partisan crusades.

Northerners in 1861 could not imagine fighting a war with party battles raging. Nor could most of them imagine acting politically except through parties. In the midst of parties, an antiparty ideal persisted, and it influenced not only a populist antagonism towards established parties and partisan practices, but it also affected the discourse and the electoral calculus of major party politicians themselves. The collapse of the Second Party System in the early 1850s was accompanied by a resurgence of antiparty impulses which, for a time, offered the most effective strategies for political mobilization. The Republican Party's rhetorical construction of a patriotic political community that transcended partisan identifications was to take on even greater significance in wartime, while the Democracy's claim to be the one true defender of the constitutional liberty of the people was to be tested to the limit.

2

The Patriotic Imperative

Their past ambivalence about the legitimacy of parties made it seem natural for Northerners in 1861 to identify partisanship as one of the evils that was responsible for the national crisis. The first year of the war, however, was to demonstrate that constructing an alternative, nonpartisan approach to politics and public life was much more difficult. Throughout the period between Lincoln's election and the spring of 1862, two theoretically opposed conceptions of politics—one rooted in the language of national unity, the other in that of partisan conflict—jostled uneasily, neither fully able to absorb the other. The assertion of national unity naturally served the interests of the administration and its supporters by delegitimizing organized opposition—whether it came from radicals who saw the war as the long-awaited moment of national redemption or from libertarian Democrats who refused to support a war of subjugation.

The Secession Crisis and the Party System

Although most observers of the political scene had predicted Lincoln's election in 1860, it was no less of a shock to Southerners when it came. They feared a president who had been elected by a party that had no ideological or organizational ties to the South and that grounded its public image in opposition to the exercise (or at least the excess) of Southern political power. Above all, the profoundly antislavery tenor of Republicans rendered them beyond the pale to most white Southerners. Lincoln's professed commitment to respect the constitutional protection afforded to slavery did not alter the fatalistic but plausible conviction of secessionists in the South that the Republican victory was a momentous watershed. For the first time in the history of the republic, a candidate had been elected without any electoral support at all in one of the two great sections of the Union. No Southerner had ever been elected president without support in the North, now a Northerner had been elected without even appearing on the ballot in several states in the Deep South. Demographics and political logic were freezing the Southern slave interest out of power. On December 20, 1860, a convention called by the South Carolina legislature passed an ordinance of secession, proclaiming the state's independence from the Union. Over the next two months, with much debate about timing and tactics, but a general and rising sense that dramatic action of some kind was needed to protect Southern interests and self-respect, other Deep South states followed suit.

These avowedly revolutionary moves were met in the North with a confused but rather muted response. Southerners had been threatening secession for a generation and, even now, many in the North assumed that this was yet another game of brinkmanship. Future leaders of the antiwar faction of the Democratic Party such as Ohio Congressman Clement Vallandigham and Samuel Medary of the Columbus *Crisis*, drafted anti-coercionist petitions and wrote pro-peace editorials. These were the men who became known as "copperheads"—a term of abuse hurled at them by their opponents who likened them to snakes in the grass. By the end of the war, with the Confederacy collapsing at the feet of the invading Union army, Copperhead warnings that the coercion of the South would destroy the old Union sounded lonely and irrelevant. But in the early spring of 1861 many voices, from across the political spectrum, opposed the resort to arms. Democratic President James Buchanan was widely ridiculed for his ineffectual declaration that, although secession was an illegal assault on the Constitution, there was no legal, constitutional way of stopping it. He explained to Congress in December 1860 that "the power to make war against a State is at variance with the whole spirit and intent of the Constitution. . . . Our Union rests upon public opinion and [can] never be connected by the blood of its citizens in civil war. If it cannot live in the affections of the people, it must one day perish."[1] Peace rallies were held in many cities. Some reportedly drew crowds of more than ten thousand. At one such public meeting in Baltimore in March, 1861, the patrician lawyer and scholar Severn Teackle Wallis, in tune with the prevailing political mood, sought to reinforce his moral authority as a speaker by telling his audience that "I am no politician" and "I belong to no party." He was "bewildered and angered," he explained, by those "who talk with sober seriousness about hanging and shooting men back into brotherhood and union with us." The Union, declared Wallis, "is a great blessing and a glorious privilege, but there is no law of God or man which will uphold the doctrine of cementing it with blood."[2]

Not all Democrats thought this way. Some, particularly supporters of Stephen A. Douglas, whose heroic but failed 1860 election campaign had been based on the claim that he was the only truly national candidate in the race, quickly took up the mantle of Unionism by castigating the Republican Party for its sectionalism. Douglas-supporting newspapers often used antiparty language in developing this line of attack. The *Cincinnati Daily Enquirer* was certain that "patriotism, honor and the national good are in one direction," while "party interests and personal prejudices" were in another. The Wilkes-Barre, Pennsylvania, *Luzerne Union* saw but one hope for the preservation of the Union: "discard party names and party platforms and come together on the broad platform of the Union."[3] Conservative newspapers that had supported the Constitutional Unionist candidate John Bell in the election pleaded for rational compromise. The Philadelphia *Public Ledger* wondered, "What is there about this question of slavery in the Territories which at this time forces it upon us as one of such a momentous issue?" and urged the Republican Party to compromise on the issue of slavery extension.[4] One of the challenges that secession immediately posed to the Republican Party leadership, then, was whether "party principle" should be placed above a compromise that might keep the Union together. The questions of the nature of parties and the legitimacy of partisanship were implicit and at times explicit in the debate that followed.

The Republican triumph in the 1860 presidential election concluded four years of steady electoral gains across the Northern states.[5] When the Civil War began, Republicans held fourteen of the eighteen governorships north of the Mason-Dixon line, controlled all but three Northern legislatures, and had won twenty-nine of the thirty-six senate seats from the Northern states. This apparent strength obscured the fragmented, precarious nature of the Republican coalition and continuing doubts—even after Lincoln's election—about the long-term viability of this new, insurgent organization. The call for the Republican Party convention in 1860 had gone out, not just to "pure" Republicans—as the radicals had wanted—but also to "members of the People's Party of Pennsylvania and of the Opposition Party of New Jersey, and all others who are willing to co-operate."[6] The senator who drafted the call commented that, without the delegates from Pennsylvania and New Jersey "we might as well have had no convention at all."[7] As a result, the 1860 platform was less radical on the slavery issue than the 1856 platform, and it placed equal emphasis on homestead legislation and a protective tariff. So long as the South remained in the Union, the Republicans were in a national minority; Lincoln was elected with just less than 40 percent of the popular vote. The party was strongly rooted only in New England and those parts of the North heavily influenced by New England migration. Given the recent upheaval in party identities, there was no reason to assume that the Republican Party could or would maintain its electoral advantage, especially if the incoming administration allowed itself to be perceived by moderate Northerners as placing party principle over the national interest.

After the election of Lincoln, conservatives within and without the Republican Party urged on the president-elect a policy of moderation. The natural process of party-building which had led to the successful appeal to the center ground in the election campaign must now be followed up by a "patriotic," conciliatory approach towards the growing secession crisis. James Gordon Bennett's *New York Herald* urged Lincoln to take notice of the "conservative masses," aligned to neither the Democrats nor the Republicans, who "wholeheartedly support the Union and oppose any man who would haul down the national flag."[8] Bennett was a brilliant, original, and intensely egotistical editor, a self-made man whose much-vaunted political independence led him and his paper to some erratic decisions. An old Jacksonian Democrat, Bennett had supported Fremont in 1856 because his dashing military background appealed to him, but opposed Lincoln in 1860, even though the latter was the more moderate of the two. During the Civil War, the *Herald* supported the Union war effort, but represented an important section of Northern public opinion with its persistent ambivalence about Lincoln and its opposition to emancipation.[9]

In the crisis of 1860–61, William H. Seward, the man who was to be Lincoln's secretary of state, emerged as the Republican leader who fought the hardest to forge a compromise. The irony of Seward's conciliatory role was that he had been denied the 1860 Republican nomination in part because he was widely perceived to be unelectably radical on the question of slavery. This misleading public image was largely due to two resonant phrases Seward had forged to describe the sectional crisis: he had invoked "an irrepressible conflict" between slavery and freedom and warned that a "higher law" than the Constitution determined that slavery was wrong. Although he consistently rejected the moral fervor of abolitionism, and despite his own Whiggish credentials, Seward had been labeled throughout the 1850s as a partisan figure who would not appeal to the conservatives whose support was essential to Republican victory. Yet, in the months between Lincoln's election and inauguration it was Seward, present on the ground in Washington while Lincoln bided his time in Springfield, who was the most visible spokesman for the incoming administration. Officially the next Secretary of State, he was widely assumed, not least by himself, to be its "prime minister," as dominant over the administration as Webster had been during the presidency of Millard Fillmore. Never one to underestimate his own importance, Seward explained to his wife that "I am the only hopeful, calm, conciliatory person" in Washington.[10] The Secretary of State elect, Henry Adams once observed, was a "genuine original," a keenly intelligent man, a wonderful raconteur with an impish sense of humor and a delight in gossip.[11] His occasional tactlessness and sense of humor did not always endear him to his earnest Republican colleagues but it was his commitment to building alliances with moderates among the former Whigs and Know-Nothings that, during the war, profoundly alienated him from the radicals in the party. On the key radical touchstone issues—the timing of emancipation and the plans for post-war Reconstruction—Seward became known as a conservative force. As a consequence the President Lincoln was never short of urgent advice to fire his Secretary of State. But although Seward and Lincoln's relationship was a complicated one, it rested on the firm foundation of mutual respect and Seward was to remain securely in office throughout Lincoln's presidency and beyond.[12] The driving and consistent theme in Seward's political career was a faith in the progress and prosperity of the American republic through economic development, expansion and social reform. He was also an instinctive pragmatist, a trait he shared with the president.

In practice Seward was a party-builder *par excellence*, yet he saw parties as transient instruments that could serve a short-term purpose but whose identity and appeal was never fixed.[13] At a dinner hosted by Stephen A. Douglas for the French minister, Henri Mercier, Seward proposed a toast: "Away with all parties, all platforms of previous committals and whatever else will stand in the way of a restoration of the American Union."[14] It should be stressed that Seward's objection, in this typically flamboyant gesture, was not to parties per se but to what he saw as the baneful, fragmenting effect of party contests in wartime. His strategy, which built on his efforts to build a southern Republican party on the ashes of the old southern Whig party, was to divide the South by strengthening border- state unionism. Through a policy that was "conciliatory, forbearing and patient" he would "open the way for the rising of a Union party in the seceding states that will bring them back into the Union."[15] The *New York Herald* lauded Seward as the "architect" of "a new party" that will arise out of the "ruins of those . . . which have . . . ceased to exist."[16]

In this project, Seward received strong support from Henry Raymond, the politically moderate editor of the increasingly influential *New York Times*. "The great question pending," declared a February 1861 editorial, is "whether Mr. Lincoln shall become the head of the great 'Union Party' of the country or whether a party upon that issue shall be permitted to grow up in hostility to his administration." In other words, who would seize the mantle of Unionism? Would the new president, and the mainstream of the Republican Party, pursue political alliances with border-state conservatives and former Whigs?[17] Privately, Raymond told Lincoln that "the Union men of the South must belong to our party,—and it seems to me important that we should open the door for them as wide as the hinges will let it swing."[18] One of Seward's correspondents from Massachusetts urged the incoming administration to "avoid all use of force" since war would surely mean the "death of the Union." And at least one Republican editor urged that the party platform be abandoned entirely in order to offer a compromise on slavery in the territories that might avert war.[19] Seward and allies like Raymond played an important role in the development of the Republican Party during the Civil War. Their sensitivity to the conservatism of public opinion and their preoccupation always to cast the war as the initiator of a grand future of national development greatly influenced Lincoln and the way in which the party's appeal was formulated.

Meanwhile, a tacit alliance developed between Republican conservatives and non-Republicans who wished to make a home for themselves in a new national conservative party. This conservative constituency included, for example, former Whigs who had supported Millard Fillmore's 1856 presidential campaign in which, running as the candidate of the American or Know-Nothing Party, he had stressed the themes of national unity and patriotism as a counterbalance to sectional extremism. One prominent Whig who had been searching for a new political home since the early 1850s was Winfield Scott, the aged General-in-Chief and former Whig presidential candidate. He advised the incoming administration, in a letter to Seward, to "throw off the old and assume a *new* designation—the Union Party" and stressed—speaking as a Virginian himself—the importance of co-operating with upper South Unionists if civil war were to be avoided. Seward indicated his concurrence with these views by forwarding the letter to Lincoln immediately.[20] Also included in this alliance were such men as Thomas Ewing of Ohio, who in 1860 supported Lincoln but not the rest of the Republican ticket, and Thomas Corwin, a former Whig from Ohio. Corwin threw his weight behind the Republican organization in that state despite his violent and unconcealed contempt for "negrophiles" like his bitter political enemy Salmon Chase, newly-appointed to be Lincoln's secretary of the treasury.

Other potential non-Republican recruits to the idea of a Union Party included supporters of the 1860 Constitutional Unionists, mainly concentrated in the Border States, such as the former presidential candidate John Bell of Tennessee and Kentucky's Thomas E. Bramlette. Southern Whigs like John A. Gilmer of North Carolina and John Minor Botts of Virginia were also prominent in promoting the Union party cause during the secession crisis, reinforcing the idea that a Union party was essential as a "bond of Union."[21] Gilmer, whose Whiggish background and willingness to compromise on the question of slavery expansion was typical of Upper South unionists, urged the president-elect to disregard extremist Republicans and "come as far South as you can."[22] Southern Unionists urged Lincoln to take "a flexible position on the territorial issue and endorse a constitutional amendment reaffirming the safety of slavery in the states." Gilmer also wrote to Thurlow Weed requesting his help in building a "great national party." Such a coalition would give the new president "a strong body of supporters in the south" and would resurrect a "bond of Union" that had been destroyed by the collapse of the second party system.[23] Southern Unionists were confident that a "hands-off" policy, supported by tangible moves towards sectional reconciliation on the part of the incoming administration, would eventually produce a counter-revolution in the Deep South and a peaceful restoration of the Union.

The pursuit of a compromise peace and the reorientation of the Republican Party—or the emasculation, depending on one's point of view—were thus completely interlinked. Gilmer delicately summed up his suggestion to President-elect Lincoln that he abandon his party's commitment to preventing the expansion of slavery as "a generous and patriotic yielding on the part of your section." While this would, he admitted, divide Lincoln from his "many party friends," he assured the president-elect that, "by the preservation of the peace of the country you will nationalize yourself and your party."[24] Similar calls for a "nationalization" of the party came from Raymond, whose *New York Times*, which had repeatedly used antiparty discourse, now urged Lincoln to reject "the party issues of the past" and embrace the "necessities of the future."[25] Raymond was among those who urged the president-elect to issue some kind of public statement reassuring Southerners and anxious northern conservatives about his intentions.[26] The key to avoiding war, in other words, was abandoning the language of party in favor of the language of nation. August Belmont, the banker and Democratic leader from New York, added his own encouragement to Seward for his efforts to make "Republicanism . . . subordinate to the Union, as everything is and ought to be," and thus to "change the proud position of the great leader of a victorious party for the more exalted and honorable one of the benefactor and savior of our country."[27]

Expectations of Party Realignment

With the identity of the Republican Party threatened, a great revolt arose. Salmon P. Chase, a former Free Soil Democrat from Ohio who was widely expected to be the radical conscience of Lincoln's new cabinet, worried that Lincoln was preparing to abandon the "great body of men who elected him." Such a disruption of the Republican Party was, Chase thought, an "imminent danger."[28] Seward's search for Southern allies made him a principal target. "God damn you, Seward!" a Republican Senator was reported as saying to him one day, "you've betrayed your principles and your party; we've followed your lead long enough."[29] A Republican congressman accused him of "starting out after a *Union Party!*" and the radical George C. Fogg wrote to Lincoln bitterly condemning Seward for contemplating the "abandonment" of the Republican Party, "and the formation of new combinations, under the name of 'Union Party' or something of that kind."[30]

In the end, the opposition of grassroots Republicans to concessions on the territorial question overwhelmed the best efforts of the compromisers. Two strands of argument justified this rejection of compromise. Most Republicans agreed that not only was it morally wrong, to acquiesce in the expansion of slavery, but also it would be an abandonment of the values of the republic if the democratically expressed wishes of the people were disregarded once the election was over. As Lincoln viewed the situation at the beginning of 1861, the question was whether to risk the break-up of the Union in order to hold together the Republican Party, or to compromise with secessionists and abandon the principle for which he and his supporters had been fighting. If it yielded on the question of slavery extension, the Republican Party, Lincoln said, in one of his colorful metaphors, would become a "mere sucked egg, all shell and no principle in it."[31] Lincoln was far too aware of the power of party organization to undermine that source of political strength. "Even if I were personally willing to barter away the moral principle involved in this contest," he told a visitor from New England, "I would go to Washington without the countenance of the men who supported me and were my friends before the election; I would be as powerless as a block of buckeye wood."[32]

Lincoln knew his party well. The Republican press vigorously supported his steadfastness on this point. The Republican Party had become, in the minds of its supporters, the means by which the ideals of the Declaration of Independence could be implemented. Very few Republicans could fairly be described as racial egalitarians, yet slavery had come to be seen by the vast majority of them as fundamentally inimical to the values of the republic, just as slavery's advocates were a mortal threat to the freedoms embodied in the Union.[33] Summing up the views of the mass of Northerners who had supported him in the election, Lincoln pointed out to the future Confederate Vice President Alexander H. Stephens that "you think slavery is *right* and ought to be extended; while we think it is *wrong* and ought to be restricted."[34]

If the Republican Party considered itself to have no less than a millennialist responsibility, such convictions energized the already converted and reinforced a strong and active core of party organizers. But did not provide a sufficient political base for the new president. As the Democratic *Cincinnati Daily Enquirer* pointed out in an open letter to the president-elect, "you will require something more than party organization (which, upon the popular vote, was in a minority of a million of the people of the whole country,) to carry you successfully, and with credit and honor, through the arduous trial (from which the boldest might shrink)."[35] Most incoming presidents re-position themselves rhetorically, claiming leadership of the nation rather than of a party or faction, and Lincoln did so as well. He sought to reassure Southerners about the use of patronage, insisting to John Gilmer that "where there are few or no Republicans, I do not expect to inquire for the politics of the appointee or whether he does or does not own slaves."[36] Above all, Lincoln entirely agreed with Seward's determination that the incoming administration must "change the question before the public from one . . . about Slavery for a question upon Union or Disunion. In other words, from what would be regarded as a Party question to one of Patriotism or Union."[37]

However successfully the Republican Party base rallied against any suggestion of abandoning party principles during the secession winter, the issue of political realignment did not go away. Far from it: by downplaying the slavery issue and appealing to a spirit of Union, supporters of the incoming administration thought that they might be able to build alliances with anti-Democratic elements in the Border States, perhaps even in the upper South. Even fervent antislavery Republicans like the radical Missourian, Carl Schurz, recognized that circumstances were "favorable to the reconstruction of parties" in the aftermath of the four-way presidential election.[38] A very similar note was sounded by George G. Fogg, a native of

New Hampshire who was the secretary to the Republican National Committee, who, on the day after the election, wrote to Lincoln about "the inevitable dissolution that is upon all the other parties."[39]

The appointments Lincoln made—particularly to his cabinet—were the most obvious means by which he could build alliances with potential allies outside the Republican camp. Some Republicans urged the president-elect to appoint his presidential rival John Bell, who one Republican congressman from Pennsylvania described as a "conservative, safe, good man."[40] Others suggested appointing prominent southern Whigs such as Robert Scott of Virginia or even Alexander Stephens of Georgia.[41] Lincoln does not appear to have seriously considered Bell and it is by no means clear that the Tennessean would in any case have accepted such an offer. (Bell did accept a Union party nomination for Congress in January 1861 after meeting with Lincoln in Washington—and he spoke out against secession. Once it had been made, he accepted the decision of his state to secede.) In practice, it was no easy matter finding plausible, willing candidates in view of the non-negotiability of the president-elect's opposition to the expansion of slavery, but through Seward's contacts, Lincoln did make an offer to John Gilmer. Although negotiations came to nothing, it still provoked unease within Republican ranks, as did the eventual appointment as Postmaster-General of Montgomery Blair of Maryland who, Lincoln was warned by Worthington G. Snethen, an angry member of that state's tiny band of Republicans, favored the "de-Republicanizing" of the party.[42] Along with Blair, Edward Bates of Missouri, who had clung to the dying embers of the old Whig party as long as he possibly could, was in the end the only other cabinet appointee who had not been a committed Republican for at least four years.[43]

The Philadelphia *Press*, which had supported Douglas, urged Lincoln to "throw himself upon the counsels of the Union men." When the appointment of Green Adams of Kentucky to a position in the Treasury department seemed to be evidence of this, the *Press* hailed the "commencement of a wise and conservative policy in reference to the distribution of patronage in the border states."[44] Of course, it was also in the administration's interest to build bridges with allies in the Border States. In Maryland, the key to such realignment appeared to be the influential figure of Henry Winter Davis, a former Know-Nothing who had supported John Bell in the 1860 presidential election and had condemned the Democratic Party as an organization of traitors. When, therefore, less than two weeks after his first letter, Worthington G. Snethen wrote again to the president-elect warning him that Blair "is for a sort of 'Union' party to take the place of the Republicans, and for dividing the patronage in this State between such Republicans as will go with him in their policy, and the Bell men of the Davis sect," Lincoln was unlikely to be dissuaded from his course of action.[45] Henry Winter Davis was later to take a lead role in the creation of a Union party in Maryland in 1861.[46] He was only one of a number of prominent Whigs who, having supported John Bell's Constitutional Union party in 1860, now committed themselves to the support of the new administration's firm stance in the face of secession.

Lincoln's willingness to cross party lines in his border-state patronage policy was not replicated in Northern states where the Republican organization was strong. All across the free states, the new administration generally made appointments in line with usual partisan practice. Within a couple of months of taking office, Lincoln had replaced 1,195 out of the 1,520 presidential appointments he personally controlled.[47] In this sense, Lincoln was acting like a traditional party leader, dispensing patronage to bind party loyalty. But in other ways, the new president tried to appear nonpartisan. In his carefully crafted inaugural address, the moral dimension of the antislavery case was played down, appearing only in the passage where the new president repeated his formulation that "one section of the country believes slavery is *right* and ought to be extended, while the other believes it is *wrong* and ought not to be extended."[48] Lincoln's first draft had been more explicit, quoting from the 1856 Republican platform's invocation of the principles of the Declaration of Independence, but his new secretary of state had intervened. Lincoln, Seward urged, should follow the example of Thomas Jefferson after the bitterly contested election of 1800 and "sink the partisan in the patriot."[49]

The Suspension of Party Conflict

When it finally came, the attack on Fort Sumter stunned the North, prompting a cathartic outpouring of patriotism after months, if not years, of mounting tension. In New Britain, Connecticut, the first war meeting—as in so many other northern towns—was the church service held on April 14, the Sunday after Sumter. Three days later the town had a full company of seventy-eight men ready for orders.[50] Men rushed to colors, encouraged by schoolteachers and ministers, by their families and by the fear of being left out while their friends joined up. It was natural in a society where the Union and the Constitution had been the subject of veneration, where the Fourth of July orations had become a whole literary genre, that appeals to patriotism should be so effective at first. In his 1864 novel, *The Test of Loyalty*, James Hiatt provided an explanation for why even Democrats signed up. The central character, a farmer who hated the Republican Party and all it stood for, was nevertheless drawn to exclaim, "The country, the country. That's what I'm thinking about. . . . To go or not to go. Here's the corn to plant and plow . . . all the season's work to do . . . [and] nobody here but father. But I want to go and help whip the secesh. Nearly all the rest of the boys are going."[51] Shortly after the firing on Fort Sumter, a New York publishing house printed a song sheet that celebrated the triumph of patriotism over party:

Bold hearts of the Union awaken
And prove you are sons of renown
All ties of your party now sever
And flock 'round your Standard so true
Compromise now? Oh never! No! Never!
The sword and the red, white and blue.[52]

Although he may have behaved like a traditional party leader when it came to patronage positions within the institutional framework of the old federal government—essentially the Treasury and the Post Office—Lincoln consolidated the strategy of making clear the nonpartisan nature of the war effort by appointing Democrats as well as Republicans to key military positions. The old regular army expanded with the appointment of dozens of commanders from the ranks of civilian life, including leading Democrats like John A. Dix, Ben Butler, Lew Wallace, and John A. McClernand. Regiments from largely Democratic neighborhoods, such as the famous "Irish brigades," were welcomed. The Lincoln administration also turned to the international contacts and expertise of leading Democratic bankers like August Belmont in their early efforts to persuade the European powers to support the Union cause.[53] In this unprecedented crisis, the line between the functions of government and private citizens blurred to an unprecedented extent. The institutions of the antebellum state—limited in its administrative capacity and staffed by party appointees—did not always have the means to respond to the challenges of mobilizing for war. The entire federal government in 1861 consisted of only ten thousand civilian employees and the regular army was only sixteen thousand strong, now much depleted by the departure of southern officers and men.

Yet by 1865 more than two and a half million men served in the Union army. This vast expansion in the scope of government was partly managed by nonpartisan private or semi-public organizations.[54] In New York, a Union Defense Committee was created by leading businessmen, half of whom were Democrats, half Republicans. Although it created confusion because it overlapped with the efforts made by the state government to recruit and supply regiments, the committee was in effect a quasi-governmental body, playing an important role in organizing New York's response to the war. Even a member of the committee, Charles Russell, remarked that it was "extraordinary that a committee of citizens, not holding office, ... should have taken in hand such important public measures."[55] The creation of the United States Sanitary Commission—a body that raised funds for military hospitals and the health and effective supply of the armies—was also a quasi-public body that gave considerable power to the wealthy and well-connected members of its committee including Unitarian minister, Henry Bellows, and Frederick Law Olmsted, the architect of New York's Central Park. The scope and authority of government expanded under the pressure of wartime in a way that bypassed the existing structures of government. And the creation of these new institutions gave the class of men who led them a distinctive wartime role that informed their view of nationalism.

In such an atmosphere, partisanship, as a means of structuring politics and mobilizing the electorate, seemed completely inappropriate. An altered political discourse that stressed the need for national unity allowed an unprecedented show of abandoning partisanship. Popular songs celebrated the virtue of nonpartisanship in wartime with lines like "No party nor clan shall divide us/ the *Union* we'll place above all."[56] An Ohio newspaper editor agreed that it seemed unpatriotic to "plot for partisan ends," at a time when citizens were sinking their differences and joining together to defend the republic.[57] A group of Pennsylvania citizens assured Lincoln that they "knew no division of parties" in their state.[58] "I take it for granted that every true American will sacrifice his prejudices for his party to his patriotism," wrote one Philadelphia pamphleteer, while a newspaper editor echoed a sentiment that appeared everywhere in the public prints when he denounced the "the licentiousness of modern partisan politics," as "an evil to be deeply deplored by every lover of his country."[59]

In elections to the city council of Philadelphia scheduled for July 1861, the suggestion of partisanship reaped electoral defeat. The press reported that a "large proportion of republicans wish to unite with other parties in the election of a Union candidate, sinking all party distinctions" but a caucus majority nominated a local party boss who lost heavily. According to newspaper reports, the turnout was low because so many Republicans, and many Democrats as well, refused to have any part in such a partisan election.[60] In New York, Democrats pledged that they now "desire to know no party but the Union party until the question is settled whether we have a government or not."[61] At a mass rally in Union Square, New York, Major Robert Anderson, the Union commander at Fort Sumter, was the star turn at an event at which the leaders of all the factions of the city's notoriously factional politics came together for what was reportedly the biggest demonstration in the history of the republic.[62] "Every right-minded man, of ordinary candor, who has no 'axe to grind,'" declared one erstwhile Republican newspaper, "will agree that while civil war is raging [it] is no time to keep up old party lines, party catches and platforms." Even Democrat Fernando Wood, who had flirted with urging his city of New York to secede if there was war, now declared, "I know no party now."[63] Emergency town meetings were held in order to coordinate the local response to the crisis and every effort was made to distance these gatherings from what the Concord, New Hampshire, *Monitor* described as any "taint of partisanship."[64]

This rush to abandon party politics was obviously prompted by the need to rally round the flag in wartime, but it drew very clearly on a long-standing antiparty discourse. "One of the most prolific sources" of the current crisis, according to a Douglas Democrat from Philadelphia, was the "official corruption" that was seemingly inseparable from partisanship. "Conventions are bought and sold; nominations are sought by the most ignorant, vicious and corrupt men in the community; bribery is openly practiced. This course is not confined to one party—it pervades all parties."[65]

Democrats and Wartime Partisanship

Far removed from the patriotic fervor in his homeland, the old Jacksonian Democrat John L. O'Sullivan, now in Europe as the American minister to Portugal, wrote to his friend, New York Democratic leader Samuel Tilden, expressing the hope that if any troops marched South they would all be Republicans. The lesson of the heart-breaking condition of the country was that "the Democratic party is the natural and the only possible government of our Democratic confederation." Tilden, though, was busy helping to raise troops and contributing his own money to the war effort. He did not reply, leaving O'Sullivan to conclude that the "black Republicans" controlling the post office must be intercepting his mail.[66]

Stephen A. Douglas, who was by some margin the best-known and most influential Democratic leader in the North, contributed to this atmosphere of nonpartisanship in the months after Sumter.[67] On April 14, Douglas met with his old Illinois rival, Abraham Lincoln, at the White House in a meeting that Douglas reported as having being about "the present and future without reference to the past."[68] A Democrat from Maryland was confident that Douglas would "shackle Black Republicanism" and "guarantee the integrity of the Union." Douglas did all he could to create exactly this impression, hurling himself into a campaign of speeches that sapped his failing strength, leading to his early death. "There are but two parties now," he said in his last speech in Springfield, Illinois, "the party of patriots and the party of traitors. [Democrats] belong to the first." Douglas played a direct role in convincing several wavering fellow Democrats in Illinois, including Congressman John A. Logan and *Chicago Times* editor Cyrus McCormick, to support the war.[69] But even after his death Douglas' influence was enduring, and his words in his final speech—words that were to be quoted and re-quoted on banners and broadsides throughout the rest of the war—reflected the response of many of the Democratic rank-and-file, who were looking for leadership to guide them through the unprecedented crisis.

As the editorial columns of normally fiercely partisan newspapers hailed the patriotic spirit that had unified the nation, local and state party conventions stopped meeting, and the Democratic Party faithful set out to recruit regiments and drum up support for the war. Democrats could, after all, draw on a generation or more of a political ideology based on the veneration of the Constitution and the individual liberties it guaranteed. Leading Democrats took to the stump to speak to hastily organized rallies for the Union. One of the most striking sound bites of the war came from John A. Dix who, as Buchanan's treasury secretary, had raised much-needed loans for the government. In a line that was repeated endlessly at rallies, on banners and in songs throughout the war, Dix issued an order to New Orleans officials in his department stating that "if any man attempts to haul down the American flag, shoot him on the spot."[70] The future Democratic governor of New York, Horatio Seymour, also spoke at rallies urging unity. Seymour at least had a record as a leader of the "Soft Shell" faction of the New York Democracy in the 1850s, which had sought reunion with the bolting "barnburners"—the Free Soil Democrats who had supported Van Buren's candidacy in 1848—and so could be expected to be unsympathetic to the Southern cause. At first sight, it was more surprising that Seymour's great Democratic rival, Daniel S. Dickinson, was also transformed into an enthusiastic supporter of the Union cause after the firing on Fort Sumter. The most prominent leader of the "Hard Shell" faction, Dickinson had probably been the Northern politicians most likely to speak out in defense of slavery and Southern rights before the war. He was so identified as a Southern sympathizer that he was a serious contender for the nomination of the Southern faction of the Democratic party, which selected John C. Breckinridge for president in 1860. During the secession crisis, he sarcastically attacked the Republicans for their pretensions to "help freedom." Their proposals, he warned, would mean "violating the Constitution [and] menacing the harmony and integrity of every bond of Union," simply because they would not allow slavery to be extended.[71] Yet, his dislike of Republican antislavery politics was grounded in his own brand of passionate nationalism and he apparently had little difficulty in standing shoulder to shoulder with former Barnburners and Republicans in support of the war.

In the West the leading War Democrats were David Tod in Ohio and John McClernand from Illinois. From Tennessee came an especially valuable ally for the administration: Senator Andrew Johnson. He was the only congressman from a seceding state to remain in Washington. An old Jacksonian Democrat who had risen from a humble background to become a leading spokesman for the poor white farmers in the mountainous eastern part of his state, Johnson had put up a spirited defense of the "peculiar institution" during the 1860 election campaign in which he had reluctantly supported the Southern-rights Democrat, John C. Breckinridge. But Johnson, like many of his constituents, was an unconditional Unionist. He had no sympathy for secession or the slave-owning class, Southern "aristocrats" like Jefferson Davis with whom he had been fighting for years. On 18 December, 1860, he made a famous speech to the U.S. Senate denouncing secession as treason—thus alienating himself from his southern colleagues and becoming a hero throughout the North. After the fall of Nashville in February 1862, Lincoln appointed Johnson military governor of Tennessee.

He tackled this difficult assignment with vigorous policies to discourage Confederate sympathizers.[72]

Johnson was not the only former Democrat to be lionized by radical antislavery men during the war. Benjamin F. Butler of Massachusetts had been the leading figure in the Breckinridge Democratic organization in that state in the 1860 election, but after the attack on Sumter he threw himself into recruiting volunteers, breathing fire on the enemies of the nation with a talent for self-publicity that would keep him in the public eye until his death in 1893. Butler was a cartoonists' dream: short and fat with a distinctive walrus moustache.[73] Daniel E. Sickles of New York had also been in the Breckinridge camp but came out as fierce nationalist.[74]

Not all Democrats wanted to abandon partisanship, though. Even in the first weeks of war, as the call to rally round the flag brought thousands to the volunteer stations, some Democrats dissented. Manton Marble, the editor of the *New York World*, which was quickly becoming the voice of the New York City Democratic elite, publicly opposed the abandonment of party organization, even in a time of national crisis. The man who most came to symbolize partisan opposition to the war was Clement L. Vallandigham of Ohio, who predicted that the "sober second thought" would calm the "surging sea of madness" and prevent "thirty million butchering each other."[75] In the southernmost counties of Ohio, Illinois, and Indiana, areas populated by Southern migrants with commercial and familial ties to neighboring slave states, opposition to the war was inevitably channeled through the local Democratic newspapers and articulated by local party leaders.[76] Resistance to calls for the suspension of party conflict was loudest of all in the Border States, where Lincoln's call for troops was deeply unpopular. The Democrats in Maryland and Delaware, led by men like Senator James A. Bayard, warned that joining Union coalitions would lead to the Democrats being "swallowed up" by the Republicans. These Democrats saw in the war policy of the Lincoln administration exactly the moralizing, meddling "Jacobin" behavior they had foreseen from a Yankee party intent on revolutionary change.

Even in the midst of unprecedented bipartisan cooperation, old enmities died hard. Republicans remained suspicious that Democrats who joined in the "chorus of the Union" were not always entirely sincere. "We have almost what looks like [a united North] but with leading Democrats hereabouts it is only an appearance—not hearty. This will throw cold water on all vigorous action of the government against the rebels," warned S. D. Pardee, a Republican politician from Connecticut who corresponded regularly with Connecticut's senior representative in the administration, Secretary of the Navy Gideon Welles. The refusal of some Democrats to abandon party organization, Pardee pointed out, "of course arises from party feeling and it can only be challenged by blotting out old party lines." He recommended that this be done by "making the only test for office *capacity, integrity and loyalty to the government.*"[77] Such comments in a private letter suggest that the calls for an abandonment of partisanship were not merely public posturing by self-interested Republicans but were based on a sincere anxiety about the threat to the war effort posed by partisan opposition.

Union Parties and the 1861 Elections

In July 1861, several thousand raw Union recruits were reduced to a shambolic rabble after the first major battle of the war, at a creek called Bull Run, near the town of Manassas in northern Virginia. Contrary to the sanguine expectations of most Northerners, the rebellion proved to be militarily and politically resilient. In the wake of this humiliating and unexpected Union defeat, supporters of the administration renewed their efforts to create new Union coalitions that would suspend partisan battles, at least for the duration of the war.[78] Different political contexts in different states created different situations. Nowhere was the ideal of suspending party conflict entirely achieved, but no state was untouched by the movement to transcend "narrow partisanship."

The congressional and state elections held in the fall of 1861 produced a plethora of overlapping labels. In only eight of the thirty-nine congressional races that year was there anything resembling a clear-cut fight between a Republican and a Democratic candidate, nominated in a regular manner. Even in those races both candidates often adopted the Union party label.[79] Elsewhere, the electoral fluidity that had been evident since before Lincoln's election combined with the rise of antipartisanship to further confuse electoral politics. The balance of forces within the Republican Party in each state had an important influence on the form that the Union movement took. The Republican name was increasingly abandoned, retained only in places that were strongly radical and where the party had a dominant political position. To many radicals, it was almost axiomatic that Union parties would be a conservative force that would hamper moves towards emancipation. And even at this early stage, there was resistance to the abandonment of Republican party organizations, which radicals felt was a plot "aimed at men of our stamp."[80] Because it was seen as an essentially conservative movement, the fusion of the Republican organization into a recognizably distinct Union party was most complete in states where the radical antislavery element in the Republican Party was comparatively weak and where there was a strong electoral imperative for cooperation with War Democrats. Beyond the evidence of voting figures, though, it is clear from the way in which electoral appeals were couched in 1861 and 1862 that both Democrats and Republicans believed that the voters were strongly sympathetic to antiparty appeals. "Straight-out" Republicans who wished to parry attempts by conservatives to create joint tickets were defensive and cautious.[81]

In Wisconsin and Connecticut, Republican and Democratic conventions met separately and nominated a Union fusion ticket, although in both cases a faction of the Democratic Party broke away and ran an independent candidate.[82] In the Republican-dominated states of Massachusetts and Iowa, party identities in 1861 remained largely untouched, even rhetorically, by the Union party movement. In Maine, Democrats were split down the middle over support for the war but both sides refused to co-operate with Union coalitions. The Democratic state convention, held only weeks after the defeat at Bull Run, narrowly passed resolutions condemning the war, prompting the pro-war men to leave the hall and nominate their own candidate for governor. Republicans gleefully exploited the situation, renominating Governor Israel Washburn who was easily re-elected in September receiving fifty-two thousand votes compared to thirty-seven thoussand for the two Democrats combined.[83] In the most Republican state in the Union, Vermont, Democratic leaders supported the suspension of party conflict for the duration but a large faction bolted and the party divided between "regulars" who opposed the administration's war measures and a small number of "War Democrats" who supported the Republican-Union platform.[84]

In Republican-dominated states, the leading party had little to lose by inviting Democrats to support its ticket.[85] In contrast, in three states where the Republican Party was very weak—California, Oregon, and Rhode Island, newly created Union parties were dominated by Douglas Democrats but eagerly supported by Republicans who saw an opportunity to exercise increased influence.[86] In these cases in particular, it does not fit the evidence to understand the emergence of Union parties as merely the Republicans in a new guise: the impetus often came from Democrats and especially from former Bell supporters, who of course had rallied under the banner of the Union party in 1860.

In Ohio and Pennsylvania, two of the biggest states in the Union, the new Union parties were genuine coalitions of Republicans and a Democratic faction led by former Douglas supporters. In Ohio, which was to hold a state election in November 1861, the Republican executive committee decided to suspend its party organization and issued a broad call for a Union convention, which met in Columbus on September 5.[87] The Democratic Party in Ohio split over support for armed "subjugation," and the pro-war faction, led by David Tod, eagerly seized the opportunity for coalition presented by the moderate Republican leadership and joined the Union movement. What one sympathetic newspaper reported as "the most harmonious state convention ever held in Ohio," nominated Tod for Governor on the first ballot.[88] This new Union Party, led by a Democrat but supported by rank-and-file Republicans, campaigned on the basis of the Crittenden-Johnson resolutions passed by the Special Session of Congress in July, which stated that the purpose of the war was to preserve the Union and the Constitution, not to subjugate the

South. The convention further reaffirmed its conservative credentials by rejecting a pro-war resolution proposed by an antislavery radical. Even Thomas Ewing, a former Whig senator, felt comfortable endorsing the Ohio Union organization as a conservative body "without a taint of abolition . . . sympathy."[89]

It quickly became clear, though, that the sine qua non of the Union movement was the assertion that continued partisan opposition by Democrats was disloyalty. James Maitland, a life-long Ohio Democrat, complained that the Union party "made great lamentations" when a Democratic convention was called to oppose Tod's candidacy. "They are endeavoring to make great political capital by saying that the Democrats are opposed to the war when it is known they were the foremost to enlist, and spend their money to sustain the Constitution," Maitland protested. Traditional suspicion of partisan opponents was hard to overcome. Maitland reported that "all the time [the Republicans] are crying Union they are removing good Union Democrats from office."[90] The new Union party still managed to sweep the state in the election, leading one newspaper to claim that it represented the "total blotting out of old party lines."[91] This was a considerable exaggeration since Democrats still polled 42 percent of the vote. But that figure represented a discernable shift of votes towards the Union Party compared with the Republican vote in 1860.[92]

The Union party that formed in Pennsylvania in the summer of 1861 was a coalition of Republicans and a faction of the Democratic Party led by John W. Forney, the editor of the Philadelphia *Press* who had supported Douglas in 1860.[93] If Douglas were still alive, declared Forney in July, 1861, "and could see the name of [the Democratic Party] flagrantly used as a cloak for treason, even in portions of the Free States, he would, in my opinion, feel that it was time to set aside a machine which has become so potent an engine of individual and general disaster."[94] Even by the standards of the confusing electoral politics of the 1850s, party labels often obscured as much as they illuminated about a candidate's political position. Consequently, pamphlets and newspapers were filled with "instructions to voters" explaining which Democrats were "reliable Unionists." The 1860 presidential election had bitterly divided Democrats in Pennsylvania and, not surprisingly, this animus corresponded closely to the division in 1861. One Douglas Democrat was prepared to claim that "it is evident to all right thinking men that all our present troubles have been brought upon us by the Breckinridge wing of the Democratic Party."[95]

In New York, there was also a confusion of overlapping platforms and tickets in the fall 1861 elections for state officers.[96] Following the battle of Bull Run, the Republican State Committee proposed creating an uncontested Union ticket. After some wrangling, the Democratic state committee refused to co-operate, fearing, not unreasonably, that it would be controlled entirely by Republicans.[97] The straight-out Democratic state convention that was then held alienated War Democrats by condemning the suspension of habeas corpus and opposing censorship of the pro-peace press. Leading Democrats like Daniel S. Dickinson and Lyman Tremain refused to be nominated on such a platform and, recognizing the power of antiparty appeals, they supported a call for a "People's Party" convention. This convention, which met at the end of September, duly ratified a platform calling for an end to partisanship and an endorsement of the war policy of the administration. The *Brooklyn Daily Eagle* hailed the new People's Party as an "antipolitician" movement.[98] In effect the War Democrat–led People's Party had outflanked the Republicans' Union party proposal. When the Republicans met in convention a week later, describing themselves as the Union Party, they adopted the platform and all but one of the candidates supported by the Democratic-dominated People's Party.[99] Confusing the picture even further, the Union ticket for elections to New York City offices in October 1861 formally excluded delegates from either of the old two parties but was actually dominated by Democrats.[100]

The basic claim of Union movements—that their opponents were disloyal—had some foundation in reality. After the initial surge of patriotic enthusiasm waned, a Democratic "Peace Movement" took off as early as August 1861, with backing from some Democratic newspapers. It was strongest in the Midwest, but even in Connecticut, the most Democratic New England state, a few Democrats denounced the war and urged citizens not to fight.[101] At public meetings white flags—and occasionally Confederate flags—were symbolically raised.[102] A conservative Republican from Hartford reported that "many of the traitors now go around armed, and [soon] the total portion of our community will have to do so in self-defense. And but a spark is now necessary to kindle a flame that can only be extinguished by much blood"[103] It is hard to be precise about the extent of the peace movement, in Connecticut or elsewhere, but it is clear that it rose and fell throughout the war, in large part as a response to events on the battlefield.[104] In Philadelphia in June 1863, a large Democratic meeting, including moderates as well as renowned peace men adopted resolutions that made no mention of suppressing the rebellion but promised that if the Democrats won the gubernatorial election they would use state authority to rebuke federal "usurpation."[105]

The 1861 election results suggest that Union organizations may have been effective at winning over some of those who had opposed Lincoln in the 1860 election. The electoral success of the Union party was most striking in Ohio, but a similar movement of voters could be observed in Wisconsin, New York, and Vermont.[106] In all of these states, the vote for Union party candidates was 5 to 15 percent higher than for Republicans in November 1860. In most places, the Democratic party retained its core support, in a few places, its organizational identity, but it was fighting in a strange new political world in which antiparty appeals dominated political discourse.[107] Democrats achieved most success in 1861 in races where they, rather than administration supporters, claimed the Union party label.

This was notably what happened in the case in Rhode Island, of course, but also in many other places as well. In a June special election in Pennsylvania, for example, a "Union Democrat" beat a candidate of the People's party—the name under which Republicans ran in that state—by winning the votes of Bell supporters who in the fall 1860 contest in the same district had accounted for 14 percent of the vote.[108] The Union party label and a platform of strong support for the war were combined in that election with warnings about the Union-endangering partisanship of radical Republicans.

Not surprisingly it was commonplace in these circumstances for newspapers to write of politics having entered a new era.[109] "We find . . . all over the country . . . a general disposition to let party bygones be bygones," reported the Springfield *Republican*.[110] "The mousing politicians who rattle the dry bones of dead parties, can make no headway," declared the Hartford *Courant*.[111] Across the North it became conventional for Republican platforms to include a "liberal" call to all "patriots," whether or not there was a genuine attempt to include Democrats on the ticket. The *Courant* was typical in characterizing the town elections in Connecticut in the fall of 1861 as a contest between "Patriots and Tories." The Union ticket in this state was predominantly Republican, but the increase in its share of the vote in 1861 seems to lend credence to the claim of the *Courant* that "besides Republicans, hundreds of honest democrats were joyous over the . . . triumph of the Union ticket."[112]

Patriotism, Partisanship, and the Meaning of the War

The hope that the war could be fought with genuine bipartisan support could be sustained only so long as the war could be characterized as an attempt merely to restore federal authority, just as President Andrew Jackson had threatened to do against the South Carolina nullifiers thirty years before. At first, the response to the attack on Fort Sumter enabled Northerners to explain the war in strongly reactive terms. One clergyman, for example, assured his congregation that the war was "strictly, on the part of the North, a war of self-defense."[113] Within a few short months though, Republicans were increasingly blatant in arguing that the war would and should reshape and rejuvenate the nation. Was this a mere "ninety-day crisis" as the *New-York Tribune* initially insisted, or was it, as the evangelical weekly, the *Independent* predicted, a "long and bloody struggle to vindicate ourselves as a nation"?[114]

During June and July 1861, the *New York Times*, the mouthpiece for moderate Republican opinion, ran a series of articles that advanced a broad vision of the consequences of the armed struggle. Taking issue with those who predicted a short war, the newspaper faced an issue that most other journals avoided, accepting that "we can no longer flatter ourselves with the axiom which has been pushed to such extreme limits, that our government rests solely on the consent of the governed." Rejecting the fiction that a few "aristocrats" had obscured the underlying unionism of the Southern people, the newspaper bluntly reminded its readers that they were "now striving by main force to reduce one third of the states to submission to a Government they claim to detest."[115] This brutal reality was to be embraced, though. Nation-building was a process that required sacrifice, perhaps over many years. The *Times* maintained that, "with this conspiracy and war commences the great era in the history of our people." The nation was "coming of age." The Republican Boston *Daily Advertiser* believed that "our nation . . . is now passing through . . . a second birth."[116]

This strident conviction that the war would be the defining moment of American national identity polarized political debate along the fault line of the larger meaning of the war. Was it a cataclysmic event, which would redeem the American republic of its sins, or was it essentially a political crisis, which should be contained as far as possible? Many Democrats were immediately on guard against the expansion of the war's purpose but were constrained by the ambiguity of taking a position in support of the war while opposing those who were determining its ultimate aims. Ohio Democrats, for example, passed a resolution declaring the cause of the war to be "fanaticism in the North and fanaticism in the South" and then declared that, although they opposed "a war of subjugation," they would nevertheless support the supply of men and money to put down the rebellion.[117] Democrats were straining to support the principle of maintaining the Union through war if necessary, while becoming increasingly uncomfortable with the aims of the war as many Republicans were beginning to articulate them.

In the hands of antislavery radicals, this nationalist language was easily converted into a moral crusade. The religious weekly, the *Independent*, for example, argued that secession and war had reversed the old equation of Union and slavery. Now it was necessary to destroy slavery in order to save the nation, a crucial link that later became the heart of the administration's fusion of emancipation and nationalism. As soon as hostilities began, the *Independent* foresaw the beginning of a long and painful, but ultimately liberating and redemptive, process. In a regular column in the *Independent* penned on this occasion from a military encampment just outside Washington, Charles Loring Brace reflected, "one can see, looming up before us, the image of a stronger government."[118] This was to be a war not merely for national survival, not merely to assert the principle that one section could not break up the government without the other's consent, but one that would create a new and very different republic. Brace appeared to view with equanimity the prospect of "perhaps years of warfare" which would "free the slaves" and "desolate the South." The editorial columns of the *Independent* echoed these views, confidently informing its readership as early as May 16 that, "the destruction of slavery and the inauguration of a new social order throughout the southern states will be . . . the result of this war."[119]

For Republicans who had been warning of the danger of the "slavocracy" for years, the diagnosis that slavery was the root cause of the current crisis was hard to resist. Even if, like President Lincoln, most Republicans at this early stage still rejected any crude attempt to use abolition as a tool of war, antislavery ideas were woven into their discourse of nationhood. A dinner in New York, organized on February 22, 1862, by the Republican State Committee, to commemorate the anniversary of Washington's birthday exemplified not only this connection between antislavery and nationalism, but also suggested the way in which antipartisan rhetoric could be used to claim for this antislavery nationalism something of the hallowed Revolutionary legacy.

At the very time that wealthy Republican dinner guests were gathering for their eight-course meal in New York, Confederates were celebrating the official inauguration of Jefferson Davis in Richmond, Virginia. The Confederate President stood in torrential rain and delivered his lengthy address next to a statue of Washington, declaring that "under the favor of Divine Providence, we hope to perpetuate the principles of our revolutionary fathers."[120] A letter read to the New York Republican dinner from the radical antislavery Senator from Massachusetts, Charles Sumner, offered a very different reading of the nation's first president than Davis would have accepted: "Let us honor the memory of Washington," Sumner wrote, "but sincerely honoring him we cannot become indifferent to those great principles of human freedom, consecrated by his life, and by the solemn act of his Last Will and Testament."[121] One of the principal speakers, Reverend Dr. Roswell D. Hitchcock, a man known for the "clarity and brilliance of his addresses, his effective delivery and personal magnetism" told the dinner guests that Washington's Farewell Address was "prescient."[122] The evils against which it warned "are now upon us, clutching at our throats." Hitchcock invoked the founders to warn against the danger of internal division. "It is not enough that we save the Union," he told the gathering. "We must save it as *patriots* and not as *partisans*. You gentlemen are Republicans. What I have been, and am, is no concern of yours. I address you tonight as an American. And I warn you solemnly against going into this holy war as Republicans. Go into it only as Americans, and with all your might." In Richmond, Jefferson Davis argued that the Confederacy was the "culmination in the history of republican government" and that the South was "in arms to renew such sacrifices as our fathers made to the holy cause of constitutional liberty." In New York, on the other hand, Henry J. Raymond, responded to a toast to "the Fathers of the Republic," by telling the diners that "we are now struggling to sustain by arms that Second Declaration of Independence, which is to deliver this country from a still more formidable power than Great Britain ever was to us—I mean the Political Dominion of Slavery."[123]

Like the Confederates, Northerners looked to the experience of the Revolution and to the values of eighteenth-century republicanism as guides to the current crisis even if the lessons they drew were radically different. Hitchcock's address to the New York dinner was typical of Republican propaganda at this time: it made the antislavery case in terms of republican government. Although slavery was "a cruel wrong to the black man" and "a fatal cancer eating its way into the very vitals of the white man," Hitchock declared that as "a local institution, destined eventually to be uprooted and disappear, we can give it tolerance." Only "as a political power, enthroned in our national Capital and dictating our national policy" was slavery a threat that had to be confronted directly. Indeed, "we have registered in heaven our oath that it shall no more have dominion over us." By casting the slavery issue in political rather than in ethical terms, Republicans reinforced the connection between the war to restore federal authority with the destruction of the Slave Power. At the same time they played down, or evaded, the challenge to white supremacy that abolition might bring.

Hitchcock's presence as the star speaker at the gathering reveals the close connection between the Republican Party and the Protestant churches. His injunctions against partyism came with greater authority than those of a "mere" politician. He used his speech, not only to make a case that "true patriots" must rise above party, but also to remind his listeners that the war was a salutary reminder of the consequences of allowing materialism and selfishness to rule over Christian morality. His peroration was a call to a Christian conception of patriotic duty: "We stand here in the breach not only for ourselves and for our children but for all mankind. Upon our shoulders is laid the task of building up a noble Christian republic, the light of whose example shall be for the guidance of all the nations of the earth."[124]

Looking back on the previous three years of political ferment, *Harper's Weekly* editor, George William Curtis, claimed in 1864 that the Union party had emerged because the Civil War was "the furnace in which old parties were fused," and "the pure gold of patriotism runs together in new combinations."[125] This purple prose obscures the more prosaic political reality that led to the experimentation with Union coalitions: the electoral weakness of the Republican party and the pressure from conservatives to create (under the aegis of the Lincoln administration) an organization purged of what they regarded as the excesses of radicalism. The creation of the Union Party was a means of bestowing on the Republican Party a "national" character, which would appeal to the influential body of self-described conservatives whose support Republican leaders, including Lincoln, deemed essential for their political future as well as for the war effort. At this early stage, radical Republicans regarded Union movements as an underhand means of diluting the party's antislavery commitment and a dangerous sop to partisan rivals. Simultaneously, as the antislavery nationalism of the New York Republicans' after-dinner speeches suggests, a discourse was emerging that wove together radical antislavery and antipartisan nationalist themes. At the same time, many partisan Democrats saw Union coalitions, not unreasonably, as a cynical attempt to reinforce Republican dominance. Some Democrats also retained the faith that a traditional partisan strategy could bring them electoral success in the 1862 elections. Even as the rhetoric of Unionism drew on an antipartisan language of national unity—and despite their partial success in some states in forging new alliances between old partisan enemies—the creation of Union coalitions did not so much end partisan conflict as reconfigure the terms in which it was conducted.

In this early phase, most politicians were unsure of how the war would affect party politics, or how durable the Union coalitions would be. Much would depend on the length of the conflict. As it became increasingly clear that the war would not be over quickly or easily, mounting tensions increasingly threatened to reignite old party lines, eventually overwhelming efforts to suppress them.

3

The Emancipation Proclamation
and the Party System

When Abraham Lincoln called together his cabinet on July 22, 1862, to inform them that he had decided to issue the Preliminary Emancipation Proclamation, Postmaster General Montgomery Blair warned of the consequences for party politics. "There is a class of partisans in the Free States endeavoring to revive old parties, who would have a club put in their hands . . . to beat the administration," he told the President.[1] Lincoln's timing, in political terms, was certainly risky. He finally issued the Proclamation on September 22, 1862, only weeks before the biggest electoral test of the administration so far: the congressional and state elections in October and November. Blair's point was not merely that the emancipation issue would polarize Northern politics, but that it would provide the justification to revive organized partisan opposition.

The Democratic Revival

Blair, it might be surmised, had particular reason to be concerned. His political career was a case study in the impact of the slavery issue on partisan alignments. An old Jacksonian Democrat from an influential Border State family, Blair, his father Francis Preston, his brother Frank, and many other Border State men, opposed slavery for the most conservative reasons. As supporters of Martin Van Buren's Free Soil Party in 1848, they had opposed slavery but favored the colonization of blacks in Africa in the hope of removing the "negro problem" from American soil for all time. The Blairs had no sympathy for abolitionism and its program of black equality. After rejoining the Democrats in the early 1850s, the Blair family had, by 1860, signed up to the new Republican Party, although their attempts to build up the party in Missouri and Maryland were less than a resounding success. From their Jacksonian heritage, the Blairs derived a fiercely nationalist rhetoric.[2] After he was appointed to Lincoln's cabinet, Montgomery Blair declared, "I am for the Union, now and forever, and against all its enemies, whether fire-eaters or abolitionists." From his base in Maryland, where secessionist feeling erupted into violence in 1861, Blair was well aware of the need for the administration to maintain the support of fervent Unionists like himself who retained a deep suspicion of the radicals and their plans. In Maryland he had been helping to build a Union organization of former Whigs, Know-Nothings, and Democrats under the banner of supporting the war to restore the Union as it was. As an old Free Soiler, Blair did not oppose the idea of freeing the slaves per se, but feared that the Emancipation Proclamation would polarize politics, making it appear that the purpose of the war was to revolutionize the South rather than merely to restore the Union.

At about this time, an exchange of letters between the President and the leading New York Democrat, August Belmont, exposed the developing fracture lines. Belmont's starting point was his fear of the effect of "the disasters in the field." "Apathy and distrust" were everywhere, he wrote, even among "men of standing and hitherto of undoubted loyalty to the Union." Belmont began by suggesting that the remedy to this desperate situation was an "energetic and unrelenting prosecution of the war to crush the rebellion"—including conscription and the raising of many more men than the President had proposed. But, he then asked, "is there no other way of saving our country, from all the horrors and calamities, which even a successful war must entail upon us?" He suggested that the "conservative men of the South" might yet be ready to negotiate terms for the restoration of the Union. The words "conquest and subjugation" were "repugnant to the American ear," he explained, and "while the Rebel leaders can keep up to their misguided followers the delusion that the North means conquest and subjugation I fear there is very little hope for any Union demonstration in the revolted States however great the dissatisfaction against the Richmond government might be." Stung by a letter Belmont had enclosed from an anonymous Southern conservative declaring that all he wanted was a restoration of the Union as it was, Lincoln sent a withering, exasperated retort: "This government cannot much longer play a game in which it stakes all, and its enemies stake nothing. Those enemies must understand that they cannot experiment for ten years trying to destroy the government, and if they fail still come back into the Union unhurt. If they expect in any contingency to ever have the Union as it was, I join with the writer in saying, 'now is the time!'"[3] Belmont's letter hit a raw nerve because Lincoln's policy in the first months of war had been predicated on the pursuit of precisely this kind of cautious strategy to rally the supposedly latent Unionism of the Southern people. While Belmont still focused on the possibility of a negotiated settlement—a dream he never renounced—Lincoln had by now recognized that the stakes of war had been raised.

During the session of Congress that ended on July 17, 1862, the Republican congressional majority enabled the party to deliver the central plank of its platform and abolish slavery in the western territories and the District of Columbia. The army was prohibited from returning fugitive slaves to masters (a common practice in the early months of the war) and in July a Confiscation Act was passed, declaring that the slaves of persons supporting the rebellion should be "forever free." The Preliminary Emancipation Proclamation, though, dramatized and clarified the lines of conflict more than any other measure. The Proclamation brought to a boil the debate over the relationship between slavery and the war that had been simmering for several months. While radical antislavery campaigners celebrated, the Proclamation focused the previously diffuse concern felt by many—including conservative Republicans—about the revolutionary changes being wrought by the war.

Montgomery Blair's warning about the revival of old parties—specifically the revival of Democratic Party organization—proved accurate. In March 1862, a meeting of congressional Democrats was held at the urging of Ohio's Clement L. Vallandigham, already emerging as one of the administration's most outspoken critics. In an "Address to the People," this meeting signaled the formal return of partisanship by denouncing co-operation with the administration and declaring that "if success . . . in a military point of view be required, the Democratic party alone can command it."[4] Democratic Party conventions met to nominate candidates for the fall elections and party newspapers vigorously defended their right to do so, indignantly denying that the Republicans had sacrificed their party at all. "It is high time that these hypocritical professions of no-party should cease, for they are too glaringly false to deceive the most simple," protested one Democratic editorial.[5] As a riposte to the endless invocation in Republican newspapers of Washington's Farewell Address, the New York World quoted a letter in which Thomas Jefferson had argued that "in every free and deliberating society, there must, from the nature of man, be opposite parties. Perhaps this party division is necessary to induce each to watch and debate to the people the proceedings of the other." Now, more than ever, with the public patronage "overgrown and enormous," the people's "rigorous scrutiny and wakeful vigilance" demanded a partisan opposition.[6] Nor was it acceptable for the administration to use patriotic appeals to stifle opposition, even in wartime. "These men are not the government; they are not the country. They are for a brief period, the instruments of conducting the affairs of the government and the country," a Democratic newspaper in Indiana reminded its readers as early as August 1861.[7]

This determination to resume "politics as usual" was not shared by all Democratic leaders. Some—among them Andrew Johnson, John McClernand, Daniel Dickinson and John A. Dix—remained deeply opposed to the revival of partisanship. These men committed themselves to work with the administration for the duration of the war, intensifying the breach with their old party colleagues. "The war is a question too great for party," Dickinson urged. "Let no political organization as such, be supported or encouraged or tolerated."[8] Republicans, of course, were quick to denounce signs that the Democrats were organizing for the fall 1862 campaigns. The Hartford Courant observed that "the revival of the Democratic party, as a party, aspiring to get possession of the government of the country is a fact that cannot fail to be noted as one of the most significant indications of the change in the current of opinion that is taking place."[9]

Just as Postmaster General Blair had predicted, Democratic Party unity gained strength from campaigns that repeated the charge that what began as a war for the Union had become a war to free the slaves. Iowa Democrats warned that the partisan, revolutionary new policy of the administration had transformed the conflict into an "abolition war, for the freedom of the Negro and the enslavement of the white race."[10] In the words of the Philadelphia *Age*—a new conservative newspaper established in early 1863—the Emancipation Proclamation was self-defeating since it left the South "no other choice but war to the knife."[11] Furthermore, the rank-and-file supporters of the Democracy—and many conservative Northerners who had never been Democrats—conceived of the United States as a white man's republic. To defend American nationhood as they understood it demanded that they oppose emancipation. Freedom—still less equal rights—for black Americans would undermine the nature of the American republic in the eyes of a large number of Northerners. A significant number of prominent Democrats continued to publicly support the Lincoln administration. But those who refused to co-operate with Republican-led Union parties charged that the extremists of the "Abolitionist Party" had transformed what could have been a consensual national war into a partisan fight. "We cannot forget," warned one Democratic candidate in the fall of 1862, "that even so beneficent a result as the restoration of the Union would be purchased at a fearful cost, if the price be the overthrow of those civil rights and remedies which constitute the most valuable part of our national inheritance, or if the freemen of this republic become accustomed to submit with tameness to the encroachments of arbitrary power."[12] Democrats fought hard in 1862 for the badge of conservative Unionism that Republicans had captured in 1861.

Chicago Tribune editor Joseph Medill anticipated that, once adopted, emancipation would strengthen the radicals' political position. "We can make ten times as strong a fight to uphold a measure once passed as to advocate it before it is law," he pointed out to a more circumspect Senator Lyman Trumbull. "Let the Democrats go before the people on the issue of re-enslavement."[13] Yet Democratic Party leaders like Ohio congressman Samuel S. "Sunset" Cox were confident that this issue could reconnect them to their core electorate and undermine the administration.[14] Their aim was to regain control of the House in the mid-term congressional elections. Lincoln would still direct the war effort under his self-proclaimed war powers, but by taking control of key congressional committees, Democrats hoped that they would be able to shape decisively both the conduct of the war and, crucially, the making of the peace.

The Democrat whose views on emancipation were potentially most relevant in the summer of 1862 was General George B. McClellan, the commander of the Army of the Potomac. Relations between Lincoln and

McClellan had often been strained—the President had never really been convinced by the General's ambitious military strategy of attacking Richmond from the East, after having first transported the mighty new Union army to the Peninsula. The cumbersome plan—well suited to McClellan's arrogant yet over-cautious personality—initially appeared successful. But then, in late June and early July, the Confederacy struck back in a series of brilliant victories led first by Joseph E. Johnston and then by Robert E. Lee. By mid-July the Union army was encamped near Harrison's Landing on the James. Yet the Army of the Potomac did not buckle in disarray as the raw Union recruits at Bull Run had done a year earlier, and their battle casualties were far lower than those of the Confederates. McClellan, whose capacity for self-deception included the habit of regularly tripling the size of the enemy's forces in his own mind, declared this strategic retreat to have been a success. Lincoln—and the Northern press—were less sure, and the President determined to visit the army in person.

This was the inauspicious moment at which McClellan decided to set out, in a letter to the President that he also released to the press, his "general views concerning the state of the rebellion; although they do not strictly relate to the situation of this Army or strictly come within the scope of my official duties." These views, he emphasized, "amount to convictions and are deeply impressed upon my mind and heart." Like Lincoln, McClellan began by declaring himself determined that "our cause"—that of "free institutions and self government"—should "never be abandoned." He then set out his understanding of the nature of the conflict and the means necessary to secure those ends in a way that revealed a growing divergence, not only between him and the President, but also between two opposing visions of the war within the North. For McClellan, the rebellion had acquired the character of a war, and as such "should be conducted upon the highest principles known to Christian Civilization," by which he meant that it "should not be a War looking to the subjugation of the people of any state, in any event." Private property should be respected, and—pointedly, in view of the Confiscation Act that Congress would shortly pass—McClellan insisted that "military power should not be allowed to interfere with the relations of servitude." The general concluded that "a system of policy thus constitutional and conservative, and pervaded by the influences of Christianity and freedom, would receive the support of almost all truly loyal men, would deeply impress the rebel masses and all foreign nations, and it might be humbly hoped that it would commend itself to the favor of the Almighty."[15] In the presidential election of 1864, this letter was to become one of the most widely reprinted campaign documents. McClellan's correspondents in the North, Democrats who regarded themselves as just as committed to the preservation of the Union as Republicans, were equally committed to the idea that reason and restraint, careful military strategy and a complete respect for the liberties—including the liberty to hold slaves—set out in the Constitution were the most effective ways to restore the Union. McClellan's Harrison's Landing letter is one of the most eloquent statements of this conservative case, written in response to the rising tide of radicalism, the growing feeling that emancipation would have to be used as a tool with which to break the rebellion.

Democrats, then, used three main lines of argument to oppose the elevation of emancipation into a war aim. First, they stressed the unconstitutionality of federal intervention. Democratic Party ideology was held together more than anything else by the faith that the purpose of the Constitution was to protect individual liberty. The strict limits to federal power were ingrained on every Democratic heart. Second, even Democrats who acknowledged the wrongs of slavery tended to regard emancipation as a dangerous social experiment, which at the very least would destroy Unionist sentiment in the Border States and within the Confederacy. This had been exactly the set of reservations that had delayed Lincoln's public acceptance of emancipation and prompted Montgomery Blair to advise the President to proceed cautiously. Democrats were therefore confident that they could build alliances with disaffected Republican conservatives by promoting this argument.

The third means by which Democrats opposed emancipation in the fall of 1862 was by exploiting deep-seated racial anxieties. Using arguments that would develop in intensity over the following two years, the anti-emancipation campaign played on fears of the prospect of "tides of Negroes" coming north, competing for jobs and status, and threatening the social order. Republican politician James G. Blaine later recalled that "the laborer of the North was disposed to regard emancipation of the slaves as tending to reduce his own wages, and as subjecting him to the disadvantage of an odious contest for precedence of race."[16] Big cities and other parts of the country with obvious class distinctions provided the most fertile ground for Democratic "race baiting." In the vitriolic New York campaign, for instance, Democrats described the Preliminary Emancipation Proclamation as a measure for the "butchery of women and children, for scenes of lust and rapine, and of arson and murder."[17] Democratic speakers habitually tied together the Preliminary Emancipation Proclamation with the President's announcement two days later that he was suspending the writ of habeas corpus throughout the North.

The threat of a black "invasion" (or "Africanization") of the North was a dominant theme in anti-emancipationist rhetoric. Politicians and editors predicted that three hundred thousand freedmen would "invade" Ohio alone, competing with white labor, filling up the poor houses and jails, and generally degrading society. In a June 1862 referendum, by a majority of more than two to one, Illinois voters endorsed a clause in a proposed state constitution that would exclude blacks from moving into the state.[18] This issue cut across party lines. Senator Lyman Trumbull of Illinois, a former Democrat, now a Unionist, explained "there is a very great aversion in the West—I know it is so in my State—against having free Negroes come

among us. Our people want nothing to do with the Negro."[19] Administration supporters tried to convince voters that after emancipation blacks
would stay in the South. Some even suggested that free blacks in the
North would migrate south once the threat of being enslaved had been
removed.[20] One Unionist editor told Salmon P. Chase that the best strategy
was to declare that blacks "don't want to come north and we don't want
them unless their coming will promote the conclusion of the war. Our
newspapers ought to advocate this view persistently, and demonstrate that
even our free colored population would go south if they were secure from
sale into slavery."[21] Chase himself, while a fervent advocate of emancipation, shared the common assumption that blacks were inherently unsuited
to the colder northern climate. "Let, therefore, the South be open to Negro
emigration by emancipation along the Gulf," he suggested, "and it is easy
to see that the blacks of the North will slide southward, and leave no question to quarrel about as far as they are concerned."[22]

Chase was not the only radical in the Republican Party who worried
about the political consequences of the "Africanization" issue in the run-up
to the fall 1862 elections. Even Governor John A. Andrew of Massachusetts,
whose antislavery credentials had been amply demonstrated three years
earlier when he had given tacit support to John Brown's raid on Harpers'
Ferry, became embroiled in this issue. In September 1862, Major General
John A. Dix wrote to the governors of three New England states asking
them to accept into their states a group of two thousand ex-slaves who had
sought refuge with the Union army. Governor Andrew responded with
a strongly argued letter, soon leaked to the public, in which he explained
that Massachusetts was, for blacks, "a strange land and climate" in which the
newcomers would "be incapable of self-help—a course certain to demor-
alize them and endanger others. Such an event would be a handle to all
traitors and to all persons evilly disposed."[23]

With timing that was appalling for the administration, the black migration issue became a crisis in Illinois at about the same time the Preliminary Emancipation Proclamation was issued. The army had been sending
refugee slaves to the military headquarters at Cairo—the southernmost
town in Illinois. Secretary of War Stanton issued an order allowing these
freedmen to be dispersed throughout the state. This appeared to violate
the state's "Negro Exclusion" law and which was certainly anathema to
mainstream public opinion. Only a handful of blacks were taken along the
Illinois Central Railroad into the central and northern parts of the state,
but the news of their coming spread with the speed of the telegraph. At
public meetings, Democratic candidates sought to capitalize on public fear
and anger. These "black locusts," Democrats charged, were "the first fruits
of emancipation."[24] The freedmen would return South as soon as slavery
was abolished and the war was over, beleaguered administration supporters promised. But they also raced to distance themselves from Stanton's
plan and privately urged the President to rescind the order. One Repub-

lican wrote to Governor Richard Yates that the "scattering of those black throngs should not be allowed if it can be avoided. The view . . . here is that if the country should become full of them they may never be removed and with the confirmed prejudices and opinions of our people against the mingling of the blacks among us we shall always have trouble."[25] Yates telegraphed the President on October 13, 1862, warning him of the impact of the refugee blacks on Unionist support; and Lincoln's close friend David Davis reported that "there is danger in the election here growing out of the large number of Republican voters who have gone to the war . . . and of the Negroes coming into the state."[26]

Many leading Republicans, including Lincoln, turned to schemes of colonization abroad as a means of evading the question of the status of freed slaves in white society altogether. Senator James R. Doolittle of Wisconsin was the leading Congressional supporter of the colonization policy. He was explicit about the political strategy behind it. It was a means of blunting any Democratic attempt to outflank the Union Party by raising the cry of "*emancipation & colonization*" against the Republican war cry of "*native abolition.*" If that happened, Doolittle warned, "The Republican Party is at once reduced to a mere handful and its power forever gone."[27] So strong was the support for colonization within the Republican Party, especially in the Midwest, that a deportation provision was included in the District of Columbia Emancipation Act in April 1862. President Lincoln made clear his continuing commitment to colonization in a well-publicized meeting with a group of blacks in August 1862. The "physical difference" between the two races was, he told them, a "great disadvantage to us both, as I think, your race suffer very greatly, many of them, by living among us, while ours suffers from your presence." Bluntly, he informed them that "there is an unwillingness on the part of our people, harsh as it may be, for you free colored people to remain with us."[28] A public commitment to colonization was a vital weapon in the public relations battle that Lincoln and his supporters were fighting to prepare the way for emancipation.[29]

The defensiveness of leading Republicans, even those who fervently supported black freedom, revealed their acute awareness of the resistance of the majority of Northerners to the idea of emancipation. Even the great antislavery senator from Massachusetts, Charles Sumner, urged in the fall of 1861 that, when it came, as he was confident it would, the freedom of the slaves should be "presented strictly as a measure of military necessity and the argument is to be thus supported rather than on grounds of philanthropy."[30] This was the essence of the Republican case made in 1862: confiscating and liberating slaves would strike a fatal blow against the rebels. Few wanted to challenge publicly the Democrats' repeated cry that "God made the White Man superior to the Black, and no legislation will undo or change the decrees of Heaven."[31] A pro-administration newspaper in Illinois was explicit: "Now we confess that we have, in common with nineteen twentieths of our people a prejudice against the nigger, but we do not hold on that account that we are bound to vote the Democratic ticket."[32]

Other conservative Republicans were alienated by the emancipation policy. One such figure was the President's old Illinois friend Orville Hickman Browning, who complained in his diary that "nothing should have been said on the subject of slavery."[33] As late as August 1862, Browning sent Lincoln enthusiastic reports of the absence of old party feeling. Not only "old line Whigs" and Republicans, but also "democrats, with hardly an exception, are your earnest supporters. They are delighted with your course, and for you against all opposition. I am much gratified at this, for we cannot get along without them."[34] The "only grumblers" he could find were a very few "ultra men . . . radicals of the *Tribune* persuasion."[35] Three months later, Browning saw a much bleaker picture. The emancipation proclamation, he told the President, had been "disastrous to us." Before it had been issued, "all loyal people were united in support of the war and the administration." The "disloyal leaders" of the Democratic party had not been able to rally the mass of Democrats, since "they had no issue without taking ground against the war, and upon that we would annihilate them." The proclamation, though, had "revived old party issues."[36]

1862 Elections

An abolitionist wrote to William Lloyd Garrison before the November 1862 elections expressing his confidence that the Democrats would be "overwhelmed."[37] He had allowed optimism to get the better of his political judgment. Candidates describing themselves as Democrats or Conservatives won thirty-five congressional seats previously held by Republicans or Unionists. In Illinois, Indiana, and Ohio, the Democratic vote increased by between 6 and 12 percent compared to the 1860 result.[38] Democrats won control of the state legislatures in Illinois and Indiana—and, most dramatically of all, they captured the Governorship of New York. The turnout was down compared to congressional races in 1860, but Republican support fell by more than the Democratic vote. The number of troops in the field who were unable to vote and generally assumed to be disproportionately Republican is part of the explanation for this decrease.

Despite these Democratic successes, Republicans too had cause to be satisfied with the elections of 1862; in truth, the electoral picture was mixed. As in the elections of 1861, there were few races in which there was a clear-cut two-party race. Almost everywhere outside a few Republican strongholds, supporters of the administration ran as Unionists (or in Pennsylvania often as People's Party candidates). But the actual composition of these Union parties—and equally the nature of their opponents—varied widely both between and within states. In the Border States, Union parties of various descriptions generally did well against Democratic opposition. In Delaware, for instance, William Cannon narrowly won the gubernatorial race, and congressional candidates running as Unconditional Unionists won just under 50 percent of the popular vote, an increase over their performance in state elections the previous year. In the Midwest, effective Union coalitions, all with a heavy representation of War Democrats, played down the emancipation issue. The Indiana Union Party, heavily influenced by conservative Democrats, called for the restoration of the Union with all the rights of the states unimpaired. In Ohio the Union Party platform ignored the slavery issue altogether and refuted the suggestion that the war would undermine state rights.[39]

It was a similar story in Connecticut, which held state elections in the spring of 1862. Governor William A. Buckingham benefited from a divided opposition. Democratic regulars adopted a set of resolutions calling for an immediate end to hostilities and condemning the administration in the strongest terms for violating civil liberties and favoring racial equality. They then nominated James C. Loomis, a prominent Peace Democrat and pro-slavery lawyer from Hartford. Disaffected War Democrats led by James Pratt resisted the call to join the state Republican organization and instead held a Union Party convention that called for an end to "crippling" partisanship and pledged to "ignore past party lines and party issues."[40] The Unionists claimed to have attracted some leading Republicans to their cause, but there is no evidence that this was so. In fact, far from welcoming the creation of a Union Party, the principal Republican newspaper in Hartford, the *Courant*, condemned the "efforts of well-meaning but ill-advised persons to get up some kind of clap trap Union Party." No doubt fearing that the new organization might draw support away from the regular Republicans, the *Courant* turned the rhetoric of antipartisanship back on the Unionists: "We want less of party more of real patriotism, fewer caucuses among designing politicians, and a more general rally to the battlefield." The *Courant* need not have worried. The Union Party renominated all but two of the Republican incumbents, and seemed only to have drawn votes from the Democrats. Buckingham, as the nominee of both the Republican and Union parties, won with a swing of 5 percent on an increased turnout.

Overall, the supporters of the administration—including Republicans, Border State Unionists, and War Democrats who had been elected on Union tickets—still retained a majority of twenty-five in the United States House of Representatives and, most noteworthy of all, they gained six seats in the Senate. According to reports from local Republican activists, Union military victories at Corinth and Perryville, and the repulsion of Lee's invasion of Maryland at the battle of Antietam in September made a huge difference to their support, perhaps accounting for the better then expected showing.

The Battle to Control the Language of Union

The most notable Democratic success story in 1862—the election of Horatio Seymour as Governor of New York—occurred in a race where the Democrats outbid the Republican candidate for the mantle of Unionism. The first move in the campaign was made on April 18, 1862, when the "Republican and Union" legislative caucus issued an address and a set of resolutions calling for a Union movement to unite "Republicans, Union Democrats and other loyal citizens" at the fall election for Governor and United States representatives.[41] This plan was positively received by some Democrats, as well as by the independent New York *Herald* and the conservative Republican *Times*. To one Democrat, the Union movement commended itself to "every man who thinks more of his country than of the worn-out issues of departed parties."[42] On May 14, a "Committee for United Political Action" met at Astor House in New York City and declared that "all honest efforts should be made to strengthen the Union movement by inviting the co-operation of all loyal citizens."[43]

In reality, however, the new Union movement was still dominated overwhelmingly by those who had supported the Republicans in 1860. A list compiled in 1862 for the editors of the New York *Evening Post* of leading Union Party supporters throughout the state revealed that, of the more than five hundred ward-level party organizers, only thirty-eight were identified as Democrats—and even that small number was marked out for particular suspicion. Against the names of the Democratic supporters of the Union Party, someone had added the warning note that "no confidential communications should be addressed to them."[44] The loyalties of party activists, a large proportion of whom had, after all, been appointed by the Republican state government were less malleable than party publicists liked to think. One such stalwart Republican, the editor of a small Republican newspaper in Brooklyn, urged his readers to be careful not to "lose their identity." Whatever "combinations" were created by a Union Party convention, Republicans, he urged, must "keep to the head of the column."[45] At the Union movement's nominating convention, tensions over the threat to the identity of the Republican Party spilled over into procedural debate as "Union" delegates opposed the assumption made by the temporary chairman that the rules that governed the previous year's Republican convention could be reapplied. One delegate from Schuyler County reminded the convention that it had gathered to "originate a new organization" and he proposed that it should make sure to distance itself from "the manipulation of any party clique."[46] The two principal candidates for the nomination personified this division. The eventual winner, with 234 convention votes on the first ballot, was James S. Wadsworth, a radical, who had been an abolitionist even before the war and was therefore, in the view of the conservative press, one of the "fanatics who had incited the rebellion."[47] The strength of the pro–Union Party vote at the Republican convention can be loosely measured by the 110 votes (roughly a quarter of the total) that went to General John A. Dix, a prominent War Democrat.[48] An additional thirty-three votes were cast for Lyman Tremaine—who was also a life-long Democrat, but a fervent supporter of the war and an early advocate of a Union Party.[49]

Exploiting divisions within the Republican/Union movement, Democrats tried to claim for themselves the mantle of Unionism. In an attempt to woo conservatives disillusioned by the nomination of Wadsworth, some Democratic newspaper editors and publicists typically referred to Seymour and the slate of candidates nominated with him as "conservatives" rather than Democrats. The success of this strategy in attracting former Whigs is indicated by the fact that prior to his nomination by the Democrats, Seymour was also nominated by a state convention of the Constitutional Union Party.[50] Seymour told a public meeting that "one wing [of the Republican Party] is conservative and patriotic, the other is violent and revolutionary."[51] The *Herald* promised that the election of Seymour would be a triumph for a new kind of politics, "the politics of moderation, conservatism . . . and common sense."[52] The destruction of old party lines was almost a daily theme in the pages of the *Herald*. In June, an editorial declared, "the departed issues of past politics are but a distant memory" and in October it was confident that "all the paltry divisions, distinctions, quibbles, claptrap and moonshine of our political parties sink into insignificance and public contempt."[53] The glue that stuck together this conservative revival was commitment to white supremacy. James Brooks, a former Whig and Know-Nothing who won the eighth congressional district in New York City, proclaimed that "this Civil War, the calamitous condition of our country, the negation of the white race and the elevation of the negro over the white man have hushed up or exiled all our past political differences."[54]

By casting himself as the conservative and patriotic candidate, and by condemning Wadsworth and his "abolitionist friends" for their destructive partisanship, Seymour effectively used the "conservative" label to forge an anti-emancipation popular front of Democrats, former Constitutional Unionists and nativists. Even powerful Republican figures like Thurlow Weed and William Seward withheld support from Wadsworth.[55] George Templeton Strong, the New York City banker, Republican activist and diarist, did not desert Wadsworth and the Republican Party. But he was ambivalent enough about the choice with which he had been faced that, tellingly, he conceded on hearing the election result that "as governor, Seymour will probably try to outbag the republicans in energetic prosecution of the war."[56] The dichotomy that New York Democrats managed to create between the "infernal republicans" and the "conservative masses" had the effect of implying that the President was sympathetic to their viewpoint. Even the Preliminary Emancipation Proclamation did not seem to dent the conviction of these conservatives that Lincoln, and selected conservative Republicans, were on their side. Lincoln, they claimed, had been forced to issue it as a "political necessity" to quiet the "baying radicals."[57]

The divisions sharply exposed by the 1862 election in New York had their roots in the different responses to the military stalemate. The cautiousness of McClellan's grand military plans brought condemnation of the idea that "strategy" alone could defeat the rebellion and calls for a radicalization of the war effort, including, inevitably, an attack on slavery. "McClellan's repose is doubtless majestic," observed Strong, "but if a couchant lion postpones his spring too long, people will begin wondering whether he is not a stuffed specimen after all."[58] George Opdyke—a self-made millionaire Republican who became mayor of the intensely Democratic city of New York in 1862 only because divisions among Democrats enabled him to win with only 34 percent of the vote—began to articulate a much more sweeping vision of the meaning of the war. The cause of the war, he claimed was "nothing less than national existence and the cause of civil liberty every-where. An aristocracy, grounded on human servitude has engaged in rebellion against a democratic government."[59] On August 27, 1862, a group of New York political leaders—including Peter Cooper, the founder of a workers' educational foundation (the Cooper Union), the banker John A. Stevens, Jr. and Mayor Opdyke—formed the National War Committee. The stated aim of this new organization was to promote enlistment in order to avoid a state draft, and at first it received generous donations from across the political spectrum. But it soon became clear that the committee's founders wanted to promote the vigorous prosecution of the war by such measures as raising troops for generals like John C. Fremont, deemed to have a sufficiently uncompromising attitude toward rebels and slavery alike. Not only Democrats like Belmont and Edwards Pierrepont, but also former Whigs and Republicans Moses Grinnell and William E. Dodge, Jr.—all of whom retained their faith in McClellan, with his pledge to win the war without revolutionizing the South—resigned from the National War Committee in protest.[60] The formation of the committee was the first institutional manifestation of division within the New York political class, which had been hitherto remarkably united, when it co-operated under the auspices of the Union Defense Committee.

Democratic victory in New York was based on the claim that the party was the legitimate and rightful protector of the Union. Aware of the precariousness of opposition politics in wartime, Democrats hoped even through the fall of 1862 that the war could be won by means of a restrained policy of restoring the status quo and respecting Southern property and society.[61] Yet events quickly demonstrated the futility of these hopes. When Abraham Lincoln fired General McClellan after the fall elections, the "Little Napoleon" moved to New York, where he was immediately drawn into Belmont's political circle, forming the nucleus of a political relationship that was to result in McClellan's challenge to Lincoln in the 1864 presidential election.[62]

In the fall of 1862, New York Democrats were not alone in playing down partisan language and stressing their loyalty to the Union in order to bring together all those who opposed the "military-abolition" party. In many states, self-styled "conservatives" succeeded in branding Republicans as dangerous and unpatriotic, as they had in New York. One of the most sustained efforts to challenge Republican radicalism in this way took place in Massachusetts, where there was a concerted effort to organize a conservative party to challenge the Republicans, and in particular to frustrate the re-election of Senator Charles Sumner.[63] With large popular majorities behind them and a radical, sophisticated elite controlling the party, Massachusetts Republicans were not interested in diluting their partisan identity and they had held aloof from Union coalitions in 1861. Consequently, Massachusetts provided the ideal political context in which Democrats could achieve some success by wooing moderate Republicans into a "nonpartisan" Unionist alliance.[64] Former Whig governor John H. Clifford and other Whig conservatives led the call for a Constitutional Union convention—the name taken by the supporters of former Whigs John Bell and the Bay State's own elder statesman Edward Everett in their presidential bid in 1860. The convention nominated candidates in the name of the People's Party, a banner that organizers felt was more likely to attract Democrats.[65] It also affirmed the Crittenden Resolutions as the basis for reunion and pledged support for the President "in his patriotic and self-sacrificing labors to save the country and put down the rebellion."[66] A sympathetic newspaper reported a "considerable number" of Republicans in this movement, which declared its aim to be the "union of all good citizens in support of the constitution."[67]

A conservative Republican newspaper, the *Springfield Republican*, deemed the People's Party a good idea in principle, and if it stood on the "broad national ground" that the Republicans should have taken, it would have a good chance of winning.[68] Radical Republicans were stung into action by this potential threat to Sumner's political position. Local politicians, ministers, and newspaper editors took to the stump in defense of their party.[69] "The People's Party," charged a Republican broadside, "is in reality designed to weaken the power of the government, by withholding a generous and hearty support to its recently declared policy [of emancipation]. It can have no other effect if successful than to encourage the leaders of the rebellion, and make them more determined and persistent in their treason."[70]

In the end, the Preliminary Emancipation Proclamation helped defeat the People's Party. Lincoln's cautious public remarks about emancipation during the spring and summer of 1862 had convinced conservatives that he would resist pressure to expand the aims of the war. But on September 22, 1862, at a stroke of his pen, Lincoln appeared to demonstrate that he shared the radicals' view of this fundamental question after all. Meeting in convention less than two weeks after the proclamation had been issued, the conservative alliance faced the prospect of being divided down the middle. Demonstrating a lawyerly ability to claim that a document implied almost the reverse of what others interpreted it to mean, the People's Party convention adopted a resolution that emphasized that part of the Proclamation in which Lincoln had reaffirmed his commitment to restoration of the Union and dismissed slave emancipation as but "one mode and manner" by which the rebellion could be crushed. They could not hide the fact, though, that their claim to moderation and nonpartisanship had been based on the argument that their radical Republican opponents, in calling for "the extermination" of slavery, were undermining the administration and thus the war effort.[71] Stepping into the apparent breach between Lincoln and the radicals, they had made support of the president the *sine qua non* of their movement, which was why they stuck to that line even after the Preliminary Emancipation Proclamation was issued.[72] One prominent conservative involved in the People's movement, Amos A. Lawrence, explained that the "signatures for the call for a 'People's Convention' were obtained in many cases by the representation that the Republicans had not expressed their determination to support the President."[73] The rug had been dramatically pulled from underneath that claim. One congregational minister argued that the Preliminary Emancipation Proclamation meant that the Republican Party should now be even more confident and overt in its radicalism.[74]

Expectations of Realignment

On one level, the reason for the relative Democratic success was simple: more Republicans than Democrats had stayed away from the polls compared to the last national round of elections in 1860.[75] Not unreasonably, many administration supporters claimed that there were more Republicans than Democrats in the army, unable to get home to vote, and several state legislatures made moves to rectify this anomaly and allow soldiers to vote in the field.[76] A few radical congressmen, blamed the reversals on the decision to "voluntarily abandon" the "Republican organization" and replace it with a "no-party Union."[77] "Fear of offending the Democracy has been at the bottom of all our disasters," argued William Pitt Fessenden of Maine.[78]

Many more drew the opposite conclusion. With its emancipation policy, the administration had offended the public by abandoning the effort to transcend partisanship. H. S. Bundy, a failed Union congressional candidate in Ohio, explained to Secretary of the Treasury Salmon P. Chase that the Proclamation had sunk his chances: "I had thought until this year that the cry of 'nigger' & 'abolitionism', were played out but they have never had as much power & effect in this part of the state as at the recent elections."[79] Chase fervently supported emancipation and had been urging the

President to act for many months. But faced with the reality of the political situation in his home state of Ohio, he now lamented that old Whigs and Democrats had ganged up on the Republicans. "The party which now opposes the National Government is not in any just sense the Democratic party, and ought not to be so called," he wrote to Benjamin F. Butler (himself a former Breckinridge Democrat who had joined the Union Party). Rather, maintained Chase, "it is simply the opposition, in which old Whigs, Know-Nothings, and Democrats unite to expel the Republicans from power."[80] He gloomily predicted that a new organization of parties would occur, brought to life in opposition to the emancipation policy.

Richard Baber, another Ohio Republican—this time on the conservative wing of the party—wrote to Lincoln directly on November 22, 1862, lamenting Lincoln's failure to live up to the conservative hopes he had inspired two years earlier. "Your speeches [before the 1860 election] gave every assurance that you had no sympathy with revolutionary politics. From that moment means were taken by the publication of your speeches . . . to rally around you all the conservative and Whig elements in the Republican party." Such conservatism, Baber argued, had enabled the people to unite "without distinction of party" and rally around the flag for "the vigorous prosecution of the war and the restoration of the Union." But now a "small clique" in the Republican Party had broken this unity and forced the President, "contrary to his own judgment," to take "positions [on] the conduct of the war, that must inevitably raise partisan issues in the loyal States and consolidate the disaffection at the South." Baber stressed that he, like the President, wished to see slavery put in a "process of ultimate extinction," but he saw the Preliminary Emancipation Proclamation as an obstacle to that end. The "political power of Slavery has been killed by the rebellion and can only be resuscitated by calling the Democratic Party to active life by means of proclamations [sic]" he argued. The proclamation "simply . . . furnished the Democrats political capital to go into the elections."[81]

Some Democrats and old-line Whigs did advocate the formation of a new national conservative party along the lines of the People's Party in Massachusetts. The *National Intelligencer,* the Washington journal that still carried the torch for the old Whig Party, declared that the new organization should be called the Constitutional Union Party, an obvious reference to the ill-fated 1860 party that had attracted some votes in the Border States and the upper South but had failed to make an impact in the North. The new party would be bound to wage war "for the Constitution and under the Constitution, in sacred regard for the sanctions of that instrument." One journalist reported that the plan was to create a "natural nucleus for the conservative men of the country."[82] It would be a truly national party, devoted to maintaining the Union at all costs, but resistant to the "dangerous social experiment" of emancipation. Some speculated in Washington in the winter of 1862–1863 that the Seward-Weed faction that had pushed so hard to compromise the core appeal of the Republican Party in 1860 would join such a movement. Weed assumed that the Republican Party could not be electorally successful in the future unless it created a base in the South and among "the men of moderation and sound-judgment," reported the *New York Times* (the newspaper edited by Weed's political ally Henry Raymond). Consequently, Weed favored the organization of a third party "composed of the moderate men of both parties," on the principle that if it was not possible to read the radicals out of the Republican Party, then they should be deserted by the rest.[83] Orville Hickman Browning also supported this idea. In a letter to former Whig Thomas Ewing, he wondered if it was "not *possible* to form a party between [the] extremes, composed of the true patriots of all parties, which would have before it, as its sole purpose, the suppression of the rebellion [and] the restoration of the Union . . . and which would draw its support from the majority of the American people?"[84]

Powerful though the wartime patriotic imperative was, creating effective co-operation between old political enemies was never easy. The key was forging a new vocabulary that rejected past badges of partisanship. As Addison C. Gibbs, a former Democrat from Oregon, concluded in a letter to the President, "there is something in a name." Renouncing old party labels was a powerful political statement. "Republicans and Douglas men are now acting together and will keep together under the name Union," reported Gibbs, "but if that name is changed the Pacific States may go copper head."[85] Anti-Republican feeling on the Democratic side ran deep, as did opposition to Democrats among former Whigs. At every turn, the difficulty of co-operation bedeviled the project of creating Union parties.

Lincoln's perspective on the prospect of realignment was influenced by the fundamental political reality that he was elected by a national electorate, whereas individual members of Congress owed their positions to constituencies that were, in most cases, strongly Republican. Most political observers assumed that the Republican Party would not endure in the form in which had been constituted in 1860—as a sectional party. Although he polled over 50 percent of the vote in almost every state he won, and his margin in the Electoral College was a comfortable one, Lincoln still polled only slightly less than 40 percent of the national popular vote. Although secession temporarily made the northern-based Republican Party dominant in Congress, the hope was, of course, that the rebel states would be restored to their former relations to the Union at some time, perhaps even before the 1864 presidential election. The impulse behind party-building in the Border States—along with the necessary political compromises that were involved—was therefore something in which the President had a greater personal investment than did most Republican congressmen. As a conservative Republican correspondent reminded Lincoln after the 1862 elections: "[You] were nominated for the Presidency without the assistance of these Congressional managers of the party—your strength lay with the masses of the people who had confidence in your honesty of purpose." The President must therefore pursue a "national" policy, must elevate himself above petty partisanship.[86]

Lincoln was highly sensitive to the importance of appearing to be "above party"—and acutely conscious of the need to build a political base in the Border States. The constant tension between the radicalism of a majority of Republican congressmen and the caution of the White House may well be, as Michael Holt has suggested, in part a product of the different political logic that applied in each case.[87] Yet, Lincoln's national vision was at least as firmly antislavery as was that of the mass of Republican supporters. To Lincoln the lessons of the 1862 election were clear: supporters of the administration should never again be cast as divisive and partisan. The language of emancipation and national redemption had to be fused with the language of antipartisanship and national unity. A radical political agenda could only be advanced within the ambit of a nationalist political discourse that rhetorically transcended partisanship.

4

The Union Leagues and the Emergence
of Antiparty Nationalism

A respected Hartford businessman and pillar of the local Presbyterian Church, James G. Batterson embodied the bourgeois respectability projected by the Whig and Republican parties. As the chairman of the Union Party state committee in Connecticut, he was also characteristic of the semi-professional, skilled political organizers who oiled the wheels of partisan electioneering in the mid-nineteenth century. In the fiercely fought elections of 1863 and 1864, Batterson and his committee followed the usual battle plan for an election campaign. They produced and distributed broadsides, organized public meetings, printed distinctively designed yellow paper ballots, and sent them out to every ward and township in the state.[1] Yet, beneath the familiarity of electoral battle, these campaigns were more than just politics as usual for Batterson. "Three Hundred and Fifty Years before the Christian era the liberty of Greece was sacrificed upon the altar of Party differences and internal strife" he reminded a political meeting:

> Jealous of each other the Grecian states ruined their united strength by failing to agree upon the administration of a central government. Party strife then as now was the hot bed of treason—and the enemies of Greece could never have power . . . had not party traitors barely betrayed and sold their country and with it their own liberty.[2]

In February 1863, Batterson wrote a circular letter to leading national figures warning them of approaching danger. "New York Bankers, Foreign Agents and Secession Emissaries are raising a large 'corruption fund,'" he told them, which would be used for the benefit of the "Breckenridge Democracy in overpowering loyal sentiment." The ballot box would soon decide "whether the people of this state are for the maintenance of law and order at home, and the preservation of our national government, or whether all shall be surrendered into the hands of Breckenridge democrats, who openly avow *hostility* and *forcible resistance* to both."[3] Although this kind of rhetoric was part of a tradition of electoral hyperbole familiar to antebellum Americans, everyone knew that the threats were real this time. Batterson was a deeply committed party organizer railing against what he saw as the destructive, treacherous partisanship of his opponents. Just as he and his fellow Republicans advocated fighting the rebels until a "just peace" was achieved, he also believed in crushing political opposition at home, so that partisanship would not bedevil the Union war effort. There is a fine line between the exaggerated language of election campaigns and the denial of the legitimacy of the opposition. For a generation, American politics had been played out on a highly charged rhetorical level. The crucial difference during the war was that the threats of violent retribution if the "wrong" side won carried credibility.

Batterson's attitudes reflected a political culture that, under the strains of war, was increasingly dominated by partisan antipartisanship. In 1863, mass membership Union Leagues emerged as the most obvious institutional embodiment of this wartime political culture, while new propaganda organizations pushed not only to delegitimize partisan opposition in wartime but also to forge a new conception of loyalty and patriotism.

The Union Leagues

The first Union League was founded in Pekin, Illinois, by a Republican Party activist, George F. Harlow. As war weariness deepened, and the restraint that had held back dissenters in the early months of the war fell away, loyal Republicans became alarmed by the resurgence in support for the Democratic Party. To combat this, they formed a secret society "whereby true Union men could be known and depended on in an emergency." The new movement gained the support of Illinois Governor Richard Yates, and quickly spread to towns and counties throughout the states. Traveling agents administered the league's oath to local political leaders and provided the new councils with league charters. By May 1863 a national convention of the Union Leagues met in Cleveland, Ohio, with delegates from eighteen states in attendance.[4] By the end of 1864 the Leagues claimed more than a million members.

The origins of the Union League movement as secret fraternities harked back to the organizational strategy of the nativist Know-Nothing lodges in 1854–1855. New members had to be voters, and each new recruit had to pledge, in an elaborate ritual involving incense, the flag, and the Bible, to "sustain the existing administration in putting down the enemies of the government" and to thwart the designs of "traitors and disloyalists."[5] In the face of what many administration supporters saw as organized disloyalty from the Democratic Party and its allies, the leagues put into practice the exhortation of John Forney's *Philadelphia Press*. In May 1863, the *Press* urged that the North unite "by any means" and called on Unionists to "silence every tongue that does not speak with respect of the cause and the flag."[6] The Leagues existed, they proclaimed, "to bind together all Loyal men, of all trades and professions, in a common union to maintain the power, glory, and integrity of the Nation."[7] Robert H. McCurdy, a member of the Loyal League of Union Citizens in New York, of which General Winfield Scott was honorary president, described the "solemn pledge of duty to the country, irrespective of party ties" that bound together the members.[8]

A nonpartisan style colored every utterance of these organizations. In their founding charters, Leagues pledged that their "only object is to unite to support of the National Government in its efforts to suppress the rebellion now being waged against its authority by a portion of the people of the Union, and not to create a political party."[9] In late 1863 the Leagues distributed a tract entitled *The Boot on the Other Leg or Loyalty Above Party*, which argued that there had been three distinct eras in the "history of parties" in the United States. The first two eras (Federalists opposed by Democrats, then Democrats opposed by Federalists and Whigs) had been succeeded by the present era "when Democrats, Federalists, Whigs, Republicans, and all other pre-existing parties were united in the administration and the Copperheads opposed them."[10] The *New York Times* headed an approving editorial on a recent Union League meeting in New York, "Partyism vs Patriotism."[11]

Union Leagues institutionalized the denial of legitimate partisanship by conflating political opposition to the Union Party with disloyalty to the United States. Calls to organize Union Leagues galvanized fears of treacherous secret organizations that were, it was alleged, plotting an armed insurrection in support of the Confederacy. "Men of the Northwest! Are you ready for Civil War?" asked an editorial in the radical *Chicago Tribune*, "the danger is imminent; the enemy is at your door . . . a Union Club or league ought to be formed in every town and placed in communication with the state central committee."[12] By the spring of 1864 the 140,000 Union league members in Illinois were organized into militia units to "resist internal rebellion."[13] They formed vigilante groups, which reported suspected disloyalists to the War Department and called for the suppression of opposition newspapers. Leagues also mobbed the offices of several small-town newspapers whose editors had expressed support for Democratic candidates or had attacked the administration.[14]

With the Leagues quickly establishing themselves as a powerful political force, conservative supporters of the administration worried, not without reason, that the Leagues were using their influence to advance a radical agenda. "The *triumph* of the *Loyal Leagues is complete,*" concluded an editorial in the *Chicago Tribune* after the Union League of America persuaded Lincoln to remove a conservative general, John M. Schofield, from command of the western Department.[15] Edwin D. Morgan, the conservative chairman of the Republican national committee for most of the war and a long-time ally of William Seward and Thurlow Weed, complained that the "real motive" of the Union Leagues "is to . . . give . . . presidential aspirants an opportunity to make speeches or what is better to write letters, and in order to suit the taste of those who get up the meetings those letters and speeches must be of the radical or high-flavored order."[16] When the radical Secretary of the Treasury Salmon P. Chase, who fought continuously with Morgan over New York patronage, sought to supplant Lincoln as his party's nominee in 1864, his friends worked hard to gain the endorsement of the Leagues for their candidate.[17] Political foes within the Union Party spread the story that Seward lost his temper about the success of the Loyal National League in New York, denouncing it as a threat to his and Thurlow Weed's political control.[18]

This well-founded perception that the Leagues represented the radical wing of the Republican Party created continual tension with others who resented their hijacking of the language of nonpartisanship and unity. On the second anniversary of the attack on Fort Sumter on April 11, 1863, the New York League organized a rally in Union Square. Delegations appeared from twenty different Loyal Leagues from across the country to mark the occasion "with due solemnity."[19] According to sympathetic news reports, thirty thousand people crowded into Union Square, gathering around six platforms, each with half a dozen speakers. But the partisan implications of such events were clear, despite the organizers' insistence that it was a nonpartisan effort to rally patriotic support for the war. The *New York Herald* reported that the only two buildings in the area not flying the American flag were "the two head-quarters of the democracy—Tammany Hall and Mozart Hall."[20] Less publicly, moderate Republicans, dismissed the nonpartisan claims of the Union Leagues and also distanced themselves from the event. Of more than sixty prominent Union men invited to speak, less than twenty accepted, and many of those who declined did so because they saw the League as a radical organization. The conservative Republican W. H. Leonard, for example, refused because he could not "associate politically with persons who applaud sentiments at variance with the restoration of the Union as it was or the preservation of the Constitution as it is."[21] The attempt of the League to conflate loyalty with adherence to its own program deeply irritated James L. Morris, a prominent New York banker who also refused an invitation to speak. "I have never been a politician," he wrote, airily dismissing the idea that the Leagues transcended politics, "and I decline to have my name used for any [such] purpose."[22]

The Leagues' construction of a patriotic national community—the claim to be the "real" nation—alienated their opponents as surely as it enthused their supporters. Samuel J. Tilden, a wealthy New York railroad lawyer who, for many years, had been active in Democratic politics, complained to a correspondent in June 1863 that the Union leagues were creating a climate in which it was impossible for normal political campaigning to take place. "Of what avail one election if we are not at liberty to discuss the measures which we may rightfully seek to have adopted or rejected by means of the election?" he asked.[23] Another New York City

Democrat, David Turnure, also resented the administration's demand that he should give "unhesitating fealty to and unquestioning endorsement of all their acts." To him, the "immaculate patriots" who carped about loyalty were simply crude partisans, who had "abolitionized" the government and were now subverting the Constitution "under the sacred mantle of patriotism."[24] Even stronger words came from the Maryland Democrat, Severn Teackle Wallis, in an ill-tempered public exchange of letters with Senator John Sherman in early 1863. "You have . . . borrowed from the vocabulary of despotism the name 'disloyalty,'" he thundered. Such a word was "not known to free institutions" but had been created by Unionists to describe the activities of those who "question . . . the wisdom . . . or, if need be, resist the corruption and usurpation of those who *temporarily* hold and prostitute power."[25]

Democratic secret societies also flourished from 1863 onward, and not surprisingly they vigorously, often violently, challenged the Union Leagues' definition of patriotism as fundamentally partisan. Democrats clung to an older vision of the nation in which loyalty demanded opposition to black emancipation in order to defend the integrity of the white man's republic. New York state Democratic chairman Dean Richmond wrote to local party workers in 1863 with instructions for canvassing and campaigning for what he described as "our campaign for the Union." A Democratic organizer in the town of Minden in Montgomery County, New York, described the battle he was waging as being between "the friends of the Constitution and the Union" and "Abolitionists."[26]

These Democratic efforts to wrap their appeal in the cloak of patriotism did not prevent some leading party members from supporting Union Leagues. In fact in some cases it legitimized their participation. The first mass public meeting of the Union League in Philadelphia in January, 1863 for example, was dominated by former Democrats. The purpose of the meeting, declared the organizers, was to "prepare the way for the union of the citizens of Philadelphia without distinction of party, in support of the war" and the star speaker, Governor Andrew Johnson of Tennessee, told the meeting "I stand before you tonight a Democrat [Applause.] I am a Democrat, as that term has been defined here tonight. I have in the whole of my life affirmed man's capacity for self-government. I have always taken the position that the world was my home and any honest man my brother [Applause.]"[27]

In another very characteristic appeal to Democrats to support the administration, Benjamin H. Brewster recalled the dilemma of the Democratic Party faced with men in national office who were "supposed to represent men with whom and measures with which they had been in open conflict for years." He went on to explain that Northern Democrats recognized that partisan battles were dangerous to the national cause, and party loyalty should not prevent them from supporting the administration:

... when they had followed Southern men to the edge of the
law for the sake of the law; when they saw that the wrath of the
Northern public was not a partisan rage but was the just sentiment of outraged men; then to hesitate was mean; to oppose and
organize opposition; to traduce officials acting in good faith under
trying circumstances, and to preach of peace, peace when there
was no peace; was treason and unmanly surrender [of] the noblest
principles that ever men bravely stood by, and in which were cen-
tered the hopes of the human race.[28]

This is an elegant statement of the Union Party's central claim: that it represented patriotism, not partisanship; principle, not prejudice.

Lincoln deliberately encouraged this strategy of equating support for
the administration with a patriotism that transcended party. Unlike his
Confederate counterpart, Jefferson Davis, Lincoln made no speaking tours
to rally home front morale, despite his proven effectiveness as a stump
speaker. Perhaps once or twice a month he would utter some brief, apparently impromptu remarks from the White House to "serenades"—gatherings of citizens who would sing a song and make speeches in his honor—
but the President made few formal speeches.[29] His brief remarks at the
ceremony to dedicate the cemetery at Gettysburg was a rare exception.
One of the most effective tools of communication available to him were
letters he wrote to individuals or groups that he made sure were widely
reprinted in the press. These provided the President with a valuable platform from which he could expound on the meaning of the war or address
particular issues.

The relative scarcity of Lincoln's words in public discourse made their
effect all the more powerful and required him to take particular care over
every word chosen. One such letter, written in the summer of 1863 to
Erastus Corning and other New York and Ohio Democrats, was notable
for its elaboration of the antiparty strategy. Corning had sent the president
copies of a series of resolutions passed by a Democratic public meeting
expressing support for the restoration of the Union but deploring Lincoln's
"unconstitutional" measures, particularly the suspension of habeas corpus.
Lincoln expressed his regret that the resolutions had been passed by men
consciously describing themselves as "'democrats' rather than 'American
citizens.'" In this time of "national peril," he continued, "I would have preferred to meet you upon a level one step higher than any party platform;
because I am sure that from such more elevated position, we could do
better battle for the country we all love" By raising the specter of partisanship, Lincoln warned, their objections threatened "more injurious consequences, than any merely personal to myself." With consummate skill,
the President added, however, that Corning and his associates may have,
through the "prejudices of the past, and selfish hopes of the future" clung

to partisanship. But he was "thankful, for the country's sake, that not all democrats have done so."[30]

Earlier in the war, radicals had resisted the language of antipartisan nationalism, believing it to be a conservative plot to narrow the space for political dissent. Now, through the instrument of the Union Leagues, radicals embraced exactly this strategy themselves, using a patriotic, antipartisan discourse to legitimize their own conception of the war. The prominence of radical Republicans in the Leagues thus marked the end of their opposition to the Union Party project more generally. This was possible, of course, because as the war continued, the radical conception of the war's meaning and purpose gained popularity. The definition of loyalty changed as the administration increasingly linked emancipation and the destruction of the Confederacy.

Despite the public prominence of leading War Democrats at Union League meetings, the bulk of the Democratic rank and file remained outside these new organizations. Internally divided between those who broadly supported the conduct of the war but opposed emancipation, and those whose opposition to the way in which the war was being fought pushed them to call for an immediate cessation of hostilities, most Democrats nevertheless held together. Indeed, the presence of an increasingly vocal partisan opposition was, of course, a prerequisite—a necessary negative reference group—for the formation of the leagues. Back in 1861, radicals had feared that no-party language was a device for isolating them. Now, precisely because the bulk of the Democratic Party was the enemy rather than partners in the coalition, the Leagues served as the means by which the powerful language of antipartyism and national unity was turned to radical ends.

Re-forging Patriotism

The mass-membership Union Leagues proclaimed a doctrine of patriotism and used it for essentially partisan ends—to delegitimize Democratic opposition and support Republican candidates in elections. Meanwhile, wealthy and intellectual elites in the three big eastern cities—Boston, New York, and Philadelphia—saw their role as cultivating a new nationalism that would transcend the factionalism and social division engendered by party politics. In early 1863, private clubs were founded in these three cities that aimed to reassert the authority of an older patrician class, which, since the development of mass politics, had felt increasingly marginalized. The clubs were to play a central role in re-formulating the antipartisan tradition in ways that helped shape Northern political culture for the rest of the war.[31]

Unlike the mass-membership Union Leagues, the Union League of Philadelphia, the New York Union League Club, and the Boston Union

Club were founded with all the appropriate accoutrements of a mid-Victorian gentlemen's club: elegant headquarters with libraries, billiard rooms and butlers. The membership of each of these organizations was barely over a thousand, but they constituted some of the most influential men in their respective cities.[32] Membership was by invitation only and determined by social status and "unqualified loyalty to the Government of the United States and unwavering support for the suppression of the rebellion." The idea was to exclude anyone suspected of Southern sympathies from business and social relations with members. "Sympathy with [armed rebellion] should in social and commercial life be met with the frown of the patriotic and the true. Disloyalty must be made unprofitable."[33] At the same time, the new clubs would help solidify the upper class, bringing together new men of business, old-style merchants and leading professionals and intellectuals in a fraternity that would help give leadership and direction to the masses.

The Union League of Philadelphia, the first of the three to be founded, was the most affluent and influential of the three big city eastern Union clubs. The poet and playwright George H. Boker, son of a well-established Philadelphia banker, was the leading spirit. Its founding membership included editor Morton McMichael, financier Jay Cooke, editor and political fixer John W. Forney, and the chairman of the Pennsylvania Republican State Central Committee, Wayne McVeigh.[34] It was a similar story in New York, where the founders of the Union League Club included prominent Unitarian minister Henry Bellows; the architect of Central Park, Frederick Law Olmsted; Oliver Wolcott Gibbs, the renowned chemist who took up a post at Harvard in 1864; and the lawyer George Templeton Strong.[35] In Boston the founders of the Union Club were all at the heart of Boston Brahmin society and the aim was to bind together radicals and conservatives in support of the Union cause in a way that transcended partisanship.[36] For McMichael, editor of the *Philadelphia North American* and a founding member of his city's group, the issue of the war was, after all, one that directly confronted the class interests of the cities business elite. "We . . . live under the national law. If that is broken down, our interests, our property, and our lives may be lost in the disorder that will ensue... Nothing but ruin awaits all business interests of ours . . . if the doctrines of the Secession leaders are to prevail."[37] Sustaining the federal government was essential to protecting court-enforced contracts and trade links with the South. Furthermore, as bankers and the monied elite of New York assumed an ever-greater responsibility for financing the war effort through buying government bonds, there was also a strong economic interest in the success of the Union war effort.[38]

The founders of the elite Union League clubs hoped to bind together an urban upper class that the sectional crisis had fractured in all three cities. In Philadelphia, a city with close commercial and familial ties to the South, the mounting sectional crisis had been highly divisive. Even after secession,

Philadelphians with Southern connections were increasingly hostile to the administration, especially after the Emancipation Proclamation. The Philadelphia Union League was confronted by a rival Central Democratic Club dominated by Copperheads like Charles Ingersoll, which on February 22, 1863—the anniversary of Washington's birthday—held a large public meeting to call for "peace and conciliation."[39] In Boston, the Union Club was designed to overcome increasingly bitter divisions within the Brahmin elite between abolitionists and the conservative "Cotton Whigs," whose Unionism accompanied a fear of the consequences of emancipation.[40]

In New York, the founders of the Union League Club sought self-consciously to counter the political power of a small but influential faction of leading Democrats. August Belmont, the investment banker who had first come to America as the agent of the Rothschilds, was the leading Democrat in the city and he was joined by lawyers Samuel L. M. Barlow and Samuel J. Tilden, and *New York World* editor Manton M. Marble.[41] These men supported the war—indeed, they had been leading players in the Union Defense Committee in 1861—but had become increasingly alienated by the evolution of the administration's war aims. In contrast, in an intensely Democratic city, where Irish immigrants were beginning to exercise political power, the founders of the Union League Club were nativists, Whigs and, latterly, Republicans. Political tensions reinforced a pre-existing cultural and economic line of division within the New York elite.

In the antebellum years, the Belmont circle had grown used to exercising political power, both nationally through their access to Washington politicians and their influential connections with European capitalists, and locally through their control of the great urban machine, Tammany Hall.[42] Belmont and his circle were committed to a decentralized polity, to free trade, unfettered capitalism, and white supremacy. Most of all, these Democratic elites were fundamentally optimistic about the rapidly expanding economy and society of mid-nineteenth-century America and were confident that the capitalist system—especially when mixed with a dose of paternalism to the white working class—could accommodate social tensions. To promulgate their views, leading New York Democrats formed the "Society for the Diffusion of Political Knowledge" in early 1863, a political education society that promoted white supremacy, defended slavery and attacked the Lincoln administration for its subversion of the constitutional limits to federal power.[43] In May 1863, a similar organization called the "Democratic Anti-Abolition State Rights Association of the City of New York" was also founded for the purpose of circulating documents, with Horatio Seymour, Thomas H. Seymour who was Governor of Connecticut, and Clement L. Vallandigham as honorary members.[44]

The founders of the Union League Club mounted a cultural as well as political critique of Belmont's national vision. Suspicious of unfettered democracy and anxious about the moral health of society, they advocated the creation of new national institutions that might disseminate culture and

Christian values and generally bind together the polity against the threat of class tensions and partisan division. They saw their Democratic opponents as failing to understand the genius of the American republic, which lay in the morality and cohesiveness of society. Belmont and his associates were "vulgar" and lacking in the moral sense and national vision to qualify them for membership of the new club, which Olmsted described in a letter to Gibbs as an association of the "legitimate descendents and arms bearers of the old dukes of our land."[45] It was, then, the explicit purpose of the Union League Club to help foster a "true American aristocracy," which in the words of one the leading historians of New York City in the Civil War, "would adapt the cultural authority of the British elite to the distinctive social and political conditions of American democracy."[46] The war provided the opportunity and, Union League Club members believed, demonstrated the necessity, for such an effort. Indeed, their credentials for national leadership would be demonstrated by the time, prestige and money they would spend on leading the mobilization effort. Thomas Wentworth Higginson, in the introduction to a compilation of biographies of Harvard men killed in the war, perfectly encapsulated the confidence of this class when he asserted that "if there is any one inference to be fairly drawn from these memoirs, as a whole, it is this: that there is no class of men in this republic from whom the response of patriotism comes more promptly and more surely than from its most highly educated class."[47] The war thus served as an impetus to the formation of a self-conscious and very particular class identity, one predicated on national leadership and fidelity to the Union cause. The great achievement of the clubs was, as Philadelphian Edwin P. Whipple later noted, "to make patriotism fashionable. Its political power consisted . . . in informing the rich and fashionable that they would lose caste if they became Copperheads."[48]

Rallying the upper class behind an avowedly nonpartisan patriotism was the first stage. The second was to exercise that leadership by instilling a new spirit of patriotism in the masses, combating the corrosive effects of war weariness, and partisan carping with a revived republicanism. The Democratic resurgence in the elections of 1862 and the increasing popular resistance to the draft and to emancipation during the spring and summer of 1863 seemed, to loyal supporters of the administration in the elite Union clubs, to pose a serious threat to the war effort. By late 1862, inflation was running more than 100 percent on basic foods like bread and eggs, adding to the discontent of urban workers. Those who suffered most from the economic stresses of wartime were disproportionately recent immigrants and Democrats, the same people who were fearful of the expanding federal state with its revolutionary emancipation policy, its attacks on individual freedom, and its coercive draft from which the wealthy were exempted. A rash of strikes, prompted by the increased bargaining position of workers in wartime in a context where their standard of living was declining, further alarmed the upper classes with the prospect of social disintegration at a time when the premium must be on unity and loyalty to the nation rather than "narrow" and "partisan" interests.[49]

The solution, members of the Union League clubs felt, was a return to the Revolutionary generation's ideal of a natural aristocracy that would contain the passions of the people. Demagoguery and the worst excesses of unfettered democracy—together with the party organization that pandered to the base impulses of the masses were, the founders of these clubs felt, threatening to undermine the old republican ideal of civic virtue and sacrifice for the common good, values that were more needed than ever. Deference and harmony between the classes were the solutions that would preserve free institutions and popular government.

Placing these new organizations "above party" was integral to this larger purpose of redefining the relationship between government and society, creating a feeling of unity, and instilling a proper patriotic feeling in the masses. Anxious to refute charges that they had created another partisan radical Republican association, the founders of the Boston Union Club made Edward Everett its honorary president. An aging scholar, orator, and sometime Whig politician, Everett had been John Bell's running mate in 1860; he was a man whose reputation was built on integrity and political moderation. One of the founding members assured the radical Republican senator from Massachusetts, Charles Sumner, that "he need not be alarmed at seeing Mr. Everett's name at the head of our club. Some of us would have had another figurehead, but it was generally admitted, and is undeniable, that the general composition of the club was so very Republican, that unless we made him prominent it would have had almost a partisan look."[50]

The Union clubs spread their patriotic message in various ways. Despite the confusing similarity of their names, the elite clubs had no *formal* connection with the mass Union Leagues. But members of the New York, Philadelphia, and Boston Union clubs were actively involved in the establishment of broader popular organizations. In New York, for example, James A. Roosevelt, a leading member of the Union Club, also became secretary of the Loyal National League, a popular organization that was part of the national network of Union Leagues. The clubs also intervened in a more direct way, raising money for the troops, sponsoring speakers, organizing mass rallies, and setting up Committees on Enlistment.[51] They also played a leading role in distributing propaganda. The Philadelphia Union League set up a Board of Publications in February 1863 with the aim of "disseminating patriotic principles amongst a larger and more distant audience." By the end of 1864, the League was able to boast in its annual report that there "was scarcely a post-town from Maine to California, which has not received a package of our publications."[52]

The Loyal Publication Society, created in New York in February 1863, was essentially an outgrowth of the Union League Club.[53] The first president was the aged president of Columbia College, Charles King, and the secretary and leading spirit was the energetic banker and Republican State Committee member, John Austin Stevens, Jr.[54] The three organizing committees included among their membership Charles Astor Bristed, greatgrandson of John Jacob Astor and Oliver Wolcott Gibbs. Francis Lieber, who had moved from South Carolina to become professor of political science at Columbia, wrote several of the pamphlets and, taking over the presidency of the organization at the end of 1863, was largely responsible for its policies.[55] Using language that disavowed partisanship, these founders declared that the purpose of their organization was to distribute "journals and documents of unquestionable loyalty," primarily to troops in the field, in order to counteract "efforts now being made by the enemies of the government and the advocates of a disgraceful PEACE."[56] The project was explicitly one of instilling a new sense of popular nationalism. "We pledge ourselves as National men devoted to the Nationality of this great people," wrote Lieber. Several of the first pamphlets published by the Loyal Publication Society urged emancipation and the use of black troops.[57] Peter Cooper argued in one pamphlet that "the act of causeless war, committed by the states now in open rebellion, has relieved our country and Government from all obligations to uphold or defend an institution so at war with natural justice and all the dearest rights of a common humanity."[58]

One of the most widely circulated pamphlets was Lieber's *No Party Now But All For Our Country*, a powerful argument that party conflict was dangerous in a time of national crisis. This claim had particular authority, coming as it did from one of the earliest defenders of the legitimacy of parties in a republic. Lieber's means of distinguishing between a party and a faction was that the former thought only of the nation while the latter pursued selfish ends, and he had stressed at great length the dangers that could accompany partisanship. Now, in 1863, he still believed that parties were "unavoidable in free countries, and may be useful if they acknowledge the country far above themselves." He came to the conclusion, though, that in a time of civil war, partisan opposition was inherently factious. The war was "no question of politics, but one of patriotism" and he who failed to support the government was a "traitor to his country." Interestingly, his argument was not limited simply to a time of war. He went on to argue that partisanship undermined a national spirit and, if it existed at all, must be carefully circumscribed and devoid of passion. As Lieber put it, partisanship "has no meaning in far the greater number of the highest and the common relations of human life." The nation, he thought, "cannot divide easily into halves, for we live in an age when the word is Nationalisation, not De-nationalisation."[59]

While the Loyal Publication Society in New York concentrated on producing and distributing original pamphlets, another organization based in Boston, the New England Loyal Publication Society, concentrated instead on re-printing "patriotic" editorials from leading newspapers and sending them in weekly batches to the editors of small-town newspapers. The two leading figures in this enterprise were John Murray Forbes, a Boston merchant and railroad financier who was well connected to the leading radical Republican politicians in Massachusetts, and the scholarly Charles Eliot Norton. A few months after he became involved in the New England Loyal Publication Society, Norton also took over the editorship of the *North American Review*—along with his friend, the poet and former *Atlantic Monthly* editor, James Russell Lowell. In both roles, Norton promoted and applied to the United States the kind of liberal nationalism that he had encountered in his long stays in London, Paris and Florence.[60]

Newspapers were the prime medium of political communication in mid-nineteenth century America. By 1860 there were 4,051 newspapers in the United States, almost all of which reported political speeches verbatim and editorialized on issues of the day. The overwhelming majority of these had a tiny circulation—sometimes under a hundred, and were often owned and produced by one man who acted as reporter, editor, typesetter, printer and distributor.[61] Even small towns on the frontier supported a weekly or twice-weekly newspaper, and towns of local political importance always had at least two dailies, generally one supporting each party. Editors were often political players in their own right. A local newspaper editor was typically an influential figure in his local community, sitting on party committees, in state legislatures, or even serving a term in the US Congress.[62] For the larger journals the practice of "exchanging" copies with other papers was one of the principal sources of information, but as an editor from Youngstown, Ohio, explained, small papers like his could not exchange with the "leading journals of the country," and he would never have the "leisure to peruse them carefully" in any case.[63]

Like the New York-based Loyal Publication Society, the Boston society was run by patrician figures who were leading supporters of the administration steeped in the language of antipartisanship. Forbes, for example, claimed that his goal was to "sink and obliterate the old party names."[64] By the beginning of 1864, Forbes and Norton began collating reprinted articles, originally posted out on slips of paper into two or three broadsides a week, with the Society's name emblazoned across the top. Only two or three thousand broadsides were printed at one time but the Society's secretary, James B. Thayer, pointed out that a single item chosen from the broadsides for insertion in a newspaper would, depending on the size of the paper's circulation, reach between five hundred and two thousand subscribers, plus the "outside constituency" of the paper who read it without subscribing to it.[65] The main area of operations for the Society was not the surrounding New England region, but the Midwest and Pennsylvania, where Forbes believed the most good could be accomplished.[66] On February 1, 1864, the Society was distributing its broadsides to 412 newspapers in Minnesota, Wisconsin, Michigan, Iowa, Illinois, Indiana, and Ohio, but only 148 to New England papers.[67] Pennsylvania received more broadsides than any other state—the society targeted ninety-four newspapers in that crucial electoral state during the 1864 campaign.[68]

Simply sending out broadsides containing pro-Union propaganda did not, of course, ensure that the message was received in the way it was intended. The limits as well as the possibilities of this patrician effort at popular education—Forbes explained that his aim was to "enlighten the working classes"—became clear in the responses to questionnaires the editors in Boston sent out on at least two occasions.[69] The editor of the Richmond, Indiana, *Palladium* wrote to the Boston offices complaining that, although "many of the articles published . . . met our view precisely," he nevertheless looked upon "the Society's efforts in *our* behalf as a species of contemptible officiousness."[70] Editors of country papers clearly saw themselves as contributors to public debate as well as messengers, and they rarely withheld their own political opinions from their paper. Their small circulation meant that they could not survive if their views were radically opposed to the bulk of their readership. When editors considered themselves more radical than their readers, they carefully waited for the most receptive moments to express their views. Above all, editors were aware of what others were writing and judged the nature of public opinion by what appeared in the editorial columns of other newspapers. On the question of the status of freedmen, for example, local editors often reported that they were holding back from discussing it, because to do so would be to stimulate controversy.[71] Sometimes, the influence of the broadsides was indirect: "I have used your publications more as a source for refreshing my own mind of the topics," wrote one Missouri editor, "and afterwards presenting them to my readers in my own form and style, [rather] than as a source of extracts."[72]

The connections among a suspicion of mass partisanship, the forging of a more vigorous nationalism, and the assertion of control by elites was illustrated in a memo to his predominatly German workers by a Pennsylvania factory owner in 1863. In a blatant attempt to influence their votes that some of his employees interpreted as a thinly veiled threat to fire them if they didn't comply, the memo began by announcing, "today I deem it right to demand of you to give more credence and confidence to me." Warning them to beware the "false views of vagabond demagogues" and "interested and bribed journalists who endeavor to propagate false and infamous views," he explained that:

> The stake is not now for this or that party, but for the existence and life of the nation, for liberty and the rights of man . . . . The true patriot has now no other choice but to vote for the candidates who are pledged to continue this war to the proposed end—to support the present administration . . . . Now the saying applies "he who is not for us is against us."

He added that he was "at all times ready to talk with every one individually, and to listen to any refutations and to correct them."[73]

Protestant churches also played a role that was rhetorically nonpartisan but which in fact could not avoid having partisan political implications.[74] Churches had the manpower, the money, and the buildings to host political meetings and to publish and distribute campaign literature. And through-out the war, churchmen led the movement to identify opposition to the administration with treason.[75] One clergyman told his congregations that "every person that could give a garment or money or influence or prayers and didn't [is] a traitor to his country."[76] When the minister of the First Episcopal Church in the small town of Kingston in upstate New York began announcing the time and place of Union Party meetings at the end of his sermon each Sunday, the local Democratic newspaper remarked that all that remained to transform it into a political club room was a portrait of the president over the pulpit and a "score of office holders beneath to give the cues for applause."[77] One elderly New York woman complained that the Reverend Corning, her local Congregationalist minister, spent every Sunday commenting on public events. "It was a harangue not exactly a sermon" she reported one Sunday. "He took no text but occupied the time in explaining and defining many terms in popular use at the present crisis. Such as patriotism." Mr. Corning, she concluded sardonically, "is a great patriot."[78]

The same patrician determination to instill in the public a fervent loyalty to the national idea also played a role in the United States Sanitary Commission.[79] Like the Union Leagues, the Sanitary Commission was an avowedly nonpartisan organization that, nevertheless, had a clear political agenda. Formed in the first months of the war by a group of wealthy New Yorkers led by the Unitarian minister and leading light in the New York Union Club, Henry W. Bellows, the Commission was to become a huge-scale quasi-governmental organization devoted to allevi-ating the suffering of soldiers while also "guiding the national instincts" and "showing the value of order and the dignity of work."[80] Although some in the army initially opposed a private group performing such a vital public role, the Sanitary Commission soon developed into an enormous national organization, whose leaders had cultural and political purposes that transcended their benevolent function.[81] Olmsted explained that the purpose of organizing aid societies was for "keeping love of the Union alive through healthy social contact, expression and labor."[82] After the war, Bellows explained that "the Sanitary Commission was not from its incep-tion a merely humanitarian or beneficent association." It necessarily "took on that appearance," he wrote, but the Commission's leaders were "men of strong political purpose, induced to take this means of giving expression to their solicitude for the national life, by discovering that the people of this country had a very much higher sense of the value of the Union . . . than [most politicians] . . . seemed to recognize."[83] For Bellows and his ilk, the strength and coherence of the political order inevitably depended on the moral health of society. War to maintain the Union was also inextricably a part of a search for a more ordered society. In *No Party Now But All For Our Country*, Francis Lieber emphasized that citizens had a duty to support the government actively, as well as desist from partisan opposition. He lauded the efforts of public-minded citizens who labored for the "great cause of liberty" by, among other things, making bandages for soldiers.[84] In other words, the conflation of the national cause with the administration brought the voluntary work of women under the auspices of organizations like the Sanitary Commission into the ambit of electoral politics.[85]

In an ideological sense, these organizations represented the flowering of a national vision that took elements of the old republican antipartisan tradition and reinforced it with a powerful new assertion of the legitimacy of established powerespecially of the nation state. Denying the right of revolution to the Southern states should have necessitated some dexterous reasoning, given the United States' revolutionary heritage. Since the Revolution—indeed arguably earlier than that—Americans had thought of their nationality in contractual terms, as a relationship based on a mutual agreement. That was the premise on which Southerners justified secession—that the federal government had broken its implicit contract with the people of the Southern states.[86] Furthermore, antebellum Americans had been accustomed to seeing revolutions as a democratic challenge to aristocracy and privilege. The European Revolutions of 1848 were still fresh in many people's memories, and most Americans had viewed the leaders of those struggles as republican heroes. Unionists were anxious to explain that the Southern cause was not comparable with the nationalist revolutions in Europe and that the Lincoln administration "wars only to preserve the institutions in which the ideas of liberty and progress are embodied."[87]

Bellows' sermon, *Unconditional Loyalty*, published in 1863, took these ideas further. Writing in the wake of the New York City draft riots of July 1863, Bellows declared straightforwardly that "the head of a nation *is* a sacred person." He tried to show that support for the Lincoln administration amounted to support for the "sacred cause of government itself." He warned critics that, by protesting about the unconstitutionality of the government's action, they threatened to "loosen every link in that chain of law and order which binds society together"; the result would be anarchy. At about the same time, Congregationalist minister Horace Bushnell defined loyalty—a word which he conceded antebellum Americans had tended to regard as "an old-world word"—not as adherence to the letter of the Constitution, but as a "moral bond created by disposing Providence, and sanctified to be the matrix of the coming nationality and the Constitution to be."[88]

This amounted to an organic conception of nationhood that was more akin to the way in which nationhood was invoked in the old world than it was to traditional American ideas. Charles Eliot Norton believed that "our nation was never in truth *founded*. . . . It was not made by man; it is no discovery or invention, but a natural growth."[89] This organic conception of nationhood had been championed in the antebellum period by Unitarians. Not surprisingly they were in the forefront of the wartime assertion that the elements of American society, like the limbs of a living body, were each dependent on the other; indeed Norton's father had been a famous Unitarian minister.[90] Another Unitarian, Bellows, wrote in 1849 that "there is no rightful authority which is not in a sense divine." In the Civil War such views became self-evident.[91] "The state is indeed divine" and the political leader of the nation was "a sacred person"[92]

Orville Dewey, at one time an assistant of Ellery Channing at the Federal Street Church in Boston, was in retirement during the war after many years of writing and lecturing as a Unitarian minister.[93] In 1863, he published a pamphlet stressing the advantages of a long war. At the outset of the war, he argued, "we had thought that, severed by the great ocean barrier from European complications, we might have the rare lot to go on for ages in undisturbed peace, in increasing abundance, wealth and luxury. . . . In our free, reckless, republican way of talking about authority, we had thought more about the right of revolution than the right of sovereignty." Such complacency was a source of corruption and degradation for, "it is more than doubtful whether in the present state of human affairs any nation could go on so without sinking into inglorious ease, into meanness, vice and ruin." The remedy was to learn the lessons of other nations: "We needed *discipline*, and especially of our *self-will*—our national vice—of which the Southern revolt is the most enormous and portentous explosion ever seen in the world." Only if Americans learned "obedience to *law* and constituted *authority*," Dewey warned, would the nation survive and prosper. "We have not felt as we ought and must the *sanctity of government* . . . the visible frame of society, all over the world, is held together only by that sacred bond." Partisanship, of course, was emblematic of this lack of discipline. "Our politics have been self-willed, factionalised and vulgar," wrote Dewey. "They must become thoughtful sincere, honest and reverent to the common weal."[94] Propounded by Northeastern elites through the pulpit and by the propaganda engines of the Loyal Publication Societies, this new nationalist vision, grounded in antipartisan assumptions, had a disproportionate influence on wartime politics. War, Unionists proclaimed, was a harsh teacher. Through the suffering of war, the American people were learning the benefits of loyalty and discipline. A common idea was to suggest that the war was a symptom of the growing pains of the nation. As a former Democratic congressman put it in a speech to a Union Party meeting, "every people who have become a first class nation have been obliged to pass through our present experience before the refractory elements in their political system have been reduced to order."[95]

Taken together, the development of the popular Union Leagues and the elite Union Clubs in 1863 significantly affected wartime political culture. The creation of national networks that, in the case of the Union Leagues, replicated many of the features of parties while claiming to be above party powerfully reinforced the Republicans' antiparty strategy. Little wonder that Democrats began to rail against the "spell" their opponents had "woven around the hearts of our people, by the cunning use of the words conservatism, patriotism, Union."[96]

5

The Army, Loyalty, and Dissent

There was a tension in nineteenth-century elections between the principle that votes should be counted fairly and voters' choices freely made, and the countervailing pressure to conform to community norms. Defining the boundary between legitimate and illegitimate efforts to shape the outcome of an election had never been easy in a political culture in which voting was a highly ritualized and public event.[1] The war made this general problem more acute. In wartime, administration supporters' assumption that partisan opposition was disloyal and therefore illegitimate made it acceptable to use the instruments of the state—especially the moral and physical power of the newly created mass citizen army—to aid the victory of loyal candidates. Loyalty Oaths in the border slave states, and the more informal loyalty tests imposed by the presence of soldiers and provost marshals at the polls in some parts of the North, gave a hard edge to the rhetorical conflation of party and nation.[2] The discourse of antiparty nationalism has to be understood in relation to the different contexts and meanings attached to wartime elections.

Defining Loyalty

To most Democrats, loyalty meant the preservation of the antebellum constitutional order—"the Constitution as it is; the Union as it was," in the words of the ubiquitous party slogan. In contrast, the new antiparty nationalism of the Union Leagues in effect conflated national loyalty with support for the administration, including its emancipation policy. In between were conservative Unionists torn between recognizing that the old antebellum order was gone, and fear of the radicalism that may take its place. Including old line Whigs and former Know-Nothings—men who had often supported Fillmore in 1856 and Bell in 1860—this moderate group supported the war and was as repelled by Copperheadism as they were by emancipation and the apparently cavalier attitude of the administration toward the Constitution. The fundamental problem of Civil War politics was this shifting definition of loyalty. Some Democrats undoubtedly pledged undying fidelity to the "Union as it was" knowing that their proposal for an armistice and negotiations on the model of the old sectional compromises would effectively mean the North losing the war. Others insisted that a true conservative policy would reunite white Southerners with their estranged Northern brethren. Although administration supporters also tried to appropriate the reassuring, preservationist language of the Constitutional Unionist tradition, in practice they branded as disloyal those opponents who wanted to uphold the Union of 1861 without giving full support to the war measures—including emancipation—which they now deemed necessary in order to suppress the rebellion. In a fluid party system, political conflict became a battle to define loyalty and patriotism, and thus determine what constituted a legitimate election.[3]

In 1862 one Ohio Democrat complained that "never since God made this world has any party been so infamously treated as has the Democratic Party since the war began. Though you give your flesh and blood to put down the rebellion, if you do not favor abolition you are denounced as a rebel sympathizer."[4] John Maitland, a rank and file Ohio Democrat, was a case in point. After spending his lifetime in the Democratic Party defending the Union and the Constitution, Maitland was shocked to find that he was being branded disloyal for his racial views. In conversation with a neighbor in the spring of 1863, Maitland had announced that he was happy to fight for the Constitution and the Union but not for "the nigger" and had been told: "Did you say Nigger! Say colored man. Why you're a traitor!"[5] As the preeminent defenders of the Jacksonian ideal of a white man's republic in which egalitarianism and individual liberty would thrive only in an exclusive, white, male community, Democrats felt profoundly threatened by the Lincoln administration's resort to emancipation.

Democrats connected their opposition to emancipation with a second, equally powerful, grievance: the draft. The federal Conscription Act of March 3, 1863, claimed Democrats, gave the federal government the right to lead citizens away "in chains" if necessary to fight a "negro war" that confirmed for them the ways in which the Lincoln administration threatened local autonomy and popular sovereignty.[6] Democratic newspapers commonly ran headlines like "Three Hundred Dollars or Your Life!" protesting against the commutation provision that provided an exemption for those who could afford to hire a substitute.[7] Emancipation and conscription, explained a Democratic newspaper in Connecticut, were both "manifestations of those colossal strides towards the establishment of despotic power on this continent, which none but fanatics of the most revolutionary and Jacobinical school would ever venture upon making even in the most turbulent and refractory times"[8] Tellingly, Democratic campaigners also repeatedly compared the draft to slavery, insisting that it was a form of "bondage" fit only for the Old World. Conscription was just the most heinous of numerous ways in which the administration threatened what Democrats had always understood to be the fundamental purpose of the

Constitution: the guarantee of individual freedom, especially from an over-bearing federal government.

In condemning the draft, violations of civil liberties, and the emancipation policy, countless Democrats who had once been fervent supporters of the war crossed over into opposition and even obstructionism. The Philadelphia *Evening Journal* was one such dissenting voice. Having declared in 1861 that it would uphold the administration in its efforts to suppress treason, by 1863 it repeatedly attacked the war which, one editorial argued, had passed into a stage that could have "no other purpose than revenge, and thirst for blood and plunder of private property." The South's military strength was greater than at any time, the author continued, while the Lincoln administration is "incapable of winning victory in the field." The newspaper was suppressed and its proprietor, Albert Bioleau, arrested and spirited away to Baltimore so that he was immune from any habeas corpus writs that might have been issued (in defiance of the President's suspension) by a Democratic judge in Philadelphia.[9] Democratic candidates in the elections that took place in the spring and fall of 1863 espoused very similar positions. Charles Carrigan, running for the fifth congressional district in Pennsylvania, explained that "when this war was first commenced, I supposed it was a war for the defense of the Union; I was in favor of it." Now, though, it was clear that the administration had transformed the war for the Union into a struggle "for the emancipation of the negro—a war for equalizing the blacks with the white race." As a result, Carrigan announced that he was "now opposed to the war on account of its brutality. . . . It whips white men . . . for the purpose of enfranchising the black man."[10]

In some cases, Republicans were absolutely right to conclude that their Democratic neighbors did not support the war. One New York Democrat told cheering groups of supporters that the North was carrying on the war for purely selfish ends.[11] Mattie Blanchard referred repeatedly to her Democratic neighbors who, she thought, were "as big a traitor as any south" and the rhetoric, overheated as it seems, reflected the reality of an increasingly vociferous peace movement in Connecticut. One prominent Democrat in that state told a party meeting in 1863 that the resolutions they had just adopted calling for an armistice "will cause a thrill in the hearts of our Southern Brethren."[12] John Wilson, a coal miner from Northeast England, found himself in a scornfully anti-Lincoln community during the war. He had traveled to America in early 1864 after losing his job at home and spent a year working in a drift mine in western Pennsylvania. In the small rural community of which he was a part, "it was not at all safe to offer a word of praise for Lincoln." Wilson recalled an incident in which an infuriated Democrat threatened at rifle point a young man who had been overheard singing the line "we will hang Jeff Davis on a sour apple tree."[13]

Republicans were right when they pointed out that professions of loyalty to a dying antebellum constitutional order were increasingly irrelevant to the issue of whether to suppress the rebellion. "The Union as it was!" quoted a Union Party broadside derisively, "Does that mean we can get back the hundreds of thousands who have been slain in battle?"[14] Democratic speakers, especially from 1863 onward, typically opposed secession and proclaimed their adherence to the nationalist vision of Washington, Jefferson, and Jackson. But many also insisted that military subjugation was the wrong way to deal with the problems the country faced and that nothing could be worth the massive loss of life and economic dislocation that the war was causing.[15] The peace faction scored some important symbolic successes in 1863, capturing the attention of Democratic platform committees and newspaper editorial writers. In February William Eaton, a Connecticut Democrat who had opposed the war from the outset, declared that Thomas Seymour, the Democratic candidate for Governor, was "a man whom the *brave men and lonely women of the South love, honor and esteem.* The conservative men of the North will grasp the demon abolition by the throat, strangle it and invite the brethren at the South to unite with us!" Another speaker was loudly cheered by a Hartford, Connecticut crowd when he declared, "*We are against the war. . . .* When Thomas J. Seymour is elected, the *President will understand what that means.*" Reading such rhetoric in their morning newspapers, Republicans like Sydney Stanley concluded that electoral politics represented nothing less than "the struggle of liberty and civilization against slavery and barbarism."[16]

The problem of defining loyalty in such shifting circumstances was illustrated by the testimony of Gustavus St Gem, an election official for a small town in Missouri, at a House of Representatives hearing into a disputed congressional election in 1862. Under oath, St Gem classed the people who voted in the 1862 election for the Democratic candidate John C. Scott in the 1862 elections as "generally disloyal, and sympathizers with the south." When asked if he knew of any act of disloyalty that a certain group of Democratic voters were guilty of, he replied "I have heard them express themselves opposed to the measures of the administration, and especially denouncing the [emancipation] proclamation." The exchange continued:

> Question: Cannot a person be opposed to the measures of the administration and yet be loyal to the government of the United States?
> Answer: Not at this time, when such measures are the means of enforcing the laws and suppressing rebellion and treason. I support every act of the administration for the purpose, without questioning it.
> Question: Cannot a person differ with the President as to what measures are necessary to put down the rebellion, and yet be loyal?
> Answer: Not if such differing would give any encouragement to rebels and traitors.

Question: How would it be if such differing did not encourage rebels and traitors?

Answer: I consider all such differing as calculated to embarrass the government, and will always more or less give encouragement to rebels.[17]

Administration loyalists' intolerance of opposition was compounded by the rising political violence during 1863, most of which was connected to the draft. Enrollment officers faced abuse, resistance and threats on their life throughout the North. At least thirty-eight employees of the Provost Marshal Bureau were killed during the war and the true figure may be even higher.[18] T. W. Bergley, a brave Union Party lecturer, reported encountering a catalogue of violence and intimidation on a speaking tour of Southern Indiana. His speech in Huntingburg was disrupted by "roughs" many of whom, he reported, were "openly shout[ing] for Jeff. Davis." The following day he was violently attacked "by a fellow called 'Mike Wotcher'" and lost the use of his left eye. When he arrived in Holland, "a number of Democrats were assembled to prevent me speaking [and] one of the worst of them 'Byron Spratly' told me 'I will kill you and any man that speaks for Lincoln.'" Bergley valiantly continued his speaking tour, although he moved into more sympathetic parts of the state, simply remarking, "poor deluded fellows!"[19] Most dramatically of all, opposition to the draft in New York in July led to one of the worst incidents of internal unrest in the history of the United States—four days of fierce rioting that had to be suppressed by a regiment of U.S. troops returning from the battle of Gettysburg. Similar incidents occurred in intensely Democratic working-class urban areas like Boston's North End and especially in the Southern counties of Illinois and Indiana.[20]

As Iver Bernstein has demonstrated in his study of the New York City draft riots, there was a party political dimension to the conflict on the streets of lower Manhattan. The working class citizens of strongly Democratic New York City felt politically marginalized and powerless in the face of a government that was threatening their liberty and fomenting unwanted social revolution.[21] Irish resistance to emancipation was driven by a racist fear of economic competition from African Americans, but it was also grounded in a political culture in which, given their experience of British rule in Ireland, the exercise of power by a centralized government was feared. Class tension also played an important role in working class Irish anti-abolitionism. Middle class, moralizing abolitionists seemed indifferent to the "wage slavery" that existed in the northern factories. A typical piece of Democratic election propaganda addressed to the "working men" of New York City in the fall of 1863 attacked the "Abolition Republican party" for "consigning to their untimely deaths five hundred thousand human beings; . . . deluged the land in blood; whitened the fields of the South with the bones of the slain; brought grief and sadness to nearly every fireside."[22] The day after the rioting began in New York, the Brooklyn *Daily Eagle* "condemned such acts as yesterday" but did so only because, "as we lay claim to a higher standard of manhood than the Negro, let us show it by obeying implicitly the laws we ourselves have made." The editor later commented that this editorial had got him into "more or less trouble," meaning that he was attacked in Republican newspapers for appearing to excuse the violence.[23] For the influential New York press, the riots were a highly significant moment in the debate about race. Overt white supremacism had now been tarnished by its association with lawless attacks on the symbols of the nation in the midst of a war. The riots also helped administration supporters to reinforce the association between treason and partisanship. The *New York Times* concluded that "there are men and women among us so besotted by party feeling as to have lost their horror of murder and cruelty, and their respect for property."[24]

Given this context, congressional and state elections in 1863 were more bitterly fought than any in the war so far but once again there was no straightforward two-party battle. Few candidates in 1863 described themselves as Republicans, while Democrats, in contrast, retreated into a familiar partisan lexicon. As always, local issues and circumstances influenced the structure of electoral conflict as different groups sought to build majorities in a fluid electoral context. In Rhode Island, for example, political factions were based on support for or opposition to the charismatic figure of William Sprague, who had been elected Governor in 1860 at the head of a fusion ticket that combined Democrats, Conservative Republicans, and 1860 Bell supporters. So powerful was Sprague's hold over Rhode Island politics that, in the April 1862 gubernatorial elections, no Republican ran against him. State assemblymen and senators calling themselves Conservatives, or Sprague Unionists, gained a large majority in the state legislature over Republicans and Peace Democrats.[25] In 1863 Sprague successfully used his personal popularity to swing a coalition of War Democrats and Whigs into supporting James Y. Smith, the Republican nominee (and Sprague's defeated rival in 1861) to succeed him as governor.[26] Elsewhere, partisan divisions were confused by the way in which Union Party tickets were put together. In Maine, the Republican state organization, under the leadership of James G. Blaine, effectively exploited the divisions in the Democratic Party and nominated a Douglas Democrat for Governor in place of the radical incumbent.[27] In New Hampshire, there was a three-way contest for the governorship: a Democratic candidate who ran on a peace platform, a conservative Republican who was uncomfortable about emancipation, and a War Democrat—the colonel of the eleventh New Hampshire Infantry—who ran as a "Unionist."[28]

The highest profile races in the fall of 1863—gubernatorial contests in Ohio and Pennsylvania—sharply illustrated the impact of the efforts to conflate loyalty with support for the administration. Both states had large numbers of conservatives, traditionally anti-Democrats but hostile to radicals, and in both states a Democratic candidate who took an antiwar position ran against a conservative Union Party nominee. In both cases the "copperhead" candidate lost, and did so in acrimonious circumstances. In Pennsylvania the Democrats ran George Woodward, a state supreme court justice who had ruled unconstitutional an antebellum law allowing soldier voting. He now denounced the "transcendental, hypocritical, canting philanthropy that would overthrow the work of the founders and set up a negro despotism upon its ruins." Woodward mobilized the Democratic base, aided by the fact that many natural Republicans were unable to vote because of service in the army, yet he lamented that he could not convince people that "no traitor blood lurks in my veins."[29] In Ohio, Clement L. Vallandigham, the best-known peace advocate in the North, ran against John Brough, a fellow Democrat who first entered political life in support of Andrew Jackson.[30] He was now the nominee of a Union Party which, although it was made up largely of Republicans, abjured all talk of "past parties." The campaigns in both states received wide national coverage and Republican editors were quick to seize the opportunity to draw conservatives into their camp by attacking their opponents for disloyalty, a strategy that had the additional benefit of allowing Union campaigns to finesse the longer-term implications of emancipation.

The Army as a Political Community

If changing definitions of loyalty facilitated the delegitimization of the Democracy, especially after the Emancipation Proclamation had been issued, the antiparty strategy was also aided by the emergence of the Union Army as a forum for political engagement quite different from any that had existed before the war. Furthermore, the patronage system gave the administration the advantage of a paid labor force to help mobilize voters.[31] During the war, government clerks were given free railroad passes in order to be able to go home and vote.[32] But the political value of traditional patronage was dwarfed in wartime by the creation of the mass citizen army. The army was a national, centralized network through which information and political propaganda could be quickly and effectively relayed and it was a community that could instill political values. As Francis P. Blair put it in a letter to Lincoln, it was "a great political, as well as war machine."[33] Acting upon this conviction, private organizations and the government and its agencies made enormous efforts to get propaganda to soldiers in the field.[34] Specially written pamphlets, copies of hometown newspapers and free issues of New York weeklies like *Harper's* were disseminated, funded, by Union League Clubs and private donations. The Post Office, under the instructions of Postmaster General Montgomery Blair, carried newspapers and Union pamphlets to the army for free, and Blair named special agents to ensure that the documents were distributed effectively to the troops.

Figure 5.1. *Pennsylvania Soldiers Voting, Army of the James.* This sketch appeared in *Harper's Weekly* on October 29, 1864. It shows Pennsylvania soldiers lining up to cast their ballots for state offices and U.S. congressmen. The Army played an important role in wartime elections, in large part because of the way in which their military experiences politicized thousands of young men. Voting in the field was itself a topic of political controversy. In several instances, the losing Democratic candidates challenged the election result alleging illegitimate interference by Union Party-supporting officers (Library of Congress, Prints and Photographs Division. Reproduction no. LC-USZ62-100635).

Literally millions of pamphlets and tracts were circulated in this way in 1863 and 1864.[35]

President Lincoln himself played a significant role in consolidating the support of soldiers. If the Union was the carrier of the values of the republic, "Father Abraham" seemed to many soldiers to personify the struggle. Regular appearances to inspect the troops, in which he would talk at length to private soldiers, and visits to hospitals to talk with the wounded, made Lincoln a visible presence. He regularly addressed groups of soldiers on their way to or from the front from an upstairs window of the White House. In addition he held perhaps two thousand or more private interviews with enlisted men who came to him with problems related to sickness, furloughs, or pay.[36] News of these meetings spread rapidly through word of mouth and through letters to local newspapers. The president had the common touch, a remarkable ability to connect to people on an individual level, to make them feel that he understood and shared their problems and concerns. As Richard J. Carwardine has put it, Lincoln became a "virtual presence" within the Union army.[37] His very ordinariness and, as the war went on, his increasingly obvious physical deterioration under the strain of wartime command reinforced his bond with the troops.

Political participation was an important manifestation of the status of the soldier as citizen. Many soldiers consciously regarded elections as solemn political festivals that affirmed republican government, a faith illustrated by the many occasions, recorded in soldiers' letters and diaries (and later in newspaper reports) in which voting took place even when it was clear that it could have no impact on who was elected. Prisoners of war held in Confederate jails rigged up polling booths on Election Day and solemnly cast their ballots. Soldiers reported how keenly their units had supported the cause by voting for Lincoln with as much zeal as if reporting the outcome of a battle.[38]

Being part of the army was to be surrounded by politics; it created a forum for political action that had not previously existed and that was beyond the boundaries of conventional partisan contests. What were they doing there, those hundreds of thousands of farmers and mechanics and small businessmen suddenly transformed into soldiers? Answering that question by talking about it, formally in debating societies that mirrored the lyceums they knew at home and informally while sitting around in camp, provided an important means of politicizing the previously unpolitical.[39] The army camps, according to one Illinoisan, were "filed with grave reasoners."[40] Political influence in the army flowed both down from the officers and also from one's peers. One Illinois regiment exercised its political muscle by resolving that all "C[ommanding] officers who do not endorse the president's proclamation of emancipation, and who will not to the utmost of their ability endorse and sustain the administration in its efforts to crush the rebellion, be politely requested to go home and let better men fill their place."[41]

For soldiers more than for civilians, the war utterly transformed the context in which electoral competition happened. Soldiers felt acutely the connectedness of the political and military campaigns. Many soldiers concurred with the sentiments of an infantryman from Connecticut who declared that he felt as if he was using the bayonet against the enemy on the field, and the ballot against the traitors in the rear.[42] "While we are watching and fighting the armed enemy in the field," warned one Union officer, "let us not forget that our enemies are *not all* in the field, nor are they *all* in the South, but that there are *many* of them lurking around and about our own dear homes, with designs as treasonable as can be formed in the breast of Jeff Davis or any of his co-conspirators."[43] The lyrics of one of the most popular soldiers' songs of the war, "Just Before the Battle Mother," took the form of a soldier's letter to his mother. It contained the line "Tell the traitors all around you/ that their cruel words we know/ in every battle kill our soldiers/ by the help they give the foe."[44] In countless letters home, soldiers—even life-long Democrats—"choked with rage" and frustration at home front dissenters. An Illinois Democrat exhorted his family to take strong measures: "Is there no grit left [in] the inhabitants or be they afraid to use their shotguns and riffles . . . [and] hang every Cussed one of the traitors as quick as you would kill a snake?"[45] In 1864, Union soldiers stationed at Vicksburg, Mississippi, passed resolutions declaring their faith in "our present President" and their wish that he be re-elected "not from any party feeling, but on account of his honesty and integrity."[46] For most soldiers, reading about politics in camp, or on the march, party conflict back home could not be anything other than factious. As a soldier in an Illinois regiment put it, "this partyism . . . is sapping the north[.] The people are very slow to learn that there are only loyal men and traitors[;] it seems to me it will be time enough to cavil about politics when our government is secure, and not before."[47] Political acts by men in uniform resonated to the folks back home. One historian has aptly described the army as a great "moral force," with enormous symbolic importance.[48] Letters home were often passed around friends and family and published in local newspapers.[49]

Mark Neely has discovered resolutions passed by Illinois regiments in 1863 threatening to march on the state capital in Springfield against the Democratic controlled legislature, should the Republican Governor Richard Yates request them to do so. The 56th Illinois, for example, resolved that "it is the duty of every citizen to lay aside all party creeds, platforms and organizations and stand firmly by the powers that be." The 88th Illinois infantry demanded that people at home "lay aside all petty jealousies and party animosities" and declared themselves ready to "obey an order from the President to march into our State with bayonets fixed to enforce the laws."[50] Altogether Neely has found resolutions of this kind from fifty-five infantry regiments, four cavalry regiments and four batteries of artillery, representing in total some fifty thousand men. Threats like these were never carried out but even so, they are a startling reminder of the vulnerability and instability within the political system. One Illinois soldier described how the privates and noncommissioned officers in his regiment had taken control of the streets of Alton, Illinois to hold a political meeting. "After supper" he wrote excitedly to his father, "we adjourned to the city hall by companies with colors and arms and these gave the biggest boost we could to the union cause." The privates and noncommissioned officers passed resolutions affirming their support for emancipation and President Lincoln. "We do not need men here who are not willing to support all the war measures of our commander in chief," he declared.[51]

There were Democrats in the army who retained their antebellum partisan affiliation. Certain regiments had been known for their Democratic loyalties since the start of the war. The Twentieth Massachusetts Infantry was one such group and, far from supporting the President, its officers wrote public letters attacking the administration that were reprinted in Democratic newspapers. Colonel John L. McNaugh lamented the lack of a George Washington among the current generation of political leaders to steer the country through its trials and tribulations. Instead, all the Union had was an "anecdote personified as a President."[52] But outside of the few regiments led and officered by committed Democrats, opponents of the administration were made to feel collective political pressure. One Democrat wrote to his local newspaper complaining about such treatment. When the men were in rank, he reported, there was an order that all who wished to vote for McClellan should take a step back and "all those who favor the re-election of Lincoln will stand fast."[53] The allegorical quality of this anecdote does not detract from its significance: enlisted men were deemed to be taking part in a political as well as a patriotic undertaking.

Soldier Voting

The Union Party's control of the apparatus of state governments over most of the North enhanced its majorities among Union troops. But in four states—Indiana, Illinois, Delaware, and New Jersey—Democratic-controlled legislatures prevented the passage of measures that would have enabled soldiers from those states to vote in the field.[54] Democrats, and some Whiggish conservative Unionists, based their opposition on the not unreasonable fear that voting in the context of military discipline would be easily corrupted. Soldier voting became one more illustration of the subversion of the Constitution by radicals, and a fear of the changing relationship between government and citizens. One Pennsylvania Democrat, opposing an 1863 constitutional amendment to allow soldier voting, vowed to protect the "purity and sanctity of the ballot."[55]

The Union Party made great political capital out of this issue, charging, with some justification that the attitude of these Democratic legislatures towards voting in the field demonstrated that they were aware of how unpopular their equivocal war policy was among fighting soldiers. "Let the ballot box show that the soldiers can vote for those who voted for them, and that the Party who refused to let soldiers in the army vote are not worthy of their ballots now."[56] One Union Party pamphlet distributed both at the front and "back home" took the form of a discussion among the soldiers from various states about their right to vote. "In becoming soldiers we certainly did not cease to be men, nor any less citizens than before we put on our uniforms, drew our swords and shouldered our guns," explained a captain in a Pennsylvania regiment. A private, in this dramatization, agreed that:

our rights should if anything be increased not lessened; for there is no use in mincing matters. Don't we do more than those who stay at home—at least more, Captain, than the *Peace* men? We have left home, with all its comforts—wives, children, sisters, mothers, fathers—to defend the old flag; risked health and life to put down those who would dash our good old Union into ruin, and, I think, we should at least be respected by those who remain behind.[57]

The pamphlet imagined a discussion among Pennsylvania troops about why the amendment to their state constitution enabling soldier voting had been delayed so long. It pointed out that in the legislature all the Republicans and Unionists had voted for the measure, and all the "Copperheads calling themselves Democrats" had opposed it, and that the same pattern of support had been visible in the popular election to ratify the amendment.

The publishers of a weekly magazine, *The Soldier's Friend*, entered into the propaganda battle with a broadside sent to army camps that called upon the "the brave men of the Army and Navy to stand by the men who have stood by them."[58] Illinois Democrats responded by arguing that the legislative committee considering the bill had not found a way of reconciling the field-voting provision with the state constitution. But the real reason for their opposition emerged clearly when they argued that "soldier–voting under the present abolition administration is the veriest mockery."[59] Regiments in states where voting in the field had been blocked actively petitioned their governments to recognize their political rights, and Union Party supporters back home took up the cause with public meetings and broadsides.[60]

Granting furloughs to known Union Party supporters from sensitive states became an important element in the administration's political strategy in October and November 1864. Union Party newspapers explained to soldiers that if they required furloughs home they should notify their Union state central committee or their congressman.[61] This clearly seemed more appropriate than approaching their commanding officer. Even in states that allowed voting in the field for national elections, residency requirements still sometimes meant that in local and state elections votes could be cast only in town meetings. In these cases, returning soldiers were sometimes issued with special orders allowing them to carry their arms to ward off anyone who tried to prevent them from exercising their right to vote.[62] In numerous instances, however, officers were given dispensation to be absent from the army during the campaigning period.[63] In some instances Democrats alleged that soldiers—for example those convalescing in hospitals in Northern cities—voted illegally, using their power to overwhelm the polls.[64]

The Union Party state committees in key battleground states like New York and Pennsylvania were given the use of navy vessels and the military telegraph to help distribute propaganda and collect ballots.[65] In Connecticut, a state that had passed a constitutional amendment to allow soldier voting, local Union Party officials were quite open about exercising partisan discretion when drawing up lists of registered soldiers.[66] In New York a fierce controversy broke out over the canvassing of state soldiers in the field. Democrats accused the administration of preventing their commissioners from distributing ballots, and each party accused the other of fraud.[67] There were many incidents of friction between canvassers and military authorities. A Democratic electoral commissioner from Connecticut was briefly arrested and placed in irons after getting into political arguments with commanding officers.[68]

The administration's attention was concentrated on the issue of soldier voting by the political situation in Illinois and Indiana where Union Party leaders were alarmed about electoral prospects. Elihu B. Washburne wrote to Lincoln from the President's hometown of Springfield, to tell him frankly that "it is no use to deceive ourselves. . . . There is imminent danger of our losing the state." The Democrats would have a majority of ten thousand, he thought, unless the soldiers were allowed home to vote.[69] On October 27, Washburne wrote again on a more confident note: "we are hard at work in this state and the prospects for our success are good, provided we get a reasonable number of the soldiers home."[70] Although the President did ensure that several thousand Illinois soldiers returned home, Washburne telegraphed the White House only five days before the election with a plea for the furlough of "four thousand Illinois soldier voters" encamped in Springfield.[71]

The Army and the Conduct of Elections

The most dramatic manifestation of the way in which the war altered the terms of electoral engagement was the unprecedented direct and active intervention of the federal government in the electoral process. Not only in the Border States but also in big eastern cities with large immigrant, Democratic-voting populations, Provost Marshals and troops were a highly visible presence at the polls, challenging voters, searching for potential draft dodgers, and watching for the pro-Confederate dissent that in practice shaded into intimidation of opponents of the administration. The foreign born were the main focus of the Provost Marshals' suspicion.[72] Immigrants who had not yet become naturalized citizens were exempt from the draft but, as Secretary of War Stanton interpreted the 1862 Militia Act, immigrants who, having taken out their first papers announcing their intention to become citizens, then exercised their right to vote would automatically become eligible for the draft.[73]

Frank King, a Democratic voter in Pennsylvania, described the scene at the polls in a congressional election in 1863:

A gentlemen there representing himself to be a deputy United States marshal, by name Jonathan Bullock, [was] acting in a very boisterous and abrupt manner, threatening to knock some down, and also threatening to smack myself over the mouth. He was also marking the names of the voters by some private mark of his— those voting the democratic ticket as having voted wrong; those the republican ticket as having voted right. It was done in a public manner—the republican who held the window-book giving the names out in that manner loud.[74]

Another witness, Enos D. Benner, complained that the self-described Provost Marshal:

would always look at the heading of the ticket. If he found it was the democratic ticket he would most generally speak of the enrolment but if it was the heading of the republican ticket he would say nothing about it; and several times have said to him, here comes a republican; he would say, I don't want him—we have him—or something to joke it off.[75]

In Bedford County, Pennsylvania, a voter reported "there were soldiers at the polls from a few minutes after they were opened until after they were closed. They said they were there for the purpose of taking any conscript that came there to vote."[76] The deputy Provost Marshal "carried a revolver" and "stood the greater part of the day on the platform at the polls.[77] A. J. Crisman, of St Clair Township in Bedford County, Pennsylvania reported a confrontation with soldiers at the polls. Approaching the polling station with thirteen other Democrats and draft dodgers, Crisman saw soldiers coming toward them with guns at the ready:

Some of the democratic leaders came to us and told us that we had better go away; some of us or some of the soldiers would be killed. At that time the soldiers were within 60, 70, maybe 80 yards of us; we went off; they halted us, but we didn't halt; we went on; there were three shots discharged. We didn't get to vote.

The same witness reported that a man was killed that night. "I didn't go to the funeral," he recalled. The same cause that kept me from the polls kept me from the funeral; I was afraid of being arrested."[78]

In the Border States, where there was a permanent military presence, the army played a direct role in the electoral process. Military authorities warned that those who voted for Democrats would have their homes or horses impressed by the army. The brother of the Democratic candidate for the Second Congressional District in Kentucky reported having seen an order of the local Union commander posted in public places "the substance of which was that horses and slaves of those men who were for 'no more men and no more money,' and their *aiders* and *supporters*, would be first pressed by the military if they needed horses or slaves. This order had a very great effect on the public."[79] The conflation of party and nation meant that only the election of a Union Party candidate could be considered by the troops guarding the polls to be a loyal, and therefore acceptable outcome. Loyalty Oaths were required of voters in slave states, adding to the discretionary power of local military authorities to obstruct voters. To administration supporters the new "ironclad" oath introduced in March 1863, which required past as well as future fidelity to the Union, was an essential weapon in the fight against secessionism and anarchy. To many conservatives, however, they were yet more evidence of the destruction of the old constitutional order and its replacement by despotism. Democratic Senator James A. Bayard of Delaware was so angered by having to take a loyalty oath that he resigned his senate seat warning that oaths were "demoralizing acts of tyranny.... The first weapons young oppression learns to handle; weapons the more odious since, though barbed and poisoned, neither strength nor courage is necessary to wield them."[80] His fears were compounded by the tendency of local military commanders to adapt oaths to suit their own purposes. Officers at the polls in Cardsville, Kentucky in 1862 reportedly required those wanting to vote to first swear to "support the policy of the present federal administration."[81] The lack of discipline of Union troops, especially in Missouri, compounded the problem.[82]

Lincoln suspended habeas corpus in Kentucky on July 5, 1864, despite the protests of leading politicians in the state from Governor Thomas E. Bramlette down, that such an "unprecedented move" was designed to "directly interfere" with the "free elections" in November.[83] Military records are filled with evidence that commanders assumed that their role was to secure votes for Lincoln. In many instances the army distributed Lincoln campaign documents.[84] The commander of the District of Western Kentucky, for example, reported that he was "canvassing this Congressional district for Mr. Lincoln with much success," although he made a plea for more forces to "hold the country securely" during the election.[85] In St Louis, soldiers were involved in a violent disturbance that broke up a Democratic meeting. According to the local Union Party press, a group of "about thirty or forty" soldiers stoned the speakers' platform, destroying transparencies bearing anti-Lincoln slogans. The meeting descended into a riot, with pitched battles between soldiers and "a mob" raging around the main hotel where the soldiers had taken refuge.[86] Every election season during the war, newspapers reported that torchlight parades had been violently attacked, or that speakers had been stoned and run out of town. Across the North, soldiers on home leave were frequently involved in attacks on Democratic newspaper offices and Democratic public meetings.[87]

There were numerous instances of the arrest of candidates, especially in the Border States and the Midwest. Kentucky Senator Lazarus Powell, a Democrat, reported that "several persons were arrested as soon as they voted the democratic ticket, and taken to Colonel John W. Foster's head-quarters; two of the persons thus arrested were imprisoned, and kept in the military prison until the next day."[88] General Stephen G. Burbridge, com-mander of Union forces in Kentucky, arrested several prominent Demo-crats a few days before the presidential election, one, John B. Houston, on the grounds that his "influence and speeches have been of a treasonable character."[89] Firmness in the Border States sent the message to Union sup-porters in the North that their vote for Lincoln was a vote for a man deter-mined to give treason no quarter in his pursuit of a Union victory.[90] This was the kind of action that was applauded by men like James Edmunds, the President of the National Union League of America (an umbrella organi-zation for the Union Leagues), who wrote to the President advising him to make a show of military strength. "I trust there will be no hesitation," he advised: "there is power behind a bold hand at this time."[91]

In the Border States and in areas that had been under Confederate occu-pation, it was necessary to take an oath of allegiance to the United States in order to be allowed to vote, a rule that was enthusiastically enforced.[92] Troops were also highly visible on the streets of New York on Election Day, 1864. General Benjamin F. Butler, after his success in subduing the occu-pied people of New Orleans, was put in charge of an operation to ensure public order. There were no reports of disturbances. "A man must be either for his country or against his country," Butler had declared, in what *Harpers'* described as a "thrilling and eloquent" speech. He acknowledged that "the present government was not the Government of my choice—I did not vote for it, or any part of it, but it is the Government of my country.... I am a traitor and a false man if I falter in my support.... No man who opposed his country in time of war ever profited."[93] The controversy surrounding the military role in the Border States also highlights the inherent confu-sion between legitimate electoral opposition and "treasonous" opposition to the government's war policy. The presence of troops at the polls had the effect of reminding the electorate that the political choice they were about to make had far more profound implications than in peacetime. But most of all, the moral authority of the army was the indispensable tool in the administration's claim to transcend party. While direct military interven-tion in election results remained very much the exception rather than the rule, the assumption that justified it—that elections were only legitimate so long as the right side won—was widespread.

6

Slavery, Reconstruction,
and the Union Party

By the end of 1863, in total contrast to a year earlier, the supporters of the administration, now more than ever wrapped in a Union Party guise, were cautiously optimistic. They looked forward to the Army of the Potomac's spring advance, hopeful that their political position in the run-up to the 1864 presidential election was strengthening. Underlying the transformation was evidence that, since the battle of Gettysburg in July, the Confederate tide was retreating. Grant's victory at Vicksburg split the Confederacy in two as the Union army gained control of the full length of the Mississippi River. And, gradually, public attitudes toward emancipation were changing. In 1863, radical antislavery campaigners were far more confident about deploying moral and humanitarian arguments than they had been a year earlier. It helped, of course, that fears of a black "invasion" following the Emancipation Proclamation had not been realized. The numbers of blacks coming north were small and those who did come were easily absorbed into the labor force as the war economy expanded. Prices were rising sharply, but so were wages. Also important in shifting popular racial attitudes was the performance of black troops. The press gave extensive coverage to the "valor" under fire of "the sable arm of the Union," notably at Milliken's Bend and Fort Wagner during June and July 1863. The recruitment of black troops had aroused a great deal of hostility at first, but once in the field, even opponents conceded that they were of more use there than back home. At the very least, conservatives argued, blacks were valuable substitutes for a drafted man. Even soldiers who retained their fervent white supremacism generally favored the use of black troops. As one put it, "may [the black man] not as well waste, and die in the nauseous swamps of the South as us?"[1] Some towns paid recruitment agents to find freed slaves who would act as substitutes so that the draft quota could be met.

The relative recovery in the political fortunes of the administration party in 1863 reflected and in turn helped to reinforce the increasing success of Republicans, led by Lincoln, in identifying their cause with that of the nation. Non-Republican conservatives were encouraged to support the administration in the interests of social order as well as military victory. So that the Republican-Union Party could present itself as the "real" nation, it turned the virulent minority of Northerners who remained unrecon-

ciled to the war into a powerful negative reference group. In the process, the meaning of national loyalty was changing. With black troops now
enlisted in the Union army and the newspapers filled with daily reports of
"contrabands"—runaway slaves—flocking to the Union lines as the army
advanced, it was becoming easier to support the radical argument that the
abolition of slavery was a patriotic, Union-saving measure.

Yet the lines of division in Northern politics remained complex and
fluid. Most Northerners continued to describe themselves as conservatives.
They were in favor of military subjugation of the South but, to a greater or
lesser extent, were nervous about the implications of emancipation and the
transformations the war was bringing to the relationship between government and citizens. In the summer of 1864, two issues—emancipation and
Reconstruction—revealed the tensions within the Union Party coalition
and helped to frame the strategic calculus of politicians in the run-up to
the presidential race.

Reconstruction and the Union Party's Southern Strategy

On June 7, 1864, in a cramped and stiflingly hot theatre in Baltimore, Abraham Lincoln was re-nominated for a second term in office. There were
no other candidates and the result had been fully expected, but when the
chairman of the convention read Lincoln's name a brass band struck up
"Hail Columbia!" and the hall erupted in uncontrolled excitement.[2] One
observer reported that "the racket was so intolerable that I involuntarily
looked up to see if the roof of the theatre was not lifted by the volume of
sound."[3] The delegates—some of whom came from the Union-occupied
South—had gathered as representatives of the National Union Party. From
New England and the Northern parts of the Midwest, where the Republican Party had dominated politics since the late 1850s, the delegations sent
to Baltimore were made up of the men who had founded the Republican
Party—and had been at similar conventions in the past to nominate Lincoln in 1860 and Fremont back in 1856. Unionists from the Border States,
War Democrats and former Whigs and Know-Nothings joined these committed Republicans.

Presbyterian pastor Robert J. Breckinridge of Kentucky, president *pro
tem* of the National Union Party convention and uncle of Confederate
General John C. Breckinridge, ended his opening speech to the convention by remarking on the heterogeneity of the past political affiliations of
the delegates. "I see before me not only primitive Republicans and primitive Abolitionists," he said, "but I see primitive Democrats and primitive
Whigs—primitive Americans, and if you will allow me to say so, I myself
am here, who all my life have been in a party to myself." This diversity, he
thought, created a new kind of party, one devoted solely to the preservation of the nation. "As a Union party, I will follow you to the ends of the

earth, and to the gates of death! But as an Abolition party—as a Republican party—as a Whig party—as a Democratic party—as an American party, I will not follow you one foot." This peroration was "cheered to the echo" by the delegates.[4] William Dennison of Ohio, in his speech accepting the position of president of the convention on the evening of the first day, reaffirmed the nonpartisan self-representation of the Union Party by declaring that "in no sense do we meet as members or representatives of either of the old political parties which bound the people, or as the champions of any principle or doctrine peculiar to either."[5]

Such rhetoric had an important function in establishing the public image of the Union Party and the presence of men like Breckinridge was evidence of the expansion of the party into the Border States. But if delegates were unanimous about their choice of presidential candidate, they divided over the purpose and future of the Union Party itself. At least in an indirect sense this was the issue at stake in the most bad-tempered conflict at the Baltimore convention: whether or not to seat the delegations from Union-occupied rebel states. Disagreement over this issue—and over the related issue of which of two rival Missouri delegations should be recognized—took up far more time than any other issue considered by the convention. Conducted through the pedantic parliamentary procedures of resolutions, amendments and "amendments to amendments" so beloved by nineteenth-century lawyer-politicians, the debate exposed a sharp divergence between those who saw the Union Party as the means of creating a new *national* organization, with roots in the restored rebel states, and those who were determined to exclude seceded states from political communion until such time as their future could be decided on Northern terms.

The background to the debate at Baltimore was the emerging conflict between Abraham Lincoln and the bulk of the Congressional Republican-Union Party over the terms on which rebel states would be readmitted to the Union. The previous December, President Lincoln had issued a "Proclamation of Amnesty and Reconstruction," according to which 10 percent of the voters of a rebel state could form a government and readmit their state to the Union by swearing an oath of loyalty to the US Constitution. The Proclamation was guided by the President's desire to stimulate and support Unionist sentiment in the South and to provide a means of rapidly establishing civil government in those parts of the Confederacy conquered by the Union army.[6] At that stage of the war, most congressional Republicans, believing that Reconstruction was a matter that had to be subordinated to the need to conquer the South, did not challenge Lincoln's leadership. Journalist Noah Brooks observed that the Proclamation "gives, probably, more general satisfaction than any message since the days of Washington," explaining that it "has pleased the radicals and satisfied the conservatives by plainly projecting a plan of reconstruction which is just to popular rights, to the cause of liberty, and to the loyal people of all sections of the Union."[7] The plan certainly had its conservative features, such as the heavy reliance on the pardon of individual Southerners. But many radicals were unperturbed by such measures and they readily approved of the loyalty oaths required of all citizens, and above all on the insistence on emancipation as a condition of reunion. Others were less convinced. On one side of the political spectrum, Wendell Phillips told audiences of abolitionists that the government should leave the freedman "on his own soil, in his own house, with the right to the ballot and the school-house within reach."[8] On the other, Democrats condemned the plan as a "despot's edict . . . a wild, unjust, and impracticable plan for the consummation of Abolition."[9]

On the basis of Lincoln's "Ten Percent Plan," administrations were formed in Arkansas, Tennessee, and Louisiana and, by the spring, anxiety was mounting in the congressional Republican Party. Radicals whose attention was increasingly turned to the rights and freedom of the ex-slave were frustrated by what they saw as the leniency given to ex-rebels. For a plan that may have appeared a strategically shrewd move six months earlier, it now increasingly appeared to many radicals, as one of the President's correspondents put it, that "only evil can result from its continuance."[10] Whitelaw Reid, Washington correspondent of the *Cincinnati Gazette*, considered that the Proclamation represented a "dangerous conservatism" and urged radicals to resist.[11] "Pure" Republicans opposed what they saw as the administration's constant efforts to, in the words of Lydia Maria Child, "conciliate the Democratic party" and by extension the rebellious South.[12] Above all, what alienated congressional Republicans was the creation of new governments in Arkansas and most notably in Louisiana that appeared to pave the way for the return of the old planter class to power under the old state constitution with scant protection for the freedmen. Whereas Lincoln's primary concern in formulating Reconstruction policy was always to help the war effort, the mood in Congress swung towards the idea of postponing the serious business of Reconstruction until the war was over. Much to Lincoln's chagrin, Congress refused to seat the congressional delegations sent from Louisiana and Arkansas, with Democrats and radicals alike now alleging that the whole purpose of Lincoln's Reconstruction plan was to create puppet regimes that would support his renomination for president and cast electoral votes in his favor in the coming presidential contest.

This was the background to the moves at the Baltimore convention, led by the radical congressman, Thaddeus Stevens of Pennsylvania, to block the recognition of the delegations from rebel states. Stevens warned that recognition in the convention would set a precedent for official recognition of those states in the Electoral College and he reminded the convention that the House Republican-Union caucus had, only days before, unanimously rejected this notion.[13] Breckinridge, who had earlier urged delegates to "organize this party thoroughly *throughout* the United States" responded bitterly that to refuse to seat delegations favorable to the "Union-Lincoln cause" would "come as nigh to playing the devil as any set of gentlemen ever did with their eyes blindfolded."[14] Horace Maynard, the leader of the Tennessee delegation, who made an impassioned plea for recognition, supported Breckinridge. "Let me say," he cried, "that for you who drink in the cool breeze of the Northern air, it is easy to rally to the flag to sustain the honor of your country." He, on the other hand, represented:

> those who have stood in the very furnace of rebellion, those who have met treason eye to eye, and face to face, and fought from the beginning for the support of the flag and the honor of our country. . . . Assembled here under that symbol which typifies our common nationality, we, the loyal people of Tennessee, claim the right to be represented in any such assemblage wherever upon this broad continent it may be met.

Rising to an emotional peroration in which he appealed to the memory of the sons of Tennessee who had died under the national flag and whose blood "has scarcely even now dried upon the sand," Maynard sat down to tumultuous applause.[15]

As big an impact as Maynard's speech seems to have made, the mood of the convention was decisively swung some hours later by the dramatic intervention of the Rev. William G. Brownlow of East Tennessee—"Parson Brownlow" as he was universally known—a slaveowning Whig minister, newspaper editor and politician whose fierce Unionism had led, briefly, to his imprisonment by the Confederate authorities in 1861 and his emergence as a national symbol of Southern loyalty to the Union. To fail to recognize the delegations from the rebel states would be, in effect, to recognize secession, he cried. "We don't recognize it in Tennessee [applause]. We deny that we have been out [applause]. We maintain that a minority first voted us out, and then a majority whipped the minority out of the state with bayonets winning over a portion of our men to their ranks."[16]

In the face of such arguments, Stevens lost the battle, complaining with a characteristically over-dramatic turn of phrase that "the applause which I have heard of the principle of . . . recognition has alarmed me more for the safety of this nation than all the armies of the rebels."[17] The delegations from Louisiana, Tennessee, and Arkansas (although not those from Florida, South Carolina, or Virginia) were admitted with full voting rights by a majority of 307 delegate votes to 167. The opposition came overwhelmingly from the New England and Pennsylvania delegations with the Border State delegations divided.[18]

The admission of the delegations from the three Union-occupied rebel states paved the way for the nomination for Vice President of Andrew Johnson, the Tennessee Unionist who had been a life-long Democrat. Vice President Hannibal Hamlin, a radical antislavery man from New England, was bitterly disappointed at the result; he had been led to believe that he would be renominated without much opposition.[19] The switch reflected political reality: New England Republicans had nowhere else to turn—and despite his disappointment Hamlin campaigned vigorously for Lincoln in the fall.[20] There were some who mistrusted Andrew Johnson's political instincts: Simon Cameron wrote privately that he would have preferred a man "reared and educated in the North."[21] But there was a powerful lobby of local Union Party politicians who recognized the strategic value of nominating a "southern man with northern principles," as one of them put it.[22] Even more visibly than the admission of the rebel state delegations, the nomination of Johnson symbolized the self-projection of the Union Party as a new, national entity, distinct from the old sectional Republican Party. There was a widespread assumption among delegates to the convention that, at least in the form in which it was constituted in 1860, the Republican Party was no longer a viable national organization, and that in the wartime context it was damaging to the national cause to maintain old party labels.

The nomination of Johnson went down well with newspapers generally sympathetic to the administration. The *New York Times* thought that "in thus selecting a War Democrat for this high distinction, the convention gave the country a substantial pledge that it was truly independent of all the old political organizations, and that it recognized no party test but that of faithful and constant devotion to the war against rebellion."[23] Most active partisans saw Johnson as a Union hero, whose humble roots and staunch support for the Union gave an easy image to sell to the electorate. It was "universally" felt that he would strengthen the ticket, reported a radical activist from Pennsylvania.[24] As they boarded the railroad trains that took them back home, pondering the long summer ahead before the election season came to life in the fall, Union Party delegates seemed confident that their appeal to national loyalty would ensure the re-election of Lincoln.

Things were not to be so simple. In June, the papers were still hopeful that despite the staggering loss of life at the inconclusive battles of the Wilderness and Spotsylvania, the new military savior of the Union would soon prevail. General Ulysses S. Grant—who, in stark contrast to McClellan was dubbed "Unconditional Surrender Grant" for his tenacity and hard-headedness—had led the Army of the Potomac to the edge of Petersburg, the city regarded as the key to unlock Richmond, the Jerusalem of the Union military crusade. In June, the Democratic opposition appeared divided and impotent. Unionists hoped that their strategy of presenting themselves as a nonpartisan, patriotic front—and with the aid of timely military victories—would sweep aside Democratic and factional opposition. The following three months in fact reignited factionalism within the ranks of the Union party, provoked challenges to Lincoln from radicals and from conservatives, and, by offering the prospect of success, reinforced the unity of the Democrats. By mid August even Lincoln was increasingly convinced that his presidency, and possibly the Union cause as well, were doomed. The military stalemate was the essential background to this pessimism, but Lincoln's summer of discontent also had political roots. Conservatives, including many leading lights in the Union Party, became increasingly disaffected by the President's continued commitment to emancipation. Meanwhile radicals, many of whom had been uneasy about the Union Party movement from the start and who were now stung by their defeat over the admission of the Arkansas, Louisiana, and Missouri delegations to the Baltimore convention, sharpened their opposition to the President's plans for Reconstruction.

The conflict over the admission of the Southern delegations at Baltimore was a precursor to a very public clash between the President Lincoln and Congress over Reconstruction. On July 2, Congress passed a bill, introduced by Henry Winter Davis in the House and Benjamin Wade in the Senate, that would have completely undermined Lincoln's Reconstruction plan. The Wade-Davis bill required a majority—not just 10 percent—of all white male citizens of a rebel state to take a loyalty oath before a new government could be recognized. To participate in the new state constitutional conventions, or in the governments that would then be formed, citizens had to swear an "iron clad" oath, not merely of future loyalty to the United States but also that they had never given aid or comfort to the rebels. All persons who had held high civil or military positions in the Confederacy were to be disfranchised and disqualified from holding office.[25] In practice, the Wade-Davis plan would have meant abandoning the governments in Louisiana and Arkansas and almost certainly postponing Reconstruction until after the war. Had Lincoln signed it, he would have lost crucial conservative support in the North and, in his view, removed a tool with which he thought he could weaken the Confederacy. As the Confederacy tenaciously fought to hold on, and the bloody battles outside Richmond continued to bring ever longer lists of the dead but few signs of a breakthrough, fewer congressional Republicans were sympathetic to the President's continuing faith in the existence of a latent Southern Unionism.

Lincoln pocket-vetoed the bill, but took the unusual step of issuing a proclamation hoping to minimize the damage within the party. He reaffirmed his commitment to a constitutional amendment abolishing slavery and explained that, although he did not want to be "inflexibly committed to any one plan of restoration," he was "fully satisfied with the system for restoration contained in the Bill" and would support any state that wished to adopt it.[26] This last point was rather disingenuous, and the President can hardly have expected his message to have placated his congressional critics. The veto of the Wade-Davis bill reinforced the view of a growing number of radicals that Lincoln, in the words of Thaddeus Stevens, was driven in his Reconstruction policy by his desire to "have the electoral votes of the seceded States."[27]

As growing numbers of Republicans plotted privately to capitalize on the President's political vulnerability and run another candidate in Lincoln's place, Wade and Davis made their protest in the most public way possible. On August 5 the *New York Tribune* published what became known as the Wade-Davis manifesto, a shrill broadside against the President, criticizing him for recognizing the "shadow governments" in Arkansas and Louisiana that they denounced as "mere creatures of his will." They predicted that similarly un-republican regimes would be established before the presidential election "in every rebel State where the United States has a camp," and that therefore the President "holds the electoral votes of the Rebel States at the dictation of his personal ambition." And then they issued a stark warning:

> If those votes turn the balance in his favor, is it to be supposed that his competitor, defeated by such means will acquiesce? If the Rebel majority assert their supremacy in those States, and send votes which elect an enemy of the Government, will we not repel his claims? And is not that civil war for the Presidency, inaugurated by the votes of Rebel States?[28]

Lincoln was shocked by the tone and the manner of this attack, concluding that they "intend openly to oppose my election."[29] Days afterward, the President's great supporter, Thurlow Weed, ruefully admitted to a correspondent, "Lincoln is gone, I suppose you know as well as I."[30]

In fact, the response to the Wade-Davis bill in the country was remarkably muted. Many congressional Republicans seemed to believe that their colleagues had gone too far. Newspaper commentary on the subject ceased after a few days, except among Democrats who gleefully seized upon it as evidence of disarray in the Union Party camp and later issued it as a campaign document.[31] If anything, the very public attack on the President served to rally some of his supporters, especially conservatives. A tract published by the Union League of Philadelphia, argued that, in his response, Lincoln had proved himself "the leader of the people and not a party. If, in this he has aroused the opposition of extremists who assisted to elect him, it but gives him an additional claim on reasonable men of all parties."[32] But Lincoln, as ever, needed to placate critics on two fronts. Concerned not to further alienate radical opinion, he resisted the temptation to respond to the Manifesto with what one correspondent of Postmaster General Blair called a "blast after the style of Jackson."[33] In the long run, Wade and Davis may have inadvertently strengthened Lincoln's position. The President's reputation as a man who was above partisanship, a claim so central to his election campaign that fall, was not at all harmed by a public spat with radicals who were clearly not in step with the public mood on this question.

Slavery and the Union Party

In November 1863, Treasury Secretary Salmon P. Chase had written to the President suggesting that the future status of the freed people should be codified in the constitutions of the rebel states as they were readmitted to the Union.[34] He was to be disappointed. Lincoln's Proclamation of Amnesty and Reconstruction did no such thing. The President never wavered in his commitment to the principle of emancipation but, even so, in radical eyes he was prepared to make too many concessions over the future status of freed people. On November 5, 1863 the President told General Nathaniel P. Banks, commander in charge of Union-occupied Louisiana, that he would not recognize a government that "repudiated the Emancipation Proclamation" but neither he would he object to any "reasonable temporary arrangement" adopted in relation to the "the landless and homeless freed people." By this he presumably meant some version of the apprenticeship system that Banks was already establishing and against which Chase had specifically warned him.[35]

In February, 1864, while Senator Pomeroy was pushing the candidacy of his friend Chase, Congress debated a proposed new Constitutional Amendment abolishing slavery. Avoiding the controversial issue of Reconstruction, the amendment reduced the political problem of freedmen to the simple proposition that they should not be returned to slavery once the war was over, a proposition on which both radical and conservative supporters of Lincoln were able to agree.[36] In the interests of securing the unity of the Union Party, moderate Republican senators rejected an amendment sponsored by Charles Sumner that would have guaranteed equality before the law to freed slaves. By separating the issue of emancipation from the politically problematic idea of equality, the constitutional abolition of slavery was presented as the final nail in the coffin of the Slave Power. In language redolent of the Republican Party's crusade to rally the North in the 1850s, Congressman Isaac Arnold denounced the Democrats as the northern minions of the southern "slave kings."[37]

Some Democrats were determined to mount a positive defense of slavery. Several publications of the Democrats' answer to the Loyal Publication Society—the Society for the Diffusion of Political Knowledge—including one by the society's president Samuel F. B. Morse—reiterated the view that slavery was biblically ordained and socially necessary.[38] The dominant response among Democratic leaders, though, was to challenge the attempt by Unionists to deny that emancipation and racial equality were part of the same package. Democratic newspapers took up with a new fervor the claim that the administration was bent on diluting the pure white blood of the American people with that of an inferior race. In February 1864, two Democratic journalists working for the New York *World* anonymously published a spoof pamphlet called *Miscegenation*—which purported to explain the Republican Party's new policy of racial amalgamation. Republicans immediately repudiated it as a hoax, but it was a brilliant means of publicizing the Democrats' central message and too tempting a target to forego. Congressional Democratic leader S. S. Cox must have known the pamphlet was not what it purported to be, yet he declared in the House of Representatives that *Miscegenation* proved that the Republican Party was "moving steadily forward to perfect social equality of black and white."[39] Democratic publicists claimed that five thousand mulatto babies had been born in Washington since 1861. This, declared a pamphlet entitled *The Lincoln Catechism*, was what "the President means by 'Rising to the Occasion.'" The "ten commandments" of this publication—a bitter satire attacking the "Abolition party"—included "thou shalt have no other God but the negro." Another directly confronted voters with the prospect of the end of the white man's republic: "thou shalt make an image of the negro and place it on the capitol as the type of the new American man."[40]

The miscegenation scare had barely begun when the elite Union League Club of New York organized the most spectacular means of displaying the war's challenge to the racial order. On March 5, 1864, the 20th Colored Regiment, funded by Union League Club members and recruited without the cooperation of Governor Seymour, marched down Broadway to Union Square, where Loyal Publication Society president Charles King told them that "you are in arms not for the freedom and law of the white race alone, but for universal law and freedom, for God implanted the right of life, liberty, and the pursuit of happiness in every being."[41] In a literal sense this march reclaimed the streets of New York for black people after the lynching and violence of the riots the previous July and it represented a remarkable transformation in the racial attitudes of the city's Union party elite. The troops were formally presented with a flag on behalf of a committee of upper-class women with the reminder that "this is also an emblem of love and honor from the daughters of this great metropolis to her brave champions in the field."[42] This was too much for the *New York Herald*, which commented that "this is a fair start for miscegenation. What the phrase 'love and honor' needs is only the little word 'obey' to become the equivalent of a marriage ceremony."[43]

Anti-emancipationist rhetoric drew, not only on the deep well of racism in the North, but also on fears of a profound breakdown of the social order. Anti-emancipationist propaganda typically invoked fears about the emancipation of women as well as blacks. Whereas previous racist imagery had typically portrayed women as the victims of sexually predatory black men, Civil War propaganda with its miscegenation rhetoric shifted gear, presenting white abolitionist women as willing sexual partners of black men.[44] One such satirical tract, the "Black Republican Prayer," invoked the "blessings of Emancipation throughout our unhappy land" so that "illustrious, sweet-scented Sambo [may] nestle in the bosom of every Abolition woman, that she may be quickened by the pure blood of the majestic African."[45] The prominence of women like the abolitionist Anna Dickinson in the Union Party campaign seemed to confirm, in the minds of Democrats, that the administration was bent on social revolution.

The Thirteenth Amendment passed the Senate on April 8, 1864, but was blocked in the House where the necessary two-thirds majority was denied by the opposition of sixty-five out of sixty-eight Democratic congressmen.[46] This defeat ensured that the amendment would play a leading role in the political skirmishing that preceded the presidential campaign. Democratic opposition in the House clarified the difference between the parties on a line of division that Republican leaders believed was to their advantage. It was this sense that the proposed amendment would unite the widest possible coalition behind the President, while simultaneously defining a clear policy difference with the Democrats, that was in the minds of the National Union Party platform committee when they came to drawing up the emancipation plank at the Baltimore convention.

The high point of the convention came when, to great acclamation, delegates endorsed a plank which, denouncing slavery as the "cause, and now . . . the strength of the rebellion," demanded in the name of "justice and national safety" its "complete extirpation from the soil of the republic."[47] Breckinridge struck the "nerve of the convention," according to one observer, when he declared that there could be no end to the war without the utter extermination of slavery—a remark greeted with "tumultuous applause."[48] Even the Methodist Episcopal chaplain who led the opening prayers concluded with the words, "Grant, we beseech Thee, that when we shall pass through this ordeal, it shall be, while the fires of the furnace have not left their smell upon our garments, they have melted off the chain of the last slave."[49] The Union Party of 1864 thus became the first mainstream party in American history to campaign for the complete abolition of slavery.

Yet even as they adopted this most radical of proposals, conservatives hoped that this commitment to emancipation could be reconciled with the Constitutional Union tradition and separated from any revolutionary-sounding commitment to racial equality. All knew that ending slavery might leave Republicans without a clear political identity. Indeed, the party that had been founded, above all, to prevent the spread of slavery in the territories would be redundant in the new political universe created by a war that swept away the peculiar institution. Seward and Weed saw the National Union Party as a step toward a moderate, nationalist party that might draw support from the South as well as the North, once the war and the divisive question of slavery had been swept away.

The strategy set out at Baltimore, then, was to keep together as wide a coalition as possible. Unionists would do this by combining support for the thirteenth amendment (the minimum demand of the radicals) with the reassurance to conservatives that this was not the old, radical Republican Party that many still blamed for fanning the fires of sectionalism before the war, but a new patriotic organization that transcended the limits of traditional partisanship, not least by reaching out to Unionists in the Border States and the South. This strategy depended, among other things, on the President's supporters being able to argue that the emancipation policy was not prolonging the war. The optimism of this view in political terms was brutally exposed in the weeks following the convention.

The Letter "To Whom It May Concern"

That summer was one of the hottest that anyone could remember. Washington was rife with the "swamp fever" that spread from the putrid Potomac River. Even Lincoln, usually robust in the face of illness, was bed-ridden for two weeks.[50] Meanwhile, the springtime hopes of an early military breakthrough dissipated in the heat. Grant and Lee appeared to be in a bloody stalemate, as the death tolls mounted. In this stifling and highly charged context, a crisis developed that threw into doubt the wisdom of incorporating the thirteenth amendment into the Union Party platform. Rumors circulated that two Confederate agents at Niagara Falls were prepared to discuss peace and reunion, so long as the insistence on emancipation was dropped. Horace Greeley of the *New York Tribune* characteristically plunged into the fray "I beg you, I implore you, to inaugurate or invite proposals for Peace forthwith," he urged the President on July 7. Under public pressure, Lincoln wrote a letter on July 18, addressed "to whom it may concern," stating the terms on which he would accept a settlement.[51] Those terms were "the restoration of the Union" but also "the abandonment of slavery." Although, in reality, as Lincoln well knew, the Confederate agents were not empowered to accept peace without disunion, the Southerners scored a propaganda triumph by sending a report of the conference to the Associated Press. They accused Lincoln of deliberately sabotaging the negotiations by prescribing conditions he knew to be unacceptable.[52]

Democrats maintained that, by insisting on emancipation as a condition of reunion, the administration was prolonging the war. The feeling grew that Lincoln could be beaten in November by any candidate who stood firmly for the Union as it had been, without the revolutionary purpose of emancipation.[53] When the Baltimore convention met in June, there was still reason to be optimistic about the progress of the war. Only a month later, pessimism about the military situation created a far more hostile environment for those—including, it now seemed, the President—who still demanded emancipation as a precondition of peace. A Democratic pamphlet that took the form of a spoof biography of "Old Abe" reveals the nature of the political capital that the president's opponents made from the issue. "He wrote a letter to whom it may concern," wrote the anonymous author sarcastically, "offering to make peace if the rebels would give up their theories, their property, their lives, and do just as he wanted them to for ever after. What more could be desired?"[54]

Of course, radical antislavery men were greatly encouraged by the letter "to whom it may concern." When it was published on August 4, the
Christian Advocate and Journal called it "one of the most dignified and appropriate acts in the records of the war."[55] The minister of Old South Church
in Boston assured the congregation that "Lincoln has exactly struck the
pulse-beat of the nation in his note 'to whom it may concern.'"[56] Harriet Beecher Stowe wrote a clarion call for antislavery men to rally round
the President: "Almighty God has granted to him that clearness of vision
which he gives to the true hearted ... to set his foot in that promised land
of freedom which is to be the patrimony of all men, black and white."[57]

Moderate supporters of the President who were the leading pro-
ponents of the Union Party strategy fretted about the political implications of the President's public commitment to emancipation as a war aim.
From Albany, Thurlow Weed reported that there had been a sharp reaction
against the administration and that Lincoln's reelection had become an
impossibility.[58] One of Weed's correspondents warned that the President's
open letter was a "Death distroying [*sic*] epidemic" that had "killed" Mr.
Lincoln.[59] The New York diarist, George Templeton Strong, thought that
Lincoln's "blunder" in his letter "to all whom it may concern" may cost
him his election: "By declaring that abandonment of slavery is a fundamental article in any negotiation for peace and settlement, he has given
the disaffected and discontented a weapon that doubles their power of
mischief." Back in Illinois, Lincoln's old friends, Leonard Swett, Elihu B.
Washburne and David Davis, were similarly pessimistic.[60] Even Forney's
Washington Chronicle pleaded with the President to abandon the Emancipation Proclamation, warning that, if he did not do, so the election would
be lost and the Union dissolved.[61]

With brazen hypocrisy given his own role in urging the President
to be more radical on slavery. Greeley scolded Lincoln on August 9 for
giving "to the general eye" the impression that the rebels were "anxious
to negotiate, and that we repulse their advances." If nothing were done
to correct this impression, he warned, "we shall be beaten out of sight
next November."[62] Greeley estimated a Democratic majority of 100,000
in New York and Pennsylvania if the election were held in August. Henry
J. Raymond wrote privately to the President telling him frankly that he
faced defeat. Public dissatisfaction, he warned, was due to "the impression
in some minds, the fear and suspicion in others, that we are not to have
peace in any event under this administration until slavery is abandoned."[63]
To a party leader in Pennsylvania, Raymond noted that the "Niagara letter
has been very adroitly and successfully used to [Mr. Lincoln's] detriment"
and despaired that "we have not a ghost of a chance in November" because
of the "*suspicion* ... that ... [he] does not seek peace, that he is fighting not
for the Union but for the *abolition of slavery*."[64]

The negative reaction to Lincoln's letter reminded administration supporters that, as enthusiastic as the public might be in principle for eman-

cipation, they would support it only if it was necessary to the defeat of the rebellion.[65] Sensing this, Raymond wrote despairingly to the President on August 8, urging him once again to offer peace on only one condition—reunion. Although Raymond was confident that such an offer would be rejected, he nevertheless urged the ploy—which would involve the public abandonment of the commitment to emancipation—as necessary to ensure victory in November. "In some way or other the suspicion is widely diffused that we can have peace with Union if we would," he told the President. "It is idle to reason with this belief—still more idle to denounce it."[66] The President may have backed off at the last moment, but his supporters used exactly this strategy publicly. Raymond played down the "to whom it may concern" letter, maintaining that it prescribed one mode of making peace, but not the only one.[67] Other administration papers eagerly took up this means of defending Lincoln from the charge that he was waging war to abolish slavery.[68]

Political Divisions

Tensions over emancipation and Reconstruction took the form of political maneuvering that sought a different form of anti-Democratic Party than that presented by the president's friends at Baltimore. Some radicals took part in a curious hybrid of a convention in Cleveland, Ohio, in May, that described itself as a meeting of the Radical Democracy. Rejecting the Union Party's overtures to the South and to conservatives, they nominated the first ever Republican presidential candidate, John C. Frémont, who had made his name as a dashing western explorer. His subsequent war record had been less than glorious (he had fallen victim to the tactical brilliance of Stonewall Jackson in 1862). But as the Major General commanding the Department of the West in August 1861, he had issued—without consulting the President—a proclamation freeing all slaves held by rebels in Missouri.[69] Lincoln countermanded the measure, but Frémont's political reputation among radicals had been reconfirmed. Frémont's greatest political support appeared to come from German settlers in the Midwest, and several prominent German-language newspapers supported him for a while, including the Illinois *Staats-Anzeiger* of Springfield.[70]

From the Union Party's point of view, a third-party candidacy might draw off enough votes from Union candidates in close states to turn the election to the Democrats. "This Fremont movement is a weak thing," wrote a friend of Andrew Johnson, "but just as strong as the Birney movement which defeated Clay in 1844."[71] Most political leaders did not, however, regard "The Pathfinder" as a serious political player. Despite being one of the most visibly unsuccessful military commanders of the war, Fremont surrounded himself with a preposterous retinue of fancily dressed European military advisers with a reputation for corruption and unprincipled ambition. As early as 1861, Northern newspapers ran mocking stories about him jostling for position for the 1864 election.[72] Partly for these reasons, Fremont's candidacy rallied few of Lincoln's opponents from within the Republican Party and he never made much of an impact on public political debate. No major newspaper gave Fremont much attention, much less editorial support, and no prominent radical Republican supported him. Radicals searching for a principled candidate to replace Lincoln were appalled by some of the men supporting Fremont who, according to a correspondent of Anna Dickinson, included "the vilest Copperheads."[73] Abolitionist Lydia Maria Child reasoned that Lincoln "is an honest man [who] conscientiously hates slavery. Fremont . . . is a selfish unprincipled adventurer."[74] Lincoln himself was not worried about Fremont's nomination. Fremont, he told his secretary, John Hay, was "like Jim Jett's brother. Jim used to say that his brother was the damnedest scoundrel that ever lived, but that in the infinite mercy of Providence, he was also the damnedest fool."[75] In fact, the main consequence of the Cleveland convention was to keep Fremont's name in discussion among radicals as a possible alternative to Lincoln, but only if he could be fully co-opted by a larger portion of the Republican Party than was present at the meeting of the "Radical Democracy."

In the end, the nomination of Fremont merely reinforced the President's position by highlighting the contrast between the narrow, apparently more "partisan," appeal of the challengers and the "national" appeal of the President. Lincoln's re-nomination by acclamation at Baltimore happened because, as the correspondence of politicians made clear, Lincoln remained more popular with the public than with congressional Republicans, and partly because the supporters of Lincoln, who identified themselves firmly with the Union Party label, were quick to claim that anything other than fervent support for the President in a time of war was unpatriotic. The Union Party was intended to be a tent big enough to embrace within it all who supported restoring the Union through "hard fighting," whatever their past political views. For some, though, the factious opposition of the radicals was an opportunity to reaffirm the conservatism of the Union Party and of Lincoln's re-election campaign. The most conservative supporters of the President, especially Border State Unionists like Montgomery Blair, actively plotted during early 1864 to "read out of the administration party those Ultra Abolitionists who were the aiders and abettors of the Secessionists in bringing on the war."[76] All seemed to agree that the future shape of party alignments was yet to be defined, and the nature of the Union Party was the battleground over which that issue was fought.

The last week of August marked the lowest ebb in the political fortunes of the Lincoln administration. One of Lincoln's private secretaries, John G. Nicolay reported a "bad state of feeling throughout the Union party about the political condition of things." Politicians in Washington worried that the lack of military success and the prospect of a new draft would make Lincoln's re-election "impossible" by a war-weary electorate unless "something is done."[77] Nicolay called these disillusioned Unionists "croakers"—but the croakers may have included the President himself.[78] On the day Lincoln received Raymond's pessimistic letter, he penned a "blind memorandum" that he asked each member of the cabinet to sign without reading. The President had asked his unwitting colleagues to sign a pledge. Because "it seems exceedingly probable that this administration will not be re-elected," Lincoln wrote on their behalf, "it will be my duty to co-operate with the president elect, so as to save the Union between the election and the Inauguration, as he will have secured his election on such grounds that he cannot possibly save it afterwards."[79] The pessimism evident in this document reflected the administration's political dependence on the military fortunes of the Union armies. It was also a recognition that political circumstances made the President's unwavering commitment to emancipation look narrow and partisan, the opposite of the intended image.

Correspondence among radicals indicates an active interest in undoing the work of the Baltimore convention and replacing Lincoln with someone who could win. Even the irrepressible General Benjamin F. Butler's name was raised.[80] "Beast Butler," as Southerners called him after the determined control he exercised as the commander of Union-occupied New Orleans, had been a supporter of Southern Rights Democrat, John C. Breckinridge, in 1860, but he had since endeared himself to firm antislavery men and was an important symbol of the war's radicalizing effect on Northern political attitudes. He lacked political credibility though, and few radicals rallied to his support. Edwin D. Morgan, the chairman of the Republican national committee, believed there "would be really strong opposition to the re-nomination of Mr. Lincoln if those against him knew in what manner to organize their party." He thought that, while opponents of Lincoln were "by no means unanimous for Mr. Chase" they would take "Grant, Fremont, Banks, or Butler more readily than Mr. Lincoln."[81]

On August 30, a meeting was held in New York organized by Mayor George Opdyke, bringing together several prominent Republican activists, politicians and editors. Francis Lieber of the Loyal Publication Society was there, as were David Dudley Field, Henry Winter Davis, and Parke Godwin of the *Evening Post*. Horace Greeley expressed interest in the movement but did not attend.[82] Other members of this network of discontent were Whitelaw Reid and Theodore Tilton of the *Independent*. These people argued that Lincoln's strength at the time of the Baltimore convention was "fictitious, and now the fiction has disappeared."[83] The product of this consultation was a circular letter, sent to Northern governors, canvassing support for a convention to meet on September 28 in Cincinnati to adopt a new candidate.[84] The plan was to forge a link between discontented Republicans and War Democrats, on the assumption that the latter group would soon be alienated by the forthcoming Democratic convention at Chicago which was expected to nominate a peace man, or produce a peace

platform, or both.[85] The group concluded that "it was useless and in-expe-
dient to attempt to run Mr. Lincoln in the hope of victory against the
blind infatuation of the masses in favor of McClellan."[86] Lincoln should be
persuaded to withdraw and a new nominee found at Cincinnati. This was
not a cabal of radicals but a symptom of a profound and widespread lack of
confidence about Lincoln's chances of re-election. On August 31, a New
York Unionist assured Secretary of the Navy Gideon Welles, that "with
the exception of an occasional man who has special interests or affiliations
there are *no* Lincoln men."[87]

Conservatives and the Chicago Convention

Meanwhile, conservative former Whigs who, since the summer of 1863,
had been attempting to effect a party realignment, plotted their own bid
to marginalize both radicals and copperheads.[88] Under the leadership of
men like the patrician Bostonian, Robert C. Winthrop, these self-described
Conservative Unionists wanted to unite conservative Republicans, War
Democrats, and old Bell-Everett Constitutional Unionists. Like those Lincoln supporters who wanted to replace the old Republican Party with
the Union Party, these conservatives wanted a firm prosecution of the war
and a "genuinely national" party that would appeal to former Whigs in
the South. A few, such as Winthrop, were even sympathetic to the idea of
emancipation, so long as it was not a condition of reunion. As a group, they
remained unconvinced by the conservative credentials of what they called
the "Military Abolition party."[89]

Conservative Unionists believed that, if they seized the initiative and
nominated a ticket for the presidential contest very early on, they could
bounce Democrats into following their lead and out-maneuver the Copperheads.[90] Former President Millard Fillmore was their preferred standard bearer but, while voicing general support, he refused to be a candidate.[91] Consequently, the national committee of the Conservative Union
Party, meeting at Philadelphia on December 24, 1863, nominated General
McClellan for president and William B. Campbell, a Mexican War hero
and former Whig governor of Tennessee, for vice-president.[92] This meeting
attracted little attention at the time, but by the end of August, 1864, politicians were sensing that a new center party that stood firmly for the Union
without the distracting and partisan issue of emancipation would be able to
steal the nationalist mantle from Lincoln. In the late summer of 1864, one
Democratic leader reported that "scores of the rank and file of the republican party" were "declaring that they have got enough of old Abe, and will
vote for any person nominated . . . [by the Democrats] if he is not an ultra
peace man."[93] George Templeton Strong thought that if the Democratic
convention had the "sagacity and patriotism . . . to nominate John A. Dix, I
believe he will be elected. Many Republicans would vote for him, perhaps

I might too."[94] With at least one eye on the expected "re-organization of politics" following the end of the war, some Democrats in the pro-war, pro-Union faction of that party made contact with disaffected Republicans like Chase whose political origins had been as Free Soil Democrats.[95]

Yet, ironically, the war-weariness in the North damaged prospects for an effective conservative alliance involving Conservative Unionists and moderate Democrats because it also had the effect of strengthened the hand of the Copperheads.[96] With the "peace at any price" party in the ascendant, the ability of pro-war Democrats to swing the platform and nomination of their party in the direction of the Conservative Unionists was lessened. The day before the Democratic convention met, a group of conservative Unionists made a futile attempt to combine the anti-Lincoln forces on a war platform. Having failed to secure Fillmore's candidacy these conservatives were prepared to support McClellan on a war platform.[97] The political force of their position was made clear in resolutions that the President has "declared his intention to change the character of the war from the single object of upholding the government to that of a direct interference with the domestic institutions of the states."[98]

When the Democrats met in convention the following day, they were confident that victory was in reach. Delegates shared a distrust of the Lincoln administration and the meddling, activist nationalism that his party seemed to represent, but were seriously divided over war policy and political strategy. In his opening speech to the Chicago convention, party chairman August Belmont attacked "four years of misrule by a sectional, fanatical and corrupt party" that had "brought our country to the very verge of ruin."[99] The tenor of the convention, reinforced by large numbers of spectators who packed the upper galleries, was rowdy and unsympathetic to War Democrats. According to the journalist, Noah Brooks, the delegates cheered every rendition of "Dixie" yet heard patriotic airs in complete silence.[100] As expected, General George B. McClellan was nominated on the first ballot. He had no previous political experience, but—especially since the publication of his Harrison's Landing letter in which he had urged Lincoln to conduct the war according to "the principles of Christian civilization"—he had made clear his ambition to lead the political fight for the conservative vision of the war.

With his commitment to reunion, McClellan was not the first choice of the party's peace wing, but they reserved their real fight for the platform. The Chicago platform committee was dominated by the peace faction in the party, including, much to the delight of Union propagandists, the arch-Copperhead Clement Vallandigham himself. Vallandigham was involved in the drafting of the resolution that committed a Democratic administration to make "immediate efforts" for the "cessation of hostilities, with a view to an ultimate convention of all the states, or other *peaceable* means, to the end that at the earliest practicable moment peace may be restored on the basis of the Federal Union of the states."[101] The cessation of hostilities was

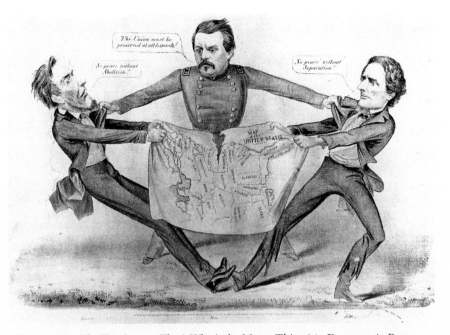

Figure 6.1. *The True Issue or That's What's the Matter.* This 1864 Democratic Party cartoon illustrates how pro-war, anti-emancipation conservatives such as the central figure here, General George B. McClellan, saw themselves—as the defenders of the old antebellum order against fanatical secessionists (represented by Jefferson Davis on the right) and fanatical abolitionists, including President Lincoln (on the left). In his July "letter to whom it may concern" setting out his terms for peace, Lincoln played into the hands of Democrats by appearing to make emancipation a precondition for reunion. The "peace plank" in the Democratic platform substantially undermined McClellan's ability to present himself as the true Unionist candidate to moderate voters, but attacking the administration's radical emancipation policy for prolonging the war and thus helping to destroy the Union remained the focus of the Democratic campaign in 1864 (Library of Congress, Prints and Photographs Division. Reproduction no. LC-USZ62-13957).

designed to "enable negotiations to take place, and if need be to protect a Convention of the States." One editorial in a leading Democratic journal argued that "the political power of [Lincoln] and the military power of [the Confederacy] will have to be displaced before the time for peace arrives. When Mr. Lincoln goes out of office the great obstacle to reunion will be removed."[102] The platform reflected the assumptions of that large section of the North that supported the Union's survival, but not the subversion of the Constitution or the massive loss of life and brutal warfare deemed necessary to suppress the rebellion. As one Democratic newspaper summarized the party's position, it favored "Union with peace, if possible, but Union and the Constitution at all hazards."[103]

Noah Brooks, in Chicago with a brief to report back personally to the President, noted that the balance of forces at the convention meant that each side depended on the other. In order to be certain of getting his nomination, the pro-McClellan delegates accepted George Pendleton, a well-known peace man, as his running mate.[104] Pendleton's presence on the ticket was a sharp reminder of the divisions in the party. It undercut the strategy of War Democrats like Belmont and Cox as well as the hopes of the Whiggish conservatives who had wanted to oppose Lincoln on a platform of waging war firmly but without the revolutionary purpose of emancipation. Furthermore, McClellan was not a natural politician; he had been so confident of receiving the nomination in Chicago that he made no serious efforts to manipulate the proceedings and was later irritated by his own lack of preparedness in not foreseeing the problems that would be created if his supporters did not control the platform committee.[105] Given the peace plank in the platform, McClellan deliberated for several days about whether to accept the nomination. Democratic national committee members agreed that, despite the pressure from the peace wing of the party, McClellan would lack national credibility if he did not make clear his support for the war. Privately, Belmont wrote to the General advising him that "it is absolutely necessary that in your reply of acceptance of the nomination you place yourself squarely and unequivocally on the ground that you will never surrender one foot of soil and that peace can only be based on the reconstruction of the Union."[106]

By presenting himself as committed to the maintenance of the Union at all costs, the General's letter of acceptance, when it eventually came, effectively repudiated the platform on which he had been nominated. McClellan's letter was the crucial factor in keeping pro-war Democrats on board. The General himself told a friend at the end of September that, without his letter, he would have been "whipped."[107] But Peace Democrats were outraged at this act of "treachery" and some even called for him to be repudiated as candidate. Republican congressman Elihu B. Washburne observed the frustration of the peace Democrats with the satisfaction of an experienced political operator who smelled victory. "The copperheads seem to be in a great snarl," he wrote to his wife. "Little Mac don't seem to go down very well with the real peace rebels, but they will have to swallow him. But we will beat them anyhow."[108]

From his vantage point within the White House, John Nicolay had been right when, at the worst moment for the re-election hopes of the President in late August, he had predicted that, "immediately upon the nominations being made at Chicago . . . the whole Republican Party throughout the country will wake up and begin a spirited campaign."[109] Supporters of the President realized that the political tide had turned. Sen-

ator Henry Wilson of Massachusetts reported that "our friends are right-
ening up in New England. The Chicago convention has aroused them to
some extent. I hope in a few weeks to find our friends at work like true
patriots."[110] The pastor of a congregational church in Connecticut wrote
to the President assuring him that, in the wake of the Chicago convention,
a "healthy reaction is now taking place in the public mind in regard to
the coming election."[111] George Templeton Strong wrote that the "general
howl against the base policy offered at Chicago is refreshing. Bitter opponents of Lincoln join in it heartily, and denounce the proposition that the
country should take its hands off the throat of half-strangled treason."[112]
Gideon Welles considered the "Chicago doings as satisfactory as we could
expect or perhaps wish." The issue framed by the Democratic platform,
he thought, was "a war upon Lincoln to make peace with Jeff Davis," a
platform that he did not think would be supported with much zeal in the
country generally, although he expected an "animated and excited contest."[113] One of Lincoln's correspondents, Samuel F. George, reported from
the Army of the Potomac near Petersburg that since the Chicago convention soldiers had been "coming over" to the support of the President in
their thousands. "My candid opinion," he wrote, "is that the soldier vote
will be all on one side."[114]

For most conservatives, the Chicago platform effectively destroyed
any lingering hope that a conservative Unionist might successfully challenge Lincoln. Furthermore, with military victory seemingly in sight at
last, the radicals and abolitionists in the Union Party seemed less dangerous
to conservative voters than the conciliators who stood behind McClellan. Before the Democratic convention even Lincoln's old friend, Orville
H. Browning had spoken in favor of McClellan but now he changed his
tune.[115] Another old Whig, Edward Everett, set the tone for many conservatives by campaigning for the President's re-election. For the man
who had given a three-hour warm-up speech before Lincoln's Gettysburg Address, voting for the re-election of the President in the midst of
a war to preserve the life of the nation was a symbol of his commitment
to the maintenance of the Constitution. Whatever the President's failings,
Everett argued, the alternative was "national dishonor."[116] Similarly, former Massachusetts governor, John H. Clifford, told his old friend Robert
Winthrop that he felt compelled to support the president. "The golden
opportunity which has been given to the Democrats by the folly of the
Republicans has been thrown away," he wrote, leaving conservatives with
no alternative but to vote for Lincoln.[117]

On the same day that news of the Chicago resolutions was wired across
the nation came the first good military news for months. On September
1, after a long siege, General Sherman's troops had finally taken Atlanta.
"The fall of Atlanta puts an entirely new aspect upon the face of affairs,"
reported a New York Union party activist.[118] Most importantly, the contrast between the sudden sense that, once again ultimate military victory

was in sight, and the condemnation of the war by Democrats as a "failure" was jarring. Leonard Swett explained that the "first gleam of hope was in the Chicago convention. The evident depression of the public caused the peace men to control that convention, and then, just as the public began to shrink from accepting it, God gave us the victory at Atlanta, which has made the ship right itself, as a ship in a storm does after a great wave has nearly capsized it."[119] A cautionary note was added by John Murray Forbes who, even after Atlanta, warned that "perhaps the War Democrats may react against the Peace party and make McClellan just as likely to save the Union as we should be."[120]

In the South, the fall of Atlanta was met with a great sense of shock; for many, the failure of the cause of Southern independence seemed, for the first time, to be likely.[121] The news also sent shock waves through the discontented Unionists who suddenly became aware of the political strength that Lincoln would gain from military success.[122] Negative responses to the circular letter sent by Greeley, Godwin and Tilton cut the ground from under those who hoped to replace Lincoln as the Union Party candidate.[123] Even Governor John A. Andrew of Massachusetts declined to endorse the radicals' program. Lincoln was "essentially lacking in the qualities of leadership" and his nomination had been a mistake, he granted; but now "correction is impossible" and "Massachusetts will vote for the Union Cause at all events and will support Mr. Lincoln so long as he remains the candidate."[124] Thurlow Weed gleefully reported that "the conspiracy against Mr. Lincoln collapsed on Monday last."[125] There was no transformation of Lincoln's reputation. Governor Joseph Gilmore of New Hampshire for example was certain that the President had "disappointed" and "had no hold on the affections of the people." But by the first week of September no one of prominence in the Union Party was arguing for a new candidate, if only because it was now "too late to change."[126] Theodore Tilton abruptly reversed his course, penned editorials in the *Independent* supporting the President and belatedly realized that Sherman's victory at Atlanta had produced a "sudden lightening of the public mind."[127] Even Horace Greeley began making campaign speeches for the Union ticket, although he made sure to avoid mentioning Lincoln by name.[128]

One final obstacle to a clear two-party fight between Lincoln and McClellan remained: John C. Fremont. Although they doubted that he would get much popular support, Union Party strategists worked hard to engineer the maverick explorer's withdrawal from the race. A third-party candidate in the race damaged the Union Party's basic strategy of polarizing the electorate by making voters chose between upholding the President and the national cause, or voting for a party that would pander to the rebels. Senator Zachariah Chandler of Michigan, a radical critic of the President, played a key role in negotiating Fremont's withdrawal in return for a tacit agreement that Montgomery Blair, the conservative Unionist from Maryland whom radicals despised, would resign from the cabinet.[129]

On September 23, Fremont announced the end of his candidacy with a grudging statement that called for Republican unity to defeat McClellan but could not resist adding that he considered the administration "politically, militarily and financially a failure" and that its "necessary continuance a cause of regret for the country." The failure of the Fremont "Radical Democracy" to galvanize the radical antislavery forces behind it was largely due to the incoherence and lack of credibility of both candidate and party. But Fremont's withdrawal was significant in terms of the shape that partisan competition would take in the election. After several months in which political insiders had predicted the emergence of a third party that, in some way, would bridge the gap between the partisan extremes, a two-party race was on the cards after all.

By September, the supporters of the administration, gathered under the umbrella of the National Union Party, had succeeded in polarizing political choices. On one side in the presidential election was a candidate committed to peace through military victory, with emancipation as an essential, if highly problematic, corollary. On the other was a candidate whose party's commitment to military reunion was questionable and whose opposition to emancipation was unshakeable. In the midst of a Civil War, the country was on the verge of the most extraordinary, bitter internal battle, one that would substantially determine the course of the war and the future of the republic. It was far from inevitable that partisan alignments should have divided along these lines. Radical distaste with the apparent caution of the Lincoln administration, especially with regard to Reconstruction, and conservative anger at the reckless pursuit of the partisan emancipation policy raised the possibility, during the summer of 1864, of alternative political alignments that might have united conservatives under one banner, in opposition to the radical experiment of the permanent abolition of slavery, with reunion achieved through military victory. The coming election was to prove the value of the Union Party designation to Republicans. By stressing their patriotism, their lack of partisanship and their determination to see the war through to victory, the party of Lincoln could build common ground among the diverse groups gathered under the umbrella of the Union party. The Democrats, meanwhile, faced a renewed assault on their patriotism and their very legitimacy as a party.

7

Emancipation and Antiparty Nationalism in the 1864 Election Campaign

A political campaign is before us," wrote the Union Party national chairman Henry Raymond, "of more terrible moment than any military campaign. One of the latter might fail and be retrieved by another. But if this campaign fails, it is irretrievable. There will be no subsequent opportunity to undo its effects. It would settle the war, decisively, fatally, forever."[1] For more than two months, an immense campaigning effort consumed the time and energy of political activists, filled public spaces with rallies, speeches and parades, and dominated the columns of newspapers.[2] Enterprising businessmen were quick to capitalize on the demand for symbols of political allegiance. The "Campaign Medal Company" of Broadway, New York City, offered trinkets "of every description" at "wholesale prices" and a New York merchant advertised "a new illuminating lamp ... so arranged as to be attached to the window" in front of which could be placed a slogan supporting either candidate. Publishers advertised for agents to sell lithographed portraits of the candidates promising "$10 a day can be made."[3] Northerners were drawn into the political battle even as Union armies were pressing on Richmond and soldiers were dying in numbers barely lower than that of the bloody summer.[4]

In one sense, the power of party organization was never more manifest than in this climactic presidential election. The Union Party national committee and the Democratic national committee were at the apex of networks of party activists at the state, town and ward level. Canvass returns were discussed avidly, wavering voters identified and efforts made to convert them to the cause. Even remote farms or hamlets were within the reach of stumping politicians and the mounds of paper propaganda sent through the mails, although the mobilization effort was by no means uniform since it depended on the energy and presence of local party agents. But if the networks of party officials and volunteers provided the organizational muscle in 1864, for Unionists at least, the familiar rites and practices of partisanship held new meanings in the context of war. In an over-heated context in which accusations of treason were a staple of political rhetoric, the presidential election campaign demonstrated the political value of the antiparty strategy embodied in the Union Party identity. Orators and pamphleteers endlessly repeated the mantra that it was not as Republicans that men were called to vote for Lincoln but as "patriots." When Ralph Waldo Emerson wrote that the Civil War was a "new glass to see our old things through," he was not specifically referring to the rituals of party politics, but the phrase aptly captures the sense in which familiar rites were invested with heightened meaning that transcended their partisan origins.

Party leaders on both sides were convinced that the contest was "wide open" and they were "playing for high stakes."[5] Both sides genuinely feared that the other might resort to arms.[6] In the week before polling day, rumors circulated among Democrats that the government would intervene militarily if it looked as if Lincoln was losing. The administration at one point appeared to believe that a plot to assassinate Lincoln was hatched that involved August Belmont, George Ticknor Curtis, and other prominent McClellan leaders.[7] For Unionists, winning the election was as crucial as winning a military battle, and the enemy was the same. In this election, politics was war by other means.

The Democratic Campaign

Democrats retained strength in parts of the Union dominated by a political culture deeply hostile to the war and emotionally and culturally in sympathy with the anti-Yankee, agrarian world represented by their Southern friends and neighbors. The southernmost counties of Illinois, Ohio and Indiana that were populated by large numbers of migrants from slave states were strongholds of the party. But Democrats were also the natural choice of discontented urban workers concerned about inflation and resentful of the draft. They also appealed to immigrants who were concerned more about jobs and food than about battles and slaves, and to isolated and sometimes transient communities of industrial workers such as coal miners in eastern Pennsylvania, who were hostile to coercive government and fearful of their increasing powerlessness in the workplace. All these groups could be rallied by an antiwar message tempered with promises of economic readjustment, and protection against concentrations of capital. These were the voters most ready to respond to the partisan code-words that had rallied them for a generation. Party leaders worked to reaffirm the party's identity as the embodiment of the "political character" of its constituent groups.[8]

Democrats still favored in 1864 the kind of limited war that most Northerners had envisaged back in 1861: one that was "prosecuted with humanity and justice," that "abstained from every measure calculated to subvert the civil Government and institutions of the insurgent States."[9] Democrats focused on the incompetent way in which the administration was handling the war. The poor care of wounded soldiers, the fatalities in army camps from disease, as well as military defeats, were all laid at the door of the government. But the problem for the Democrats in attacking the government's record, even on nonmilitary matters, was that it was hard to avoid appearing to benefit from Union military failure. Many Democrats did try to minimize Union military victories but, after the fall of Atlanta, these kinds of attack lacked the credibility they had in the summer.[10] Recognizing the electoral danger of outright opposition to the war, one Illinois newspaper tried, deftly but defensively, to claim that the Chicago convention had meant to describe the war, not as a military failure, but as a political failure. Indeed, it was precisely because the armies had been so successful that "the democratic party arraigns Abraham Lincoln for official misconduct and imbecility. Had the soldiers failed in their duty ... then we could not have blamed Abraham Lincoln for the failure to restore the Union."[11]

The September draft call, which should have been powerful ammunition for Democrats, simply highlighted the dilemma that faced them in trying to expand their base. While it was easy to rally ingrained and vehement (indeed often violent) opposition to the administration by attacking the draft, it was precisely this sort of issue that distanced the Democrats from the moderate center. The "terrible conscription law is drawing its chord still stronger and closer about our homes" warned one newspaper. "All conscription or other forced service of the citizen to the state is contrary to the genius and principles of republican government."[12] This was a powerful appeal, but one directed to a stubborn minority: those who felt themselves to be outside the mainstream of patriotic Northern society. The strength of the Democrats in urban centers with large immigrant populations, like New York, was a product of the ability of local party leaders in those places to give a sense of protection to vulnerable communities against external threats such as the demands of the state or the prospect of labor competition with freed blacks. The commutation provision, whereby a drafted man could hire a substitute to fight in his place, was especially disliked in poor communities. Republican newspaper editors, charged Democrats, were "very generous with men and money, but are very careful that they nor theirs do not go to war. If they are drafted they will hire some crippled nigger to take their place."[13] Democratic leaders were aware of the political dangers of becoming too identified with antidraft sentiment. The hundreds of thousands of men who volunteered to fight, and their families and friends, were offended by the pleas of those who had refused. Antidraft agitation simply stigmatized the Democrats as the party of negativism, rather than of potential power.

Recognizing this problem, a majority of national Democratic Party leaders agreed that, notwithstanding the "peace plank" of the party platform, a pro-war message was essential if the party was to avoid large-scale defections.[14] For three years, the party had been confronted with accusations of disloyalty. They had lost many of their best-known leaders, and some prominent Democrats now marched to the tune of the Union Party as "War Democrats." The gains the party had made in the 1862 elections had been eroded in 1863 and in spring elections early in 1864. Yet, party leaders knew, conservative Unionists, many of whom were former Whigs, shared their hostility to the administration even while being fervent supporters of the Union. The best chance of Democratic success in the presidential election was to capitalize on the popular sense of discontent about the perceived incompetence and zealotry of the administration without alienating conservatives who felt there should be no compromise with traitors. War Democratic newspapers, especially in the East, were anxious to appeal to what they believed was a "conservative majority" opposed to emancipation and constitutional change. Many were optimistic that a candidate who stood firmly for the Union could beat Lincoln in November.[15]

By reminding voters of their traditional devotion to the Constitution, Democrats sought to resist the powerful attempt by supporters of the administration to redefine the line of partisan division.[16] "In the name of all that is sacred and glorious in our past history as a nation," the leading Democratic newspaper in Ohio urged voters to support "the only party who in the present as in the past carry the flag and keep step to the music of the Union!"[17] Democratic newspapers reprinted the rousing peroration to Daniel Webster's "second reply to Hayne," the speech familiar in the lexicon of antebellum American politics for its final line: "Liberty and Union, now and forever, one and inseparable!" Democratic meetings were told: "you are fighting for the preservation of the Union!"[18] For the prowar faction of the Democratic Party, loud proclamations of loyalty were a recognition of the power of the accusation of treason.

A few conservative Unionists maintained their faith in McClellan despite the Chicago peace plank. The most prominent by far was Robert C. Winthrop. A sixth-generation descendent of John Winthrop, the first governor of the Massachusetts Bay Colony, Robert Winthrop had been a leader of the "Cotton" faction of Massachusetts Whigs who sought to conciliate the South before the war. He was deeply conservative (indeed he once observed that "I have something in me of the Hampden and the Falkland, but not a particle of the Cromwell") and, as a protégé of Daniel Webster, he was also a passionate Unionist. Despite being approached by a moderate faction of Bay State Republicans, he felt unable to join the new party in the 1850s because of its antisouthern rhetoric, which he feared would exacerbate the sectional crisis.[19] A supporter of Fillmore in 1856 and of Bell and Everett's Constitutional Union Party ticket in 1860, when war came, Winthrop argued that rebellion was "unnatural" and fervently supported the war.[20] Yet, by 1864 his worst fears about the sectional extremism of the Republican Party seemed to be realized. Fearing that Lincoln's reelection would prolong the war because of the administration's determination to place social revolution in the South ahead of preserving the Union, Winthrop supported McClellan, the first occasion in his long political career that he supported a Democrat. Although he approvingly discerned some "conservative leanings" in Lincoln, he condemned the "political exigencies" and "party trammels" that had led the President away from the "brave, prudent and patriotic" policy he should have followed.

In a well-reported speech, which McClellan praised as the most "calm dignified & able & exhaustive exposition of the questions at issue" during the entire campaign, Winthrop set out the conservative case against Lincoln.[21] Military victories were welcome, but they were not in themselves sufficient to restore peace. The policies of the administration, he charged, were calculated "to extinguish every spark of Union sentiment in the Southern States; that it has been calculated to drive those states finally out of the Union, instead of being adapted to draw them back to their old allegiance." Winthrop represented the Republicans as dangerous radicals who had no vested interest in restoring the Union because it would deprive them of national political power:

> The Republican Party have so thriven and fattened on this rebellion, and it has brought them such an overflowing harvest of power, patronage, offices, contracts and spoils, and they have become so enamored of the vast and overshadowing influence which belongs to an existing administration at such an hour, that they are in danger of forgetting that the country is bleeding and dying in their hands.

He wished wholeheartedly that the institution of African slavery could be safely and legitimately brought to an end, but he believed that the sudden, "sweeping, forcible emancipation" would result in "mischief and misery for the black race as well as the white." Noting that the eighty-third anniversary of the surrender at Yorktown was almost upon them, Winthrop dreamed that "even now the associations of that day might overpower and disarm the unnatural hostility of our adversaries, and that the soldiers of the North and South might be seen like the soldiers in the old Roman story, rushing into each other's embrace under the old flag of our fathers!"[22] This rhetoric of conciliation fits into a long tradition that had sustained antebellum efforts at sectional compromise. After the war, such sentimental patriotism again became fashionable. But in 1864, it resonated only with a minority of Northerners. Winthrop carried few of his conservative friends with him. Old Whig colleagues turned against him.[23] The *New York Times* argued that "the student of history hereafter will hear with profound surprise that the purest of the New England Puritans, in the great crisis of his country's history, placed himself on the side of oppression against the party of liberty, excusing slavery."[24] Winthrop complained that "a very insolent tone prevails [in Boston] towards all who cannot find it in their conscience to support Lincoln."[25]

The core of the mainstream Democratic case was that the "consolidationists" of the Republican Party were destroying the decentralized, limited government created by the Founders.[26] Drawing on the party's self-image as the protector of the constitutional liberties of the people, Democratic leaders reminded voters that, with regard to the Constitution, their party, "since its foundation, [has] steadfastly denied that circumstances should affect the application or enforcement of the cardinal doctrines it professed."[27] For the *Brooklyn Daily Eagle*, the "main ground on which the Democratic Party" claimed "the support of the American people" was the promise to restore the Union *"under the Constitution."*[28] Democrats seized on Washington's Birthday and the Fourth of July, as they had in the antebellum period, as opportunities to identify their party with the nation as a whole, rather than narrow, partisan interests.[29] The war was not an excuse for abandoning the guarantees of free government contained in the Constitution, which was "as binding in war as it is in peace."[30] The Democratic congressman, "Sunset" Cox, encapsulated the view of most Lincoln opponents when he declared, "under no circumstances conceivable by the human mind would I ever violate the Constitution for any purpose."[31]

The supporters of McClellan mocked the Union Party's claim to be above partisanship and angrily refuted the assertion that national loyalty meant silent acquiescence in the subversion of the Constitution, the preservation of which had been the original justification for war. Echoing the hyperbole of the Revolutionary generation's attacks on the government of George III, Democratic campaign literature claimed that Lincoln had assumed the powers of a tyrant, creating "an Absolute state asserting all the prerogatives of an infallible church."[32] The "fanatical" Lincoln administration had turned the government of the United States into "a military despotism," and suspension of habeas corpus meant that "every man who is not [a supporter of the administration] … is not a freeman."[33] According to a pamphlet one of the "crimes" of the President was his ordering the "seizure [of] clergymen while at prayer, on accusation of treason."[34]

The administration's "suppression of internal dissent" was no more than could be expected from a party that owed its strength to the "persecuting, intolerant, hateful and malignant … Puritan spirit of New England." According to the *Chicago Times*, "it was sour, narrow-minded and illiberal."[35] Democratic Congressman James Brooks made the same point when he lamented that "this is now a New England Government and in the main in the hands of New England men."[36] Indeed, the enormous expansion of the federal government demonstrated to Democrats that the Lincoln administration was the embodiment of all that the party had been struggling against on behalf of the people since the age of Andrew Jackson. Democrats had always opposed "oneidea-ism": abolitionism; free soilism; sectionalism, which they saw as efforts to use governmental power to impose one vision of how society should be run. In wartime they added to this list "shoddyism": the corruption of war contractors that was symptomatic of the "Federalist" instincts of centralizing, elitist Republicans.[37]

Their appeal was summed up in the slogan: "the Union as it was, the Constitution as it is." But even when they were talking about the Constitution and individual liberties, Democrats were also talking about race. The implications of the party's position were sometimes spelled out by the more populist campaigners by adding a third clause to the slogan: "and the nigger where he was." Unlike previous elections, Democrats in 1864 rarely emphasized the defense of slavery for its own sake, appealing instead to racism and fear of a social revolution that seemed to be a harbinger of other frightening changes.[38] But for Cox it was "so obvious as to be not worth restating" that "our past seventy years refute" the idea that "slavery was the cause of this war." Indeed, according to the Springfield *Illinois State Register*, the Union "would be preserved unbroken still had it not been that the people in an evil hour for themselves and for the world, elected an abolitionist—a sectionalist—to the chief magistracy of a hitherto undivided and happy republic."[39] For many Democrats, a magnanimous, statesmanlike appeal to the patriotism of Southerners could, even now, end the war. Instead, the reckless partisanship of the administration had given the rebels no choice but to fight to the death.[40]

A cartoon in the Democratic *Cleveland Plain Dealer* in September showed McClellan calmly crossing a stream astride a strapping black horse called "Democracy," while Lincoln, on an emaciated pony called "Abolition" staggered over a waterfall to his doom. "Want to swap horses?" enquired McClellan. "No time to swap now," replied Lincoln, as he plunged the nation into a watery grave.[41] The metaphor that to vote for McClellan was like swapping horses while crossing a stream was much used by the Unionists. The cartoon captured the basic proposition underlying all Democratic arguments: black emancipation was fundamentally at odds with the aim of national preservation.

Delegitimizing the Opposition

"Under ordinary circumstances," confessed Henry Raymond at the start of the campaign, "it would be next to impossible to re-elect any President who, in the absence of overshadowing ability should have to shoulder all the responsibilities, failures, short-comings and personal disappointments of a four-year administration."[42] After all, no President had won a second term since Andrew Jackson in 1832. These were not ordinary circumstances, however, and what gave hope to Raymond and the Union campaign was the enormous advantage of advocating the re-election of an administration in the midst of a great national crisis. A campaign that appealed to popular antipartisanship could connect the Union Party to voters whose past loyalties were to the Democrats, and who had been repelled by the strong negative connotations of the Republican label.[43]

The military metaphors that had been familiar in antebellum election campaigns now referred to a real crisis that could plausibly be defined as a "contest for the life of the nation." Unionist literature continually compared the military and the political campaign currently being waged, arguing that "for four summers the loyal North has been firing *bullets* at the rebellion. The time has now come to fire *ballots.*"[44] This was a time when more was "at stake in ballots than in bullets," as Raymond put it in the *New York Times*: "The test is on us. The crisis summons. To your tents, O Israel!"[45] In other words, the Union Party insisted that voters held the power to determine whether the rebellion should succeed or fail. Rather than a referendum on who should control the government, voting for Lincoln was a test of loyalty to the cause, "an opportunity for us all to act a part scarcely less important than that played out on the battlefields."[46] Indeed, a Union Party election victory in November would "paralyze the arm of the Rebellion," according to the appeal of the party's National Committee.[47] "The Southern people know we have the *power* to overmaster them," explained a campaign newspaper, confident that the military tide had decisively turned. "What is especially needful is that they should also know that we have the *determination.*"[48] The cautiousness of McClellan's military leadership, it was suggested, displayed an effete obsession with "strategy." Ingenious strategies could not win wars, trumpeted Union Party tracts, only "manly . . . determined . . . hard fighting" of the kind exemplified by General Sherman.[49]

Against a backdrop of deep war-weariness, the summer months had forced the administration to be defensive about the relationship between war and emancipation. But by September, the turn in military fortunes combined with the politically disastrous "peace plank" of the Chicago platform to enable the Union Party to go on the offensive. A typical Union Party broadside explicitly compared the two platforms. Both were printed in full, followed by a list of "points of contrast" with a rhetorical question asking "fellow-citizens" to "answer wisely": "Which of these positions is the most patriotic?"[50] The broadside contrasted the Chicago "peace plank" with the Baltimore resolution demanding that the rebellion must be quelled by "force of arms" and concluded, "the first is *surrender*—the last VICTORY!" A lasting peace that secured American nationhood, or a cowardly and inconclusive submission to rebels: *"Which do you prefer?"*[51] In private, Union Party leaders declared themselves to be amazed that the Democrats had acted as "foolishly and as blindly" as they had.[52] The strategy of identifying the Democratic Party exclusively with its peace wing was explained by a correspondent of Simon Cameron: "We should flood the country with caricatures of the rebel convention at Chicago with McClellan in the centre and Voorhees, Vallandigham and Woods, and Alex. Long looking over his shoulders with their peculiar sentiments spread as streamers from their mouths."[53] The Democratic platform, declared the keynote "appeal" of the National Union committee, "gives a silent approval of the Rebellion itself, and an open condemnation of the war waged for its suppression."[54] A Loyal Publication Society pamphlet pointed out that the Democrats "have nothing but expressions of contumely for the sacred

Figure 7.1. *A Thrilling Incident During Voting—18th Ward, Philadelphia, October 11.*
This emotive piece of Union Party propaganda purports to depict an actual incident at a polling place in Philadelphia during congressional elections in October
1864. Its purpose is to show that old party allegiances were irrelevant in wartime.
A caption beneath the drawing described the scene: "An old man over seventy
years of age advanced to the window, leaning tremblingly on his staff, when an
officious copperhead vote distributor approached him and thrusting a ticket in
his face said, 'Here is an old Jackson Democrat who always votes a straight ticket.'
The old man opened the ballot and held it with trembling fingers until he had
read one or two of the names, when he flung it from him with loathing and in
a voice husky with emotion exclaimed: 'I despise you more than I hate the rebel
who sent his bullet through my dead son's heart! You miserable creature! Do you
expect me to dishonor my poor boy's memory, and vote for men who charges
American soldiers, fighting for their country, with being hirelings and murder-
ers?'" (Library of Congress, Prints and Photographs Division. Reproduction no.
LC-USZ62-89566).

war."[55] Not only did this leave Democrats wide open to the accusation
that they wanted peace at any price, but nowhere else in the platform was
"proper" respect paid to the soldiers in the field. While the Baltimore platform of the Union Party demanded for them "the highest thanks and hon-
ors which a grateful nation can bestow," the Chicago platform expressed
only "sympathy." Most damning of all was that nowhere did the Chicago

platform condemn the rebellion. Instead, as Union propaganda was quick to point out, it had nothing but criticism for the government that was trying to put the rebellion down.[56]

It was the next logical step in the argument for Unionists to claim that leaders of the "unholy rebellion" would welcome McClellan's election. One reprinted speech exhorted its readers to consider the "ancient maxim" that "it is wise to learn from our foes." If the rebels prefer McClellan, "we can have no stronger reason for preferring Lincoln."[57] Headlines like "the last hope of the rebellion—the election of McClellan" encapsulated the way in which the Union party press portrayed the opposition.[58] The Washington correspondent of the New York Times, William Swinton, claimed in a widely circulated pamphlet that the Democratic Party had the "entire sympathy and moral support" of the leaders of the rebellion.[59] Abram Dittenhoeffer, a young Lincoln campaigner from New York, described McClellan in stump speeches as "the leader of the Confederate forces."[60] Massachusetts Republican George S. Boutwell challenged a packed meeting in Boston's Faneuil Hall to refute the "irrefutable proposition" that "the resolution at Chicago meets with the approval of the rebels in arms against the government."[61] Most Confederates did, in fact, see McClellan's candidacy (despite his warlike letter of acceptance) as their last, best hope for achieving independence, and Unionists seized upon any evidence from Southern newspapers that indicated this.[62]

As the campaign intensified through October, Union Party campaigners became ever more confident about labeling Democrats as traitors, and they seized upon every scrap of evidence that could link prominent members of the party to covert Confederate operations. In Pennsylvania, the Union Party ran scare stories about the implications of having a hostile nation on the state's Southern border.[63] One broadside warned of "a military system which will put every man in the army for years!, destruction of the public credit requiring taxation which will consume the substance of poor and rich! [and] yearly invasions, destroying property and paralyzing industry!"[64] Union campaigners, aware of the hardships induced by wartime inflation, argued that the economic consequences of disunion would be serious. The North would have to take upon itself the entire war debt with no gains to show for it in terms of a stable reunited Union.[65] Such tactics provided a distraction from Democrats success at exploiting popular dislike of the new draft announced in September.[66]

Identifying the Democrats with "treason" and asserting that they were "in arms for the destruction of the Union" was not merely shrill background noise, but integral to Union Party campaign strategy.[67] Often, the link between Democrats and treason was merely a rhetorical device—Benedict Arnold, the Revolutionary who defected to the British, was compared to leading Democrats in a number of Union Party tracts.[68] But the claim that Democrats were actively involved in treasonous plots to aid the Confederacy was also made. The activities of secret southern–sympathizing brotherhoods such as the Sons of Liberty and the Knights of the Golden Circle were, Unionists claimed, plotting to establish a Northwestern confederacy that would ally itself with the South. Governor Oliver P. Morton of Indiana was most prominent among those Unionist politicians who highlighted the issue of domestic treason and linked it to alleged Democratic disloyalty. At the end of August 1864, he ordered the arrest of Harrison Dodd, the grand commander of the Sons of Liberty in Indiana, who had been implicated in an abortive attempt to seize the state arsenal and raise a general insurrection in the state. Found with guns and ammunition and incriminating documents, and together with some hearsay about his treasonous intentions, Dodd was charged with conspiracy to aid the rebellion, and conspiracy to overthrow the government of the United States. He had been arrested on his return from the Democratic convention in Chicago, and there was abundant evidence of his personal connection with many prominent Democrats.[69] Along with Lambdin P. Milligan, a lawyer from Huntington, Indiana, and three others, he faced trial before a military commission rather than a civil court. Beginning on September 22, the trial was heavily covered by Union Party newspapers. Three weeks later, on October 16, Judge Advocate General Joseph Holt's report on the activities of treasonous secret societies was published and became one of the most widely circulated campaign documents.[70] "Judea produced but one Judas Iscariot," Holt wrote in the opening peroration, "but there has arisen together in our land an entire brood of such traitors . . . all struggling with the same relentless malignity for the dismemberment of the Union."[71]

The scholarship of Frank Klement and others has demonstrated that scare stories about secret disloyal conspiracies did not reflect reality. Far from a serious threat to the Union, organized disloyalty in the North more often resembled a comic-opera fantasy. Yet, far-fetched as these conspiracy scare stories may seem, there was enough evidence to convince Union Party supporters that they should be taken seriously, and they may well have eroded partisan support for the Democrats by undermining their claims to be loyal.[72] They provided, in other words, a vivid illustration of the Union Party's claim that partisanship and patriotism were incompatible.[73] Antebellum party politicians had constructed meaningful narratives by warning that the opposing party was part of a conspiracy to destroy the liberty of the people. Both parties created a "dramatic vision" that depicted the other as a dragon to be slain. Such heightened discourse was, of course, a particular feature of the politics of the 1850s and such a conspiratorial view of the world was central to the rise of the Republicans.[74] The Union Party allegation that the Democrats were engaged in sedition fitted naturally into this paranoid style.[75]

Partisan Antipartisanship

The Union Leagues had provided the template for an antiparty campaign strategy through effective grassroots organization and grand spectacle. The return home of companies of soldiers (often furloughed in order to be able to vote) was frequently the occasion for a pro-Lincoln meeting. Eight thousand of the "loyal citizens" of Douglas County, Illinois, for example, gathered in Tuscola on September 23, 1864, to "show their appreciation of the services rendered their boys in blue." After prayers and a musical interlude by the Tuscola Glee Club and two local brass bands, the local Union party congressional candidate spoke for more than an hour, castigating the Chicago platform, and reminding his audience that "we have duties at home as imperative as those in the field." In a perfect expression of the mutually reinforcing symbolism of party and nation, the evening ended with the soldiers marching to the front of the gathering to the cheers of the crowd and symbolically depositing ballots for Lincoln.[76]

Everywhere, Union Party state platforms played down past party associations, denied that the election was a "party contest," avoided stands on specific issues unrelated to the war, and used their antiparty appeal to persuade former Democrats that they transcended party in their selfless devotion to the Union.[77] "In times like these, the world moves fast" explained one pamphlet. "In the great crucible of civil war, old-time prejudices and worn-out convictions are melted and dissipated like dross."[78] Union Party discourse in 1864 played on the antebellum tradition that equated partisanship with irrationality, appealing instead to the "logic of facts" and the "dictates of reason."[79] The issues now confronting the people of the Union in this election demanded "higher than a party view," argued one Lincoln supporter, "it demands unbiased action in the light of truth for the common good."[80] "On the whole," began a typical pro-Lincoln tract, "we may confidently appeal to intelligent and candid men of all parties to say whether a larger amount of hard work was ever done by an administration. … Even its severest critics must admit that, compared with the preceding incumbents of the cabinet offices, their record as diligent and patriotic servants of the country is as pure as new-fallen snow"[81] The Republican New Hampshire state central committee, when urging local clubs to hold regular public meetings expressed confidence that "the questions which are now at issue are plain and unmistakable." If the "people resident in each town" discussed these issues with their "friends and neighbors," they "will not fail to arrive at correct results. The Union men of the state have nothing to lose and everything to gain by discussion and should carry it on incessantly, in school district meetings, in private gatherings, in public meetings, among Republicans and among Democrats, and whether or not aided by speakers from abroad, until truth shall triumph and be acknowledged as the result of the debate."[82]

Given the apocalyptic confrontation consuming the nation, the Union Party became, in the imagination of Yankee Protestants, no less than the means of national redemption. It seemed to many observers that clergymen took the lead in the election campaign, opening Union Party mass meetings with prayers and making speeches in support of the President.[83] Sermons were frequently printed and circulated, just as Sunday services became a distribution outlet for pro-Lincoln broadsides.[84] The New York correspondent of the *Boston Journal* reported that, on the Sunday before the presidential election, "nearly every pulpit . . . resounded with patriotic appeals. Most of them were draped with the American flag."[85] One clergyman wrote to Lincoln, promising that "we . . . are doing what we can for you and the country."[86] Lincoln reciprocated, recognizing the importance of his Protestant constituency through frequent meetings with church leaders and editors of the religious press. A Proclamation calling for a national day of thanksgiving and prayer for the military victories also played to this constituency. The Union Party press interpreted it as a symbol of Lincoln's firm trust that "God was the arbiter of all human events."[87] The *New York Tribune* urged every minister to read the Proclamation from the pulpit, calling a prayer for a "*righteous* peace" a "Christian duty."[88] Summing up the contribution of the churches to the creation of an antiparty nationalist discourse, one minister told his congregation after the 1864 election that "it is not the triumph of Abraham Lincoln we celebrate, nor the victory of any political party; it is the predominance of patriotism, and the conquest of the grandest ideas which ever inspired a nation."[89]

The antiparty themes of the corruption of party machines and partisanship's evisceration of manly independence were prominent. One pamphlet described party politics as "one of the great sins of the day," another as a "synonym for all that is mean and low."[90] Charles Wright, for example, published a short essay in Boston called *Our Political Practice: The Usurpations of Vice through the Popular Negligence*, which drew on republican themes about the degenerative effect of partisanship on the republic. He argued that "our government is in the way of ruin not merely from the war—for that we could manage if we were virtuous—but from our rottenness in the Representative relation. Our rule is mainly one of self, under mere spoilsmen."[91] Meanwhile, the Union Party represented its candidates as "stouthearted inflexible men," who transcended "mere politics"; they were "fresh from the loins of the people" and thus not "tainted by party intrigue."[92] One of the most popular Union Party campaign songs contained the lines:

Let us drown all party feeling
And for the "Many in One" unite
Soon we'll set our foes all reeling
Leaving victory with the right[93]

And another, sung to the tune of "When Johnny comes marching home," had the refrain:

We'll not be bound by party ties, Hurrah! Hurrah!
For open now we have our eyes, Hurrah! Hurrah![94]

It is often claimed that the key to a party's electoral victory in the nineteenth century "party period" was mobilizing its core supporters.[95] In the fluid politics of the Civil War North, and with Unionists appealing to an antiparty nationalism, that rule did not hold true. In the small town of Collinsville, Connecticut, which had produced a small majority for the Democrats in the spring state elections in 1864, the local Union Party chairman was furious with a visiting speaker who had "done us positive harm" with a speech that consisted of nothing but "abuse of McClellan and the Copperheads and that of smallest kind." In one of several increasingly agitated letters to state Union Party chairman James Batterson, the town committee chairman explained that "the object of speaking is to win votes from our opponents." Narrow partisanship was counterproductive. "We want an able, candid and eloquent speech and if the speaker be of Democratic antecedents all the better—He can make appeals that our old line Whigs and Republicans cannot do . . . We must have [another] meeting to counteract the ill effects of the meeting last evening."[96]

Even a radical like Henry Wilson told a Union rally in New York—the report of which was later circulated as a campaign document—that "he came not here to-night to defend the Republican party." Instead the re-election of Lincoln and candidates on the Union Party slate by "honest Democrats as well as Republicans" would ensure the "maintenance of the nationality of our country."[97] The appearance at this meeting of Union general Joseph "Fighting Joe" Hooker was used to make the same point. Of the "democratic party which voted against Lincoln four years ago, there are tens of thousands like [former democrat] 'Fighting Joe'," pointed out Senator Wilson.[98]

Union Party publicists worked hard to persuade as many former Democratic voters as possible that the Union Party represented the best in the Democratic political tradition. Claiming to be in the nationalist tradition of Andrew Jackson, a widely published picture distributed by administration supporters contrasted the "Democracy of 1832" with that of 1864. In one half, a fiery President Jackson imposes his physical presence upon a penitent Calhoun and other South Carolina nullifiers. The other half of the image shows Jeff Davis lording it over "Little Mac," who cravenly implores that "we should like to have Union and Peace, dear Mr. Davis, but if such is not your pleasure then please state your terms for a friendly separation."[99] One ambitious Union campaign broadside stressed the antislavery achievements of Democrats in the past and argued that their natural home was with the Union Party.[100] Rather than merely reinforcing preexisting party loyalties, Union propaganda was designed to persuade habitual non-Republicans with flattery and threats. This poster slogan, for instance, had the punchy sound-bite quality of a modern-day bumpersticker: "Are you a Democrat? So is Andrew Johnson of Tennessee."[101]

In some states a small faction of the Democratic Party seceded and formed "War Democratic" state committees, which tried to mobilize the Democratic rank and file to support Lincoln.[102] Pamphlets with titles like *Country Before Party: The Voice of the Loyal Democrats* argued that "the self-styled 'Regular Democracy' has become thoroughly Vallandighamised" and now "stands in an attitude of virtual hostility to the country."[103] War Democrats attacked the "pretended Democrats" who "labor incessantly to belittle our victories, magnify our reversals and give hope and courage to those who are in arms against us." And they publicized the remarks of 'loyal Democrats' like John A. Dix, who produced one of the Union Party publicists' favorite sound bites: "If any man attempts to haul down the American flag, shoot him on the spot!"[104] The claim was that "real Democrats" worthy of the Democratic tradition had joined the Union Party.[105] A meeting of the War Democrats at the Cooper Union in New York in 1864 was described by the *New York Herald* as a "political movement of greater importance than any of the ordinary *partizan* assemblages of the day."[106] An estimated five thousand War Democrats crowded into the hall to hear Edwards Pierrepont declare, "we do not turn Republicans to fight this war. We fight for our government—for patriotism—not for party."[107] David Coddington, a leading War Democrat appealed to a widespread feeling that the war had changed the rules of the political game. "Do not the virtues of war and the vicissitudes of the war admonish us to remember that while both parties are falling and dying upon the same bloody field, struck down by the same dark hand, for the same bright cause." Both parties, he argued, "should adjourn their less urgent differences and unite upon the one fearful overshadowing necessity, so that citizen and soldier, partisan and patriot, Republican and Democrat" could unite together for victory. Democratic leaders had so "shaped the canvass that we dare not change our rulers for fear of changing our institutions."[108] Union leaders were confident that many former Democrats intended to support Lincoln through the forum of "Union" Democratic organizations. "Every day and every hour patriotic Democrats are coming to us and asking for meetings and documents," reported the chairman of a War Democratic organization in Ohio.[109]

The Fusion of Nationalism, Antipartyism, and Emancipation

The antipartisan language of the campaign for Lincoln's re-election enabled nationalist rhetoric to be imbued with antislavery principles. The fundamental connection between the antipartisanship of the Union campaign and their conception of the nation was revealed in an archetypical summary of the differences between the parties offered by a Baptist minister.

The Democratic campaign represented "selfishness, bigotry, partisanship, treason, ignorance and bondage," declared the Rev. Apsey of Bennington, Vermont, while the Unionists stood for "liberty, law, principle, justice, patriotism and self-sacrifice."[110] Patriotism was contrasted with partisanship; the corruption of faction was blamed for having led the country to Armageddon and having "duped" the "ignorant" into supporting the Democratic Party. The self-sacrifice and principle of disinterested patriots were contrasted with the personal moral weaknesses of selfishness, which was a failure to think in terms of the larger "national" community, and the bigotry that resulted from "blind partisanship" rather than "unselfish devotion" to a higher cause. Similarly, the alleged faith in law and justice of the Unionists was contrasted with the treason of the Democrats. This was the wider cultural and political context in which the drama of black freedom was played out.

In the dramatic vision of Unionists, the coming of the war was in itself seen as a failure of national character. Northerners who resisted the call for loyalty even at such a critical moment in the life of the nation were tarnished with the same badge of dishonor as the rebels in arms. The taunts made in 1864 against the "ignorant" Democrats who would "unthinkingly" support their party were contrasted with the Unionists' emphasis on the ideal of responsible, respectable citizens, engaging in rational-critical discourse about politics. For Union Party leaders, wartime politics had demonstrated that the respectable people of the North could respond to a higher level of politics, one that appealed to what Lincoln called "the better angels of their nature" over the base and corrupting influence of party. Many Unionists hoped that the experience of war, by generating patriotism, loyalty to a higher cause, and shared suffering, would bind the body politic together in the face of the partisan divisiveness of the Democrats.[111] "If the voters stoop so low" as to elect McClellan, one wrote, they will have proved their "incapacity to govern themselves."[112] For some of those who had been at the forefront of the campaign to instill a proper sense of patriotism in the Northern people, then, the wartime appeal to transcend party also provided a template for political mobilization and an idealized construction of social harmony and a loyal, patriotic citizenry that was to outlast the surrender at Appomattox. The war, many Northerners hoped, had revived the republican virtues necessary for the maintenance of the republic.

To those Lincoln supporters who believed that this was a war for "Christian civilization, for God's pure truth," emancipation was an atonement for sin, an honoring of God's highest purposes. The nation, thus redeemed, would be "henceforth the crowning national work of the Almighty, the wonder of the world."[113] One Presbyterian Minister spoke of "our soil made sacred by such a baptism of fraternal blood."[114] This belief in a greater moral good gave meaning to the suffering and loss of life and reinforced the connection between patriotic sacrifice and the end of slavery. "Never before," claimed the Missouri radical Charles Drake, "have people brought such sacrifices to their country's altar as those with which this people have taught the world what patriotism means."[115]

Lincoln's own public statements about emancipation suggest that the President was developing a profound understanding of the moral connection between emancipation and the war. His own ambiguous religious faith did not prevent him from being deeply aware of the power of the biblical tradition and of the need to anchor the case for emancipation in something more substantial than pragmatism. "We know that, by His divine law, nations, like individuals, are subjected to punishments and chastisements in this world," Lincoln wrote in a proclamation calling for a national day of fasting in 1863. "May we not justly fear that the awful calamity of civil war, which now desolates the land, may be but a punishment, inflicted upon us, for our presumptuous sins, to the needful end of our national reformation as a whole People?"[116] Emancipation thus was the means to redemption. In April 1864, anticipating the themes of his second inaugural address, Lincoln wrote to a Kentucky newspaper editor on the subject of emancipation, speculating that "if God now wills the removal of a great wrong, and wills also that we of the North as well as you of the South shall pay for our complicity in that wrong, impartial history will find therein new causes to attest and revere the justice and goodness of God."[117]

The President was capable of giving a moral lead, but the antislavery case was principally made by abolitionists and from the pulpit. During the fall of 1864, in communities across the North, ministers told their congregations that the war was a punishment for the sin of slavery, and that the "blessings of heaven" on the nation would only come if slavery were removed. A sermon by a New York Presbyterian minister proclaimed that "Christ himself...sends us the sword, because of our manifold offenses; but then [after the emancipation of the slaves] will he give us peace."[118] Some of this more passionate abolitionist language appeared in mainstream Union Party campaign material. *The President Lincoln Campaign Songster* included a campaign song called *The scourged back*, which invoked the image of "A wilderness of scars!/ A field by tangled furrows torn and riven!" and ended with an appeal to natural justice:

> Send such men back to chains?
> Not while a conscious nation feels and thinks!
> Not till each freeman's lifted right arm shrinks!
> Not till the perjured land that dares it sinks!
> And God no longer reigns![119]

Abolitionist journals like William Lloyd Garrison's *Liberator* also provided support for Lincoln during the 1864 election campaign, even though some abolitionists, most notably Wendell Phillips, were publicly hostile to the President's re-election because of what they saw as his conservatism.[120]

Nevertheless, although many Northerners had come to accept that slavery, as the cause of the rebellion, should be eradicated, the word "abolitionism" retained frightening connotations. As the presidential campaign was getting under way, the conservative New York Republican George Templeton Strong confessed that he never called himself an abolitionist "without a feeling that I am saying something rather reckless and audacious."[121] The campaign for Lincoln's re-election therefore had to steer a careful path. It had to support the ending of slavery, embodied in its endorsement of the proposed Thirteenth Amendment, but at the same time it needed to reassure voters that emancipation was not a threat. Part of the solution was to downplay the moral case against slavery. Although, for many radicals, emancipation was a moral question that bestowed dignity and nobility on the war, most Lincoln supporters emphasized that the purpose of the struggle—the preservation of free institutions and the maintenance of a coherent national entity—remained the same. Emancipation was about means not ends.

Some Unionists took this position to the extreme of denying that emancipation was a relevant issue in the election at all. In his letter accepting nomination to run for Congress on the Union Party ticket, James G. Blaine wrote that "the controlling and absorbing issue before the American people is whether the federal Union shall be saved or lost. In comparison with that all other issues and controversies are subordinate."[122] The issue, Unionists repeated, was Union or dis-union, the maintenance of national integrity and honor, or national disintegration and disgrace. Emancipation, after all was—as the "letter to whom it may concern" had demonstrated—a potentially serious political liability for a coalition that was so broad. By down playing their antislavery credentials, William H. Seward, Henry Raymond and like-minded men at all levels of the party organization with whom they corresponded, hoped to keep on board conservatives and border state men who still regarded emancipation as the symptom of an irresponsible radicalism in the Republican Party. "The struggle for the Presidency demanded harmony," Blaine explained later, "and by common consent agitation on the question [of emancipation] was abandoned."[123]

Sherman's great victory at Atlanta and the Chicago convention's commitment to pursue a policy of an armistice followed by negotiations with the rebels made it far easier than it would otherwise have been to "abandon" the emancipation issue. A sudden return of public optimism about the war made the conservatives more receptive to the idea that changing horses in mid-stream would be folly. No longer forced to be defensive about the military situation, supporters of the administration were free to concentrate their attacks on the Democrats and the threat to the national cause that they represented. The McClellan-Pendleton ticket, insisted Lincoln supporters, could only be supported by people who thought that the "Government ought to stop the war and hereafter deal with the rebels by negotiation only."[124] The strategy was explained by a Union Party leader in Pennsylvania who urged his state central committee to "inaugurate a most vigorous campaign [which will] put the other party at once on the defensive as to their treasonable purposes" and so take the heat off the emancipation issue.[125]

Taking a broad overview of Union Party campaign material, it would be inaccurate, however, to suggest that the attempt to evade the question of emancipation was successful. When the issue of slavery was addressed, Unionists more often drew an implicit distinction between the "political" abolitionism of antebellum times and the "practical" abolitionism that justified the freedom of the slave in the interests of the nation.[126] In a letter to Theodore Tilton, the editor of the influential Congregationalist weekly, the *Independent,* one New York businessman outlined the approach of Unionist publicists by explaining that "the term *Abolitionist* has two very distinct and different meanings." The first was a term applied to the set of dangerous radicals who had agitated for years but had contributed nothing to the emancipation of the slaves. In the second sense, abolitionist "applies to every honorable citizen who may wish that slavery might be abolished throughout the land, if it could be done by the Southern states themselves, in a manner that would be an advantage to the Blacks to be emancipated." In this second sense of the term, the correspondent argued that "the great mass of the northern people are abolitionists and may...very properly swear that they are so."[127] Circumstances were such that the dangers of emancipation now seemed to be outweighed by the foolhardiness of the alternative: letting the slave-owners maintain the system that had brought the nation to the brink of destruction.

While Democrats told Northerners that abolitionism threatened their republican liberties, Unionists insisted that the reverse was true: the destruction of slavery was a natural and necessary means of preserving the Union and the individual rights it guaranteed. The Republican Party had been telling Northerners for almost a decade that freedom was inherent in the promise of the Revolution and that the institution of slavery violated the most basic tenets of republican independence and self-will. In this view, the ending of slavery was no more than the last act in a drama that had begun in 1776.[128] The concessions to the slave interest in the Constitution—the three-fifths clause and the fugitive slave clause— were described as "a cloud on the horizon" that would lead ultimately yet inexorably to the "Slaveholders' rebellion of 1861."[129] Lincoln, whose speeches made a critical contribution to the fusion of antislavery politics and nationalism, had made clear since the 1850s his view that slavery was a violation of the promise of the Declaration of Independence.[130] By 1864 these ideas had gained credibility; the war pitted the values of slaveholders against the life of the nation and what Union Party state platforms often described as "the heritage of freedom" shared by all Americans.[131]

War, according to one Union Party campaign song was "God's Lightening glance, the purifying flame" that would make the "Flag of Freedom be worthy of its name."[132] In Union Party campaign literature, the President was portrayed as having bestowed the blessing of emancipation on the nation, as a step towards the "new birth of freedom" which he had promised in the Gettysburg Address. In several prints and cartoons, the goddess Liberty was pictured together with Lincoln and a copy of the Emancipation Proclamation.[133] The same antislavery ideas that had once frightened conservative Northerners by seeming to jeopardize national unity were now draped in the authority of the government and juxtaposed with rebels striving to destroy the Union.

The Unionists thus built a campaign that implicitly transformed emancipation into an aspect of nation-building: slavery must die because it threatened the life of the nation. John Murray Forbes, who described himself as "essentially a conservative," confessed that he was "more antislavery because slavery is antirepublican, antipeace, antimaterial progress, anticivilization than upon the higher and purer ground that it is wicked and unjust to the slave. I have no special love for the African, anymore than for the low-class Irish."[134] But the continuance of slavery had become incompatible with the maintenance of free institutions.[135] Even hardened supporters of slavery gradually came to see that the Union could not survive with slavery intact. The consequences of allowing slavery to continue would be "eternal contention between North and South."[136] "Men, who, three years ago would have periled their lives to preserve from reform the institutions of the South," wrote one anonymous Philadelphia pamphleteer, "now acknowledge in those institutions the deep-rooted cause of our troubles, and have resolved that the downfall of the rebellion shall carry with it all that gave the rebellion vitality."[137] John Brough, formerly a Democrat and now the Union Party governor of Ohio, told supporters at a campaign rally in September that he would not have gone quite so far as the President in his letter "to whom it may concern." "I will not say I will continue the war to free every Negro in bondage," he insisted, in a characteristic line of argument that distanced the Union Party campaign from the radical implications of Lincoln's apparent position, "but I will say, no more shall slavery be represented in the councils of my country."[138] The issue before the voters was a choice between a "humiliating" peace that would "make slavery perpetual" or a peace that would be "enduring" in which emancipation was implicit.[139] To those who believed that the war was the result of a Slave Power conspiracy, it was evident that any lasting peace must be one that involved the destruction of the political power of the slave-owners. "If the Southern people had not rebelled against this government, [slavery] might have gradually died out," explained a Union Party campaign broadside. But since the war *had* come, "we can only again be a united people by the total extinction of slavery."[140]

A speech by William Seward on September 3, in his hometown of
Auburn, New York, illustrates this careful defense of emancipation within
the context of a nationalist discourse.[141] He appealed to those voters
who accepted emancipation as a final settlement of the sectional crisis,
but who were nevertheless fundamentally conservative on the question
of race. He made no mention of the Baltimore convention's enthusiastic
endorsement of the proposed abolition amendment. Instead he insisted
that while the rebels waged war, military measures affecting slavery—
meaning the Emancipation Proclamation—would continue. His listeners—and the many more readers of the reprinted speech—were left in
no doubt that Seward saw slavery as the cornerstone of the rebellion
and therefore its removal as a natural element in the process of preserving the nation. But, Seward said, as soon as the Confederates laid down
their arms, all such questions would "pass over to the arbitrament of
the courts of law and to the councils of legislation."[142] In part, this was
a deliberate attempt to counteract the damage that had been done to
the administration's credibility with conservatives by Lincoln's letter "to
whom it may concern." For this reason, the speech intensified the hostility of those radicals who were disinclined to support the President
anyway. But the absence of an alternative candidate meant that radicals had nowhere else to turn and, despite their complaints, Seward had
neatly set the tone for the campaign.[143] He had not explicitly endorsed
the proposed Thirteenth Amendment but he had declared his faith that
constitutional action could solve the slavery problem. Most importantly,
he had assured conservatives that a commitment to emancipation would
not prolong the war while hinting that, nevertheless, he saw the ending
of slavery as an inseparable element in the process of nation-building.
Hugh McCulloch, Seward's future cabinet colleague as Secretary of the
Treasury under Johnson, observed thoughtfully that the speech had been
"captivating and *adroit!*"[144]

The nationalist ideology embraced by the Union Party enabled them
to defend what would previously have been regarded as dangerously radical
positions with conservative arguments. Before the war William Seward had
acquired political notoriety by appealing to a "higher law" than the Constitution. In 1864, radicals also openly departed from traditional constitutionalism by advocating the right of the people to shape their government
according to the demands of natural justice. The abolitionist, Lydia Maria
Child, for example, rebutted Democratic attacks on the legitimacy of the
proposed Thirteenth Amendment with the argument that the "best feature
of a Republican government is the power to modify it according to the
needs of the people."[145] This view of the relationship between the Constitution and the nation was no longer one that marked out radicals, however.
True conservatism, argued many Union Party advocates, lay in defending
and preserving the nation rather than the letter of the Constitution. A former Whig, Robert J. Breckinridge, declared that if the Constitution were

"torn into ten thousand pieces the nation would be as much a nation as it was before the constitution was made—a nation always, that declared its independence as a united people, and lived as a united people until now—a nation independent of all particular institutions under which they lived, capable of modeling them precisely as their interests require."[146] In a similar vein, Henry Stanbery, a self-proclaimed "conservative" defended the President from accusations of tyranny by explaining that "while he may have been careless of the constitution, *he has been very careful of the nation... If he has torn the garment, he has taken precious care of the body, and is not the body better than the raiment?*"[147]

In this way, conservatives made common ground with radical antislavery campaigners who argued that "Emancipation is now within our grasp. Will you reply that we have no right to seize it; that the constitution stands in our way?"[148] The radical antislavery message was also reinforced by the conservative theme of duty to established authority. Echoing Henry W. Bellows' 1863 pamphlet, *Unconditional Loyalty*, one Presbyterian minister told his congregation that the struggle against the slaveholding rebels was a moral one not only because slavery was contrary to God's law, but also because the Confederates had committed treason against a government instituted not just by men, but "by divine authority."[149]

The Union Party's conservative conception of loyalty and social order produced a radical transformation of racial attitudes. It is true that persistent white racism was undoubtedly a powerful force in limiting the acceptability of emancipation. Unionist publicists were careful to distinguish emancipation from the much more dangerous issue of equal rights for freed men and women. One Unionist pamphleteer explained that the "future condition of the Negro" was not his concern: "Let that be left to Philanthropists." The *President Lincoln Campaign Songster* even included a ditty with the refrain:

> The Negro free or slave
> We care no pin about,
> But for the flag our fathers gave
> We mean to fight it out.[150]

Even so, the acceptance of black emancipation as part of the process of nation building was accompanied by a significant shift in the public image of blacks, as well as a related reconceptualization of the ideal of the loyal citizen. Union Party cartoons showed black soldiers in a condescending but sympathetic way. The "Sambo" idiom and childish caricature, familiar to white audiences for decades, were unaltered, but now these images also emphasized the loyalty of black soldiers to the higher cause of the preservation of the Union.

One cartoon in *Harper's Weekly* satirized a call by the *Richmond Enquirer* for the Confederacy to employ slaves as soldiers by depicting a fictional "impetuous charge of the first colored rebel regiment." It showed

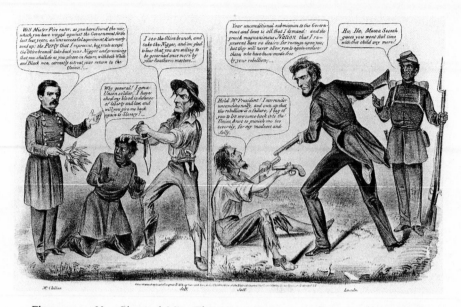

Figure 7.2. *Your Plan and Mine.* This Union Party print from the 1864 election campaign contrasting Lincoln and McClellan indicates how, while declaring themselves to be "above party," supporters of Lincoln could link the subjugation of the rebels to the ending of slavery. Lincoln, on the right, represents "the nation," offers no quarter to Jefferson Davis, and rewards the loyalty of black troops by redeeming the promise of freedom (Library of Congress, Prints and Photographs Division. Reproduction no. LC-LC-USZ62-36201).

childlike slave soldiers in rebel uniforms gleefully throwing down their weapons and swarming the Union lines calling "Hurrah for Massa Linkum!"[151] Contrasting the positions of McClellan and Lincoln, a cartoon published by the lithographers Currier and Ives in October confronted the electorate with the dishonor of returning to slavery those who had fought gallantly in the army. The cartoon (figure 7.2) is split into two panels above the banner title "Your Plan and Mine." On the left is a vision of McClellan's peace plan, on the right, Lincoln's. On the right hand side, President Lincoln, towering over a submissive Jeff Davis and pinning him to the ground with a bayonet, tells the Confederate leader that "the great and magnanimous *Nation* that I represent have no desire for revenge upon you, but they will never allow you to again enslave those who have been made free by your rebellion." In contrast, on the left, a penitent McClellan offers an olive branch to a victorious rebel leader and tells him "the *Party* that I represent beg you to accept this olive branch ... and promising that you shall do as you please in the future, with both white and Black men, earnestly entreat you to return to the Union." The cartoon is a comprehensive expression of the Union Party case. It casts the different attitudes to the South in the context of the narrow partisanship of McClellan and the great, national spirit of Lincoln. It also deals with the issue of emancipation by linking it firmly to the fate of the nation, for there is a third figure in each panel: a uniformed black soldier. On the left hand panel, the black man is on his knees, with a rebel bowie knife to his head. McClellan tells the rebel to "take this Nigger," while the soldier cries "Why general! I am a Union Soldier! I have shed my blood in defense of liberty and law and will you give me back again to slavery?" On the right hand side, a very different fate awaits the black soldier. Standing not center stage, but in the background behind Lincoln, still with gun in his hand and his Union kepi perched on his head, he celebrates Lincoln's firmness with the rebels with the words "Ha Ha, Massa Sesech, guess you won't fool aroun' with this child any more!"[152]

The shift in racial attitudes observable in the Union Party campaign also has to be understood in terms of the ethnocultural base of the Union Party and particularly a virulent anti-Irish animus. The Democratic Party, it was claimed, was "engaged in exciting sedition, employing ... as its principal instruments aliens, and recently naturalized aliens."[153] One of the most revealing of Thomas Nast's many didactic images produced during the campaign was subtitled "Citizens Voting." It depicted a respectable, bearded gentleman voting for Lincoln, whilst a dirty, scruffy, ape-like Irishman voted for McClellan. The crude nativist prejudices that this image revealed were linked to allegations that foreign, antirepublican interests controlled the Democratic Party. Ingeniously conflating anti-Irish with anti-English sentiments Unionists suggested that Irish opposition to the war was playing into the hands of the British: tempting the simian Irishman with a bag of gold was a rotund John Bull figure with a copy of the London *Times* in his pocket. In another cartoon, an Irishman was depicted with Neanderthal features, and carrying a club. He responded to McClellan with the words "All right General! If yere in favor of resistin the draft, killing the nagurs and pace wid the Southerners, Ill knock any man on the head that'll vote agin ye."[154] As an article in *Atlantic Monthly* in October 1864 put it, "the emancipated negro is at least as industrious and thrifty as the Celt, takes more pride in self-support, is far more eager for education, and has fewer vices. It is impossible to name any standard of requisites for the full rights of citizenship which will give a vote to the Celt and exclude the Negro."[155] In turn, Irish immigrants were portrayed as being motivated by religious conviction and cultural hostility as well as by loyalty to local party machines. This amounted to a radical challenge to antebellum conceptions of citizenship and equal rights, which had been defined in racial terms. Unionists elevated loyalty and patriotic sacrifice into the primary signifiers of qualification for American citizenship.

In his annual message to Congress in December 1864, Abraham Lincoln argued that his own re-election had seen "the voice of the people now, for the first time, heard upon the question" of slavery.[156] This appears to be a deeply disingenuous statement if meaningful political discourse about slavery is assumed to be focused on the plight of slaves. As Michael Vorenberg has pointed out, Frederick Douglass was right to complain that slavery, "though wounded, dying and despised, is still able to bind the tongues of our republican orators" and his powerful image of the Negro as "the deformed child, which is put out of the room when company comes" was an understandable and accurate response to the racial ambiguities and moral evasions of the election campaign.[157] Lincoln's claim stands, however. The 1864 Union Party campaign was a vital staging post in the revolution in Northern antislavery attitudes. Challenging the views of many Democrats, old line Whigs and conservative Republicans who saw the emancipation policy of the administration as being fundamentally at odds with the cause of national preservation, Lincoln effectively bound together antislavery and nationalist discourses. Unionists—whether or not they previously had been antislavery advocates—now conceptualized American nationhood in a way that embraced the end of slavery. The "*patriotic* policy of the President," concluded William E. Chandler, chairman of the New Hampshire Union Party, "is to unite men of varying shades of sentiment upon a policy radical enough *to destroy slavery*, conservative enough *to save the nation*."[158]

The old antebellum constitutional order, so revered by Democrats and conservative ex-Whigs like Winthrop, was a fatal casualty of the war. Although they recognized that truth, Unionists avoided the trap of appearing too revolutionary. They managed the trick of employing the preservationist language of the old Constitutional Union tradition while reconfiguring its meaning into what amounted to a fundamentally new conception of national loyalty. By redefining patriotism, Unionists in 1864 tarnished their opponents, who proudly maintained their patriotic faith in the old order, with the badge of disloyalty. The nationalist ideology of the 1864 Union Party reinforced fundamentally conservative notions about loyalty, discipline and patriotic duty but also downplayed race as the basis of citizenship. Antipartisanship provided the rhetorical tools with which this could be done: it helped to distance the Union Party from the perceived sectionalism and radicalism of the antebellum Republicans and offered loyalty to a transformed and redeemed American republic as an alternative to "narrow" and "destructive" partisanship. The "precious blood shed" on the battle-field was justified and given meaning by the appeal to the "life-principle" of "nationality," a matter too lofty for "mere party concerns."[159]

The Lessons of Election Day

"On the eve of the Great Election," wrote Mary Hawley, an elderly resident of Poughkeepsie, New York, "all seems hushed and still as if the very existence of our nationality depended on a single breath."[160] The day itself, Tuesday, November 8, was wet and gloomy across the Northern states. Nathan Abbott, a New Hampshire farmer, recorded his election day activities: "Had 4 bushels of corn ground at the mill—attended our Ward meeting to vote for President and Vice President—finished spreading the manure."[161] The mood in the big cities where troops had been deployed was also strangely anticlimactic. From Philadelphia, one well-to-do Union lady observed that "you would never dream that anything important was going on here today—things look as quiet as on any other rainy day."[162]

For weeks, politicians had been pouring over canvass returns and talking to local party organizers, trying to get a picture of the popular mood.[163] The intensity of the campaign was partly a reflection of a palpable sense of uncertainty about the result. Political leaders in both parties believed that, as Francis Lieber later recalled, "many voters were undecided until the last minute."[164] "Three weeks ago our friends everywhere were despondent, almost to the point of giving up the contest in despair," wrote the President's private secretary, John Nicolay, on September 11. "Now they are hopeful, jubilant, hard at work, and confident of success."[165] Many Democratic politicians, however, sincerely believed right up until polling day that McClellan stood an excellent chance of winning.[166] The Democratic congressmen S. S. Cox told McClellan that only fraud could prevent his victory.[167] Because of the rolling electoral timetable, the period from the Chicago convention to the presidential election on November 8 was punctuated by state elections that were widely regarded as reliable indicator of how the nation as a whole might vote. Vermont voted for state officers on September 5, Maine on September 13. The most important "bellwether" tests, however, were the elections for state officers and for congressmen on October 11 in Ohio, Indiana, and Pennsylvania. These big states would reveal whether McClellan had managed to persuade sufficient numbers of conservative voters to support his candidacy. Of these "October States," Governor Morton's campaign for re-election in Indiana offered the best chance of a Democratic victory—one local Unionist warned that "Indiana may be as troublesome to Lincoln as South Carolina."[168] But although the President refused Morton's repeated and increasingly hysterical requests to suspend the draft until after Election Day, the Union Party carried the election with a small majority, prompting a storm of protest from Democrats who claimed that the results were fraudulent.[169] New Hampshire Republican leader, William Chandler, was grimly confident that the October results, narrow as they were, ensured that "the country is to be saved by the intelligence and patriotism of the people."[170]

Political observers had other means of gauging public opinion, even in places where no actual votes were cast. One issue of the *Ohio State Journal* for instance contains a story about a vote taken on the New York Central Railroad on a train of thirteen cars. Two hundred and ninety passengers expressed support for the President, ninety-five for McClellan, one for Fremont, and two provocative (or darkly ironic) souls declared for Jeff Davis. The same issue also reported six other polls with roughly similar results often carried out on trains or steamboats.[171] Gambling on the result of the election was common, and the odds given were also a reflection of the way in which close observers felt that the public mood was shifting. Seward's friend and protégé, Sam Blatchford, regularly informed the Secretary of State on where the "betting men" were putting their money. By the middle of September, he reported that the tide was firmly running in the President's direction, although there was still "great excitement" about the result.[172] Politicians believed that there was a swing towards Lincoln in the last two weeks of the campaign and the betting odds also indicated that this was the case. Although a week before the election betting shops in New York City were still only offering even bets on who would carry New York State, the odds had moved to 10-6 in favor of Lincoln's re-election in the nation as a whole.[173]

From Lincoln's contacts in the key states came confident predictions of victory. Alexander McClure reported from Pennsylvania that "the work is as well done as it can be done, & well enough I have no doubt. We shall carry the state by from 5,000 to 10,000 on the home vote, and it may be more, unless all signs are deceptive."[174] Divisions in the Democratic Party probably contributed to the failure of their campaign to capture the public mood. Lincoln's private secretary, John G. Nicolay, thought that the confused message that the Democrats were sending out was their greatest handicap. McClellan, he recognized, had lost a lot of support in the West by repudiating the peace plank, but he would have lost even more support in the East, had he not done so.[175] As Nicolay put it, "little Mac's blanket was too short—if he pulled it up over his head his feet would stick out—if he kept his feet covered he would have cold ears."[176]

Despite these positive indications, Lincoln was anxious on election day. He told journalist Noah Brooks that "about this thing I am far from certain; I wish I were certain."[177] In the evening, the President hurried to the War Department, where he was used to spending many anxious hours following telegraphed reports from the military front. Results were slow to come in because the wire transmission was interrupted by stormy weather. At ten o'clock the message came through that Lincoln had carried Baltimore by a landslide. This was swiftly followed by a report that New York State had been carried by ten thousand. Lincoln "received this news with much incredulity" and was more prepared to believe a subsequent message from Horace Greeley to say that New York was safe for the Union by four thousand votes. By midnight, it was clear that Lincoln had taken

Pennsylvania, Ohio, and Indiana of the big "battleground" states. He had also won Connecticut (very narrowly) and Wisconsin as well as the reliable New England states. There was no news from Lincoln's home state of Illinois—reliable results were not received from the Midwest until two days later—but with sufficient Electoral College votes already in the bag, the little crowd in the telegraph office congratulated the President. He "took the matter very calmly, showing not the least elation or excitement, but said that he would admit that he was glad to be relieved of all suspense, and that he was grateful that the verdict of the people was likely to be so full, clear and unmistakable that there could be no dispute."[178] When all the results were in, it was clear that Lincoln had gained 55 percent of the popular vote and all but three states (Kentucky, New Jersey, and Delaware), which translated into 212 Electoral College votes against McClellan's 21.[179]

Returning to the White House at about two in the morning, the President made some dignified but circumspect remarks to a small crowd waiting by the gates. "I cannot at this hour say what has been the result of the election," he claimed, rather disingenuously, "but whatever it may be I have no desire to modify this opinion—that all who have labored today on behalf of the Union organization, have wrought for the best interests of their country and the world, not only for the present, but for all future ages.... It is no pleasure to me to triumph over anyone; but I give thanks to the Almighty for this evidence of the people's resolution to stand by free government and the rights of humanity."[180]

As Lincoln spoke that damp November morning, he and his audience knew that four years of Civil War were nearing an end. A month after Lincoln's second inauguration, the last Confederate army surrendered and the great experiment of separate Southern nationhood with slavery as its cornerstone came to an end. By that time, Congress—amidst scenes of great jubilation—had finally passed the Thirteenth Amendment to the Constitution, which, when ratified later that year by the requisite number of states, abolished slavery as a legal institution in the United States. The election of 1864 was, in a very real sense, the last moment when those two great results of the war—the ending of slavery and the triumphant consolidation of American nationhood—might have been delayed, perhaps even avoided altogether: the hyperbolic language of the Union campaign was not empty rhetoric. Had McClellan managed to galvanize a conservative majority in opposition to the "military-abolition" party, as August Belmont and other moderate Democrat leaders hoped he might, his election, dependent as it would have been on the support of the peace party, would have been a boost to the flagging confidence of the Confederacy.[181] Even had McClellan had the political strength to ignore the platform pledge to seek an armistice followed by peace talks, his administration certainly would not have formally endorsed the destruction of slavery. Little wonder that, looking back on a lifetime of political activism, Charles Francis Adams, Jr., thought that of nine presidential elections that he remembered only that of 1864 seemed to have the significance attached to it at the time.[182]

Given the advantages that the administration had during the campaign, and the difficulties faced by the Democrats, some supporters saw Lincoln's comfortable but not overwhelming victory as less convincing than it might have been. Carl Schurz, for example, later recalled that "the size of the majority did not come up to the expectations of Lincoln's friends."[183] But most Lincoln supporters rejoiced that his election had saved them from "national disfigurement and disgrace." Their conviction that the Democrats had constituted a treasonous and illegitimate opposition was not revised in the slightest. The Executive Committee of the Pennsylvania Union Party, for example, had no doubt that the internal threat from the Democrats remained despite the election result. Alarmed by rumors—entirely unfounded as it turned out—that McClellan was to be given a military position once again, the committee petitioned the President just two days after the election warning him that "any attempt to restore [McClellan] to confidence and power now would only be offering another opportunity to domestic traitors to distract our loyal people and destroy the country."[184] To George Templeton Strong, the extinction of the Democratic Party, which, he conceded, was unlikely given its "immense vitality," would be a "great blessing." It has been an "ancient *imperium in imperio* with its own settled rules, usages, and traditions of political immorality, not worse, perhaps, than those of other parties, but better established, more powerful and more fruitful of public mischief."[185]

The fundamental paradox of wartime politics—the veneration of the process of election combined with the conviction that only one side could legitimately win—was on display in the aftermath of the November election as never before. Having defined the war as a "people's conflict," a struggle to maintain government of, for and by the people, the process of election was in 1864, as it had been in 1861, the symbol of all the North was fighting for. Yet if the "wrong side" won, the cause would in any case have been lost.

As they celebrated victory, most Northerners were prepared, for the first time, to incorporate a cautious endorsement of black freedom into their conception of American nationhood. The war, and its eventual outcome, consolidated among a majority of the Northern population what had once been only the view of committed Republicans—that the contest had been between two "civilizations [so] diverse they cannot be harmonized."[186] What had once been dangerous and radical became, by war's end, the hegemonic, conservative view. By threatening the life of the nation, slavery had signed its own death warrant. Emancipation, and with it the incorporation of blacks into the republican polity, became an essential corollary of patriotism, not a partisan pledge.

The claim to transcend party had the effect, at war's end, of making Northern politics seem retrospectively more consensual, less fraught with alternative possibilities than was in fact the case. The Union Party's claim to be the embodiment of the entire nation created a powerful myth of national purpose and social cohesion. Lincoln's re-election, followed four months later by the final defeat of the Confederacy, ensured that the war would be concluded and remembered as Lincoln wanted it to be: as a new birth of freedom for the republic. The enduring power of his rhetoric is a tribute to the effectiveness of nationalism as a political strategy.

Conclusion

In counting up the casualties of war, Unionists could confidently add "copperheadism" to slavery and secessionism. George Templeton Strong commented sarcastically that now even Democratic National Committee chairman, August Belmont, would be sending in his name to join the Union League Club.[1] As Union Party propagandists had been warning since at least 1862, the electoral battle against dissenters at home was as much a part of the struggle to preserve the nation as the military battle against the rebels. In a letter to Abraham Lincoln in which he outlined the hearty endorsement by the men of the Army of the Potomac for the President, Henry Hoffman concluded, "soldiers are quite as dangerous to Rebels in the rear as in front."[2] Union Party supporters assumed, as soon as the 1864 election result was known, that "our great struggle for national existence is past."[3]

The intense party conflict between Federalists and Jeffersonians had—in popular memory at least—come to an end after the War of 1812, during which Federalists had revealed their inherent lack of patriotism through their antiwar dissent. In the same way, Unionists now looked forward to a "new era of good feeling" spreading its "benignant wings" over the land.[4] There was much talk of a partisan realignment that would bring together the vast majority of the political nation behind a vision of patriotic consensus and national reconciliation. Many of the same figures who had campaigned for a nonpartisan Union Party in 1860-61 made similar calls at the end of the war. Moderate Republican leaders like Seward and Raymond saw the Union Party as a strategic step towards a new organization that would embrace a national conservative constituency. Seward spoke enthusiastically of a "great coming together" of the parties once the divisive issue of slavery was dispensed with by the Thirteenth Amendment.[5] He told friends and supporters that he was looking forward to a "grand alliance that would dominate the future political scene."[6]

The passage of the Thirteenth Amendment abolishing slavery reconfirmed to many the redundancy of old party labels. Ironically, the realization of the dream of radical antislavery idealists—the redemption of the nation from the sin of slavery—was also widely assumed to mark the final nail in the coffin of the Republican Party that had been the institutional embodiment of their crusade. In the debate on the amendment one Democratic congressman predicted that, "upon the consummation of this measure, a new organization of parties will be inevitable." And the New York *Herald* reported that there were "rumors ... of a new party, composed of the conservative elements of both of the old parties, leaving the extreme men of each out by themselves." This meant, it continued, that "we can now look forward to a reconstruction of the Union, of our political parties, and of Northern and Southern society upon a harmonious footing."[7] The supporters of the Lincoln administration, *Harper's Weekly* pointed out, included "Edward Everett, General Butler, John A. Griswold, Thurlow Weed and Charles Sumner who were respectively leaders of the Bell-Everett, the Breckinridge, the Douglas parties and both wings of the Republican Party before the war." The conclusion was obvious, it seemed. Four years of war, in which parties had proven themselves the enemy of harmony and patriotism had taught Americans a valuable lesson. "Old party lines do not separate us" proclaimed *Harper's*, with satisfaction, "we are at the end of parties."[8]

The Significance of the Union Party

It is conventional to observe that the Civil War consolidated the two-party system of Republicans and Democrats. Such a judgment, however, requires a retrospective view of party development from the standpoint of, at the earliest, the late 1870s. Few northerners expected that the Republican Party would survive the war in a recognizable form. Civil War politicians well understood that, to say the least, the war dramatically disrupted a pattern of partisan loyalties that had in any case been in a considerable state of flux throughout the previous decade. It was in this context that the antiparty Union appeal was so effective. Behind a patriotic banner and with the cry of "No Party Now, But All For Our Country!" ringing in their ears, many former Know-Nothings, Whigs, and War Democrats rallied to Lincoln's aid. A comparison of the 1864 election results with those of 1860 demonstrates that the Republican/Union Party strategy of appealing to Bell-Everett supporters was largely successful. Edward Everett himself, after an exhausting campaign in which he had traversed the northeastern states speaking on Lincoln's behalf, concluded that his old supporters had endorsed the President.[9] He felt that former Constitutional Unionists had tipped the balance in New York and Pennsylvania. The *New York Times* agreed with this analysis, pointing out that the total votes Lincoln received in most counties in New York State were roughly equivalent to the Lincoln and Bell vote in 1860.[10]

The Union party also played a significant role in establishing a new partisan dividing line in the Border States—and in other parts of the North that had been deeply hostile to the Republicans. Baltimore, for example, stood firmly behind Lincoln—although Democrats explained this with reference to the strong military presence in the city on polling day.[11] The war also strengthened the position of Republicans in the big "swing" states of Illinois, Indiana, Ohio, and Pennsylvania as well as in small western states like Iowa.[12] The Union Party represented a significant reconfiguration of politics in Pennsylvania and was a powerful means of extending support for the administration beyond the confines of Republican die-hards like Thaddeus Stevens. John W. Forney's close alliance with Lincoln throughout the war was conditional on Lincoln's recognition of the coalitional nature of the Pennsylvania Union Party. On one occasion he reminded Lincoln that he could not conduct his administration without consulting the leading Democratic "patriotic minds" or rewarding "them [with] certain official positions." He urged the president to "set an example" that would acknowledge that the Union majority in Pennsylvania depended on Democratic votes.[13] The impact of the Union Party was particularly dramatic in California. At the start of the war, a group of moderate Republicans and Douglas Democrats, calling themselves 'the Irrepressible Union Party' met at a convention at Sacramento, but the newspapers reported a "slim" attendance and the New York *Tribune* concluded that "the Union men of California do not intend to abandon their party organizations, either as Republicans or Democrats."[14] California would not see a significant realignment until late 1862, when the Preliminary Emancipation Proclamation divided the Democrats down the middle, and led to the creation of a Union Party that was an effective merger of the pro-emancipation Democrats with the Republicans.[15]

The Union Party was also crucial in providing a political framework that could provide at least a notional link between fledgling Unionist movements in occupied rebel states and a bigger national movement.[16] In the end, Lincoln was able to win in November without the Electoral College votes of any Confederate States, but there is no doubt that not just Lincoln but many other supporters of the Union Party as well assumed that any future partisan re-alignment would have to include the South, and the Union Party was the model for such a development. Lincoln's political interests, as President, were not synonymous with those of congressional Republicans, many of whom came from districts where Republicans were in a heavy majority. Their ability to wield national power depended on excluding Southern states for as long as possible, until they had had time to build a different kind of society in the defeated South.[17] Lincoln's political authority, on the other hand, inevitably required him to seek a broader constituency of support, not only among former Whigs and Nativists who were brought into his Union coalition, and not only in the Border States, but also in the ex-Confederacy, among those Southern Unionists in whom he had invested such faith for so long. It was exactly this sort of coalition that President Andrew Johnson attempted to marshal, with far less skill and with such fateful results, after 1865.

The Union Party appeal also helped to consolidate the support of soldiers for Abraham Lincoln. In November 1864, they gave him an estimated 78 percent of their ballots (as compared to 53 percent of the civilian vote) and, at least in New York and Connecticut, their support probably made the crucial difference that carried those states for the Union Party.[18] The demographic and ethnic profile of soldiers—especially the volunteers who made up the vast bulk of the Union army—made them more likely to be Republicans than Democrats. It is also undoubtedly the case that intimidation and interference of various kinds meant that a certain amount of bravery was required to cast a Democratic ballot in the army.[19] Among the most important reasons for the support Lincoln received from the army, though, was that fighting for the Union was a powerful experience that politicized many young men who had previously been unmoved by politics. Moreover, distanced from the pressures of their communities, soldiers were open to the influence, both direct and indirect, of their officers and comrades and, whatever their past political associations may have been, many were apt to see the Northern party battle through the sobering lens of their enemies: if Confederates were praying for McClellan's victory, Lincoln must be sustained.[20] What was true of soldiers was also true to a lesser extent of the Northern people as a whole. Antiparty patriotic appeals helped to socialize habitual Democratic and former Whig voters, for most of whom the Republican label had negative, antinational connotations, into supporting the administration and, in some cases severing forever their past political ties.

The Party System and the Union War Effort

Civil War politicians simply could not conceive of a legitimate role for a "loyal opposition." After the attack on Sumter, even the most obstreperous critics of the Republican Party joined the calls for the abandonment of party conflict for the duration of war, and state and local elections throughout most of 1861 were marked by an absence of the familiar partisan rituals. Once it became evident that the war would not be over in a matter of weeks, however, and, most especially, once the Lincoln administration resorted to emancipation and conscription, Northerners quickly returned to the tools of political combat with which they were familiar. Those who remained loyal to the Lincoln administration—including many who had not voted for Lincoln in 1860—were genuinely shocked by such expressions of partisan opposition in time of war.

If the underlying ambiguity of partisanship in American political culture combined with the pressure for unity in wartime to make the position of a loyal opposition near untenable, Democrats were further frustrated by the workings of the Constitution. It is often observed that, although designed by men who thought them dangerous to the republic, parties were essential to the operation of the American Constitution.[21] Relations between the President and Congress, the operation of the Electoral College, as well as the political links between the federal government and state and local officials, all depend on party organization. Yet in wartime, the Constitution served as an obstacle to the development of a party system and especially to the formation of the concept of a loyal opposition. The relentless timetable of elections—in an age before the modern concentration of major elections in early November—kept party organization alive and provided power bases at the local level. But unlike in a parliamentary system, the separate election of the executive meant that these elections could never give the party that did not control the White House meaningful national power. Lincoln's assumption of additional power in wartime made this even more true. Even if the opposition party had been able to win a majority in the House of Representatives in the 1862 elections (and despite gains, they fell some way short of this goal), they would still have faced a Republican president who, as commander in chief in wartime, had effective control of war policy. This, of course, as Mark Neely and others have pointed out, was why the presidential election of 1864 was by far the most important political battle of the war. At last here was the opportunity for a political revolution in the North that would also determine the course of the war itself.[22]

The difficulties confronting an opposition party in wartime were further compounded by the limited development of a federal government bureaucracy. While partisanship was suspect, by the same token no truly nonpartisan war effort was conceivable because in a very real sense the party—principally through the distribution of patronage—*became* the government in the mid-nineteenth century. In Britain mass political parties emerged in the mid-nineteenth century within the context of a strong ruling class, an emerging professional civil service and with a monarchy that stood, theoretically at least, above politics.[23] The United States, of course, lacked equivalent institutions, having instead only an appeal to patriotic symbols. American political culture thus created both an inbuilt resistance to the dangers of parties and yet provided no meaningful nonpartisan alternative organizing principle or nonpartisan national institutions. This explains why the claims to nonpartisanship of the Union Leagues and the Loyal Publication Society were treated with contempt by those who disagreed with them and also why the administration had not the slightest moral qualms about using the federal bureaucracy and the army for partisan ends.

This wartime blurring of the line between partisan and nonpartisan activities, helps to put in context the question asked by Eric McKitrick in his influential comparative essay on the Union and Confederate political experience: how did the political process, and in particular the persistence of partisan conflict, influence the Northern war effort?[24] McKitrick suggested that one of the reasons why the North was able to contain internal dissent more effectively than the Confederacy was because a rigid two-party system provided a framework in which dissenters had a safety-valve in the form of the Democratic Party and the administration had a ready means by which they could bind together their supporters. Whereas Jefferson Davis faced an inchoate opposition and had no means of compelling loyalty other than by general appeals to patriotic virtue, Abraham Lincoln had the advantage of being at once both a national figurehead and also a party leader. In McKitrick's view, therefore, the persistence of two-party politics in wartime gave a distinct advantage to the North not only because of the positive benefits for the administration of a network of party loyalists, but also because there was something inherent in the process of inter-party competition that moderated the excesses and unrestrained oppositionism that, he claimed, characterized the Confederate political experience. In his study of the Democratic Party during the Civil War era Joel Silbey has filled out this picture of a functional and efficient two-party system by arguing that, in spite of the pressures of wartime, Democrats were a "loyal opposition," a minority but a "respectable" one. They maintained an impressive degree of party unity, held onto the bulk of their voting base and, most importantly, retained their fundamental loyalty to the Constitution and the maintenance of the Union.[25] Northern public opinion was the single most important determinant of the result of the war. Confederates recognized very clearly that their only chance of victory was to persuade the North that the cost of war was not worth paying.[26] So the question of how popular faith in the war was maintained—not only why the North resorted to arms in the face of secession but why, in the face of military setbacks, internal division and great sacrifice, it carried on fighting—goes to the heart of an explanation of why the North won the Civil War.

In the last few years a challenge to the McKitrick thesis has been mounted. First, recent work by Gary Gallagher and George C. Rable has emphasized the coherence, resilience and internal strength of the Confederacy.[27] Although it is true that in certain respects, Jefferson Davis's nonpartisan approach may well have resulted in weaker appointments, for example to his cabinet, than Lincoln made, it is now clear that in many other respects he was far from the hapless figure that he was once regarded as being. Indeed it can be argued that in terms of the co-ordination of manpower and resources, the efficiency of the Confederate government, even without a party system, exceeded that of the Lincoln administration, at least in the early stages of the war. The reason why party politics was abandoned in the Confederacy was because Southerners were convinced that partisanship was incompatible with patriotism. Even with the Confederacy on its last legs, Southerners were proud that what Rable calls their "revolution against politics" had not disintegrated into partisanship.[28] This book has argued that Northerners shared many of these antiparty assumptions. They may not have entered the war as revolutionaries—even ones that, like the Confederates, conceived of their revolution as a restoration of the republican virtue of the eighteenth century—but they shared Southerners' critique of parties and they most certainly prized the virtue of patriotism and endorsed the ideal of unity. Whatever may be the merits of McKitrick's positive analysis of the structural and institutional value of party politics in wartime, it is indisputably the case that no one who lived through the Civil War, either in the North or the South, would have shared his rose-tinted view.[29] On the contrary, Northerners regarded the persistence of party conflict as a serious threat rather than an aid to their war effort. The highly visible antiwar dissent in the form of draft rioting and assaults on Provost Marshals, or community protection for deserters, were assumed by Lincoln supporters to be intimately related to Democratic oppositionism.

To be fair, it is important to state that McKitrick's is a functional-ist analysis, so the perceptions of people at the time do not in themselves necessarily invalidate it. But a powerfully argued recent study by Mark E. Neely, Jr. has opened up a second front against the McKitrick thesis by suggesting that contemporaries were absolutely right to believe that the two-party system was a hindrance.[30] Indeed, in Neely's view, an excess of partisanship blighted the Northern war effort. Documenting the genuine anxieties of Republicans about the treasonous nature of their opponents, Neely stresses such factors as the partisan distortions of the war by pre-professional newspaper reporters to explain how party conflict depressed civilian morale and made the war harder to win.

In spite of the strength of Neely's case, McKitrick's perception that the political process was one of the principal mechanisms that managed dis-sent and mobilized loyalty is largely borne out by this study, although not in quite the way McKitrick implied. McKitrick's argument that Lincoln's ability to draw on the support of a partisan organization gave him a source of political strength not available to Jefferson Davis is particularly insightful. Although the Republican Party was a fragmented and ideologically dif-fuse organization, many of whose radical members provided more difficult opposition than anything the Democrats could muster, the Lincoln admin-istration undoubtedly benefited from the power of the party, in an orga-nizational sense at least. The network of active partisans who undertook the prosaic business of conducting a canvass to determine likely supporters and "doubtful" voters, distributed campaign pamphlets, organized meet-ings and, on election day, cajoled voters to the polls, provided a powerful mechanism for communicating ideas and influencing public opinion.[31]

But it was not loyalty to the Republican party per se that provided the instrument by which commitment to the war effort could be maintained so much as the administration's exploitation of an antipartisan discourse of loyalty and dissent. It was the adoption of the Union party label by Repub-licans—and the conflation of support for the administration with patrio-tism through such agencies as the army, the churches, the Union Leagues, and the publication societies—that was the defining element of the north-ern political experience in wartime. These developments provided a pub-lic space that, by claiming to be above partisanship and removed from the selfishness and corruption of politics, broadened the base of support for the war. At the same time, calls for an abandonment of party politics delegiti-mized partisan opposition and sought to circumscribe the limits of acceptable speech and behavior in the public sphere. Without the Union party strategy, the war may not have been won.

From the point of view of the supporters of the administration, contested elections were dangerous. Had the most important contests, especially the election of 1864, not been won by the Union party, the consequences would have been almost as momentous for the course of the war and the history of the United States as even the most lurid contemporary account claimed that it would. To point to the advantages to the administration of being able to harness the power of party is emphatically not the same thing, therefore, as demonstrating the advantage of a *two-party system*. The administration rallied a coalition of voters not only—not even *primarily*—by means of partisan appeals, but by discrediting the Democrats on the grounds of their partisan—and therefore inherently unpatriotic—opposition. In an environment in which party identities and alignments were malleable, administration supporters bound together a winning coalition in the presidential election of 1864, not by appeals to party loyalty but to patriotism and a desire for unity. As a private in a New York regiment told his wife, "I wouldn't vote a *republican* ticket merely because it *was* republican but I should most assuredly vote for the Union, and those that would maintain it, let the principle appear under any name whatsoever."[32]

To sum up the case made in this book: the Lincoln administration distanced itself from the negative, radical connotations with which it had been associated in 1860, stigmatized Democrats as disloyal, and attached to themselves the symbols of nationhood—in short, they adopted an anti-party nationalism—this strategy provided the organizational and ideological context in which the North could continue to support the war even after the escalation of the war aims and the military reversals of 1862.

McKitrick's argument recognized neither the essential fluidity of party identities nor the way in which the rhetoric of nonpartisanship shaped the mobilization strategies of politicians.[33] There was simply no clear-cut two-party system in most of the North, throughout most of the war. Even so, his suggestion that competitive party politics helped to moderate extremism by compelling politicians to appeal to the moderate center ground is worth re-examination. After all, an influential section of the leadership of the Democratic Party, especially in the Eastern states, did indeed recognize the electoral imperative to moderate the party's message. There is evidence, especially in the 1864 election campaign, that the Democracy in many places deliberately played down their more shrill denunciations of the war. One Democratic newspaper, for example, appealed to "honest political opponents, who, relinquishing party ties, will unite with us."[34] Some Democrats recognized that they had to "say good bye to by gones"; and the resolutions passed by local and state parties in 1864, in recognition of the dominance of the war, played down or ignored entirely many traditional party issues.[35] Furthermore, as McKitrick correctly points out, the Democratic governors of New York and New Jersey did not place significant obstacles in the way of the war effort, despite the attempts of Union Party publicists to portray Governor Seymour as a friend of the New York City draft rioters. Indeed, it might be added that Governor Seymour's record of mobilizing troops was a great deal more impressive than that of the Union Party governor of Pennsylvania, Andrew Curtin, who consistently objected to the implementation of federal conscription in his state.[36] In this case at least, party loyalty did not guarantee effective federal-state co-operation. But for the most part, Democratic politicians conceptualized mobilization in exactly the same way as they had before the war—as a rallying cry for the faithful. This may have reinforced the affinity of some Northerners for the party, but in the face of the antiparty nationalism of the administration it alienated conservative Republicans and former Whigs who, in other circumstances, would have been willing to support a party that combined a fervent Unionism with a repudiation of the radical agenda of a large section of the Republican Party.[37] Even to the limited extent that the pressure to make electoral appeals to the center ground moderated partisan language, it did so within an electoral framework that frequently confused the clarity of the two-party choice and in a political culture in which partisanship was viewed as inherently factious.

McKitrick's assumption that everyone understood the "rules of the game"—that, in his words, the authorities could "always round up the local Democrats, as many a time they did, and in case of error there was always a formula for saving face all round: it was 'just politics'"—simply does not capture the paranoid political discourse of wartime or the shifting political identities traced in this book.[38] It was not the presence of a loyal opposition that aided the Union war effort—or even an "opposition that was under constant suspicion of being only partly loyal" that "channeled" dissent into manageable forms—so much as the ability of the Lincoln administration to create a united patriotic front, a Union party bound together by the conviction that it was the means of delivering national salvation. To a degree, Republicans believed this of themselves already—to them, their party had always been a righteous crusade for national redemption. The achievement of the Lincoln administration was to expand this appeal to those who had previously regarded the Republican label with anxiety and contempt, to make it, in Lincoln's words, a home for all "noble men, whom no partizan malice, or partizan hope, can make false to the nation's life."[39] Dissent in the North—most dramatically in the form of the July 1863 New York City draft riots, but also in the everyday form of the persistent threat of copperheadism—had the effect of binding together conservative and radical Unionists in a common cause. Democratic party organization was castigated as factious. The antipartyism of the Union organization rhetorically transformed every election into a test of loyalty, a process aided by the strength and visibility of the Democrats' peace wing.

The Lessons of Wartime Politics

The war highlighted the best and the worst features of republican govern-ment. In the end, the republic had survived and, Unionists concluded, it had done so because of the faith, the patriotism, the loyalty of a majority of its citizens. Yet if antebellum Northerners had worried, in the tradi-tion of the antipartisan leaders of the early republic, that parties were inherently factious, the Democratic opposition during the war exempli-fied their fears. If, using the idioms of party warfare in the 1840s and 50s, they had seen party organization as the tool of corrupt men and dem-agogues, and the demands of partisanship undermining rational debate and independent thought, then draft rioting and disloyalty in wartime provided yet more evidence to justify their fears. In April 1863, an edi-torial in the *New York Times* reminded readers of a familiar theme: "until rebellion is crushed and the safety of the country put beyond reasonable peril, the duty of every true man is to forget party." On this occasion though, the *Times* went on to speculate about the longer-term impact of the war on parties. "When this deadly rebellion is once conquered [sic], and civil affairs resume their ordinary course, party will again present itself to engage the public mind" it predicted. But, crucially, "it would not come in the old shape." The *Times* was confident that the "natural operation of the severe trials the Government is now undergoing" would ensure that parties would be "*purged and purified* in new forms when the crucial test is over." Indeed, the editorial elaborated, "one of the great providential ends secured by this terrible strife" would be that "the old party corruptions shall, in some good measure, cease; that the public soul, in its renewed patriotism, shall realize, as it has not before, what deadly agencies they are and no more tolerate them."[40]

The author of this piece was to be disappointed. Instead of a puri-fied politics, the Gilded Age ushered in a new era of partisan excess. In response, some of those who had taken the lead in creating war-time nonpartisan organizations like the Union Leagues and the Loyal Publication Society again revolted against mass politics, forming the Liberal Republican and Mugwump movements. The Union Leagues had seemed to represent an idealized relationship between citizens and government—one based on patriotism rather than partisan passion. In the same way the propaganda efforts of the Loyal Publication Societ-ies appealed to voters as independent-minded citizens above party ties. The disillusionment of these Gilded Age antipartisans was prompted by the way in which the post-war Republican party failed to live up to the model of the nonpartisan, wartime Union party, and became almost as bad as the Democrats in its use of patronage and its crude efforts to reward supporters with policies that might be inimical to the true national interest.

Anxieties about the role of parties were, as antipartyism had on one level always been, a response to fears about democracy itself.[41] Three years after the war was over, the elite Union League of Philadelphia announced an essay competition. Entrants had to propose legal remedies for the "grave defects existing under the present system of voluntary [political] organization." The shortlisted essays all dwelt at length on the corrosive effects of party organization on republican values. "In too many instances, the party ticket is moulded by the hands of a few . . . determined and unprincipled political managers in the interests of persistent office-seekers," argued W. E. Barber, who won first prize. The corruption of party organization, together with the "noisome odors" and the "ribaldry and blasphemies" of party meetings alienated the "sober, industrious, self-respecting, and God-fearing men."[42] Another essayist added to this indictment of party organization the deleterious effects of the "perturbations of the moment," by which he meant "all those influences which affect men in crowds against the calm conclusions of their individual judgment." Mass meetings organized by parties enervated the rational critical faculties of the citizen-voter, he concluded.[43] For one essayist, the only solution to these problems was to render parties unnecessary as a means of organizing the people by setting up a system based on the ideal of a New England town meeting. A chief executive appointed by Congress, as in a parliamentary system, would replace a directly elected president. Congress would also be indirectly elected by the members of state legislatures, who, in turn would be selected by "the smallest and ultimate" constituency—meetings of no more than three hundred people that would select their delegates in a face to face meeting. The author of this grand plan to resuscitate direct democracy saw the Athenian city-states as the ideal, but he also stressed that this plan would return the American republic closer to the vision of the founders.[44]

As the gentlemen of the Philadelphia Union League Club soberly judged their essays, the parties were gathering strength for another presidential election campaign and within a few more years still, the Republican Party had adopted the telling but inaccurate label "Grand Old Party." The Civil War, of course, did not lead to the "end of parties." Indeed, ironically, the war provided the inspiration, the source of recrimination, and the lines of division for the mass parties of the Gilded Age with their distinctive symbols, songs, and traditions. Wartime issues animated party politicians until the end of the century. For Republicans, the Union campaign of 1864 was idealized as the moment when the battle lines were clearly drawn and the right side won. In their dramatic imagination, every subsequent Democrat was as traitorous as McClellan and Jeff Davis. Most of all, an appeal to the memory of Abraham Lincoln—sanctified in death as he had never been in life—served to rally the party faithful. The Civil War added another tier to the pantheon of those national heroes who were also partisan symbols. And yet even as the power of parties has waxed and waned, American political culture has retained a dread of corruption and a yearning for harmony. The tension between liberty and unity cannot and should not ever be fully resolved. It was the peculiar fate of Northerners in the Civil War to have to grapple with this abstract problem in a very real way.

Notes

PREFACE

1. The argument that party politics was an advantage to the North and its absence a hindrance to the South was expressed in its most extended form by Eric McKitrick, "Party Politics and the Union and Confederate War Efforts," in William Nisbet Chambers and Walter Dean Burnham, eds. *The American Party Systems: Stages of Political Development* (New York: Oxford University Press, 1967), 117–51. The two best one-volume surveys of the Civil War both incorporate McKitrick's argument. See Peter J. Parish, *The American Civil War* (London: Eyre Methuen, 1975), 199–225; and James M. McPherson, *Battle Cry of Freedom: The Civil War Era* (New York: Oxford University Press, 1988), 689–91. For a further discussion of this theme see the conclusion.

2. Roy P. Basler, Marion Dolores Platt, and Lloyd A. Dunlap, eds, *The Collected Works of Abraham Lincoln* (8 vols. New Brunswick, N.J.: Rutgers University Press, 1953–1955), 5: 537.

INTRODUCTION

1. Stephen C. Foster, "That's What's the Matter!" (New York: H. De Marsan, [n. d.]), *American Songs and Ballads*, ser. 4, vol. 4, Rare Book and Special Collections Division, Library of Congress.

2. *Hartford (Connecticut) Weekly Courant*, September 14, 1861.

3. Francis Lieber, *No Party Now But All For Our Country* (New York: Loyal Publication Society, 1863).

4. *Cleveland Herald*, October 6, quoted in the *Chicago Tribune*, October 8, 1864; "Enarc." [pseudo.], "Lines to a copperhead," (n.p., n.d.), American Song Sheets, ser. 1, vol. 5, Rare Book and Special Collections Division, Library of Congress. For a discussion of the symbolic and psychological significance of party activity within a cultural context, see the following: Jean H. Baker, "The Ceremonies of Politics: Nineteenth-Century Rituals of National Affirmation," in *A Master's Due: Essays in Honor of David Donald*, ed. William J. Cooper, Jr., Michael F. Holt, and John McCardell (Baton Rouge: Louisiana State University Press, 1985), 161–78; Jean H. Baker, *Affairs of Party: The Political Culture of the Northern Democrats in the Mid–Nineteenth Century* (Ithaca, N.Y.: Cornell University Press, 1983); Frank O'Gorman, "The Social Meaning of Elections," *Past and Present* 135 (1992), 79–115; and Daniel Walker Howe, *The Political Culture of the American Whigs* (Chicago: University of Chicago Press, 1979).

5. A malleable concept, political culture has gradually become the accepted currency among eighteenth- and nineteenth-century political historians as a shorthand way of describing the lens through which groups of political actors

interpret the process of politics. In developing the use of this term, historians have been heavily influenced by the anthropologist Clifford Geertz, who wrote of man as "an animal suspended in webs of significance he himself has spun" and "culture to be those webs." Clifford Geertz, *The Interpretation of Culture: Selected Essays* (New York: Basic Books, 1973), 5. To analyze these "webs of significance" is inevitably to become immersed in the way in which words are used in political discourse. For a history of the concept of "political culture" as used by historians of nineteenth-century America, see Glen Gendzel, "Political Culture: Genealogy of a Concept," *Journal of Interdisciplinary History* 37 (1997): 225–50; Meg Jacobs and Julien E. Zelizer, "The Democratic Experiment: New Directions in American Political History," in *The Democratic Experiment: New Directions in American Political History*, ed. Meg Jacobs, William J. Novak, and Julien E. Zelizer (Princeton, N.J.: Princeton University Press, 2003), 1–19; Joanne B. Freeman, "The Culture of Politics: The Politics of Culture," *The Journal of Policy History* 16 (2004): 137–43.

6. As David Waldstreicher has written of the early republic, the rituals of national celebration, while aspiring "to a unity beyond political division," were rooted in the needs and perspectives of particular groups and so were never merely a "reflection of ideological consensus." David Waldstreicher, *In the Midst of Perpetual Fetes: The Making of American Nationalism, 1776–1820* (Chapel Hill: University of North Carolina Press, 1997), 8. See also Baker, "The Ceremonies of Politics," 165–69.

7. For a description of the process of voting in the Civil War era, see Richard Franklin Bensel, *The American Ballot Box in the Mid Nineteenth Century* (New York: Cambridge University Press, 2004).

8. William Claflin to Joseph Holt, October 20, 1862, Joseph Holt Papers, Library of Congress.

9. T. J. Barnett, *Abraham Lincoln, The People's Candidate* (n.p.: Union State Central Committee, 1864).

10. William H. Seward to Thurlow Weed, 1 April 1862, Thurlow Weed Papers, University of Rochester.

11. *Harper's Weekly*, November 12, 1864.

12. *Pittsburgh Gazette*, April 16, 1864.

13. This phrase comes from Samuel T. Spear, *Our country and its cause. A discourse preached October 2nd, 1864, in the South Presbyterian Church, of Brooklyn* (New York, 1864). This is one of many published sermons that use very similar language. For an overview of the role of churches in wartime politics, see Richard J. Carwardine, *Lincoln* (London: Pearson Education, 2003), 267–74; James H. Moorhead, *American Apocalypse: Yankee Protestants and the American Civil War, 1860–1869* (New Haven, Conn.: Yale University Press, 1978).

14. As in, for example, this extract from the diary of Sydney Stanley, a leading Hartford Republican: "The defeat at Fredericksburg conquored the northern states. After that most unfortunate event the tories began to show themselves much more bold and confident than previously; the patriots were depressed in proportion, and the multitude who are swayed by the feelings of the moment, true to their instincts, began to want peace however disgraceful." Stanley Diary 26 March 1863, Sydney Stanley Papers, Watkinson Library, Trinity College, Hartford, Conn.

15. On the development of national organizations and their role in shaping American nationality in the Civil War, see George M. Frederickson, *Inner Civil War: Northern Intellectuals and the Crisis of the Union* (New York: Harper & Row, 1965),

98–113, 217–39; Melinda Lawson, *Patriot Fires: Forging a New American National-ism in the Civil War North* (Lawrence: University of Kansas Press, 2002); Michael S. Green, *Freedom, Union and Power: The Ideology of the Republican Party in the Civil War* (New York: Fordham University Press, 2004), 300–30; and Peter Dobkin Hall, *The Organization of American Culture: Private Institutions, Elites, and the Origins of American Nationality* (New York: New York University Press, 1982), 220–39. On the impact of the war on bourgeois class formation, see Sven Beckert's study of the New York upper class: Sven Beckert, *Monied Metropolis: New York City and the Consolidation of the American Bourgeoisie* (New York: Cambridge University Press, 2001), 81–144.

16. Mattie Blanchard to Caleb Blanchard, March 26, 1863, in *Yankee Correspon-dence: Letters between New England Soldiers and the Home Front*, ed. Nina Silber and Mary Beth Sievens (Charlottesville: University of Virginia Press), 115.

17. This question of the stability or malleability of party support in the war has been the subject of much scholarly debate. Joel Silbey has argued that the war itself wrought relatively little change in the dynamics of the party system. After the re-alignments of the mid–1850s, he suggests, "the electorate had become locked in." Joel H. Silbey, *A Respectable Minority: The Democratic Party in the Civil War Era* (New York: Norton, 1977), xi, 157, 175. See also Silbey's calculation of Democratic electoral support on page 151. His figures do not include Border States where the electoral situation could not be characterized as a continuation of the antebellum party system, and where the Republican Party had, in any case, never existed in any strength. Other studies that indicate relative partisan stability at the state level include Dale Baum, *The Civil War Party System: The Case of Massachusetts* (Chapel Hill: University of North Carolina Press, 1984); and Robert Cook, *Baptism of Fire: The Republican Party in Iowa* (Ames: Iowa State University Press, 1994). Other stud-ies of wartime politics paint a less clear-cut picture. Paul Kleppner, for example, has demonstrated that especially in the Midwest, the realignment of the 1850s con-tinued until the late 1860s and that there were large fluctuations in party support, as well as a notable "drop–off," especially among Republican voters, in the 1862 elections. Paul Kleppner, *The Third Party System: Parties, Voters and Political Culture* (Chapel Hill: University of North Carolina Press, 1979), 73–88. See especially the table on page 77. Studies that see party politics as fluid in wartime include Lex Renda, *Running on the Record: Civil War Era Politics in New Hampshire* (Charlottes-ville: University of Virginia Press, 1997). Until the 1960s, most scholarship on Civil War politics focused on the internal factionalism within the Republican Party, especially the tension between Lincoln and the radicals in Congress. For example, see William F. Zornow, *Lincoln and the Party Divided* (Norman: University of Okla-homa Press, 1954), and T. Harry Williams, *Lincoln and the Radicals* (Madison: Uni-versity of Wisconsin Press, 1941). For a recent historiographical overview of war-time politics, see Michael F. Holt, "An Elusive Synthesis," in James McPherson and William J. Cooper, Jr., eds, *Writing the Civil War: The Quest to Understand* (Columbia: University of South Carolina Press, 1998), 112–34.

18. Michael F. Holt, "Change and Continuity in the Party Period" in Byron E. Shafer and Anthony J. Badger, eds, *Contesting Democracy: Substance and Structure in American Political History, 1775–2000* (Lawrence: University of Kansas Press, 2001), 93–115.

19. Holt, "An Elusive Synthesis," 125. On the break–down of the Second Party System see Eric Foner, *Free Soil, Free Labor, Free Men: The Ideology of the Republican Party before the Civil War* (New York: Oxford University Press, 1970); William E.

Gienapp, *The Origins of the Republican Party, 1852–1856* (New York: Oxford University Press, 1986); Michael F. Holt, *The Political Crisis of the 1850s* (New York, Wiley, 1980); Holt, *The Rise and Fall of the American Whig Party and the Onset of the Civil War* (New York: Oxford University Press, 1999).

20. For many years the standard work on Northern politics in wartime was James A. Rawley, *The Politics of Union* (Hinsdale, Ill.: Dryden Press, 1974). For a more recent, revisionist account that argues that the party system was an obstacle to the Union war effort, see Mark E. Neely, Jr., *The Union Divided: Party Conflict in the Civil War North* (Cambridge, Mass.: Harvard University Press, 2002). On wartime Republicans, see Xi Wang, *The Trial of Democracy: Black Suffrage and Northern Republicans, 1860–1910* (Athens: University of Georgia Press, 1997); Green, *Freedom, Union and Power;* William C. Harris, *With Charity For All: Lincoln and the Restoration of the Union* (Lexington: University of Kentucky Press, 1999); Heather Cox Richardson, *The Greatest Nation of the Earth: Republican Economic Policies during the Civil War* (Cambridge, Mass.: Harvard University Press, 1997). Three recent biographies of Lincoln also offer insights into wartime politics: William E. Gienapp, *Abraham Lincoln and Civil War America: A Biography* (New York: Oxford University Press, 2002); Allen C. Guelzo, *Abraham Lincoln: Redeemer President* (Grand Rapids, Mich.: Eerdmans, 1999); Carwardine, *Lincoln.* On the Democrats, see Frank L. Klement, *The Copperheads in the Middle West* (Chicago: University of Chicago Press, 1960); Klement, *The Limits of Dissent: Klement L. Vallandigham and the Civil War* (Lexington: University of Kentucky Press, 1970); Klement, *Dark Lanterns: Secret Political Societies, Conspiracies and Treason Trials in the Civil War* (Baton Rouge: Lousiana State University Press, 1984); Leonard P. Curry, "Congressional Democrats: 1861–1863," *Civil War History* 12 (1966): 213–29; Jean H. Baker, "A Loyal Opposition: Northern Democrats and the Thirty-Seventh Congress," *Civil War History* 25 (1979): 139–55; Baker, *Affairs of Party*; Silbey, *A Respectable Minority.* 21. S. C. Pomeroy, *Speech . . . on the Platform and Party of the future and National Freedom secured by an amended Constitution, delivered in the Senate of the United States, March 10, 1864* (Washington, 1864).

22. Most historians have played down the significance of the Union party label. A notable exception is Michael F. Holt. See Holt, "Abraham Lincoln and the Politics of Union," in John L. Thomas, ed., *Abraham Lincoln and the American Political Tradition* (Amherst: University of Massachusetts Press, 1986). The article was reprinted in Michael F. Holt, *Political Parties and American Political Development from the Age of Jackson to the Age of Lincoln* (Baton Rouge: Louisiana State University Press, 1992), 323–54. Another insightful exploration of the political value of the Union label is Green, *Freedom, Union and Power,* 253–99.

23. *Chicago Tribune*, March 5, 1863.

CHAPTER I

1. *The New York Times,* July 7, 1861.

2. See George C. Rable, *The Confederate Republic: A Revolution Against Politics* (Chapel Hill: University of North Carolina Press, 1994).

3. *Richmond Whig,* August 6, 1861, reprinted in the *New York Times,* August 21, 1861.

4. See for example the essays in William Nisbet Chambers and Walter Dean Burnham, eds. *The American Party Systems: Stages of Political Development* (New York: Oxford University Press, 1967).

5. *New York Times*, April 24, 1863.

6. Jean H. Baker, *Affairs of Party: The Political Culture of the Northern Democrats in the Mid–nineteenth Century* (Ithaca, N.Y.: Cornell University Press, 1983).

7. This is an argument made persuasively by Richard Franklin Bensel, *The American Ballot Box in the Mid-Nineteenth Century* (New York: Cambridge University Press, 2004).

8. The term the "party period" was first coined by Richard L. McCormick, *The Party Period and Public Policy: American Politics from the Age of Jackson to the Progressive Period* (New York: Oxford University Press, 1986), but has also been used by Joel Silbey, *The Partisan Imperative: the Dynamics of American Politics before the Civil War* (New York: Oxford University Press, 1985).

9. The political scientist Stephen Skowronek has described the United States in this period as a country of "courts and parties." Skowronek, *Building a New American State: The Expansion of National Administrative Capacities, 1877–1920* (New York: Cambridge University Press, 1982), 24–52.

10. Samuel Hays, "Society and Politics: Politics and Society," *Journal of Interdisciplinary History* 15 (Winter 1985).

11. Michael Schudson, *The Good Citizen: a History of American Civic Life* (New York: Martin Kessler Books, 1998).

12. Benjamin F. Butler, "Representative Democracy in the United States" (Albany, 1841), 28–29, quoted in Silbey, *American Political Nation*, 35. On Butler, who should not be confused with his namesake the Civil War general, see William D. Driscoll, *Benjamin F. Butler: Lawyer and Regency Politician* (New York: Garland, 1987). The most famous justification for the creation of the Democratic party was penned by the man who is often seen as the father of party machines: Martin Van Buren, *Inquiry into the origin and course of Political Parties in the United States* (New York: Hurd and Houghton, 1867). Van Buren was passionate about the Democratic party's achievements but a close reading reveals that he was less certain about the value of a party system.

13. Frederick Grimké, *The Nature and Tendency of Free Institutions* (Cincinatti: H. W. Derby, 1848. Reprint, John William Ward, ed., Cambridge, Mass.: Harvard University Press, 1968), 172–73. See Richard Hofstadter, *Idea of a Party System: The Rise of Legitemate Opposition in the United States, 1780–1840* (Berkely: University of California Press, 1969), 263–66.

14. Francis Lieber, *Manual of Political Ethics* (2 vols., Boston: C. C. Little and J. Brown, 1838–1839). Lieber records in a footnote in II: 434 one of the first usages of the term "Her Majesty's Loyal Opposition" to describe Sir Robert Peel's Tory party in January 1838, only six months before the publication of the first volume of Lieber's work.

15. Lieber, *Manual of Political Ethics*, II: 414.

16. Lieber, *Manual of Political Ethics*, II: 434.

17. Glenn C. Altschuler and Stuart M. Blumin's attempts to understand the "social space that politics occupied" has led them to conclude that high electoral turnout in the mid–nineteenth century was not an indication of a deep popular partisanship and that the hoopla of election campaigns were regarded by voters with cynicism. Glenn C. Altschuler and Stuart M. Blumin, "Limits of Political Engagement in Antebellum America: A New Look at the Golden Age of Participatory Democracy," *Journal of American History* 84 (December 1997): 855–85; and Altschuler and Blumin, *Rude Republic: Americans and Their Politics in the Nineteenth*

century (Princeton, N.J.: Princeton University Press, 2000). Bensel, *The American Ballot Box*, stresses the importance of party agents in the voting process, and concludes that most voters were not motivated by public policy choices, but came to the polls as a way of expressing their membership of a particular community. Bensel's argument is similar to Altschuler and Blumin's in many ways, but he is able to delve more deeply into the motivations of at least a handful of apathetic or uninformed voters who nevertheless bothered to turn up to the polls thanks to his use of testimony from contested election hearings. Philip J. Ethington describes the "hibernation" of the parties between elections in *The Public City: The Political Construction of Urban Life in San Francisco, 1850–1900* (New York: Cambridge University Press, 1994), 70–71. The word "hibernation" was first used with reference to American political parties outside election season by Maurice Duverger in the classic work on parties: *Political Parties: Their Organization and Activity in the Modern State*, trans. Barbara North and Robert North (New York: Science Editions, 1963), 24. Ronald Formisano and Mark Voss-Hubbard have argued that the persistence of anti–party attitudes undermines the easy assumption that it was partisanship that generated high levels of political engagement. See Ronald P. Formisano, "The 'Party Period' Revisited," *Journal of American History* 86 (June 1999): 93–120; Mark Voss-Hubbard, "The 'Third Party Tradition' Reconsidered: Third Parties and American Public Life, 1830–1900," *Journal of American History* 86 (June 1999): 121–50.

18. Mark Voss-Hubbard, *Beyond Party: Cultures of Antipartisanship in Northern Politics Before the Civil War* (Baltimore: Johns Hopkins University Press, 2002) and Voss-Hubbard, "The 'Third Party Tradition'."

19. Ronald P. Formisano, 'The "Party Period" Revisited', 93–120; Voss-Hubbard, "Third Party Tradition" 121–50. For a stout defense of the importance of parties as a means of structuring popular participation in political life see Michael F. Holt, "The Primacy of Party Reasserted," *Journal of American History* 86 (June 1999): 151–57.

20. The two essential studies of northern Know-Nothingism are Tyler Anbinder, *Nativism and Slavery: The Northern Know-Nothings and the Politics of the 1850s* (New York: Oxford University Press, 1992) and Voss-Hubbard, *Beyond Party*.

21. Voss-Hubbard, *Beyond Party*, 4.

22. Quoted in Voss-Hubbard, 5.

23. Quoted in David Donald, *Lincoln's Herndon* (New York: A. A. Knopf, 1948), 31.

24. Culver Haygood Smith, *The Press, Politics, and Patronage: The American Government's Use of Newspapers, 1789–1875* (Athens: University of Georgia Press, 1977), 34–36.

25. See Michael F. Holt, *The Political Crisis of the 1850s* (New York: Wiley, 1978), and J. Mills Thornton, *Politics and Power in a Slave Society: Alabama, 1800–1860* (Baton Rouge: Louisiana State University Press, 1978).

26. See Mark W. Summers, *The Plundering Generation: Corruption and the Crisis of the Union, 1849–1861* (New York: Oxford University Press, 1987).

27. *Daily Alta California*, October 18, 1849, quoted in Philip J. Ethington, *The Public City*, 66–67.

28. Hofstadter, *Idea of a Party System*.

29. On the development of the idea of party in the United States see Gerald Leonard, *The Invention of Party Politics: Federalism, Popular Sovereignty and Constitu-*

tional Development in Jacksonian Illinois (Chapel Hill: University of North Carolina Press, 2003), 18–50.

30. Quoted in Hofstadter, *Idea of a Party System*, 96.

31. George Washington, "Farewell Address," in *Messages and Papers of the Presidents*, ed. James D. Richardson, 20 vols. (New York: Bureau of National Literature, 1917), 1: 209.

32. Lieber, *Manual of Political Ethics*, 2: 413.

33. Lieber, *Manual of Political Ethics*, 2: 421–2.

34. Lieber, *Manual of Political Ethics*, 2: 444.

35. The creation of an ideal–type of a "responsible two-party system" is particularly associated with E. E. Schattschneider, *Party Government* (New York: Rinehart, 1942).

36. On the evangelical origins of anti-partyism see Richard J. Carwardine, *Evangelicals and Politics in Antebellum America* (New Haven, Conn.: Yale University Press, 1993) 7–8, 64, 77, 94; Ronald P. Formisano, *The Birth of Mass Political Parties: Michigan, 1827–1861* (Princeton: N.J.: Princeton University Press, 1971), 56–80; Formisano, "Political Character, Anti–partyism and the Second Party System," *American Quarterly* 21 (Winter 1969): 707–8; Daniel Walker Howe, *The Unitarian Conscience: Harvard Moral Philosophy, 1805–1861* (Cambridge, Mass., 1970), 207; Ralph Ketcham, *Presidents Above Party: The First American Presidency, 1789–1829* (Chapel Hill: University of North Carolina Press, 1984), 157.

37. Carwardine, *Evangelicals and Politics*, 8.

38. Ibid. 39. Kimberly K. Smith, *The Dominion of Voice: Riot, Reason and Romance in Antebellum Politics* (Lawrence: Kansas University Press, 1999), 154.

40. *Mechanics Free Press*, April 16, 1831, quoted in Smith, *Dominion of Voice*, 155.

41. James M. Henderson to James G. Batterson, 29 October 1864, Batterson Papers, Connecticut Historical Society, Hartford.

42. *American Banner*, April 26, 1851, quoted in Smith, *Dominion of Voice*, 128.

43. *Mechanics Free Press*, April 16, 1831, quoted in Smith, *Dominion of Voice*, 128–29.

44. There are Hogarthian elements in Bingham's paintings—red–faced drunks and ludicrous over-indulgence—but they provide character and color to the margins rather than being the main focus. On Bingham see Nancy Rash, *The Paintings and Politics of George Caleb Bingham* (New Haven, Conn.: Yale University Press, 1991); John Demos, "George Caleb Bingham: The Artist as Social Historian," *American Quarterly* 17 (Summer 1965): 218–28.

45. Smith, *Dominion of Voice*, 157.

46. David Waldstreicher, *In the Midst of Perpetual Fetes: The Making of American Nationalism, 1776–1820* (Chapel Hill: University of North Carolina Press, 1997), 201. On formation of parties in early republic, see Richard Hofstadter, *The Idea of a Party System: The Rise of Legitimate Opposition in the United States, 1780–1840* (Berkeley: University of California Press, 1969); Michael Wallace, "Changing Concepts of Party in the United States: New York, 1815–1828," *American Historical Review* 74 (1968): 453–91; William N. Chambers and Phillip C. Davis, "Party Competition, and Mass Participation: The Case of the Democratizing Party System, 1824–1852," in Joel H. Silbey, Allan G. Bogue, and William H. Flannigan, eds, *The History of American Electoral Behavior* (Princeton, N.J.: Princeton University Press, 1978), 174–97; William G. Shade, "Political Pluralism and Party Development: The Creation of a Modern Party System, 1815–1852," in Paul Kleppner, ed., *The Evolution of Ameri-*

can Electoral Systems (Westport, Conn.: Greenwood Press, 1981), 77–112; Ronald P. Formisano, *The Transformation of Political Culture: Massachusetts Parties, 1790s–1840s* (New York: Oxford University Press, 1983); Formisano, "Boston, 1800–1840: From Deferential-Participant to Party Politics" in Formisano and Constance K. Burns, eds., *Boston, 1700–1980: The Evolution of Urban Politics* (Westport, Conn.: Greenwood Press, 1984), 29–57; Richard P. McCormick, *The Second American Party System: Party Formation in the Jacksonian Era* (Chapel Hill: University of North Carolina Press, 1966); Lee Benson, *The Concept of Jacksonian Democracy: New York as a Test Case* (Princeton, N.J.: Princeton University Press, 1967); and Michael F. Holt, "The Election of 1840, Voter Mobilization, and the Emergence of the Second American Party System: A Reappraisal of Jacksonian Voting Behavior," in his *Political Parties and American Political Development from the Age of Jackson to the Age of Lincoln* (Baton Rouge: Louisiana State University Press, 1991), 151–91. A functional analysis of political parties that highlights their role as organizers of the political sphere is presented in Joel H. Silbey, *The American Political Nation, 1838–1893* (Palo Alto, Calif.: Stanford University Press, 1991).

47. Waldstreicher, *In the Midst of Perpetual Fetes*, 201.

48. Hofstadter, *Idea of Party*, 96–102.

49. Waldstreicher, *In the Midst of Perpetual Fetes*, 179.

50. Len Travers, *Celebrating the Fourth: Independence Day and the Rites of Nationalism in the Early Republic* (Amherst: University of Massachusetts Press, 1997); Simon P. Newman, *Parades and the Politics of the Street: Festive Culture in the Early American Republic* (Philadelphia: University of Pennsylvania Press, 1997).

51. Quoted in Waldstreicher, *In the Midst of Perpetual Fetes*, 194.

52. Formisano, "Political Character, Anti-partyism and the Second Party System"; Marc W. Kruman, "The Second American Party System and the Transformation of Revolutionary Republicanism," *Journal of the Early Republic* 12 (Winter 1992): 509–37; Leonard, *The Invention of Party Politics*, 18–51; Edward L. Mayo, "Republicanism, Anti-partyism, and Jacksonian Party Politics: A View from the Nation's Capital," *American Quarterly* 31:1 (Spring 1979): 3–20; Michael J. Heale, *The Presidential Quest: Candidates and Images in American Political Culture: 1787–1852* (New York: Longman, 1982), 37–82.

53. Thus, even while condemning the partisanship of his opponents, the 1852 Whig presidential candidate, Winfield Scott, legitimized his adherence to the Whig party by explaining that "brought up in the principles of the Revolution—of Jefferson, Madison etc—under whom in youth I commenced my life, I have always been called—I have ever professed myself, simply a Republican or Whig which with me was the same thing." *American Banner,* July 26, 1851, quoted in Smith, *Dominion of Voice*, 156. Jackson quoted in Marvin Myers, *The Jacksonian Persuasion: Politics and Belief* (Palo Alto, Calif.: Stanford University Press, 1959), 24.

54. *Indiana State Sentinel*, December 2, 1847, quoted in Joel H. Silbey, *The American Political Nation*, 60.

55. The early history of nominating conventions in presidential contests is charted in James S. Chase, *The Emergence of the Presidential Nominating Convention, 1789–1832* (Urbana: University of Illinois Press, 1973).

56. As Anne C. Rose has put it, "Self-righteous condemnation of opponents resembled the shoptalk of political insiders, who successfully turned their doubts about their own legitimacy into aggressive partisan weapons." Anne C. Rose, *Victorian America and the Civil War* (New York: Cambridge University Press, 1992), 208.

57. Kruman, "The Second American Party System," 522.

58. *National Gazette and Literary Register,* January 8 and 11, 1830, quoted in Smith, *The Dominion of Voice,* 153.

59. Michael Schudson, *Discovering the News: A Social History of American Newspapers* (New York: Basic Books, 1978), 22.

60. Annotation in scrapbook, Thomas Kinsella Papers, New York Public Library.

61. Schudson, *Discovering the News,* 22.

62. *The Letters of Wyoming, to the People of the United States, on the Presidential Election, and in Favor of Andrew Jackson. Originally Published in the Colombian Observer* (Philadelphia, 1824), quoted in Heale, *The Presidential Quest,* 58.

63. *New York Times,* June 18, 1864; *Cincinnati Daily Enquirer,* July 28, 1864; *Chicago Tribune,* September 2, 1864.

64. *Philadelphia Evening Bulletin,* June 1, 1847, quoted in Smith, *The Dominion of Voice,* 157.

65. "Free Soil Chorus" in *The Free Soil Minstrel* (New York: Martyn and Ely, [1848]). See also "Hurrah! For Our Cause" also in *The Free Soil Minstrel.*

66. William P. Dale, "A Good Time Coming" in *The Young Men's Republican Vocalist* (New York: A. Morris, 1860); Thomas Drew, "The Fine Old Fossil Bachelor" in *The Campaign of 1856. Fremont Songs for the People. Original and Selected* (Boston: John P. Jewett and Co., 1856).

67. Holt, *Rise and Fall of the American Whigs,* 30–32, 270–73; Howe, *Political Culture of the American Whigs,* 43–68, 126; John Ashworth, *"Agrarians" and "Aristocrats": Party Political Ideology in the United States, 1837–1846* (London: Royal Historical Society, 1983), 205–18; Formisano, "Political Character," pp. 683–709; Formisano, *The Birth of Mass Political Parties,* 56–80.

68. "For Harrison Huzza" in *Tippecanoe Song Book: A Collection of Log Cabin and Patriotic Melodies* (Philadelphia: Marshall, Williams and Butler, [1840]). For similar sentiments in the 1840 and 1844 campaigns see "Whig Girls of 1840" in the *National Clay Minstrel and Frelinghuysen Melodist* (Philadelphia: George Hood, [1844], "Song of the Ohio Boys" in *The Log Cabin Songbook: A Collection of Popular and Patriotic Songs* (New York: The Log Cabin Office, [1840]).

69. "Know Ye the Land?" in *The Log Cabin Songbook.*

70. John Maxim, "Harrison Song" in *Songs for the People, or Tippecanoe Melodies* (New York: James P. Giffing, [1840]).

71. Holt, *Rise and Fall of the American Whigs,* 31.

72. As quoted in Holt, *Rise and Fall of the American Whigs,* 31.

73. Raleigh, North Carolina, *Register,* October 9, 1840, quoted in Marc Kruman, *Parties and Politics in North Carolina, 1836–1865* (Baton Rouge: Louisiana State University Press), 3.

74. Harrison quoted in Howe, ed. *The American Whigs: An Anthology* (New York: Wiley, 1973), 77.

75. Carwardine, *Evangelicals and Politics,* 8.

76. The quote is from Kleppner, *The Third Electoral System,* 78. Holt, *The Rise and Fall of the American Whig Party,* 30–32.

77. Resolutions of a "Grand Rally of the People" in Lynn, Massachusetts, cited in Voss-Hubbard, *Beyond Party,* 191.

78. Draft editorial, 1856, Gideon Welles Papers, Connecticut Historical Society, quoted in Holt, *Political Crisis of the 1850s,* 176.

79. Quoted in Voss-Hubbard, *Beyond Party*, 197.

80. Holt, *Political Crisis of the 1850s*, 163–169, 175–76. Joel Silbey provides a contrary view in chapter 11 of *The American Political Nation*, 196–214, which focuses on those who dissented from the political norms he describes. However, Silbey's concern is with those he describes as "outsiders"—challengers to two-party hegemony who resorted to third-party "guerrilla" tactics. "Their schismatic behavior," he writes, "roiled the political waters but did not re-channel the mainstream of two-party politics," 197. The standard work on the ideology of the Republican party in the 1850s is Eric Foner, *Free Soil, Free Labor, Free Men: The Ideology of the Republican Party Before the Civil War* (New York: Oxford University Press, 1970). On relations with Know- Nothings, see William E. Gienapp, "Nativism and the Creation of a Republican Majority in the North before the Civil War," *Journal of American History* 72 (1985): 529–59.

81. See Philip S. Paludan, *The Presidency of Abraham Lincoln* (Lawrence: University Press of Kansas, 1994), 97–135.

82. Susan-Mary Grant, *North Over South: Northern Nationalism and American Identity in the Antebellum Era* (Lawrence: University of Kansas Press, 2000).

83. Baker, *Affairs of Party*, 317.

84. Thomas Courtnay to Robert Gill, October 15, 1858, Frederick Brune Papers, Maryland Historical Society, Baltimore, quoted in Baker, *Affairs of Party*, 325. On the role of parties in New York City in this period see also Amy Bridges, *A City in the Republic: Antebellum New York and the Origins of Machine Politics* (New York: Cambridge University Press, 1984); and Mary P. Ryan, *Civic Wars: Democracy and Public Life in the American City during the Nineteenth Century* (Berkeley: University of California Press, 1997).

85. Holt, *Rise and Fall of the American Whigs*, 963–65.

86. *Speech of Hon. John J. Crittenden, Strong Appeal to the Reason of the Country. Thursday, September 13, 1860*. Collection of Broadsides, Houghton Library, Harvard University.

87. Robert Kelley, *The Transatlantic Persuasion: The Liberal-Democratic Mind in the Age of Gladstone* (New York: Alfred A. Knopf, 1969), xix.

CHAPTER 2

1. Robert W. Johannsen, *Stephen A. Douglas* (New York: Oxford University Press, 1973), 832.

2. Severn Teackle Wallis, *The Writings of Severn Teackle Wallis*, 4 vols. (Baltimore: John Murphy, 1896), 2: 140, 136. Wallis' attempt to reinforce his authority by denying his own partisanship was implausible. He had begun his political career in opposition to Andrew Jackson but had gravitated to the Democratic Party when the Whigs collapsed. He warned "the people of the South will not . . . submit to have religion and morality manufactured for them by Massachusetts. We will never consent to accept Plymouth Rock as the touchstone of right and truth" (141).

3. Howard Cecil Perkins. *Northern Editorials on Secession*, 2 vols. (New York: D. Appleton–Century, 1942), 2: 275.

4. Philadelphia *Public Ledger* January 1, 1861, in Perkins, *Northern Editorials*, vol. 1, 247.

5. On the Republican Party in the 1850s see William E. Gienapp, *The Origins of the Republican Party, 1852–1856* (New York: Oxford University Press, 1986); Michael F. Holt, *The Political Crisis of the 1850s* (New York: Wiley, 1980); Eric Foner, *The Ideology of the Republican Party Before the Civil War* (New York: Oxford University Press, 1970).

6. David M. Potter, *Lincoln and His Party in the Secession Crisis* (New Haven, Conn.: Yale University Press, 1942), 29–30.

7. Senator J. R. Doolittle, quoted in Potter, *Lincoln and His Party*, 30 n14.

8. *Daily National Intelligencer*, January 13, February 15, 1861; *New York Herald*, December 21, 1860. On pressure on the Republican Party to 'nationalize' its electoral base see Richard H. Abbott, *The Republican Party and the South, 1855–1877: The First Southern Strategy* (Chapel Hill: University of North Carolina Press, 1986).

9. Douglas Fermer, *James Gordon Bennett and the New York Herald: A Study of Editorial Opinion in the Civil War Era 1854–1867* (London: Royal Historical Society, 1986).

10. Glydon G. Van Deusen, *William Henry Seward* (New York: Oxford University Press, 1967), 246.

11. Adams is quoted in John M. Taylor, *William Henry Seward: Lincoln's Right Hand Man* (New York: Harper Collins, 1991), 130.

12. On the relationship between Lincoln and Seward see David Herbert Donald, *"We Are Lincoln Men": Abraham Lincoln and His Friends* (New York: Simon & Schuster, 2003), 140–76. For a less cordial perspective on this close relationship from a man who observed them both at close quarters see Gideon Welles, *Lincoln and Seward. Remarks upon the memorial address of Chas. Francis Adams, on the late William H. Seward, with incidents and comments illustrative of the measures and policy of the administration of Abraham Lincoln. And views as to the relative positions of the late President and secretary of state* (New York, Sheldon & Company, 1874).

13. Seward had spent the years leading up to the war using his patronage powers as a senator and his extensive networks of correspondents to help build the new Republican Party in close alliance with Thurlow Weed—an Albany, New York, newspaper editor and one of the greatest political fixers of the day. See Van Deusen, *William Henry Seward*; Taylor, *William Henry Seward*.

14. Burton J. Hendrick, *Lincoln's War Cabinet* (Boston: Little, Brown, 1946), 148.

15. Seward to Lincoln, January 27, 1861, Abraham Lincoln Papers, Manuscripts Division, Library of Congress.

16. New York *Herald*, March 1, 1861, quoted in Daniel W. Crofts, "The Union party of 1861 and the Secession Crisis," *Perspectives in American History* 11 (1977–78), 359.

17. *New York Times*, February 26, 1861.

18. Henry J. Raymond to Lincoln, December 14, 1860, Lincoln Papers.

19. J.M. Chamberlain to Seward, April 15, 1861, Seward Papers, University of Rochester Library, Rochester, New York: For a pro-compromise edition, see *Newberryport Herald* in Perkins, ed., *Northern Editorials*, 2: 654–58.

20. Scott to Seward, March 3, 1861, Lincoln Papers; see also Thurlow Weed to Lincoln, January 10, 1861, Lincoln Papers.

21. On the Union Party of 1860–1861 and the attitude of many Whigs and moderate border-state Unionists to the Republican Party see Daniel W. Crofts,

Reluctant Confederates: Upper South Unionists in the Secession Crisis (Chapel Hill: University of North Carolina Press, 1989), 215–89.

22. John A. Gilmer to Abraham Lincoln, December 29, 1860, Lincoln Papers.

23. John A. Gilmer to Thurlow Weed, January 12, 1861, Weed Papers, University of Rochester; New York *Times*, February 26, 1861, quoted in Crofts, "Union Party of 1861," 358.

24. John A. Gilmer to Abraham Lincoln, December 10 and December 29, 1860, Lincoln Papers.

25. New York *Times,* February 26, 1861. Similar appeals appeared in the New York *Herald*, February 28 and March 1, 1861.

26. Henry Raymond to Abraham Lincoln, November 14, 1860, Lincoln Papers.

27. August Belmont to William H. Seward, January 17, 1861, Seward Papers.

28. Salmon Chase to Lincoln, January 28, 1861, Lincoln Papers.

29. Van Deusen, *William Henry Seward*, 249.

30. Van Deusen, *William Henry* Seward, 249; Daniel W. Crofts, *Reluctant Confederates: Upper South Unionists in the Secession Crisis* (Chapel Hill: University of North Carolina Press, 1989), 271; George C. Fogg to Lincoln, February 5, 1861, Abraham Lincoln Papers, cited in Holt, "Abraham Lincoln and the Politics of Union."

31. Don E. Fehrenbacher and Virginia Fehrenbacher, *Recollected Words of Abraham Lincoln* (Palo Alto, Calif.: Stanford University Press, 1996), 436.

32. John G. Nicolay and John Hay, *Abraham Lincoln: A History*, 10 vols. (New York: Century, 1890) 3: 280. The New Englander was unnamed.

33. On the role of antislavery idealism in Republican thought see Eric Foner, *Free Soil, Free Labor, Free Men: The Ideology of the Republican Party Before the Civil War* (New York: Oxford University Press, 1970) and Harry V. Jaffa, *A New Birth of Freedom: Abraham Lincoln and the Coming of the Civil War* (Banham, Md.: Bowman and Littlefield, 2000).

34. Roy P. Basler, Marion Dolores Platt, and Lloyd A. Dunlap, eds., *The Collected Works of Abraham Lincoln,* 9 vols. (New Brunswick, N. J.: Rutgers University Press, 1953–55), 4:160.

35. *Cincinnati Daily Enquirer*, February 10, 1861, in Perkins, ed., *Northern Editorials on Secession*.

36. Lincoln to John A. Gilmer, December 15, 1860, Basler, ed., *Collected Works of Abraham Lincoln*, 4: 152.

37. William Seward to Abraham Lincoln, April 1, 1861, Lincoln Papers.

38. Carl Schurz to Lincoln, November 7, 1860, Abraham Lincoln Papers.

39. George G. Fogg to Abraham Lincoln, Wednesday, November 7, 1860, Lincoln Papers.

40. James K. Moorhead to Abraham Lincoln, November 23, 1860, Lincoln Papers. For similar advice, see George N. Eckert to Abraham Lincoln, November 14, 1860, Lincoln Papers.

41. David Davis to Abraham Lincoln, November 19, 1860; John D. Defrees to Abraham Lincoln, December 15, 1860, Lincoln Papers.

42. Worthington G. Snethen to Lincoln, November 26, 1860; Joseph Calvert to Lincoln, December 28, 1860, Lincoln Papers.

43. Along with Senator John Bell, Bates had attended the "rather forlorn" Whig party convention in 1856 that nominated Millard Fillmore for president. Michael F.

Holt, *The Rise and Fall of the American Whig Party: Jackson Politics and the Onset of the Civil War* (New York: Oxford University Press, 1999), 977.

44. Philadelphia *Press*, March 21, 1861, quoted in Harry J. Carman and Reinhard Luthin, *Lincoln and the Patronage* (New York: Columbia University Press, 1943), 187.

45. Worthington G. Snethen to Abraham Lincoln, December 8, 1860, Lincoln Papers.

46. Gerald S. Henig, *Henry Winter Davis: Antebellum and Civil War Congressman from Maryland* (New York: Twayne, 1973); Jean H. Baker, *The Politics of Continuity: Maryland Political Parties from 1858 to 1870* (Baltimore: Johns Hopkins University Press, 1973).

47. Paludan, *The Lincoln Presidency*, 35–36; Paul Van Riper and Keith A. Sutherland, "The Northern Civil Service: 1861–1865," *Civil War History* 11 (1965): 351–69; Carman and Luthin, *Lincoln and the Patronage*, 331.

48. Abraham Lincoln, "First Inaugural Address," March 4, 1861, in Basler, ed., *Collected Works of Abraham Lincoln*, 4: 258.

49. Nicolay and Hay, *Lincoln*, 3: 319–23.

50. J. Robert Lane, *A Political History of Connecticut During the Civil War* (Washington, D.C.: Catholic University of America Press, 1941), 175.

51. James Hiatt, *The Test of Loyalty* (Indianapolis: Merrill and Smith, 1864), 8.

52. "The Sword and the Red, White and Blue" (New York: H. De Marsan, 1861), *American Songs and Ballads*, ser. 4, vol. 4, Library of Congress.

53. Irving Katz, *August Belmont: A Political Biography* (New York: Columbia University Press, 1968), 100–103.

54. See Peter Dobkin Hall, *The Organization of American Culture, 1700–1900: Private Institutions, Elites, and the Origins of American Nationality* (New York: New York University Press, 1982), 220–39.

55. Russell quoted in Sven Beckert, *Monied Metropolis: New York City and the Consolidation of the American Bourgeoisie* (New York: Cambridge University Press, 2001), 116; Ernest A. McKay, *Civil War and New York City* (Syracuse: Syracuse University Press, 1990), 78–79.

56. "The true Jersey blue," by T. T. Price, M.D. (n., [1861]), Civil War Song Sheets, ser. 1, vol. 3, Rare Book and Special Collections Division, Library of Congress.

57. *Cincinnati Daily Enquirer*, October 11, 1861.

58. "Philadelphia Citizens" to Lincoln, April 15, 1861, Lincoln Papers.

59. John Campbell, *Unionists versus Traitors. The Political Parties of Philadelphia; or the nominees that ought to be elected in 1861* (Philadelphia, n., 1861), 8; Lancaster (Pa.) *Daily Evening Express* Jan 17, 1861, in Perkins, ed. *Northern Editorials on Secession*, 2: 1046–7.

60. Boston *Daily Advertiser*, July 4, 1861; Philadelphia *North American*, June 27, 29, July 3, 1861.

61. E.B. Holmes to Lincoln, April 20, 1861, Lincoln Papers.

62. *New York Times*, April 21, 1861; Earnest McKay, *The Civil War and New York City*, 62–64.

63. Quoted in Joel Silbey, *A Respectable Minority: The Democratic Party in the Civil War Era, 1860–1868* (New York: W. W. Norton, 1977), 39. On Wood's political journey see Jerome Mushkat, *Fernando Wood: A Political Biography* (Kent, Ohio: Kent

State University Press, 1990) and Tyler G. Anbinder, "Fernando Wood and New York City's Secession from the Union: A Political Reappraisal," *New York History* 68 (1987): 67–92.

64. See for example Concord [NH] *Monitor*, May 23, 1861.

65. Campbell, *Unionists versus Traitors*, 7.

66. John L. O'Sullivan to Samuel J. Tilden, May 6, June 5, 1861 in John G. Bigelow, ed, *Letters and Literary Memorials of Samuel J. Tilden*, 2 vols. (New York, 1908): vol. 1. 157–59, 160–62. See also McKay, *Civil War and New York City*, 61; Jerome Mushkat, *The Reconstruction of the New York Democracy, 1861–1874* (Rutherford, N.J.: Farleigh Dickinson University Press, 1981).

67. Robert W. Johannsen, "The Douglas Democracy and the Crisis of Disunion," *Civil War History* 9 (1963): 229–47; Joel Silbey, *A Respectable Minority*, 39–42

68. Johannsen, *Douglas*, 859–60; Carwardine, *Lincoln*, 161–2.

69. Christopher Dell, *Lincoln and the War Democrats: The Grand Erosion of Conservative Tradition* (Rutherford, N.J.: Farleigh Dickinson University Press, 1975), 68–70.

70. This phrase was used repeatedly in Republican Party election propaganda throughout the war. See for example "Rally Round the Old Flag!" Broadside (1862?) in the Collection of Broadsides, Houghton Library, Harvard University.

71. John R. Dickinson, ed., *Speeches, Correspondence etc., of the late Daniel S. Dickinson of New York*, 2 vols. (New York: Putnam, 1867), 2:550–51.

72. Hans L. Trefousse, *Andrew Johnson: A Biography* (New York: Norton, 1989).

73. Hans L. Trefousse, *Ben Butler: The South Called Him Beast!* (New York: Twayne, 1957).

74. Breckinridge, a native Kentuckian, worked hard for a sectional compromise even after the attack on Sumter, before finally fleeing to Virginia in the fall of 1861, where he took up a commission as a brigadier general in the Confederate army, a decision that left many of his northern supporters with a sense of betrayal. See William C. Davis, *Breckinridge: Statesman, Soldier, Symbol* (Baton Rouge: Louisiana State University Press, 1974).

75. Klement, *Limits of Dissent*, 62–63.

76. See, for example, Kenneth M. Stampp, *Indiana Politics during the Civil War* (Indianapolis, 1949).

77. S. D. Pardee to Gideon Welles, April 17, 1861. Welles Papers, Library of Congress.

78. For a survey of attempts to create Union parties in the fall of 1861 see Dell, *Lincoln and the War Democrats*, 102–23.

79. Based on Michael Holt's calculations in his "A Moving Target: President Lincoln Confronts a Two–Party System Still in the Making," paper delivered to the Annual Symposium of the Abraham Lincoln Association, February 2004, 14. See also Michael J. Dubin, *United States Congressional Elections, 1788–1997: the Official Results of the Elections of the 1st Through 105th Congresses* (Jefferson, N.C.: McFarland, 1998), 189–190.

80. Benjamin F. Biggs to George W. Julian, January 16, 1861, quoted in Michael F. Holt, "Abraham Lincoln and the Politics of Union," in his *Political Parties and American Political Development from the Age of Jackson to the Age of Lincoln* (Baton Rouge: Louisiana State University Press, 1992), 337n17.

81. See for instance, in the case of Massachusetts: Boston *Post*, June 23, September 19, 1862; Boston *Courier*, June 17, 1962; Springfield *Republican*, August 15, 1862; Boston *Daily Advertiser*, September 15, 23, 1862.

82. *Connecticut Courant*, December 9, 13, 1861, January 9, 17, 1862; *Tribune Almanac*, 1863.

83. Dell, *Lincoln and the War Democrats*, 107–8.

84. *New York Times*, June 29, 1861; *New York Daily Tribune*, June 27, 1861; Burlington (Vermont), *Sentinel*, August 2, 1861. Faced with a three-way choice, Vermont voters overwhelmingly supported the Republican candidate, endorsed by leading Democrats, who polled 78 per cent of the vote, an unprecedented total even in a state where the Democracy had been weak since the early 1850s.

85. As an editorial in the *New York Tribune* dryly pointed out, "The especial liberality of asking the other party to support your party's candidate for the country's sake is not superhuman." *New York Daily Tribune*, June 28, 1861.

86. In Rhode Island, a resolution favoring a "full and sincere" union of all political parties was first offered in the state assembly by a prominent local Democrat, Ellis R. Potter. *Connecticut Courant*, August 31, 1861.

87. George H. Porter, *Ohio Politics during the Civil War* (New York: Columbia University Press, 1911), 88.

88. Cincinnati *Enquirer*, September 10, quoted in the *Connecticut Courant*, September 14, 1861.

89. Edward C. Smith, *The Borderland in the Civil War* (New York: Macmillan, 1927), 88, 90; George H. Porter, *Ohio Politics during the Civil War* (New York, 1911), 88; Ewing quoted in Dell, *Lincoln and the War Democrats*, 110–11; *Connecticut Courant*, August 31, 1861.

90. James Maitland to E.M. Mast, August 28, 1861, Maitland Papers, Gilder Lehrman Collection, Morgan Library, New York (GLC 3523.10 no. 34).

91. *Connecticut Courant*, September 14, 1861.

92. David Todd won 206,997 votes, or 57.7 percent of the total. His Democratic opponent won Hugh J. Jewett won 151,774 or 42.3 percent. In October 1860, Republican congressional candidates averaged 54 percent of the vote and won 13 of the 21 congressional districts. Abraham Lincoln won 52.3 percent in November 1860. Dubin, *United States Congressional Elections*, 188.

93. Dell, *Lincoln and the War Democrats*, 111; Philadelphia *Press*, July 26, September 2, October 9, 1861; *New York Herald* September 3; *Daily National Intelligencer*, October 3, 1861. The simmering feud between Forney and Republican governor Andrew G. Curtin—and his Machiavellian henchman, the former Know-Nothing Alexander K. McClure—ensured that the Pennsylvania Union party was to present Lincoln with some of the most difficult patronage problems of his administration. See Carman and Luthin, *Lincoln and the Patronage*, 136–39.

94. John W. Forney, *Eulogy upon Stephen A. Douglas, Delivered at the Smithsonian Institute, Washington, July 3, 1861* (Philadelphia, 1861), 7–8.

95. Campbell, *Unionists versus Traitors*, 13.

96. *Tribune Almanac and Political Register for 1861* (New York, 1862), 56–64.

97. Dell, *Lincoln and the War Democrats*, 116; Dickinson, *Speeches*, 2: 550–551.

98. *Brooklyn Daily Eagle*, October 1, 1861.

99. *New York Times*, August 21, 1861; *New York Daily Tribune*, September 12, 18, 28, 1861. What is extraordinary about this particular coalition is that it had the support of all the major metropolitan dailies in New York, including the *Tribune*.

100. *New York Times*, October 10, 1861.

101. The main Democratic newspaper in the state, the Hartford *Times* described the peace movement as "purely spontaneous . . . springing up from the hearts of

the honest farmers of the country towns, and only looking to what they sincerely believe to be for the country's good." The *Times* quoted in the Hartford *Courant*, Aug 30, 1861.

102. Lane, *Political History of Connecticut*, 177–78

103. Pratt to Welles, Aug 14, 1861, Welles Papers, Library of Congress.

104. Other factors were undoubtedly also at work. A leading Republican in Connecticut thought that the apparent success of peace agitators could be put down to "many an old farmer who can't get last years prices for his butter and eggs." Mark Howard to Welles, August 28, 1861, Welles Papers.

105. *North American Inquirer*, June 2, 1863.

106. *The Tribune Almanac for 1861* (New York, 1862); *New York Times*, October 8, November 9, 1861; *Boston Daily Advertiser*, October 12, November 9, 1861.

107. Joel Silbey, *A Respectable Minority*, 56–59.

108. *Philadelphia Free Press*, June 17, 1861; Campbell, *Unionists versus Traitors*.

109. See, for instance, *New York Tribune* October 8, 1861; *Boston Daily Advertiser*, October 17, 1861; Concord (New Hampshire) *Monitor*, July 2, 1864; *Connecticut Courant*, August 12, 1861

110. Springfield (Mass.) *Republican*, October 12, 1861.

111. *Connecticut Courant*, August 12, 1861.

112. *Connecticut Courant*, November 30, 1861.

113. George B. Ide, 'The War for the Union a Righteous War' in Ide, *Battle Echoes, or, Lessons from the War* (Boston, 1866), 21.

114. *New York Times*, April 15, 1861, quoted in Perkins, ed., *Northern Editorials on Secession* 2: 735, 808; *Independent*, May 2, 1861. On the Northern reaction to Sumter see Peter J. Parish, *The American Civil War* (New York: Holmes & Meier, 1975), 103–28; James M. McPherson, *Battle Cry of Freedom: The Civil War Era* (New York: Oxford University Press, 1988), 308–11; Allen C. Guelzo, *The Crisis of the American Republic: A History of the Civil War and Reconstruction Era* (New York: St. Martin's Press, 1995), 102–15; Earl J. Hess, *Liberty, Virtue and Progress: Northerners and their War for the Union* (New York: New York University Press, 1988), 23–31.

115. "The Era in Our National History," *New York Times*, July 9, 1861.

116. *New York Times*, August 2, 1861; Boston *Daily Advertiser*, July 4, 1861.

117. James Maitland to E.M. Mast, August 9, 1861, Maitland Papers, Gilder Lehrman Collection (GLC: 3523.10, no. 33).

118. 'Notes and Comments from the National Capital,' by Charles L. Brace, *The Independent*, May 16, 1861.

119. *The Independent*, May 16, 1861.

120. George C. Rable, *The Confederate Republic: A Revolution Against Politics* (Chapel Hill: University of North Carolina Press, 1994), 121–22.

121. *Speeches delivered at the Republican Union festival, in commemoration of the birth of Washington* (New York: Putnam, 1862).

122. Robert T. Handy, *A History of Union Theological Seminary in New York* (New York: Columbia University Press, 1987), 56. Hitchcock was a Congregationalist minister, the holder of the Washburn Chair of Church History and later the president of the Union Theological Seminary in New York City.

123. Rable, *Confederate Republic*, 122. In his message to the gathering, Governor Edwin D. Morgan of New York added that no one "at this time [can] read Washington's Farewell Address . . . without a deeper and more abiding impression that ever before of the wisdom of that Patriot and Statesman."

124. *Speeches delivered at the Republican Union festival, in commemoration of the birth of Washington* (New York: Putnam, 1862)

125. *Harper's Weekly*, September 10, 1864.

CHAPTER 3

1. 1.Howard K. Beale, ed., *Diary of Gideon Welles: Secretary of the Navy under Lincoln and Johnson*, 3 vols. (New York: W.W. Norton, 1960), 1:143–44.

2. William Ernest Smith, *The Francis Preston Blair Family in Politics*, 2 vols. (New York: Macmillan, 1933); William E. Parrish, *Frank Blair: Lincoln's Conservative* (Columbia: University of Missouri Press, 1998).

3. August Belmont to Thurlow Weed, May 9, 1862 in August Belmont, *A Few Letters and Speeches of the Late Civil War* (privately printed, New York, 1870), 68–70; Lincoln to Belmont, July 31, 1862, Basler, ed., *Collected Works of Abraham Lincoln*, 5: 350–51; and Belmont to Lincoln August 10, 1862, Lincoln Papers. On Lincoln's evolving attitudes toward Reconstruction and his faith in Southern Unionism see William C. Harris, *With Charity for All: Lincoln and the Reconstruction of the Union* (Lexington: University of Kentucky Press, 1997).

4. Vallandigham, *Speeches, Arguments, Addresses and Letters of Clement L. Vallandigham* (New York: J.Walter, 1864), 362–69.

5. *Indianapolis Daily State Sentinel*, April 16, 1862, quoted in Lawson, *Patriot Fires*, 91.

6. *New York World*, September 23, 1862, quoted in Lawson, *Patriot Fires*, 91.

7. *Indianapolis Daily State Sentinel*, August 10, 1861, quoted in Lawson, *Patriot Fires*, 92.

8. Dickinson, *Speeches and Letters*, 211, quoted in Silbey, *Respectable Minority*, 56.

9. Hartford *Courant*, July 3, 1862.

10. Olynthus B. Clark, *The Politics of Iowa during the Civil War and Reconstruction* (Iowa City, Iowa: Clio Press, 1911), 148.

11. Philadelphia *Age*, March 30, 1863.

12. Open letter from Nelson J.Waterbury to the Electors of the Eighth Congressional District, New York, in *Documents Relative to the Withdrawal of Nelson J. Waterbury from the Canvass in the Eighth Congressional District, New York, November 1862* (New York: Baptist & Taylor, 1862), pp. 5–6.

13. Joseph Medill to Lyman Trumbull, June 5, 1862, Lyman Trumbull Papers, Manuscript Division, Library of Congress.

14. S. S. Cox's nickname was acquired when, as a young editor of the *Ohio Statesman* in 1853 he penned a ludicrously effusive description of a sunset. See David Lindsey, *"Sunset" Cox: Irrepressible Democrat* (Detroit: Wayne State University Press, 1959).

15. George B. McClellan to Abraham Lincoln, July 7, 1862, Abraham Lincoln Papers, Manuscripts Division, Library of Congress.

16. James G. Blaine, *Twenty Years of Congress: From Lincoln to Garfield*, 2 vols. (Norwich, Conn.: Henry Bill Publishing, 1884), 1: 353.

17. *New York World*, October 23, 1862.

18. At the same time, Illinois voters turned down a new Constitution. See V. Jaques Voegeli, *Free but Not Equal: The Midwest and the Negro during the Civil War* (Chicago: University of Chicago Press, 1967), 17; James D. Bilotta, *Race and the Rise of the Republican Party, 1848–1865* (New York: P. Lang, 1992).

19. Quoted in Voegli, *Free But Not Equal*, 18.

20. See for instance, *Frank Leslie's Illustrated Newspaper*, November 1, 1862.

21. Quoted in John Niven, *Salmon P. Chase: A Biography* (New York, 1995), 345.

22. Chase to Benjamin P. Butler, July 31, 1862, Chase Papers, Manuscripts Division, Library of Congress.

23. Quoted in Voegli, *Free But Not Equal*, 58–59.

24. *Chicago Times*, September 23, 27, October 9, 1862, quoted in Voegli, *Free But Not Equal*, 60. For a fuller summary of the Illinois black scare on which my account is based see Voegli, 59–62.

25. A. Kitchell to Richard Yates, October 9, 1862, Yates Papers, Illinois State Historical Society.

26. David Davis to Abraham Lincoln, October 14, 1862, Lincoln Papers.

27. James R. Doolittle to Mary Doolittle, April 4, 1862, Doolittle Papers, Manuscripts Division, Library of Congress.

28. Abraham Lincoln, "Address on Colonization to a Deputation of Negroes," August 14, 1862, in Basler, ed., *Collected Works of Abraham Lincoln*, 5: 371.

29. On the political maneuvering that led up to the Emancipation Proclamation see Michael Voreneberg, *Final Freedom: The Civil War, the Abolition of Slavery and the Thirteenth Amendment* (New York: Cambridge University Press, 2001), 36–48

30. Sumner to John Jay, November 10, 1861, in Edward L. Pierce, *Memoir and Letters of Charles Sumner*, 4 vols. (Boston: Roberts Bros., 1887–1893), 4: 49.

31. Congressman Richardson (Illinois), speech to the US House of Representatives, *Congressional Globe*, 37th Cong., 2d sess., p. 2207, quoted in Voegli, *Free But Not Equal*, 15.

32. *Illinois State Journal* (Springfield) March 22, 1862.

33. Orville Hickman Browning, *Diary*, Theodore Calvin Pease and James G. Randall, eds., 2 vols. (Springfield: Illinois State Historical Library, 1925), 1: 578. Entry for October 14, 1862. On Browning see Maurice Baxter, *Orville H. Browning, Lincoln's Friend and Critic* (Bloomington: Indiana University Press, 1957); and David H. Donald, *We Are Lincoln Men: Abraham Lincoln and His Friends* (New York: Simon and Shuster, 2003), 101–39.

34. Orville H. Browning to Abraham Lincoln, August 25, 1862, Lincoln Papers.

35. Browning illustrated these remarks by claiming that an old Democratic acquaintance had waxed lyrical about the nonpartisan, patriotic course taken by the President. "It has been a hard struggle for me to come to the support of a Republican Administration," said the Democrat, according to Browning. "It has been a hard struggle for the Democratic party. We were afraid of Mr. Lincoln, but his firm, honest, patriotic course has won our hearts, and now nine out of every ten of us, every where, would vote for him. He has resisted factions, and shown that he can be President himself, and the President of *all* the people. I have two sons in the war, and am now ready to go myself." Orville H. Browning to Abraham Lincoln, 11 August 1862, Lincoln Papers.

36. *Diary of Orville Hickman Browning*, 589 [Entry for November 28, 1862].

37. Oliver Johnson to William Lloyd Garrison, September 25, 1862, William Lloyd Garrison Papers, Manuscripts Division, Boston Public Library.

38. The increase in Illinois was 6.37 percent; in Indiana it was 9.09 percent; and in Ohio it was 11.84 percent. Unionists held only 5 out of 19 congressional seats in

Ohio, 4 out of 11 in Indiana and 5 of 14 in Illinois. Calculated from congressional election results in Dubin, *Congressional Elections*, 193–96.

39. *Tribune Almanac and Political Register for 1862* (New York, 1863).

40. Lane, *Political History of Connecticut*, 185.

41. The address was formulated at a meeting in Albany on April 18; *New York Daily Tribune*, April 19, 1862.

42. Letter from Judge Willed, Democratic state senator from Saratoga district, *New York Daily Tribune*, May 5, 1862.

43. *New York Daily Tribune*, May 16, 1862.

44. "List of Union Men in New York State," compiled by H. R. Low for the editors of the *Evening Post*, 1862, New-York Historical Society [under catalog heading 'Union Party'].

45. Undated clipping from the Brooklyn *Star*, in the Thomas Kinsella Papers, New York Public Library.

46. Thomas G. Alvord, quoted in the *New York Herald*, September 25, 1862; *New-York Daily Tribune*, September 25, 26, 1862. Alvord was a War Democrat who had been the chairman of the 1861 People's Party convention. He was a member of Mozart Hall, and a close friend of Fernando Wood, the Democratic Mayor of New York City, a man whose name would later become a byword for Copperheadism. Dell, *Lincoln and the War Democrats*, 116.

47. *New York Herald*, September 3, 1862.

48. Sydney D. Brummer, *Political History of New York During the Period of the Civil War* (New York: Columbia University Press, 1911), 56–72; *New York Herald*, September 25, 26, 1862; *New York Times*, September 25, 26, 27, 1862; *Daily National Intelligencer*, September 27, 1862. Two votes were also cast for another life-long Democrat, Daniel S. Dickinson.

49. Dell, *Lincoln and the War Democrats*, 116; *New York Herald*, July 17, 1861.

50. Michael Holt, "A Moving Target: President Lincoln Confronts a Two-Party System Still in the Making," Paper delivered to the Abraham Lincoln Association Symposium, 2004, 11.

51. Quoted in Silbey, *A Respectable Minority*, 49.

52. *New York Herald*, October 26, 1862.

53. *New York Herald*, June 22, October 9, 1862.

54. James Brooks, quoted in Bernstein, *New York City Draft Riots*, 146. Brooks' victory was made possible by the withdrawal of the Democratic candidate, Nelson J. Waterbury, who was pressured to stand down so that only one conservative candidate would run against the Republican. In explaining why he was standing down, Waterbury explained that "I yield to the supreme duty which every man owes to his country—in order to prevent the possible loss of our District." *Documents Relative to the Withdrawal of Nelson J. Waterbury from the Canvass in the Eighth Congressional District, New York, November 1862* (New York: Baptist & Taylor, 1862).

55. *Albany Evening Journal*, September 30, October 21, November 5, 1862; Van Deusen, *William Henry Seward*, 289.

56. Allan Nevins and Milton H. Thomas, eds., *The Diary of George Templeton Strong*, 3 vols. (New York, 1952), 3:270.

57. *National Intelligencer*, November 5, 1862, *New York Herald*, October 3, 1862.

58. Strong, *Diary*, 2:267.

59. Quoted in Beckert, *Monied Metropolis*, 126.

60. This account of the formation of the National War Committee is drawn from George Winston Smith, "The National War Committee of the Citizens of New York," *New York History* 28 (October 1947): 440–457; New York Herald, August 28, 1862; Beckert, *Monied Metropolis*, 126–27; Iver Bernstein, *New York City Draft Riots: Their Significance for American Society and Politics in the Age of the Civil War* (New York: Oxford University Press, 1990), 146.

61. Beckert, *Monied Metropolis*, 126; Katz, *August Belmont*, 111–12.

62. Katz, *August Belmont*, 116–49.

63. Springfield *Republican*, September 9, 12, 15, 19, 1862.

64. Dale Baum, *The Civil War Party System: The Case of Massachusetts* (Chapel Hill: University of North Carolina Press, 1984), 64; David H. Donald, *Charles Sumner and the Rights of Man* (New York: Knopf, 1970), 78–79, 81–82; *National Intelligencer*, November 11, 13, 1862; Richard Henry Dana, *Speeches in Stirring Times,* and Richard Henry Dana III ed., *Letters to a Son* (Boston: Houghton Mifflin, 1910), 126–29.

65. *Boston Post*, August 5, 1862, *Boston Daily Courier*, September 4, September 9, 1864. The Republican State committee met in Boston on July 31, and issued a call for a Republican state convention at Worcester to be held on September 10. The objection of conservatives was to the commitment in the call for convention delegates to emancipation. See *Boston Daily Courier*, August 1, 1862.

66. Boston *Daily Advertiser*, October 8, 1862.

67. Boston *Daily Advertiser*, October 8, 1862.

68. *Springfield Republican*, September 20, 1862. See also *Boston Daily Journal*, September 22, 1862.

69. Boston *Daily Advertiser*, October 12, 1862.

70. 'Stand by the President! Sustain the Government!' [broadside published by the Republican County Committee, Worcester, Massachusetts, October 25, 1862] Collection of Pamphlets and Broadsides, Houghton Library, Harvard University.

71. *Appleton's Annual Cyclopeadia* for 1862.

72. Edward Everett to Charles Francis Adams, September 30, 1862, Adams Family Papers, Massachusetts Historical Society.

73. Amos A. Lawrence to Alexander H. Rice, October 27, 1862, Amos A. Lawrence Papers, Massachusetts Historical Society.

74. S. Holmes to Charles Sumner, October 6, 1862, Charles Sumner Papers, Houghton Library, Harvard University.

75. See Paul Kleppner, *The Third Electoral System, 1853–1892: Parties, Voters, and Political Cultures* (Chapel Hill: University of North Carolina Press, 1979), 84.

76. Lincoln to Schurz, Basler, ed., *Collected Works*, V, 493–95, 509–11.

77. John Sherman to William T. Sherman, November 16, 1862, quoted in Michael F. Holt, "Abraham Lincoln and the Politics of Union."

78. William Pitt Fessenden to John Murray Forbes, November 13, 1862 in John Murray Forbes, *Letters and recollections of John Murray Forbes* ed. Sarah Forbes Hughes, 2 vols. (Boston: Houghton Mifflin, 1899).

79. H. S. Bundy to Salmon P. Chase, October 18, 1862, Chase Papers.

80. Salmon P. Chase to Benjamin F. Butler, December 14, 1862, *Private and Official Correspondence of Benjamin F. Butler*, 5 vols. (Norwood, Mass.: Plimpton Press, II: 542–43, cited in William C. Harris, "Conservative Unionists and the Presidential Election of 1864," *Civil War History* 37 (1992): 302.

81. Richard P. L. Baber to Abraham Lincoln, November 22, 1862, Lincoln Papers.

82. *New York Herald*, May 17, 1862; Glyndon G. Van Deusen, *William Henry Seward*, 202.

83. *New York Times*, June 29, 1862.

84. Orville H. Browning to William B. Campbell, June 15, 1863, quoted in Harris, "Conservative Unionists," 303.

85. Addison C. Gibbs to Abraham Lincoln, September 24, 1863, Lincoln Papers.

86. Richard P. L. Baber to Abraham Lincoln, November 22, 1862, Lincoln Papers.

87. This is an argument elaborated by Michael F. Holt, "Abraham Lincoln and the Politics of Union."

CHAPTER 4

1. The James G. Batterson Papers at the Connecticut Historical Society contain his correspondence on all these matters. See for example: Henry J. Raymond to James G. Batterson, undated [Oct, 1864]; H. H. Starkweather to Batterson, October 27, 1864; J. M. Sperry to Batterson, October 20, 1864; William Buckingham to Batterson, October 10; D. N. Cooley to Batterson, October 10, 1864.

2. Fragment of a speech, undated, Batterson Papers.

3. James G. Batterson to Hon. Charles Sumner et al., February 20, 1863, Collection of Broadsides, Houghton Library, Harvard University.

4. Melinda Lawson, *Patriot Fires: Forging a New American Nationalism in the Civil War North* (Lawrence: University of Kansas Press, 2002), 89.

5. *Installation ceremony, for the use of subordinate councils of the Union League of America in Illinois. By authority of the State Grand Council* [Springfield: Union League of America, 1863]. Illinois State Historical Library.

6. *Philadelphia Press*, May 8, 1863.

7. *The Loyal National League* (New York, [1863]); [New York Public Library].

8. Robert H. McCurdy to [illegible], April 7, 1863, Papers of the Loyal League of Union Citizens, New-York Historical Society.

9. *Constitution and By-Laws of the Union League of Loyal Men of the 19th Ward, Brooklyn* (New York, 1863).

10. *The Boot on the Other Leg or Loyalty Above Party* (Philadelphia: Philadelphia Union League, 1863).

11. *New York Times*, April 24, 1863.

12. *Chicago Tribune*, February 27, 1863.

13. H. G. McPike to Lyman Trumbull, February 6, 1863, Trumbull Papers.

14. Union League of Springfield, Illinois, to Abraham Lincoln, March 17, 1863, Union League of York, Pennsylvania, to Abraham Lincoln, December 16, 1863, February 9, 1864, James Edmunds to Edwin M. Stanton, March 1, 1864, in the Lincoln Papers.

15. *Chicago Tribune*, December 22, 1863. In December 1863 a three-man delegation was sent from the convention of the Union League of America (meeting in Washington) to the President seeking the removal of General John M. Schofield, a conservative in his attitude both to the rebels and slavery. Despite having refused to dismiss Schofield three months earlier when requested to do so by the Missouri

Union League under the control of B. Gratz Brown and Charles Drake, Lincoln this time acceded to the demand.

16. E. D. Morgan to George Morgan, April 12, 1863, Morgan Papers, New York State Library, Albany.

17. John Austin Stevens, Jr., a prominent Chase supporter, was the president of the New York League (as well as secretary of the New York Loyal Publication Society) and Mark Howard, another Chase man, was president of the Connecticut Union League.

18. [Illegible] to Montgomery Blair, May 2, 1863, Montgomery Blair Papers, Blair Family Collection, Manuscripts Collection, Library of Congress.

19. *The Loyal National League* (New York, [1863]).

20. *The Sumter anniversary, 1863. Opinions of loyalists concerning the great question of the times* (New York, 1863), 4–7. *New York Herald,* April 15, 1863.

21. W. H. Leonard to James A. Roosevelt, April 4, 1863, John A. Stevens Papers, New York Historical Society.

22. James L. Morris to James A. Roosevelt, May 5, 1863, John A. Stevens Papers.

23. Samuel J. Tilden to unknown, June 11, 1863, Box 6, Papers of Samuel J. Tilden, New York Public Library.

24. David M. Turnure, Journal for 1863, New-York Historical Society.

25. Severn Teackle Wallis, *Writings of Severn Teackle Wallis,* 4 vols. (Baltimore: John Murphy, 1896), 2: 266.

26. Poll Book, Montgomery County, New York, enclosing letter from Dean Richmond [1863], New-York Historical Society.

27. *Immense Meeting in Favor of the Union* (Philadelphia, [1863]), pamphlet in the Houghton Library, Harvard University.

28. Ibid.

29. Carwardine, *Lincoln,* 257–160.

30. Basler, ed., *Collected Works of Abraham Lincoln,* 6: 267–68.

31. George Fredrickson, discussing this phenomenon has described the emergence of a "doctrine of loyalty" in 1863. Fredrickson, *Inner Civil War,* 130–50. On the issue of loyalty on the Northern home front see also Jorg Nagler, "Loyalty and Dissent: The Home Front in the American Civil War" and Philip A. Paludan, "'The Better Angels of Our Nature': Lincoln, Propaganda and Public Opinion in the North during the Civil War" in Stig Förster and Jörg Nagler, *On the Road to Total War: The American Civil War and the German Wars of Unification, 1861–1871* (New York: Cambridge University Press, 1997), 331–56, 357–76.

32. The Union League of Philadelphia, for instance, had 1129 members in December 1864. *Chronicle of the Union league of Philadelphia, 1862 to 1902* (Philadelphia: Union League, 1902); Maxwell Whiteman, *Gentlemen in Crisis: The First Century of the Union League of Philadelphia, 1862–1962* (Philadelphia: Union League, 1975); Ernest A. McKay, *The Civil War and New York City* (Syracuse: Syracuse University Press, 1990), 240–43; Reginald Townsend, *Mother of Clubs, Being the History of the First Hundred Years of the Union Club of the City of New York* (New York: W. E. Rudge, 1936). These clubs were not formally a part of the Grand National Council of the Union League of America, but they co-operated with the national organization.

33. *Address by the Union League of Philadelphia to Citizens of Pennsylvania, in favor of the Re-election of Abraham Lincoln* (Philadelphia: Union League, 1864); Lawson, *Patriot Fires,* 103.

34. Union League of Philadelphia, *First Annual Report of the Board of Directors of the Union League of Philadelphia, December 14, 1863* (Philadelphia: Union League, 1863).

35. Henry W. Bellows, *Historical Sketch of the Union League Club of New York* (New York: G. P. Putnam's Sons, 1879).

36. S. Lothrop Thorndike, *A Brief Sketch of the History of the Union Club of Boston* (Boston, n.p., 1893), 5–8.

37. *Philadelphia North American and United States Gazette*, April 11, 1861, quoted in Lawson, *Patriot Fires*, 102.

38. Beckert, *Monied Metropolis*, 114.

39. J. Matthew Gallman, *Mastering Wartime: A Social History of Philadelphia During the Civil War* (New York: Cambridge University Press, 1990), 95–96; Nicholas B. Wainwright, "The Loyal Opposition in Philadelphia," *Pennsylvania Magazine of History and Biography* 88 (July 1964): 298–99. On Philadelphia elites and the Civil War see also William Dusinberre, *Civil War Issues in Philadelphia*, 156; Whiteman, *Gentlemen in Crisis*, 18–28.

40. Richard H Abbott, *Cotton and Capital: Boston Businessmen and Antislavery Reform, 1854–1868* (Amherst: University of Massachusetts Press, 1991), 100–4.

41. On Marble's political role see George McJimsey, *Genteel Partisan: Manton Marble, 1834–1917* (Ames: Iowa State University Press, 1971).

42. A leading upper-class Democrat, Edwards Pierrepont served as Grand Sachem of Tammany Hall, according to Bernstein, *New York City Draft Riots*, 129. He later became a prominent War Democrat, supporting Lincoln's re-election in 1864.

43. Beckert, *Monied Metropolis*, 132–33.

44. *The Democratic Anti-Abolition State Rights Association of the City of New York* (New York, 1863).

45. Quoted in Lawson, *Patriot Fires*, 106. See also Bernstein, *New York City Draft Riots*, 125–61.

46. Berstein, *The New York City Draft Riots*, 159.

47. Thomas Wentworth Higginson, ed., *Harvard Memorial Biographies*, 2 vols. (Cambridge, Mass.: Harvard University Press, 1867), 1: v.

48. Quoted in George Parsons Lathrop, *History of the Union League of Philadelphia, From its Origin and Foundation to the Year 1882* (Philadelphia, 1884), 42.

49. Foner, *Reconstruction: America's Unfinished Revolution, 1863–1877* (New York: Harper and Row, 1988), 31; Bernstein, *New York City Draft Riots*, 100–104.

50. In fact, as it was, partisan Democrats playing on racial stereotypes, dubbed the organization "the Sambo Club." John Murray Forbes to Charles Sumner, 4 March 1863, Charles Sumner Papers, Houghton Library, Harvard University. Everett told his friend Henry W. Bellows, the Unitarian minister who was a member of the New York Union League Club, that he was "almost the only person of what are called rather vaguely 'conservative' associations who has joined the club." Edward Everett to Henry W. Bellows, March 6, 1863, Henry W. Bellows Papers, Massachusetts Historical Society.

51. Union League of Philadelphia, *Second Annual Report of the Board of Directors of the Union League of Philadelphia, December 12, 1864* (Philadelphia: Union League, 1864), 6.

52. *First Annual Report of the Directors of the Union League of Philadelphia*, 6–7.

53. Frank Freidel, "The Loyal Publication Society: A pro-Union Propaganda Agency," *Mississippi Valley Historical Review* 26 (1939): 359–76.

54. *First Annual Report of the Directors of the Union League of Philadelphia,* 9–10.

55. Freidel, "Loyal Publication Society," 362; First Annual Report of the Board of Directors of the Union League of Philadelphia, 6–7; Loyal Publication Society, Proceedings at the First Anniversary Meeting, 11–14; Frank Freidel, *Francis Lieber: Nineteenth Century Liberal* (Baton Rouge: Louisiana State University Press, 1947).

56. Loyal Publication Society, [John A. Stevens, Jr., secretary], *Proceedings at the First Anniversary Meeting of the Loyal Publication Society* (New York, 1864), 8.

57. *Emancipation is Peace* (New York: Loyal Publication Society, 1863); see also *The Death of Slavery, Letter from Peter Cooper to Governor Seymour* (New York: Loyal Publication Society, 1863); *Patriotism* (New York: Loyal Publication Society, 1863).

58. *Letter from Peter Cooper on Slave Emancipation* (New York: Loyal Publication Society, 1863).

59. Lieber, *No Party Now But all For Our Country,* 3.

60. James Turner, *The Liberal Education of Charles Eliot Norton* (Baltimore: Johns Hopkins University Press, 1999).

61. These newspapers produced 928 million copies annually. S. N. D. North, *History and Present Conditions of the Newspaper and Periodical Press of the United States* (Washington: General Printing Office, 1880), 187. This represented more than threefold increase in just twenty years. In 1840 there had been 1,403 newspapers. Precise figures for the number of newspapers in the Loyal states in 1864 are not available, but in 1860 it has been estimated that over three-quarters of all newspapers published in the United States were in the Northern states. See Frank Luther Mott, *American Journalism: A History of Newspapers in the United States through 250 Years, 1690 to 1940* (New York: Macmillan, 1947), 329–59.

62. See, for instance, Charles T. Congdon, *Reminiscences of a Journalist* (Boston: J. R. Osgood, 1880), 210–11, 310–11; Mott, *American Journalism,* 205; Bingham Duncan, *Whitelaw Reid: Journalist, Politician, Diplomat* (Athens: University of Georgia Press, 1975), 23.

63. From the Youngstown (Ohio) *Register, Report of the Executive Committee of the New England Loyal Publication Society, May 1, 1865* (Boston, 1865). The executive committee of the new organization included among its members Samuel G. Ward, a friend of Emerson and the Boston agent of Barings' Bank, and Norton, who was to take over from Forbes as editor. Forbes to Samuel G. Ward, January 22, 1863, New England Loyal Publication Society MSS, Boston Public Library; Circular letter signed by J. M. Forbes, Samuel G. Ward, Charles Eliot Norton, Martin Brimmer, March 9, 1863, New England Loyal Publication Society MSS. For a list of the members of the executive committee see George Winston Smith, "Broadsides for Freedom: Civil War Propaganda in New England," *The New England Quarterly* (September 1948), 292–93.

64. John Murray Forbes to William Curtis Noyes, August 12, 1862, in Forbes, ed., *Letters and Recollections,* 327

65. James B. Thayer to William Endicott, Jr., February 1, 1864, New England Loyal Publication Society Papers, Boston Public Library.

66. John M. Forbes to Charles Eliot Norton, undated New England Loyal Publication Society Papers.

67. *Report of the Executive Committee of the New England Loyal Publication Society, May 1, 1865* (Boston, 1865).

68. "Public Library's Prize," Boston *Evening Transcript,* February 7, 1903. During the 1864 election campaign itself the Society stepped up both the rate of

publication and the circulation figures. In October the Society published its own newspaper, *The Campaign for the Union*, which was distributed two or three times a week throughout Boston and the state. There was a concerted effort to distribute the paper for free, but subscribers were also sought, and all readers encouraged to spread information on how the publication could be obtained. Circular 'from the publishers,' enclosed in the holdings of *The Campaign for the Union*, Boston Public Library.

69. Forbes, *Letters and Recollections*, 1: 327; New England Loyal Publication Society Papers.

70. The broadsides were not wasted. The editor went on to report that the blank reverse side of the Society's publications were very useful "for writing editorials, notices, etc." They also made excellent wrapping paper, it seemed and "we used divers of them for mailing the Palladium." From the Richmond (Indiana) *Palladium, Report of the Executive Committee of the New England Loyal Publication Society*, 12–13.

71. Charles Eliot Norton to J. M. Forbes, July 12, 1864, New England Loyal Publication Society MSS.

72. From the editor of the Kansas City (Mo.) *Commerce, Report of the Executive Committee of the New England Loyal Publication Society*, 11.

73. Carrigan vs. Thayer. Memorial of Charles Carrigan, contesting the right of M. Russell Thayer to a seat as a representative from the Fifth Congressional District of the State of Pennsylvania in the Thirty-eighth congress. December 8, 1863. *Congressional Serial Set* 1199 (38th Cong., 1st sess.), House of Representatives Misc. Doc. 17, 199–200.

74. Richard J. Carwardine, *Lincoln* (London: Pearson Education, 2003), 287–89; Allen C. Guelzo, *Abraham Lincoln: Redeemer President* (Grand Rapids, Mich.: William B. Eerdmans, 1999), 394–96; James H. Moorhead, *American Apocalypse: Yankee Protestants and the Civil War, 1860–1869* (New Haven, Conn., 1978), 158–62; Richard J. Carwardine, "Lincoln, Evangelical Religion and American Political Culture in the Era of the Civil War," *Journal of the Abraham Lincoln Association* 18 (1997): 27–55; Dale Baum, *The Civil War Party System: the Case of Massachusetts, 1846–1876* (Chapel Hill: University of North Carolina Press, 1984), 95–100

75. James H. Moorhead, *American Apocalypse: Yankee Protestants and the American Civil War* (New Haven, Conn.: Yale University Press, 1978), 152; *Appleton's Annual Cyclopaedia and Register of Important Events . . . for 1864* (New York, 1865), 680–684.

76. Mary Kelley to James Kelley, January 30, 1862, Kelley Correspondence, Gilder Lehrman Collection.

77. Quoted in Altschuler and Blumin, *Rude Republic*, 168.

78. Mary Hawley Diary, entry for November 24, 1864, New York Historical Society.

79. On the Sanitary and Christian Commissions see George M. Fredrickson, *The Inner Civil War: Northern Intellectuals and the Crisis of the Union* (New York: Harper & Row, 1965), 98–112; Robert H. Bremner, *The Public Good: Philanthropy and Welfare in the Civil War Era* (New York: Knopf, 1980), 39–46, 54–62; William Q. Maxwell, *Lincoln's Fifth Wheel: The Sanitary Commission* (New York: Longmans, Green, 1956); Jeannie Attie, "Warwork and the Crisis of Domesticity in the North," in Catherine Clinton and Nina Silber, eds., *Divided Houses: Gender and the Civil War* (New York: Oxford University Press, 1992), 247–59.

80. Katherine Prescott Wormeley, *The United States Sanitary Commission: A Sketch of its Purposes and its Work* (Boston: Little, Brown, 1863), 253–54.

81. Frederick L. Olmsted to Abraham Lincoln, September 30, 1861, Lincoln Papers; Lincoln to Winfield Scott, September 30, 1861, Basler, ed., *Collected Works of Abraham Lincoln*, 4: 543

82. Quoted by Attie, "Warwork and the Crisis of Domesticity in the North," 250.

83. Henry W. Bellows, *The Advantage of Testing Our Principles, Compensatory of the Evils of Serious Times, a Discourse of February 17, 1861* (Philadelphia, 1861), cited in Fredrickson, *The Inner Civil War*, 58–59. Henry W. Bellows, *Historical Sketch of the Union League Club of New York* (New York: Union League Club, 1879), 5.

84. Francis Lieber, *No Party Now But All For Our Country* (New York, 1863), 331–56, 357–76.

85. Friends and neighbors regarded women as making political statements when they decided to work—or not to work—for a Soldiers Aid association. Local organizers complained bitterly of obstructionism in Democratic towns. While attempting to encourage the establishment of a local branch in a town in Southern Ohio, one organizer complained, "this is a Democratic town of the Messrs Breckenridge, Stevens, and Jeff Davis persuasion. As a result the Sanitary Commission is left out in the cold." Attie, *Patriotic Toil*, 140.

86. Paul C. Nagel, *One Nation Indivisible: The Union in American Thought, 1776–1861* (New York: Oxford University Press, 1964); Fredrickson, *Inner Civil War*, 130–65; Hall, *Organization of American Culture*, 220–39.

87. *New York Evening Post*, April 12, 1864.

88. Horace Bushnell, "The Doctrine of Loyalty," *New Englander* XXII (July 1863), 564–71, quoted in Fredrickson, *Inner Civil War*, 138.

89. Charles Eliot Norton, "American Political Ideas," *North American Review* 101 (October 1865), quoted in Lawson, *Patriot Fires*, 124.

90. Daniel Walker Howe, *The Unitarian Conscience*, 125–31.

91. Quoted in Bernstein, *The New York City Draft Riots*, 156.

92. Henry W. Bellows, *Unconditional Loyalty* (New York: A. D. F. Randolph, 1863). See also Bellows, *The State and the Nation-Sacred to Christian Citizens. A Sermon, etc.* (New York: James Miller, 1861) and Bellows, *The War to End only when the Rebellion ceases* (New York: A. D. F. Randolph, [1863]).

93. On Dewey see Conrad Wright, *The Liberal Christians: Essays on American Unitarian History* (Boston: Beacon Press, 1970), 62–80.

94. Orville Dewey, *A Talk with the Camp* (New York, 1863).

95. Hiram Walbridge, *Speech delivered before the Convention of the War Democracy, Cooper Institute, New York, Tuesday, November 1, 1864* (New York, 1864).

96. *New York Herald*, November 5, 1864.

CHAPTER 5

1. On the practice of elections in the nineteenth-century see Robert Wiebe, *Self-Rule: A Cultural History of American Democracy* (Chicago: University of Chicago Press, 1995; Michael Schudson, *The Good Citizen: A History of American Civic Life* (New York: Free Press, 1998); Richard F. Bensel, *The American Ballot Box in the Mid-Nineteenth Century* (New York: Cambridge University Press); Alexander Keyssar, *The Right to Vote: The Contested History of Democracy in the United States* (New York:

Basic Books, 2000). As Richard Bensel's study of the process of voting in the Civil War era has shown, "men placed their bodies in the path of opponents attempting to approach the voting window. They shoved, poked, threatened, grabbed, and sometimes stabbed or shot those they saw as politically damned. But, whatever they did, men at the polls rarely engaged in an open and free debate of the issues that divided them." Bensel concludes that, paradoxically, "the polling place, in nineteenth-century America, was often one of the less democratic sites in the nation." *The American Ballot Box*, 290, 292.

2. Harold M. Hyman, *Era of the Oath: Northern Loyalty Tests During the Civil War and Reconstruction* (Philadelphia: University of Pennsylvania Press, 1954); Philip J. Avillo, Jr., "Ballots for the Faithful: The Oath and the Emergence of Slave State Republican Congressmen, 1861–1867," *Civil War History* 22 (June 1976): 164–74.

3. On the ambiguities of defining loyalty see Bensel, *American Ballot Box*, 223–28; Hubert W. Wubben, *Civil War Iowa and the Copperhead Movement* (Ames: Iowa State University Press, 1980), 223–25.

4. Allan Thurman to the Ohio Democratic State convention in 1862, quoted in William F. Zornow, *Lincoln and the Party Divided* (Norman: University of Oklahoma Press, 1954), 160.

5. John Maitland to James Maitland, April 6, 1863, Maitland Papers, Gilder Lehrman Collection on deposit at the New York Historical Society (GLC: 3523.10 no. 62).

6. New Haven *Register*, March 11, 1863.

7. James W. Geary, *We Need Men: The Union Draft in the Civil War* (Dekalb: Northern Illinois University Press, 1991), 104–8.

8. New Haven *Register* March 7, 1863.

9. William Dusinberre, *Civil War Issues in Philadelphia* (Philadelphia: University of Pennsylvania Press, 1965), 154–55.

10. *Philadelphia Age*, August 8, 1863.

11. Alexander B. Johnson, *The Approaching Presidential Election* (Utica, N.Y., 1864).

12. Newspaper readership was, of course, a prominent badge of partisan identification. In Blanchard's Connecticut, the readers of the Hartford *Times* had marked themselves out as disloyal. The kind who "get over to the store and have a glorious time over the news if it is in favor of the south . . . I hope there will be a time when they will be punished for treason. Mattie Blanchard to Caleb Blanchard, 26 March 1863, in Nina Silber and Mary Beth Sievens, eds., *Yankee Correspondence: Civil War Letter between New England Soldiers and the Home Front* (Charlottesville: University of Virginia Press, 1996), 115.

13. John Wilson, *Memories of a Labour Leader: The Autobiography of John Wilson* (London: T. F. Unwin, 1910), 172. Wilson also describes the joking celebration in Broad Top, Pennsylvania, at the news of Lincoln's assassination. He was later to become the founding president of the Durham Miners' Association and Liberal MP for Durham City.

14. *The Only Alternative: A Tract for the Times. By a Plain Man* (Philadelphia, 1864).

15. One historian has estimated that in Pennsylvania half of the state's Democrats supported an armistice and a peace convention in the spring of 1864. Arnold Shankman, *The Pennsylvania Antiwar Movement, 1861–1865* (Rutherford, N.J.: Fairleigh Dickinson University Press 1980), 217–19.

16. Sydney Stanley Diary, entry for October 2, 1863, Stanley Papers, Watkinson Library, Trinity College, Hartford, Connecticut.

17. "Memorial of James Lindsay, contesting the right of John G. Scott to represent the 3rd Congressional District of Missouri. December 16, 1863," *Congressional Serial Set* 1200, 38th Cong., 1st sess., House of Representatives Misc. Doc. 43, 120–21. James Moore, another Missouri election official classified rebel and Unionist voters confidently, with one confusing exception who was noted down as "Union when sober, rebel when drunk." Ibid., 52.

18. Joan E. Cashin, "Deserters, Civilians and Draft Resistance in the North" in Cashin, ed., *The War Was You and Me: Civilians in the American Civil War* (Princeton, N.J: Princeton University Press, 2002), 274.

19. T. W. Bergley to Elihu B. Washburne, October 3, 1864, Washburne Papers.

20. On draft resistance in the Pennsylvania coal fields see Grace Palladino, *Another Civil War: Labor, Capital and the State in the Anthracite Regions of Pennsylvania, 1840–1868* (Urbana: Illinois University Press, 1990), 98. For descriptions of violent opposition to the war in the West, often focused on opposition to the draft see, for example: *Chicago Tribune,* June 12, 1863, September 12, 15, 19, 1862; *Daily Illinois State Register,* September 12, 1862; Citizens of Randolph County to Richard Yates, August 23, 1864; James Montgomery to Richard Yates, August 27, 1864, Richard Yates Papers, Illinois State Historical Library. A. E. McNall to O. M. Hatch, October 17, 1864, O. M. Hatch Papers, Illinois State Historical Library. On draft riots in the eastern cities see William Hanna, "The Boston Draft Riot," *Civil War History,* 36 (1990): 260–75; *New York Times,* July 20, 1863; *Independent,* July 28, 1863.

21. Bernstein, *The New York City Draft Riots.*

22. *Address of the Workingmen's United Political Association of the City and County of New York* (New York, n.d.), 4.

23. Annotated book of clippings from the *Brooklyn Daily Eagle,* Thomas Kinsella Papers, New York Public Library.

24. *New York Times,* July 21, 1863.

25. *Boston Daily Advertiser,* April 17, 1862.

26. Providence (Rhode Island) *Post,* February 12, 18, 28, 1863. About four thousand fewer votes were cast in 1863 than in 1861. Smith received 10,828 compared to 7,537 for his Democratic opponent, William C. Cozzens. John L. Moore, Jon P. Preimesberger, and David R. Tarr, eds, *Congressional Quarterly Guide to US Elections* (Washington D.C.: CQ Press, 2001), 524.

27. Samuel Cony replaced Abner Coburn as Governor. Dell, *Lincoln and the War Democrats,* 240–41; *US Elections,* 504.

28. Concord (NH) *Monitor,* January 12, 29, February 19, 1863; Manchester (NH), *Democrat and Republican,* February 19, 1863; Boston *Daily Advertiser,* February 26, 1862.

29. George Woodward to Jeremiah Black, September 10, 1863, Jeremiah S. Black Papers, Library of Congress.

30. Arnold Shankman, "Soldier votes and Clement L. Vallandigham in the 1863 Ohio Gubernatorial Election," *Ohio History* 82 (1973): 88–104.

31. The Washington correspondent of the leading Democratic paper in Indianapolis complained, "the National Republican Committee have taken full possession of all the Capitol buildings, and the committee rooms of the Senate and House of Representatives are filled with clerks, busy in mailing Lincoln documents all over the loyal States." These federal employees, he noted, "continue to

draw their salaries while engaged in re–electing Abraham Lincoln. They neglect the business of the country for which only they ought to be paid." Indianapolis *Daily State Sentinel*, October 12, 1864, quoted in Harry J. Carman and Reinhard Luthin, *Lincoln and the Patronage* (New York: Columbia University Press, 1943), 287; *Chicago Tribune*, September 30, 1864.

32. Edwin B. Stanton to Lincoln, September 29, 1863, Lincoln Papers.

33. Francis P. Blair to Abraham Lincoln, December 18, 1862, Lincoln Papers

34. A. H. Markland to Montgomery Blair, September 14, 1864, Lincoln Papers

35. Loyal Publication Society of New York, *Proceedings at the Second Anniversary Meeting*, 19; William Swinton, *A few plain words with the rank and file of the Union armies* (Washington, 1864). On the role of the Union League Club in New York see Circular to the State Council and the subordinate Councils of the Loyal Union League in the State of New York, October 24, 1864, in the Lincoln Papers. On the financing of this effort see Albert G. Richardson to Abraham Lincoln, October 24, 1864, Lincoln Papers. In just one week, in the run up to the 1864 presidential election, one agent of the Union party national committee estimated that "nearly a million" documents had been sent to troops. George T. Brown to Lyman Trumbull, November 5, 1864, Trumbull Papers.

36. Davis, *Lincoln's Men*, 130.

37. Carwardine, *Lincoln*, 275.

38. John W. Northrop, *Diary of Prison Life* (transcript), [November] 16, 1864, Western Reserve Historical Society, quoted in Joseph Allen Frank, *With Ballot and Bayonet: The Political Socialization of Civil War Soldiers* (Athens: University of Georgia Press, 1998), 93.

39. On the political role of Civil War soldiers see Frank, *Political Socialization of Civil War Soldiers*; James M. McPherson, *For Cause and Comrades: Why Men Fought in the Civil War* (New York: Oxford University Press, 1997).

40. J. M. Palmer to D. Davis, November 26, 1862, Lincoln Papers, cited in Carwardine, *Lincoln*, 277.

41. Charles Pearce to Father, March 15, 1863 (GLC 0066.115), Pearce Papers, Gilder Lehrman Collection.

42. Frey to [illegible], [1864], Augustus Beardsley Frey Letters, Illinois State Historical Society, Springfield.

43. Fragment of a handwritten speech by an unknown Union Officer, Gilder Lehrman Collection (GLC 03738).

44. George F. Root, "Just Before the Battle Mother" (Chicago: Root and Cady, 1864).

45. F. M. Sparks to Richard Yates, April 21, 1863, Yates Family Papers, Illinois State historical Library, Springfield.

46. *New York Times*, April 23, 1864.

47. Charles Pearce to Father March 15, 1863 (GLC 00066.115), Gilder Lehrman Collection.

48. Carwardine, *Lincoln*, 274.

49. For a discussion of the advantages and propriety of publishing private letters in newspapers "if they [will] do some good" see John P. Jones to wife, February 8, 1863, John Jones Collection (GLC 5981), Gilder Lehrman Collection. On the political significance of soldiers see William C. Davis, *Lincoln's Men: How President Lincoln became a father to an army and a nation* (New York: Free Press, 1999), 192–227.

50. Mark Neely, *The Union Divided: The Civil War and the Two-Party System* (Cambridge, Mass.: Harvard University Press, 2002)

51. Charles Pearce to Father March 15, 1863, Pierce Papers, Gilder Lehrman Collection (GLC 00066.115).

52. Quoted in Frank, *With Ballot and Bayonet*, 91.

53. "Letter from a soldier," printed in the *Daily Illinois State Register*, September 30, 1864.

54. On Soldier voting see Josiah Henry Benton, *Voting in the field* (Boston: Plimpton Press, 1915); T. Harry Williams, "Voters in Blue," *Mississippi Valley Historical Review* 31 (1944): 187–204; Oscar O. Winther, "Soldier Voting in the Election of 1864," *New York History* 25 (1944); Jonathan W. White, "Citizens and Soldiers: Party Competition and the Debate in Pennsylvania over Permitting Soldiers to Vote, 1861–1864," *American Nineteenth Century History* 5.2 (Summer 2004), 47–70. For the texts of election laws regulating the voting of soldiers in the field see "Contested Congressional Election in the Thirteenth District of Ohio. Charles Follett vs. Columbus Delano, election held on October 11, 1864," *Congressional Serial Set* 1270, House of Representatives Misc. Doc. 8, 41–44; "Contested Congressional Election in the Fifth District of Michigan. August C. Baldwin vs., Rowland E. Trowbridge, election held on November 8, 1864," *Congressional Serial Set* 1270: House of Representatives Misc. Doc. 10. 30–36.

55. Quoted in White, "Citizens and Soldiers," 57.

56. *How Shall Soldiers Vote?* (The New York State Central Committee of "The Boys in Blue," Rooms 16 and 17, Astor House, New York, 1864).

57. *Political Dialogues: Soldiers on their right to vote and the men they should support* (Washington, 1864).

58. *How Shall Soldiers Vote?*

59. *Daily Illinois State Register*, July 29, October 27, 1864.

60. See for example, Petition of May 7, 1864, by Drury Township Voters, Yates Family Papers, Illinois State Historical Library, Springfield.

61. See for instance *Connecticut Courant*, October 13, November 7, 1864.

62. Benton, *Voting in the Field*, 221. Even in states where voting was permitted in the field there was pressure for furloughs to be made in order for those who had come of age since enlisting to go home and register. In Connecticut, for example, it was constitutionally necessary for soldiers to register in person if their family had moved from the town in which the serviceman had resided at the time of his enlistment. See James Dixon to Edwin M. Stanton, August 11, 1864, Stanton Papers; Amos J. Trent to James G. Batterson, October 3, 1864; N. N. Haley to Batterson, October 6, 1864; George Leavens to Batterson, October 24, 26, 1864, Batterson Papers; Erastus Cotton to William A. Buckingham, Buckingham Papers, Manuscripts Collection, Connecticut Historical Society Library. The most revealing indication of Lincoln's approach to furloughs is his letter to Sherman in which he explained "the loss of Indiana to the friends of the government would go far towards losing the *whole Union cause*." Roy P. Basler, *The Collected Works of Abraham Lincoln* (8 vols.: New Brunswick, 1953), 8: 11; see also Lincoln to Oliver P. Morton, ibid, 46.

63. In September, 1864, for example, Congressman Washburne became extremely anxious about the vote in his home district of Galena, Illinois. As well as adding his voice to that of Governor Yates and *Chicago Times* editor Joseph Medill,

who were vigorously urging the President to furlough Illinois troops home for the election, Washburne also requested that his friend Brigadier General Augustus L. Chetalian receive a leave of absence to help him campaign. The leave was granted. Elihu B. Washburne, MSS diary, October 22, 1864, Elihu B. Washburne Papers, Washburn Collection, Washburn Norlands Library, quoted in Nelson, "The early life and congressional career of Elihu B. Washburne," 362; Joseph Medill to Elihu B. Washburne, October 4, 1864, Washburne Papers, Library of Congress; F.W. Hutchinson to Richard Yates, September 29, 1864; M. Schaeffer to Richard Yates, September 30, 1864; J. Richards to Richard Yates, August 21, 1864, Richard Yates Papers, Illinois State Historical Society.

64. " Memorial of Charles Carrigan, contesting the right of M. Russell Thayer to a seat as a representative from the Fifth Congressional District of the State of Pennsylvania in the Thirty-eighth congress. December 8, 1863," *Congressional Serial Set* 1199 (38th Cong., 1st sess.), House of Representatives Misc. Doc. 17, 41.

65. Basler, ed., *Collected works of Abraham Lincoln*, 8: 43.

66. Rufus Griswold to James G. Batterson, October 27, 1864, James G. Batterson Papers, Manuscripts Collection, Connecticut Historical Society Library. For a thorough discussion of the problem of soldier voting, pressure for furloughs, and the implications of the state's field voting law see Samuel T. McSeveney, "Re-electing Lincoln: The Union Party Campaign and the Military Vote in Connecticut," *Civil War History* 32 (1986): 139–58.

67. Stewart Mitchell, *Horatio Seymour of New York* (Cambridge, Mass.: Harvard University Press, 1938), 376–381; Zornow, *Lincoln and the Party Divided*, 183, 203–4.

68. H. T. Blake to William A. Buckingham, October 23, 1864, Buckingham Papers.

69. Elihu B. Washburne to Lincoln, October 17, 1864, Lincoln Papers.

70. Elihu B. Washburne to Lincoln, October 27, 1864, Lincoln Papers.

71. Washburne to Lincoln, November 3, 1864, Lincoln Papers.

72. On the intimidation of voters in the Border States by soldiers and Provost Marshalls see Richard Franklin Bensel, *The American Ballot Box in the Mid-Nineteenth Century* (New York: Cambridge University Press, 2004), 217–85; Altschuler and Blumin, *Rude Republic*, 174–75; Phillip J. Avillo, Jr., "Ballots for the Faithful: The Oath and the Emergence of Slave State Republican Congressmen, 1861–1867," *Civil War History* 22 (June 1976): 164–74.

73. Eugene C. Murdock, *One Million Men: The Civil War Draft in the North* (Madison: State Historical Society of Wisconsin, 1971), 6, 308; *Official Records of the Union and Confederate Armies*, series III, vol. II (Washington: Government Printing Office, 1899), 369.

74. "John Kline vs. Leonard Myers, 3rd Congressional District of Pennsylvania, referred to the Committee of Elections, February 4, 1864," *Congressional Serial Set* 1199 (38th Cong., 1st sess.), House Misc. Doc. 26, 21.

75. For similar allegations in the fifth congressional district in Pennsylvania in the fall 1863 elections see "Carrigan vs. Thayer," *Congressional Serial Set* 1199 (38th Cong., 1st sess.), Misc. Doc. 17, 40.

76. William H. Koontz vs. Alexander H. Coffroth, 16th Congressional District of Pennsylvania, Serial Set vol. no. 1271: 39th Cong., 1st sess. (1865–1866), vol. 3, House of Representatives Misc. Doc. 117, 84.

77. Ibid., 188.

78. Ibid., 190.

79. John H. McHenry Jr., vs. George H. Yeaman. Memorial of John H. McHenry, Jr., contesting the seat of the Hon. George H. Yeaman, representative from the Second Congressional District of Kentucky, December 14, 1863. *Congressional Serial Set* 1200 (38th Cong., 1st sess.) House of Representatives Misc. Doc. 36, 48. For supporting testimony see ibid., 12–13, 16–17, 22, 42–48, 50–51, 53, 64, 68, 73–74.

80. *Congressional Globe* 38th Cong., 1st sess., January 19, 1864, p. 245. For a discussion of the test oath issue in the senate see Harold M. Hyman, *Era of the Oath: Northern Loyalty during the Civil War and Reconstruction* (Philadelphia: University of Pennsylvania Press, 1954), 25–32.

81. "Yeaman vs McHenry," *Congressional Serial Set* 1200: 28th Cong., 1st sess. (1863): House of Representatives Misc. Doc. 36, 15.

82. On the lack of discipline among Union troops in Missouri throughout the war see Michael Fellman, *Inside War: The Guerrilla Conflict in Missouri during the American Civil War* (New York: Oxford University Press, 1989), 81–82.

83. Thomas E. Bramlette to Abraham Lincoln, September 3, 1864 in *The War of the Rebellion: A Compilation of the Official Records of the Union and Confederate Armies* (128 vols.: Washington, D.C., 1880–1901), Ser. III, vol. 4. *Union Correspondence Etc.* Serial no. 125, 689.

84. *Official Records*, Ser I, vol. 39, pt. III, *Correspondence,* Serial No. 79, 393.

85. Brig.–Gen. S. Meredith to Bvt. Maj. Gen. S. G. Burbridge, October 25, 1864 in *Official Records*, Ser. I, vol. 39, pt. III, *Correspondence.* Serial No. 79, 437.

86. *St. Louis Democrat*, September 16, 1864; *Chicago Tribune*, September 17, 1864.

87. *New York Times*, March 13, 1864; *Chicago Tribune*, December 12, 1863; *Cincinnati Daily Commercial*, October 8, 1863; *Cleveland Plain Dealer*, October 8, 1863. Allan Nevins has estimated that approximately three hundred newspapers were closed at any one time during the last year and a half of the war. Allan Nevins, *The War for the Union,* 4 vols. (New York: Scribner, 1959–1971), IV: 128.

88. "Yeaman vs McHenry," *Congressional Serial Set* 1200: 28th Cong., 1st sess. (1863): House of Representatives Misc. Doc. 36, 33.

89. Lincoln dryly responded, "if that had been deemed sufficient cause of arrest, I should have heard of more than one arrest in Kentucky on election day." Lincoln to Thomas E. Bramlette and Lincoln to Stephen G. Burbridge, both November 10, 1864 in Basler, ed., *Collected Works of Abraham Lincoln*, 8: 98–99; *Official Records*, ser. I, vol. 39, pt. 3, *Correspondence*, serial no. 79, 739–40; Burbridge to Lincoln, November 11, 1864, Lincoln Papers; Bramlette to U. S. Grant, November 9, 1864, *Official Records*, ser. I, vol. 39, pt. 3; *Correspondence*, serial no. 79, 725.

90. Lincoln went out of his way to emphasize that none of his military orders was designed to influence the electoral process, and Mark E. Neely has rightly emphasized the electoral liability to the administration of being perceived as high–handed with civil liberties. Mark E. Neely Jr., *The Fate of Liberty: Abraham Lincoln and Civil Liberties* (New York: Oxford University Press, 1991), 92. Frank L. Klement is the historian who has been most critical of the administration. See Klement, *The Copperheads in the Middle West* (University of Chicago Press, 1960), 18–23; and *Dark Lanterns: Secret Political Societies, Conspiracies and Treason Trials in the Civil War* (Baton Rouge: Louisiana State University Press, 1984).

91. James Edmunds to Abraham Lincoln, 1 November 2, 1864, Lincoln Papers.

92. Phillips Avillo, Jr., "Ballots for the Faithful: The Oath and the Emergence of Slave State Republican Congressmen, 1861–1867," *Civil War History* (1976): 164–74.

93. Benjamin F. Butler, *The Character and Results of the War: How to Prosecute It and How to End It, A Thrilling and Eloquent Speech* (Philadelphia, 1863); *Harper's Weekly*, July 25, 1863.

CHAPTER 6

1. John P. Jones to wife February 8, 1863, John Jones Collection (GLC 5981), Gilder Lehrman Collection.

2. Other candidates, notably Salmon P. Chase, had been in the frame earlier in the year. At the convention itself, General Grant received the votes of the radical Missouri delegation, but they changed their votes under pressure to ensure that the nomination was unanimous.

3. Noah Brooks, "Two War-Time Conventions," *The Century Magazine* XLIX (March, 1895), 723–24. Another observer later recalled that the "deep feeling of the American people . . . felt that not to renominate Mr. Lincoln would be a sort of concession to the enemy." The scenes of jubilation at Baltimore were inspired by the feeling that in renominating the President a blow had been struck at the rebellion. Andrew D. White, *Autobiography*, 2 vols (New York: Century, 1905), 1:120.

4. *Proceedings of the first three Republican national conventions of 1856, 1860 and 1864: including proceedings of the antecedent national convention held at Pittsburg, in February, 1856, as reported by Horace Greeley* (Minneapolis: C.W. Johnson, 1893), 180; Brooks, "Two War–Time Conventions," 723.

5. *Proceedings of the First Three Republican Conventions*, 196.

6. "Proclamation of Amnesty and Reconstruction," December 8, 1863 in Basler, ed., *Collected Works of Abraham Lincoln*, 7:51. On Lincoln's proclamation see William C. Harris, *With Charity for All: Lincoln and the Restoration of the Union* (Lexington: University of Kentucky Press, 1997), 129–42.

7. Quoted in Harris, *With Charity For All*, 130.

8. Quoted in Harris, *With Charity For All*, 137.

9. *New York News*, quoted in Harris, *With Charity For All*, 137.

10. Bland W. Ballard to Abraham Lincoln, June 11, 1864, Lincoln Papers.

11. Whitelaw Reid to Anna E. Dickinson, April 3, 1864, Anna E. Dickinson Papers, Manuscripts Division, Library of Congress. See also Simon Nash to John Sherman, February 4, 1864, John Sherman Papers, Manuscripts Division, Library of Congress; *Independent*, December 10, 1863.

12. Lydia Maria Child to Gerrit Smith, April 22, 1864, Gerrit Smith Papers, quoted in Victor B. Howard, *Religion and the Radical Republican Movement, 1860–1870* (Lexington: University of Kentucky Press, 1990), 73.

13. *Proceedings of the First Three Republican Conventions*, 187–88.

14. Ibid., 178.

15. Ibid., 188–89.

16. Ibid., 198–89.

17. Ibid., 190.

18. Ibid., 222.

19. James G. Blaine to Hannibal Hamlin, June 4, 1864; R. Beale to Hamlin, June 5, 1864, Hannibal Hamlin Papers, Library of Congress. On Johnson's nomi-

nation see Don E. Fehrenbacher, "The Making of a Myth: Lincoln and the Vice-Presidential Nomination in 1864." *Civil War History* 41 (December 1995): 273–90.

20. H. Draper Hunt, *Hannibal Hamlin of Maine: Lincoln's First Vice-President* (Syracuse: Syracuse University Press, 1969).

21. Simon Cameron to William Pitt Fessenden, June 15, 1864, Hannibal Hamlin Papers, Butler Library, Columbia University, New York.

22. John Reeves to William Henry Seward, June 2, 1864, Seward Papers.

23. *New York Times,* June 9, 1864.

24. John A. Hiestand to Thaddeus Stevens, June 15, 1864, Thaddeus Stevens Papers, Manuscript Division, Library of Congress.

25. Harris, *With Charity For All*, 186–87.

26. Proclamation Concerning Reconstruction, July 8, 1864, in Basler, ed., *Collected Works of Abraham Lincoln*, 7: 433–34.

27. Thaddeus Stevens to Edward McPherson, July 10, 1864, Thaddeus Stevens Papers, cited in Harris, *With Charity For All*, 189.

28. "Wade-Davis Manifesto," in Harold Hyman, ed., *Radical Republicans and Reconstruction* (Indianapolis: Bobbs-Merrill, 1967), 137–47.

29. Lincoln cited in Harris, *With Charity For All*, 189.

30. Cited in Harris, *With Charity For All*, 190.

31. Noah Brooks to John G. Nicolay, August 29, 1864, Lincoln Papers.

32. Union League of Philadelphia, *Abraham Lincoln* (Philadelphia: Union League, 1864).

33. P. H. Agan to Montgomery Blair, August 8, 1864, Lincoln Papers.

34. Chase to Lincoln, November 23, 1863, Lincoln Papers.

35. Lincoln to Nathaniel P. Banks, November 5, 1863 in Basler, ed., *Collected Works of Abraham Lincoln*, 7:1–2; Salmon P. Chase to Lincoln, 25 November 1863, Lincoln Papers, cited in Harris, *With Charity for All*, 130.

36. This is a point made by Michael Vorenberg, *Final Freedom*, 91.

37. Isaac N. Arnold, *Reconstruction: Liberty the Corner-stone, and Lincoln the Architect. Speech of Hon. Isaac N. Arnold, of Illinois. Delivered in the House of Representatives, March 19, 1864* (Washington, 1864).

38. John D. Hopkins, *Bible View of Slavery* (New York: Papers of the Society for the Diffusion of Political Knowledge, 1864); Samuel F. B. Morse, *An argument on the ethical position of slavery in the social system and its relation to the politics of the day* (New York: Papers of the Society for the Diffusion of Political Knowledge, 1863). The SPDK had been formed *before* the Loyal Publication Society, at the very start of 1863.

39. Samuel S. Cox, *Miscegenation or Amalgamation. Fate of the Freeman. Speech of Samuel S. Cox of Ohio Delivered in the House of Representatives, February 17, 1864* (Washington, 1864).

40. *The Lincoln Catechism, wherein the Eccentricities and Beauties of Despotism are fully set forth* (n.p., n.d.).

41. Henry Bellows, *Historical Sketch of the Union League Club of New York: Its Origin, Organization, and Work, 1863–1879* (New York; G. P. Putnam's sons, 1879), 56.

42. Bellows, *Historical Sketch*; Beckert, *Monied Metroplis*, 135.

43. *New York Herald,* March 6, 1864.

44. This is a point made by Michael Vorenberg, *Final Freedom*, 127–36.

45. Sidney Kaplan, "The Miscegenation Issue in the Election of 1864," *Journal of Negro History* 34 (1949): 274–343.

46. This and the following two paragraphs draw heavily on Michael Vorenberg, *Final Freedom*, 90–114.

47. Kirk H. Porter and Donald B. Johnson, eds, *National Party Platforms, 1840–1956* (Urbana: University of Illinois Press, 1956).

48. Whitelaw Reid, "Agate" letter in the *Cincinnati Gazette*, June 8, 1864, Reid Family Papers, Library of Congress.

49. *Proceedings of the First Three Republican Conventions*, 182.

50. John G. Nicolay to Therena Bates, August 14, 1864, John G. Nicolay Papers, Library of Congress.

51. Basler, ed., *Collected Works of Abraham Lincoln*, 8: 451.

52. Nelson, *Bullets, Ballots and Rhetoric*, 67; McPherson, *Battle Cry of Freedom*, 764.

53. [Washington, DC], *Daily National Intelligencer* Nov. 5, 1864; Robert Charles Winthrop, *Speech at the Great Ratification Meeting in Union Square, New York, September 17, 1864* (Democratic Campaign Document No. 9: New York, 1864); Winthrop, *Great Speech of Hon. Robert Charles Winthrop, at New London, Connecticut, October 18, 1864. The Principles and Interests of the Republican party against the Union. The Election of McClellan the Only Hope of Union and Peace* (Democratic Campaign Document No. 23: New York, 1864).

54. *Only Authentic Life of Abraham Lincoln, alias 'Old Abe'. A Son of the West. With an account of his birth and education, his railsplitting and flat–boating, his joke–cutting and soldiering, with some allusions to his journeys from Springfield to Washington and BACK again* (n.p., n.d.), Illinois State Historical Library.

55. *Christian Advocate and Journal*, August 4, 1864.

56. *Boston Daily Journal*, August 5, 1864, quoted in Howard, *Religion and the Radical Republican Movement*, 81. See also George May Powell to Emma C. Small, August 9, 1864, George May Powell Papers (GLC 687), Gilder Lehrman Collection.

57. Harriet Beecher Stowe, *Abraham Lincoln* (n.p., n.d.).

58. Weed to Frederick Seward, August 26, 1864 and G. W. Holley to William H. Seward, August 27, 1864, Seward Papers; Weed to David Davis, February 9, 1864, Davis Family Papers.

59. T. S. Faxton to Weed, August 10, 1864, Weed Papers; G. W. Holley to Seward, June 2, 1864 and Thurlow Weed to Frederick W. Seward, August 26, 1864, Seward Papers; David Davis to Thurlow Weed, August 19, 1864, Davis Papers; Glyndon G. Van Deusen, *Thurlow Weed: Wizard of the Lobby* (Boston, 1947), 310; John H. and Lawanda Cox, *Politics, Principle and Prejudice*, 3–4.

60. Leonard Swett to David Davis, August 23, 1864, Leonard Swett Collection, David Davis Family Papers, Illinois State Historical Library; David Davis to Joseph H. Scranton, August 1, 1864, David Davis Family Papers; Elihu B. Washburne to Adele Washburne, September 11, 1864, Elihu B. Washburne Papers, Washburn Collection, Washburn Norlands Library.

61. *Washington Chronicle*, August 17, 1864.

62. Greeley to Lincoln, August 9, 1864, Lincoln Papers.

63. Henry J. Raymond to Lincoln, August 22, 1864, Lincoln Papers.

64. Henry J. Raymond to Simon Cameron, August 19, and August 21, 1864, Cameron Papers.

65. The extent of public interest in the "To whom it may concern" letter may be judged by the publication of a broadside in San Francisco in September 1864 that reprinted editorials from a selection of eastern newspapers so that "the true

significance of the 'to whom it may concern' document may be understood." "To Unconditional Union Voters," San Francisco, September, 1864. Collection of Broadsides, Houghton Library, Harvard University.

66. Raymond to Lincoln, August 8, 1864, Lincoln Papers. On August 17 Lincoln appeared to shift his ground slightly in a draft of a long letter to a Democratic newspaper editor, Charles D. Robinson. "To me it seems plain," wrote the president, "that saying reunion and abandonment of slavery would be considered, if offered, is not saying that nothing else or less would be considered, if offered." But the letter was never sent. Lincoln held to his public position that slavery should not exist in a reunified nation. And even in this letter Lincoln still argued that abandoning emancipation was not only wrong but also impossible. Giving up emancipation as a war aim, involving as it would the forsaking of black support for the Union, would simply be "giving a large force to the enemy, for nothing in return." Basler, ed., *Collected Works of Abraham Lincoln* 7: 499. James A. Rawley, *Turning Points*, 185–188, Richard N. Current in *The Lincoln Nobody Knows* (ch. 10) argues that Lincoln was ultimately prepared to abandon (or at least compromise) emancipation in order to secure Union victory.

67. *New York Times*, August 21, 1864.

68. *Springfield Republican*, August 25, 1864; *Chicago Tribune*, August 23, 1864.

69. Allan Nevins, *Frémont: Pathmarker of the West* (New York: Longmans, 1955)

70. Robert S. Harper, *Lincoln and the Press* (New York: McGraw-Hill, 1951), 304; On the German support for Fremont in Missouri and the Midwest in general, see Montgomery Blair to Abraham Lincoln, July 18, 1863, Montgomery Blair Papers, Blair Family Collection.

71. George Lincoln to Andrew Johnson, June 11, 1864, Andrew Johnson Papers, Library of Congress.

72. *Frank Leslie's Illustrated Newspaper*, October 26, 1861.

73. Benjamin F. Prescott to Anna Dickinson, June 10, 1864, Anna Dickinson Papers.

74. Lydia Maria Child to Eliza Scudder, n.d., 1864, in Lydia Maria Child, *Letters of Lydia Maria Child*, John G. Whittier, ed. (Boston: Houghton, Mifflin, 1882), 183–84.

75. Tyler Dennett, ed., *Lincoln and the Civil War in the Diaries and Letters of John Hay* (New York: Dodd, Mead, 1939), 183.

76. Montgomery Blair to Abram Wakeman, March 19, 1864, Blair Papers.

77. For pessimistic assessments of the chances of Lincoln's re-election, both of which feature the Wade-Davis bill as one of the key indicators of the divisions that were undermining his strength see Mark W. Delahay to Abraham Lincoln, August 24, 1864; George B. Senter to John G. Nicolay, August 10, 1864, Lincoln Papers.

78. John G. Nicolay to Therena Bates, August 21, 1864, Nicolay Papers.

79. Basler, ed., *Collected Works of Abraham Lincoln* 7: 514.

80. Edgar Conkling to Benjamin F. Butler, July 18, 1864 in *Private and Official Correspondence of General Benjamin F. Butler, During the Period of the Civil War* (4 vols. Norwood, Mass.: Plimpton Press, 1917), 4: 510; Russell Everett to Simon Cameron, August 23, 1864, Cameron Papers; Zornow, *Lincoln and the Party Divided*, 110; Long, *Jewel of Liberty*, 192–94.

81. Edwin D. Morgan to Thurlow Weed, March 6, 1864, Edwin D. Morgan Papers, New York State Library.

82. George Wilkes to Elihu B. Washburne, August 31, 1864, Washburne Papers.

83. Harper, *Lincoln and the Press*, 309.

84. A copy of the letter, which was signed by Horace Greeley, Parke Godwin, and Theodore Tilton together with a dozen replies from Governors are in the John A. Stevens Papers in the New-York Historical Society. James C. Conkling forwarded a copy to Abraham Lincoln, September 5, 1864, Lincoln Papers.

85. Zornow, *Lincoln and the Party Divided*, 114.

86. George Wilkes to Elihu Washburne, August 31, 1864, Washburne Papers.

87. Henry H. Elliot to Gideon Welles, August 31, 1864, Welles Papers.

88. This and the following paragraph draw heavily on William C. Harris, "Conservative Unionists and the Presidential Election of 1864," *Civil War History* 38: 298–318.

89. Harris, "Conservative Unionists," 301; *National Intelligencer*, November 1, 6, 1862; Robert C. Winthrop, Jr., *A Memoir of Robert C. Winthrop* (Boston: Little, Brown, 1897), 228–29, 252–53.

90. Harris, "Conservative Unionists," 305; James T. Noble to Millard Fillmore, November 25, 1863, Fillmore Papers, Buffalo and Erie County Historical Society.

91. Millard Fillmore to Ephraim Hutchens, February 9, 1863; R. F. Stevens to Millard Fillmore, August 5, 1863; Leslie Combs to Fillmore, August 7, 1863, Fillmore Papers.

92. Millard Fillmore to Mrs. Ellen McClellan, April 24, 1864; S. Ellsworth to Fillmore, April 4, 15, 29, 1864, Fillmore Papers; Stephen W. Sears, *George B. McClellan: The Young Napoleon* (New York: Ticknor & Fields, 1988), 345–47, 350, 354–55.

93. Cyrus Hall McCormick to Manton Marble, August 17, 1864, Manton Marble Papers, Library of Congress.

94. Allen Nevins and Milton H. Thomas, eds, *The Diary of George Templeton Strong: The Civil War* (New York: Macmillan, 1952), 478.

95. James M. Ashley to Salmon P. Chase, August 5, 1864, Chase Papers.

96. James T. Noble to Fillmore, June 9, 1864; John Bell Robinson to Fillmore, August 8, 1864; A. B. Norton to Fillmore, August 6, 1864; Benjamin Ogle Taylor to Fillmore, July 24, 1864; James B. Colegrove to Fillmore, July 21, 1864, Fillmore Papers.

97. S. Ellsworth to Millard Fillmore, April 29, 1864; John R. Johnston to Millard Fillmore, June 4; Millard Fillmore to J. R. Riddle, July 5, 1864; A. B. Norton to Millard Fillmore, August 6, 1864, Fillmore Papers.

98. *Constitutional Union*, October 20, 1864, quoted in Harris, "Conservative Unionists," 310; *Chicago Times* August 29, 1864; New York *Evening Post*, August 30, 1864.

99. *New York Herald,* August 30, 1864.

100. Noah Brooks to John G. Nicolay, August 29, 1864, Lincoln Papers.

101. Kirk H. Porter and Donald B. Johnson, eds., *National Party Platforms, 1840–1956* (Urbana: University of Illinois Press, 1956).

102. Albany (NY) *Atlas and Argus*, September 4, 1864.

103. Albany (NY), *Atlas and Argus*, September 9, 1864; *Boston Post*, September 3, 1864; *Detroit Free Press*, September 6, 1864.

104. Noah Brooks to John G. Nicolay, August 29, September 2, 1864, Lincoln Papers.

105. McClellan to S. L. M. Barlow, August 28, 1864; McClellan to William C. Prime, October 20, 1864, George B. McClellan Papers, Manuscripts Division, Library of Congress.

106. Belmont to McClellan, September 3, 1864, McClellan Papers.

107. George B. McClellan to Samuel S. Cox, September 24, 1864, Thomas F. Madigan Collection, Rare Books and Manuscripts Division, New York Public Library in Stephen W. Sears, ed., *The Civil War Papers of George B. McClellan: Selected Correspondence, 1860–1865* (New York: Ticknor & Fields, 1989), 603. See also, Stephen W. Sears, "McClellan and the Peace Plank of 1864: a reappraisal," *Civil War History*: 36 (1990), 57–64.

108. Elihu B. Washburne to Adele Washburne, September 11, 1864, Washburne Papers.

109. Jon G. Nicolay to Therena Bates, August 29, 1864, Nicolay Papers.

110. Henry Wilson to Abraham Lincoln, September 5, 1864, Lincoln Papers.

111. John P. Gulliver to Abraham Lincoln, September 12, 1864, Lincoln Papers.

112. George Templeton Strong diary entry for September 5, 1864. Nevins, ed, *Diary of George Templeton Strong*, 481.

113. Gideon Welles to "my dear wife," September 4, 1864, Welles Papers.

114. Samuel F. George to Abraham Lincoln, September 7, 1864, Lincoln Papers.

115. Britton A. Hill to Abraham Lincoln, Monday, October 3, 1864, Lincoln Papers. On Browning see David H. Donald, *"We Are Lincoln Men": Abraham Lincoln and His Friends* (New York: Simon & Schuster, 2003), 101–39.

116. Edward Everett, *Address Delivered in Faneuil Hall, October 19, 1864. "The duty of supporting the government in the present crisis of affairs."* New England Loyal Publication Society Pamphlet No. 237 (Boston, 1864); an annotated copy of the speech cut from the *Boston Daily Advertiser* October 22, 1864 is enclosed in the John A. Clifford Papers, Massachusetts Historical Society.

117. John H. Clifford to Robert C. Winthrop, September 13, 1864, Robert C. Winthrop Papers, Massachusetts Historical Society. For similar responses from disappointed conservatives see also [Pennsylvania Senator] Edgar Cowan to Jeremiah Black, September 12, 1864, Jeremiah Black Papers, Manuscript Division, Library of Congress.

118. Henry H. Elliot to Gideon Welles, September 3, 1864, Welles Papers.

119. Quoted in Long, *Jewel of Liberty*, 236.

120. J. M. Forbes to Gustavus V. Fox, September 6, 1864 in *Letters and Recollections of John Murray Forbes*, 1: 101.

121. The fall of Atlanta was recognized as a serious blow to their cause by Confederates in part at least because of the effect it would have on Lincoln's electoral chances in the North. See Larry E. Nelson, *Bullets, Ballots and Rhetoric*, 117–225.

122. Henry H. Elliot to Gideon Welles, September 3, 1864, Welles Papers.

123. Parke Goodwin and Theodore Tilton to John Andrew, September 2, 1864; John Murray Forbes to John Andrew, September 2, 1864; Theodore Tilton to John Andrew, September 5, 1864, John A, Andrew Papers, Massachusetts Historical Society; Richard Yates to Greeley, Goodwin and Tilton, September 6, 1864, Richard Yates Papers, Illinois State Historical Library; James C. Conkling to Abraham Lincoln, September 6, 1864, Lincoln Papers.

124. Henry G. Pearson, *The Life of John A. Andrew, Governor of Massachusetts, 1861–1865*, 2 vols. (Boston: Houghton, Mifflin, 1904) 2: 162–63.

125. Thurlow Weed to William H. Seward, September 10, 1864, Lincoln Papers.

126. Letters to Horace Greeley, Parke Godwin, and Theodore Tilton from John A. Andrew, September 3, 1864; from Joseph Gilmore, September 5, 1864; and from

William A. Buckingham (September 3, 1864) are all in the John A. Stevens Papers, New–York Historical Society.

127. Theodore Tilton to John G. Nicolay, September 6, 1864, Lincoln Papers.

128. L. E. Chittenden to Lincoln, October 6, 1864, Lincoln Papers.

129. Henry W. Davis to Zachariah Chandler, August 24, 1864; Zachariah Chandler to his wife, August 27, 28, September 2, 6, 8, 24, 1864; Benjamin F. Wade to Chandler, October 2, 1864, Zachariah Chandler Papers, Manuscripts Division, Library of Congress; Lincoln to Blair, September 23, 1864 in Basler, ed., *Collected Works of Abraham Lincoln*. For debate about Chandler's role see Winfred A. Harbison, "Zachariah Chandler's Part in the Reelection of Abraham Lincoln," *Mississippi Valley Historical Review* 22 (1935): 268–70; Hans L. Trefousse, "Zachariah Chandler and the Withdrawal of Fremont in 1864: New Answer to an Old Riddle." *Lincoln Herald*, 70 (1968), 181–88. For responses and analysis from Blair's friends on hearing of his resignation see E. Cowles to Blair, September 24, 1864; Francis G. Pratt to Blair, September 26, 1864; A. B. Swayne to Blair, September 24, 1864, Montgomery Blair Papers.

CHAPTER 7

1. *New York Times*, September 3, 1864.

2. For a firsthand account of the campaign see Abram Dittenhoeffer, *How We Elected Lincoln: personal recollections of Lincoln and men of his time, by Abram J. Dittenhoefer, a campaigner for Lincoln in 1860 and a Lincoln elector in 1864* (New York: Harper & Brothers, 1916)

3. Frank Leslie's Illustrated Newspaper, October 1, October 29, June 16, 1864.

4. Even in as apparently as crucial an election as that of 1864, some party activists privately worried that their efforts met with dispiriting indifference: "Our village badly needs stirring up by an eloquent convincing speaker," reported a Connecticut Unionist party organizer. Frank Blair to James G. Batterson, September 27, 1864, Batterson Papers, Connecticut Historical Society.

5. Thomas E. Smith to Elihu B. Washburne, September 19, 1864, Washburne Papers; M. A. Croft to Simon Cameron, September 27, 1864, Simon Cameron Papers, Manuscripts Division, Library of Congress. John G. Nicolay, Lincoln's private secretary conveyed the sense of uncertainty about the election in his regular letters to his fiancée, Therena Bates. See for instance Nicolay to Therena Bates, September 11 and October 2, 1864, John G. Nicolay Papers, Library of Congress.

6. *Chicago Tribune*, September 8, 1864.

7. McClellan suspected "a conspiracy by the administration going beyond interference with the soldier vote" according to Stephen W. Sears, *The Civil War Papers of George B. McClellan: Selected Correspondence, 1860–1865* (New York: Ticknor & Fields, 1989), 617. On the suspected plot to assassinate Lincoln see Allan Pinkerton to McClellan, October 26, 1864, McClellan Papers, in which the private detective stated that he had information of "the gravest consequence to the McClellan campaign." The grave information, passed on to Edward H. Wright, McClellan's "confidential friend" was the knowledge that senior figures in the administration believed there to be an assassination plot and were planning preemptive arrests. See also Wright to George Ticknor Curtis, December 28, 1864, McClellan Papers.

8. Kleppner, *Third Party System*, 86; Shade, *Banks or No Banks*, 172–73.

9. Time and again Democratic campaign documents quoted Lincoln's inaugural address and other speeches in 1861 in which he pledged not to violate the institutions of the South. See William David Clark Murdock, *An Address to the Democratic Party on the Present Crisis and the Next Presidential Election* (Washington, 1864), 22.

10. They claimed that the stalemate at Petersburg, for instance, disproved assertions that the war was nearly over: "We were told at the commencement of this war that 75,000 men would wipe the rebellion out in three months; afterwards we were told that 300,000 men would close the war in six months; this failing, 600,000 more with the other calls, were put into the field, and still the war is no nearer an end than two years ago. This rebellion has been on "its last legs," has had its "back bone" broken, ever since it commenced, according to the Republican creed, and yet it stands defiant as ever." Portsmouth (N.H.) *Journal*, October 8, 1864, quoted in Lex Renda, *Running on the Record: Civil War Politics in New Hampshire* (Charlottesville: University of Virginia Press, 1997), 129.

11. *Daily Illinois State Register*, October 27, 1864.

12. Columbus (Ohio) *Crisis*, July 22, 1863, quoted in Joel H. Silbey, *A Respectable Minority: The Democratic Party in the Civil War Era, 1860–1868* (New York: Norton, 1977), 73.

13. *Cleveland Plain Dealer*, October 13, 1864.

14. Whitelaw Reid, librarian of the House of Representatives and one of the first eastern correspondents for the newly founded Western Associated Press, provided a shrewd analysis of Democratic prospects in his "Agate" letter of November 3, 1864. Reid Family Papers, Library of Congress.

15. *Daily National Intelligencer*, November 5, 1864; *Brooklyn Daily Eagle*, October 18, 1864.

16. Kleppner, *Third Party System*, 87.

17. *Cleveland Plain Dealer*, November 7, 1864.

18. *Cleveland Plain Dealer*, November 5, 1864.

19. The remark about his conservatism is quoted in Robert C. Winthrop Jr., *A Memoir of Robert C. Winthrop* (Boston: Houghton, Mifflin, 1897), 205. John Greenleaf Whittier, an old Henry Clay Whig considered that Winthrop's prestige was sufficient to sway New England Whigs who were suspicious of the new Republican Party, so much so that "the destiny of the North" was in Winthrop's hands. Ibid. 171.

20. Thomas H. O'Connor, *Lords of the Loom: The Cotton Whigs and the Coming of the Civil War* (New York: Scribner, 1968); David H. Donald, *Charles Sumner and the Coming of the Civil War* (New York: Knopf, 1960), 143–50, 273–74.

21. McClellan to Robert C. Winthrop, 22 October 1864, Winthrop Family Papers, Massachusetts Historical Society.

22. Robert Charles Winthrop, *Great Speech of Robert C. Winthrop, at New London, Conn., October 18. The Principals and Interests of the Republican party against the Union. The Election of McClellan the Only Hope for Union and Peace.* (Democratic Campaign document, no. 23: New York, 1864). The pamphlet is reprinted in Frank Friedel, ed., *Union Pamphlets of the Civil War, 1861–1865*, 2 vols (Cambridge, Mass., 1967), 2: 1076–1117. Quotations from 1081, 1082. See also Robert C. Winthrop, *Speech at the Great Ratification Meeting in Union Square, New York, September 17, 1864* (Democratic Campaign Document no. 9: New York, 1864).

23. There were other conservative Whig voices in support of McClellan but none as prominent as Winthrop. See, Anon., *A Political Conservative Circular, from an "Old Line Webster Whig" of Forty Years VOTING experience, in support of constitutional freedom and sound CONSERVATIVE principles; with reasons for opposing the RE–ELECTION of Abraham Lincoln, for his gross violation of both spirit and provisions of the same* (n.p., n.d.)

24. *New York Times,* November 5, 1864.

25. Winthrop quoted in Winthrop, *Memoir,* 238

26. Henry McCloskey, speech to a "Mass Meeting of the Democracy," reported in the *Brooklyn Daily Eagle,* October 25, 1864.

27. *New York World,* February 25, 1864.

28. *Brooklyn Daily Eagle,* October 29, 1864.

29. Baker, *Affairs of Party,* 318.

30. *Cincinnati Daily Enquirer,* October 7, 1864.

31. Quoted in Silbey, *A Respectable Minority,* 79. See also Manton M. Marble's pamphlet attacking the Lincoln administration for the suppression of the *New York World:* Marble, *Freedom of the Press Wantonly Violated* (New York, n.p.: 1864).

32. Albany (N.Y.) *Atlas and Argus,* July 28, 1864.

33. William David Clark Murdock, *An Address to the Democratic Party on the Present Crisis and the Next Presidential Election* (Washington, 1864), 22; *New York World,* September 13, 1864.

34. *Mr. Lincoln's Arbitrary Arrests: The Acts which the Baltimore Platform Approves* (Democratic Campaign Document no. 13: New York, 1864), 5. The *New York World* illustrated this argument by comparing President Lincoln to the man who not only tells another that smoking a pipe or cigar is a "nasty pernicious practice, but [who] knocks it out of his mouth." *New York World,* June 30, 1864.

35. *Chicago Times,* November 11, 1863, quoted in Silbey, *A Respectable Minority,* 75. See also *Cincinnati Daily Enquirer,* January 1, 1864; *New York World,* April 14, 1864.

36. James Brooks, *Speech of the Hon. James Brooks of New York on the President's Message, in the House of Representatives, December 1864* (n.p., n.d.).

37. For an especially excoriating attack on the alleged corruption of the administration, see *Corruptions and frauds of Lincoln's administration.* [Democratic] Campaign document no. 14. New York, 1864. The New York banker James Gallatin repeatedly attacked Lincoln for financial corruption and waste as well as other matters. See, for example, James Gallatin, *Address by Hon. James Gallatin, before the Democratic Union Association, October 18, 1864: 'George McClellan as a Patriot, a Warrior, and a Statesman.'* New York, 1864.

38. A little booklet called *Campaign Songs for Christian Patriots and True Democrats* written by the Reverend William Potts, and published in New York in October 1864, contained a number of songs that lamented the sacrifice of white Northerners on the false altar of black freedom. The refrain of one song summed up the party's message very well:

> Would twelve million white men slay
> To make four million Negroes free?
> The human slaughter stop, I pray
> Work for true Democracy!

Rev William Potts, *Campaign Songs for Christian Patriots and True Democrats* (New York, 1864). On Democratic ideology in the Civil War see Baker, *Affairs of Party*; Vorenberg, *Final Freedom* and Silbey, *Respectable Minority*.

39. Samuel S. Cox, *Puritanism in Politics: A Speech before the Democratic Union Association in January 1863 in New York City* (New York, 1863), reprinted in *Eight Years in Congress*, 286; *Daily Illinois State Register*, September 30, 1864.

40. See for instance: *The President's usurpations. The president's ultimatum to the propositions of the Confederate commissioners asking for peace* (n.p., n.d.), Illinois State Historical Library; George F. Comstock, *Speech of Judge George F. Comstock delivered at the Brooklyn Academy of Music* (McClellan Campaign Document No. 2: New York, 1864); Comstock, '*Let us reason together' by George F. Comstock of Syracuse, late justice of the Court of Appeals* (Papers from the Society for the Diffusion of Political Knowledge No. 18: New York, 1864).

41. *Cleveland Plain Dealer*, September 10, 1864.

42. Henry J. Raymond to Simon Cameron, August 21, 1864, Cameron Papers.

43. Kleppner, *Third Party System*, 79. For comments on the value of antipartisanship to expand the voter base of the Republican party see Alexander K. McClure, *Old time notes of Pennsylvania: a connected and chronological record of the commercial, industrial and educational advancement of Pennsylvania, and the inner history of all political movements since the adoption of the constitution of 1838* 2 vols. Library ed. (Philadelphia: John C. Winston, 1905), 2: 60.

44. *Worcester Palladium*, [date unknown], quoted in *The Campaign for the Union*, November 3, 1864.

45. *New York Times*, September 3, 1864, quoted in John C. Waugh, *Reelecting Lincoln: The Battle for the 1864 Presidency* (New York, 1998), 310.

46. Charles Drake, *Speech of Hon. Charles Drake delivered before the National Union Association of Cincinnati, October 1, 1864* (n.p., 1864).

47. "The Presidential Election: Appeal of the National Union Committee to the People of the United States" (New York, 1864), Collection of Broadsides, Houghton Library, Harvard University.

48. The quote continues "Give Abraham Lincoln the overwhelming majority he should and can receive, and its moral effect will tell more toward giving the rebellion its quietus than all the grandest victories in the field we have yet achieved." "Not the time to surrender!," in the *Campaign for the Union*, November 5, 1864.

49. On the strategy of hard fighting see Mark Grimsley, *The Hard Hand of War: Union Military Policy Toward Southern Civilians, 1861–1865* (New York: Cambridge University Press, 1995). Confederate General John B. Hood had written to Sherman protesting about his declared policy of removing the civilian population from their homes. The Loyal Publication Society published Sherman's public reply in which he castigated Hood's hypocrisy: "In the name of common sense, I ask you not to appeal to a just God in such a sacrilegious manner—you, who, in the midst of peace and prosperity, have plunged a nation into civil war, 'dark and cruel' war, who dared and badgered us to battle, insulted our flag, seized our arsenals and forts that were left in the honorable custody of a peaceful ordnance sergeant, seized and made prisoners of war the very garrisons sent to protect your people against Negroes and Indians, long before any overt act was committed by the (to you) hateful Lincoln government." *Sherman vs Hood* (Loyal Publication Society pamphlet no. 61: New York, 1864).

50. "How shall we end the rebellion: shall we coax it, or crush it?," Broadside issued by the National Union Executive Committee, Astor House, New York, [1864]. Collection of political broadsides, Houghton Library, Harvard University.

51. Union Congressional Committee, *Shall We Have An Armistice?* (Washington, 1864).

52. Martin Ryerson to William H. Seward, October 15, 1864, Seward Papers.

53. Sam Purviance to Simon Cameron, September 1, 1864, Cameron Papers.

54. National Union Committee, *The Presidential Election: Appeal of the National Union Committee to the People of the United States* (New York, 1864)

55. Swinton, *The War for the Union.*

56. Charles Astor Bristed, *The Cowards' Convention*, Loyal Publication Society Pamphlet No. 68 (New York, 1864).

57. Henry Stanbery, *The ballot and the bullet: how to save the nation. Address of Henry Stanbery, esq.. delivered in Newport, Kentucky, Saturday evening, September 17, 1864* (Cincinnati, 1864), 3.

58. *The Campaign for the Union*, November 3, 1864. See also "The Real Chicago Platform, as expounded by the Democratic Orators at Chicago," Henry Horner Lincoln Collection, Illinois State Historical Library Broadsides Collection; *The Chicago Copperhead Convention* (Union Congressional Committee: Washington, 1864); *The Great Surrender to the Rebels in Arms: The Armistice* (Union Congressional Committee: Washington, 1864).

59. Swinton, *The War for the Union.*

60. Dittenhoeffer, *How We Elected Lincoln*, 87.

61. George S. Boutwell, "Chicago Convention of 1864: A Speech at Faneuil Hall, September 6, 1864" in his *Speeches and papers of George S. Boutwell relating to the rebellion and the overthrow of slavery* (Boston, 1867), 347–55.

62. For evidence supporting this point see McPherson, *Battle Cry of Freedom*, 803. However, many Southerners recognized that the election of a conservative like McClellan would pose new and perhaps insurmountable threat to the survival of the Confederacy. If the Democrats came to power in Washington and adopted conciliatory policies while offering constitutional guarantees for states rights and slavery, some Southern states might be induced to return to the Union for the sake of peace. See Larry E. Nelson, *Bullets, Ballots and Rhetoric: Confederate Policy for the United States Presidential Election of 1864* (Tuscaloosa: University of Alabama Press, 1980), 128–30.

63. Poster issued by the State Committee of the National Union Party in Pennsylvania. Civil War Library and Museum, Philadelphia.

64. "The Democratic Times," Broadside in the Alfred Whital Stern Collection of Lincolniana, Library of Congress.

65. *Springfield Republican* [date unknown] quoted in the *Campaign for the Union*, November 5, 1864.

66. The Illinois Governor, at least, was particularly worried about the negative effect of the draft. Richard Yates to Abraham Lincoln, August 21, 1864, Richard Yates Papers, Illinois State Historical Library.

67. *Voter's Catechism: Plain questions and answers for the campaign* (n.p., [1864]).

68. See for example, Loyal Publication Society pamphlet no. 61, which compared Arnold to New York Governor Horatio Seymour.

69. Kenneth M. Stampp, "The Milligan Case and the Election of 1864 in Indiana," *The Mississippi Valley Historical Review* 31 (1944), 50; William F. Zornow, *Lincoln*

and the Party Divided (Norman: University of Oklahoma Press, 1954), 154–58; Frank L. Klement, *The Copperheads in the Middle West* (Chicago: University of Chicago Press, 1960), 190; Frank L. Klement, *Dark Lanterns: Secret Political Societies, Conspiracies, and Treason Trials in the Civil War* (Baton Rouge: Louisiana State University Press, 1984).

70. Joseph Holt, *Report of the Judge Advocate-General on the 'Order of the American Knights' or 'Sons of Liberty': A Western conspiracy in aid of the Southern rebellion* (Washington, 1864). The Union Congressional Committee published extracts from the report: *Copperhead Conspiracy in the North-West. An expose of the treasonable order of the 'Sons of Liberty'* (Union Congressional Committee: Washington, 1864).

71. Joseph Holt, *Report of the Judge Advocate-General.*

72. See Strong *Diary*, 478.

73. In private correspondence, Union Party supporters were genuinely convinced that the consequences of a Democratic victory would be the collapse of the Union. See, for example, Thomas E. Smith to Elihu B. Washburne, September 19, 1864, Washburne Papers; M. A. Croft to Simon Cameron, September 27, 1864, Simon Cameron Papers, Manuscripts Division, Library of Congress. John G. Nicolay, Lincoln's private secretary conveyed the sense of uncertainty about the election in his regular letters to his fiancée, Therena Bates. See for instance Nicolay to Therena Bates, September 11, and October 2, 1864, John G. Nicolay Papers, Library of Congress.

74. For a full explanation of the capacity of republicanism to polarize political debate see Holt, *The Political Crisis of the 1850s.*

75. See Richard Hofstadter, "The Paranoid Style in American Politics" in *The Paranoid Style in American Politics and Other Essays* (New York: Knopf, 1965).

76. *Chicago Tribune*, September 26, 1864.

77. For a survey of state party platforms, see *New York Times*, September 13, 1864. See also James G. Blaine, *Letter of acceptance.* n.p., [1864], Alfred Whital Stern Collection, Library of Congress.

78. *The will of the people*, published by the Philadelphia Union League, tract no. 18 (Philadelphia, 1864). For similar arguments, see *How Shall We End the Rebellion: Shall We Coax It or Crush It?* (National Union Executive Committee: New York, 1864); and Coffin, N. W. et al. *A vigorous prosecution of the war the only guaranty of an honorable peace!* Boston, 1864.

79. See, for example, a pamphlet published by New York Unionists, *Pretexts of the Rebels and their sympathizers refuted by the logic of facts . . .* (New York, 1864)

80. "Mountaineer" [pseudonym for Charles Wright], *Our Political Practice. The Usurpations of Vice through the popular negligence.* (Boston, 1864)

81. *The "Only Alternative": A Tract for the Times by a plain man* (Philadelphia, 1864).

82. Union Republican Party of New Hampshire, circular, 26 September 1864, in the Abraham Lincoln Papers, Library of Congress.

83. *Boston Journal*, September 24, 27, 28, 29, October 11, 13, 18, 31, 1864; *Boston Daily Advertiser*, September 7, 21, October 6, 10, 29, 1864; *Boston Evening Transcript*, October 20, 1864; Boston *Commonwealth*, September 9, 1864. On the activism of the clergy in other states see *Pittsburgh Gazette*, September 11, 15, October 7, 10, 25, 17, 1864; *New York Tribune*, September 22, 1864; *Chicago Tribune*, September 22, October 31, 1864; *Connecticut Courant*, October 12, 26, 1864.

84. An example of a sermon that was reproduced by the Union League is Rev. Samuel T. Spear *Our Country and its Cause. A Discourse Preached October 2nd, 1864, in the South Presbyterian Church, of Brooklyn* (New York, 1864). Sermons published by and distributed by other loyal organizations included Rev. R. D. Hitchcock, *Thanksgiving for Victories. Discourse by Rev. R. D. Hitchcock* (New York, 1864). The National Union Committee also engaged Henry Ward Beecher to speak on behalf of Lincoln in the last two weeks of the campaign. *New York Tribune*, October 17, 24, 1864; *New York Times*, October 23, 31, 1864

85. *Boston Journal*, November 7, 1864.

86. J. R. Sikes to Abraham Lincoln, September 10, 1864. See also Benjamin B. French to Lincoln, October 11, 1864; George W. Eggleston to Lincoln, October 25, 1864; Joseph B. Maxfield to Lincoln, October 21, 1864, Benjamin Tatham to Isaac Newton, October 28, 1864, Lincoln Papers.

87. Basler, ed., *Collected Works of Abraham Lincoln*, VII: 533.

88. *New York Tribune*, September 5, 1864.

89. Rev. William S. Apsey, *Causes for National Thanksgiving: a discourse delivered in the First Baptist Church, Bennington, November 24th, 1864, by the Rev. Wm. S. Apsey, Pastor of the Church* (n.p. [1864]).

90. *A Workingman's reasons for the re-election of Abraham Lincoln.* [Philadelphia, 1864], in the New York Public Library; *The Nation's Sin and the Nation's Duty* (Philadelphia Union League pamphlet no. 41, Philadelphia, 1864).

91. 'Mountaineer' [Charles Wright, pseudo.], *Our political practice: The usurpations of vice through the popular negligence* (Boston, 1864).

92. M. A. Croft to Simon Cameron, August 31, 1864, Cameron Papers, Library of Congress; *New York Times*, June 18, 1864; *Cincinnati Daily Enquirer*, July 28, 1864; *Chicago Tribune*, September 2, 1864. John C. Hamilton was loudly cheered by a Union meeting when he began with the words "I am neither a partisan nor a politician . . . and so I am compelled to be and am a Unionist. John C. Hamilton, *Coercion Completed, or treason triumphant. Remarks by John C. Hamilton, September 1864* (Loyal Publication Society Pamphlet No. 66: New York, 1864).

93. 'On the Chicago Surrender' by Bayard Taylor from *The Lincoln and Johnson Campaign Songster* (Philadelphia, 1864), Collection of Pamphlets and Broadsides, Houghton Library, Harvard University.

94. 'In praise of Abraham' from *The Lincoln and Johnson Campaign Songster* (Philadelphia, 1864), Collection of Pamphlets and Broadsides, Houghton Library, Harvard University

95. See for example, Joel Silbey, *The American Political Nation.* 96. [unknown] to James G. Batterson October 28, 1864, Batterson Papers, Connecticut Historical Society. The counterproductive partisanship of the orator being berated by the unnamed Committee chairman must have been especially frustrating since it had evidently been difficult to get any speakers at all. Ten days beforehand, the chairman had written to Batterson beside himself with frustration: "Do you want our Town to give a copperhead majority next month[?] If you don't then send . . . *good Union Speakers* out here soon. The Copperheads [are] at work like *devils*. They have any quantity of papers to distribute among the Doubtful ones. *Whereas I have none.*" If nothing was done soon, he warned, "we shall [all] go to the D–l." [unknown] to James G. Batterson October 19, 1864, Batterson Papers, Connecticut Historical Society.

97. Speech of Sen. Henry Wilson at the Academy of Music, Brooklyn, October 1864, Campaign Document No. 1 of the Central Union Club of Brooklyn (New York, 1864), 4.

98. Ibid., 5.

99. Cartoon in the Stern Collection of Lincolniana, Library of Congress, Prints and Broadsides Collection, Box 4, pt. 2, no. 30.

100. "Who are the Real Democrats?," address of the Democratic [Loyal] League. (n.d., n.p.) Collection of Pamphlets, Election of 1864, Houghton Library, Harvard University. See also "The Real Chicago Platform, as expounded by the Democratic Orators at Chicago," Collection of Broadsides, Houghton Library, Harvard University.

101. *The Campaign for the Union*, November 2, 1864.

102. The War Democratic Committee of New York, for example, published a number of pamphlets including *Country Before Party: The Voice of the Loyal Democrats* (War Democratic State Committee: New York, 1864) and *Speech of Hon. Edwards Pierrepont, delivered at the convention and mass meeting of the Democracy opposed to the Chicago Convention, held at the Cooper Institute, New York, November 1, 1864* (War Democratic State Committee of New York: New York, 1864).

103. *Country Before Party: The Voice of the Loyal Democrats* (War Democratic State Committee: New York, 1864).

104. "Honest War Democrats: Read What Democrats Say," Campaign Document of the Central Union Club of Brooklyn (New York, 1864). Dix's remark was repeated in many Union documents. For instance "Rally Round the Old Flag!!," broadside in the collection of political broadsides, Houghton Library, Harvard University. An oft-used tactic was to appropriate the memory of Stephen Douglas in order to claim that Democrats who continued to oppose the administration were nothing but "poor traitors." See "Who Shall be Vice-President?: Shall he be a loyal or a disloyal man?," pamphlet published by the National Union Executive Committee, Astor House, New York, 1864. See also the speech of Benjamin F. Butler at Concord New Hampshire, July 21, 1863, reported in *Harper's Weekly*, July 25, 1863.

105. In a stump speech Congressman John A. Bingham of Ohio described those who did not as "hypocritical pretenders of Democracy . . . they call themselves Democrats; they are simply northern traitors . . . they are no more Democrats than the Devil himself." *Cincinnati Daily Gazette*, September 8, 1863.

106. *New York Herald*, undated, quoted in *The Campaign for the Union*, November 5, 1864. [This was a Union Party campaign newspaper published in Boston in October and November 1864. Holdings in the Boston Public Library.] Reports also appeared in, for example: Pittsburgh *Gazette*, June 9, 1864; *New York Times*, June 9, 1864; *Chicago Tribune*, June 10, 1864; *Proceedings of the Grand Meeting of the War Democracy in the Cooper Union* (New York, 1864); Hiram Walbridge, *Speech of Gen. Hiram Walbridge, delivered before the convention of the War Democracy at Cooper Institute, New York, Tuesday, November 1, 1864* (New York, 1864); Collections of the Illinois State Historical Library; *Pittsburgh Gazette*, November 3, 1864. A digest of War Democratic letters and speeches is provided in a pamphlet published by the Philadelphia Union League: *A Savory Dish for Loyal Men* (Philadelphia, 1863).

107. *Speech of Hon. Edwards Pierrepont, delivered at the convention and mass meeting of the Democracy opposed to the Chicago Convention, held at the Cooper Institute, New York, November 1, 1864* (War Democratic State Committee of New York: New York, 1864).

108. David S. Coddington, *The Crisis and the Man*, 4, 6. The Union Leagues circulated a broadside reproducing a letter by George B. Loring of Salem, Massachusetts, a "life-long Democrat" whose "patriotism will not permit him to sacrifice country for party" and who was therefore urging the reelection of Lincoln. 'Another Life-Long Democrat Testifies to the Truth,' Henry Horner Lincoln Collection, Illinois State Historical Society Broadsides.

109. George A. Brandreth to Benjamin F. Wade, October 15, 1864, Wade Papers, Library of Congress.

110. *Causes for National Thanksgiving*, "A discourse delivered in the First Baptist Church, Bennington, November 24th, 1864, by the Rev. Wm. S. Apsey, Pastor of the Church" (n.p., [1864]), Collection of Political Pamphlets, Election of 1864, Houghton Library, Harvard University.

111. See George M. Frederickson, *The Inner Civil War: Northern Intellectuals and the Crisis of the Union* (New York: Harper & Row, 1965), 101–5.

112. The *"Only Alternative": A tract for the times by a plain man* (Philadelphia, 1864)

113. *Chicago Tribune*, September 28, 1864.

114. Rev. R. D. Hitchcock, *Thanksgiving for Victories* (New York, 1864).

115. Charles D. Drake, *Speech of the Honorable Charles D. Drake, delivered before the National Union Association at Cincinnati, October 1, 1864* (n.p. [1864]).

116. Basler, ed., *Collected Works of Abraham Lincoln*, 6: 156.

117. Lincoln to Albert G. Hodges, April 4, 1864 in Basler, ed., *Collected Works of Abraham Lincoln*, 7:281–82.

118. Rev. R. D. Hitchcock, *Thanksgiving for Victories* (New York, 1864).

119. "The Scourged Back," in *The President Lincoln Campaign Songster* (Philadelphia, 1864), Pamphlets and Broadsides Collection, Houghton Library, Harvard University.

120. James M. McPherson, *The Struggle for Equality: Abolitionists and the Negro in the Civil War and Reconstruction* (Princeton, N.J.: Princeton University Press:, 1964), 260–86.

121. Strong *Diary*, 474 (entry for August 19, 1864).

122. James G. Blaine, "Letter of Acceptance," Broadside in the Alfred Whital Stern Collection of Lincolniana, Library of Congress.

123. Blaine, *Twenty Years of Congress from Lincoln to Garfield: with a review of the events which led to the political revolution of 1860* (2 vols: Norwich, Conn., 1884), 2: 43. For similar comments see I. P. M. Epping to William H. Seward, 30 September 1864, Seward Papers, University of Rochester; Schuyler Colfax to Edwin M. Stanton, 29 August 1864, Stanton Papers, Library of Congress

124. *New York Evening Post*, September 28, 1864.

125. Sam Purviance to Simon Cameron, September 1, 1864, Cameron Papers.

126. For the clearest statement of this distinction see John Murray Forbes, "By a Conservative who believes in Abolition as a Military Necessity," *Boston Daily Advertiser*, September 27, 1862. This article was republished in several newspapers during the 1864 campaign, and was released as a broadside. *New York Evening Post*, September 21, 1864; *Chicago Tribune*, October 12, 1864; Broadsides Collection, Houghton Library, Harvard University; John Murray Forbes to Francis P. Blair, Sr., September 18, 1864, Blair Family Papers.

127. J. W. Gerrard to Theodore Tilton, April 26, 1860, Theodore Tilton Papers, New York Historical Society. Tilton was appointed assistant editor of the *Independent* in 1861, although he conducted most of the editorial duties, and in 1863 he

formally took over the role. Gerrard was a New York businessman who had made a public offer to give a hundred dollars to any abolitionist who was prepared to put up a similar sum of his own money buying the freedom of a slave. Since of course Gerrard did not expect anyone to take up the offer, the rather dubious point of this ploy was to try to prove that abolitionists—in the radical sense of the term—were more interested in social disruption and fighting political battles than they were in actually securing the freedom of slaves.

128. See for instance a broadside that compared Benedict Arnold to Horatio Seymour. "Benedict Arnold and Horatio Seymour," Henry Horner Lincoln Collection, Illinois State Historical Library Broadsides Collection.

129. *The "Only Alternative": A Tract for the times by a plain man* (Philadelphia, 1864).

130. On the antislavery origins of the Republican Party see Graham Peck, "The Social and Cultural Origins of Sectional Politics: Illinois from Statehood to Civil War," PhD diss., Northwestern University, 2002; Harry V. Jaffa, *A New Birth of Freedom: Abraham Lincoln and the Coming of the Civil War* (Banham, Md.: Bowman and Littlefield, 2000).

131. Lane, *Political History*, 222.

132. "What Are We Fighting For?," *The President Lincoln Campaign Songster* (Philadelphia, 1864).

133. "Platforms Illustrated," Broadside, Alfred Whital Stern Collection of Lincolniana, Library of Congress; "Uncle Abe's Valentine sent by Columbia: An envelope of Broken Chains," original drawing in the Alfred Whital Stern Collection, Library of Congress.

134. John Murray Forbes, *Letters and recollections of John Murray Forbes*, Sarah Forbes Hughes, ed., 2 vols. (Boston, 1899).

135. Edward Mansfield, *The Issues and Duties of the Day* (Cincinnati, 1864). A Presbyterian Minister from New York assured his congregation that there was no point in wasting time talking about the Emancipation Proclamation because 'the bondsmen would have snatched their freedom' anyway. Rev. R. D. Hitchcock, *Thanksgiving for Victories* (New York, 1864), 3.

136. 'Slavery and the Next President,' Broadside in the Abraham Lincoln Papers, Library of Congress, enclosed October 25, 1864.

137. Philadelphia Union League, *The Will of the People* (Philadelphia, 1864).

138. John Brough, *The defenders of the Country and its enemies. The Chicago platform dissected. Speech of Governor John Brough, delivered at Circleville, Ohio, September 3, 1864* (Cincinnati, 1864).

139. *New Hampshire Statesman*, January 22, 1864.

140. 'Slavery and the Next President,' Broadside in the Lincoln Papers, enclosed October 25, 1864.

141. The speech was reprinted, for example in *New York Times*, Sept. 4, 5, 1864; *New York Evening Post*, Sept. 5, 1864; *Albany Evening Journal*, Sept. 4, 5, 1864; *Boston Daily Advertiser*, Sept. 8, 1864; *Cleveland Plain Dealer*, Sept. 5, 9, 1864; *Chicago Tribune*, Sept. 7, 1864.

142. William H. Seward, *Issues of the conflict—terms of peace. Speech of William H. Seward, on the occasion of the fall of Atlanta, at Auburn, Saturday, Sept. 3, 1864* (Washington, 1864).

143. For radical discontent see Lucius Fairchild to Abraham Lincoln, September 13, 1864, Lincoln Papers; Henry T. Cheever to William H. Seward, Septem-

ber 10, 1864; John D. Baldwin to Frederick Seward, September 10, 1864. For thoughts on Seward's purpose see Frederick Seward to Baldwin, September 24, 1864, Seward Papers; Boston *Commonwealth*, September 16, 1864; John Cox and Lawanda Cox, *Politics, Principles and Prejudice, 1865–1866* (New York, 1963), 4.

144. Hugh McCulloch to Seward, September 8, 1864, Seward Papers.

145. Lydia Maria Child to George W. Julian, January 30, 1862, quoted in Earl J. Hess, *Liberty, Virtue and Progress: Northerners and Their War for the Union* (New York, 1988), 94.

146. Speech of Robert J. Breckinridge, *Proceedings of the National Union Convention*, 6.

147. Henry Stanbery, *The ballot and the bullet: how to save the nation. Address of Henry Stanbery, esq.. delivered in Newport, Kentucky, Saturday evening, September 17, 1864* (Cincinnati, 1864).

148. *The Campaign for the Union*, November 2, 1864.

149. Spear, *Our Country and its Cause*, 1.

150. "We will fight it out," *The President Lincoln Campaign Songster* (Philadelphia, 1864).

151. *Harper's Weekly*, October 22, 1864.

152. "Your Plan and Mine," Broadside (New York, 1864), Collection of Broadsides, Houghton Library, Harvard University.

153. John C. Hamilton, *Coercion Completed or Treason Triumphant* (Loyal Publication Society: New York, 1864), 9.

154. "The Chicago Platform and it candidate," cartoon in the Collection of Broadsides, Houghton Library, Harvard University.

155. Review of Robert Dale Owen's *The Wrong of Slavery*, *Atlantic Monthly* XIV (October 1864), 517.

156. Abraham Lincoln, Annual Message to Congress, December 6, 1864, in Basler, ed., *Collected Works of Abraham Lincoln*, 8: 149.

157. Douglass to Theodore Tilton, Oct. 15, 1864, *The Life and Writings of Frederick Douglass*, ed. Philip S. Foner (New York: International Publishers, 1952), 3:422–24.

158. William E. Chandler to Montgomery Blair, November 20, 1863, Blair Papers.

159. Charles Drake, *Speech of Hon. Charles Drake delivered before the National Union Association of Cincinnati, October 1, 1864* (n.p., 1864); William Swinton, *The War for the Union: The First, Second, Third, and Fourth Years of the War* (Loyal Publication Society Pamphlet no. 62: New York, 1864).

160. Mary Hawley Diary, entry for November 7, 1864, New-York Historical Society.

161. Entry for November 8, 1864. Nathan Kilbourn Abbott diaries, vol. 7, New Hampshire Historical Society.

162. Elizabeth Blair Lee, *Wartime Washington: The Civil War Letters of Elizabeth Blair Lee*, Virginia Jeans Laas, ed. (Urbana: University of Illinois Press, 1991), 441.

163. See for example M. B. Brown to Elihu B. Washburne, October 18, 1864, Washburne Papers, Library of Congress; Frederick H. Brandes to Abraham Lincoln, September 5, 1864, Lincoln Papers, Library of Congress.

164. "Address" of Francis Lieber, President of the Loyal Publication Society, *Proceedings of the Second Anniversary Meeting of the Loyal Publication Society February 11, 1865* (New York, 1865), 3.

165. John G. Nicolay to Therena Bates, September 11, 1864, Nicolay Papers.

166. For optimistic assessments of the Democrats' chances see William C. Prime to McClellan, October 20, 1864, Horatio Seymour to McClellan, October 23, 1864; S. L. M. Barlow to McClellan, October 27, 1864, McClellan Papers.

167. S. S. Cox to McClellan, October 27, 1864, McClellan Papers.

168. S. Fletcher to Andrew Johnson, July 30, 1864, Andrew Johnson Papers, Manuscripts Division, Library of Congress.

169. William C. Prime to McClellan, October 20, 1864, McClellan Papers.

170. Chandler quoted in Zornow, *Lincoln and the Party Divided* (Norman: University of Oklahoma Press, 1954), 194. The closeness of the result in Pennsylvania worried Lincoln, even if it satisfied Chandler. On the day that the results came in Lincoln sat in his favorite chair in the War department telegraph office and worked out how the presidential election might go. Being as pessimistic as seemed reasonable given the results that week, he awarded McClellan New York, Pennsylvania and Illinois of the big battleground states, and assumed his own victory in Ohio and Indiana. Given his probable victory in New England (including marginal Connecticut), Iowa, Kansas, Wisconsin, Minnesota, West Virginia, and Michigan, and assuming his victory in the far West, Lincoln reckoned that he still had enough electoral college votes to win: 117 to 114. Someone—perhaps John G. Nicolay—later added the three electoral college votes of Nevada, that achieved statehood on October 31, 1864, giving him a projected total of 120. McClellan, he thought, would win New Jersey, Delaware, Missouri, Kentucky, and Maryland in addition to New York and Pennsylvania. The inclusion of Missouri in McClellan's column is interesting. Seventy percent of the popular vote there went to Lincoln in the end, although in the fraught politics of that state, where the military played a lead role in the organization of the campaign and the supervision of the election, popular sentiments must have been hard to judge. The Union Party in Missouri was so factionally riven that a low turnout was also possible. Basler, ed., *Collected Works of Abraham, Lincoln*, 7: 46.

171. *Daily Ohio State Journal*, September 23, 1864. Lincoln noted the results of a poll conducted on the train from Pittsburgh to Harrisburg on September 13 that gave him 172 votes against 66 for McClellan and seven for Fremont. Basler, ed., *Collected Works of Abraham Lincoln*, 8: 3. There were never any recorded "don't knows" in these early versions of the opinion poll, even though canvassers knew that voters sometimes changed their minds or didn't bother to vote. This may be evidence of the passionate engagement of voters in the campaign, or it may be that "don't knows" were cajoled into making a choice.

172. Sam Blatchford to William H. Seward, September 17, October 18, 1864, Seward Papers.

173. Whitelaw Reid, "Agate" letter, November 3, 1864, Reid Family Papers.

174. Basler, *Collected Works*, 8: 81.

175. John G. Nicolay to Therena Bates, September 11, 1864, Nicolay Papers.

176. John G. Nicolay to Therena Bates, September 4, 1864, Nicolay Papers.

177. Noah Brooks, *Washington DC in Lincoln's Time: A memoir of the Civil War era by the newspaper man who knew Lincoln best*, Herbert Mitgang, ed. (Athens: University of Georgia Press, 1989), 196.

178. Brooks, *Washington DC*, 197.

179. In nine states (Maine, New Hampshire, Wisconsin, Michigan, Connecticut, Minnesota, New York, Pennsylvania, and Vermont) Lincoln's share of the vote was lower than in 1860 despite an increased turnout and fewer opponents.

Lincoln won Missouri and Maryland, states he had lost in 1860, as well as West Virginia (the counties of which had split their vote between Bell and Douglas in 1860), Kansas (which was admitted to statehood in 1861) and Nevada (which was admitted as a state only just in time to cast its vote in November 1864). He won about the same number of votes in New Jersey as he had in 1860 on a slightly higher turnout, but lost the state by a five percent margin. In states where in 1860 there had been a sizeable vote for Breckinridge and Bell, Lincoln tended to win a majority of the Bell voters, while Breckinridge voters went for McClellan. Altogether, Lincoln won 339,308 more votes than he had in 1860. About a third of this increase was due to the Border States, where Lincoln improved dramatically on his derisory 1860 performance, winning an extra 124,584 votes in Maryland, Missouri, Delaware, and Kentucky. This breaks down as 26,422 extra votes in Kentucky, 55,963 in Missouri and 37,859 in Maryland and 4,340 in Delaware. There was also a significant proportional increase in the far West (amounting to an extra 33,748 votes in California, Nevada and Oregon). All figures are from *Congressional Quarterly's Guide to US Elections* (Washington, 2nd ed., 1985), 763–768, 488–535, supplemented by *Tribune Almanac* for the years 1861, 1862 and 1863 (New York). George Templeton Strong was right to see a clear ethnocultural pattern underlying these results. In the "Irish Fourteenth" ward in New York, Lincoln polled only 859 out of 5008 votes and in the neighboring "Bloody Sixth" ward he did even worse, polling only 326 votes against 3,475 for McClellan, or 8.5 percent of the vote. *New York Times*, November 10, 1864. On the fourteenth and sixth wards see Iver Bernstein, *The New York City Draft Riots: Their Significance for American Society and Politics in the Age of the Civil War* (New York, 1990), 24–25; Tyler Anbinder, *Five Points the 19th-century New York City neighborhood that invented tap dance, stole elections, and became the world's most notorious slum* (New York: Free Press, 2001). Irish immigrants retained their traditional allegiance to the Democratic Party, even when they were enlisted in the army. "Irish" regiments returned high levels of support for McClellan, such as the Boston "Irish Brigade," See Thomas H. O'Connor, *Civil War Boston: Home Front and Battlefield* (Boston: Northeastern University Press, 1997), 136. Newspapers are a useful source for ward level election results. See *Boston Daily Advertiser*, September 26, 29, 30; October 14; November 6, 8, 1861; January 13, 29; April 6, 17; June 12, 18; September 16; October 28, 30; November 9, 1862; October 12; November 7, 11; December 3, 1863: *New York Tribune*, September 28; October 12; November 9, 1862. The most heavily Irish wards of Boston returned the highest vote for McClellan in the nation and, overall, Lincoln lost most of the counties where at least one third of the population was foreign born. *New York Times*, November 9, 10, 11, 12, 1864; *Boston Daily Advertiser*, November 9, 10, 1864. Even in a strongly Republican state like Iowa, Lincoln lost in two counties where there was a high foreign-born population, and polled less well in two others than he did in the state as a whole. The greatest Union strength in the Midwest, then, came from the "Yankee" counties—those areas that had been settled by people from the Eastern seaboard, especially New England. The counties of northeastern Ohio, for example, gave Lincoln very strong support, whereas the southernmost counties tended to be more evenly divided. This familiar pattern had been visible during the Second Party system. In Illinois and Indiana, the divide was even more obvious: Lincoln received over 65 percent of the vote in many northern counties, whose population was largely "Yankee" in origin, and lost a majority of counties in the Copperhead—supporting Southern parts of the state. See Kleppner, *Third Electoral System*, 84; Cook, *Baptism of Fire*, 154.

180. Basler, ed., *Collected Works of Abraham Lincoln*, 8: 96.

181. On Confederate hopes for a McClellan victory see Nelson, *Bullets, Ballots and Rhetoric*.

182. Charles Francis Adams, Jr., *Individuality in Politics: A Lecture delivered in Steinway Hall, New York, Wednesday Evening, April 21, 1880* (New York: Indpendent Republican Association, 1880), 11–13.

183. Quoted by Zornow, *Lincoln and the Party Divided*, 215.

184. Philadelphia Union Central Committee, November 10, 1864 (Resolution opposed to command for General McClellan; signed by Simon Cameron and A. W. Benecket), Lincoln Papers.

185. Strong *Diary*, 513.

186. George H. Corey, *Wisdom and War: A Discourse Delivered Before the Department of the Potomac, Grand Army of the Republic* (Washington, D.C.: Gibson Brothers, 1889), quoted in Hess, *Liberty, Virtue and Progress*, 104.

CONCLUSION

1. Strong *Diary*, 580.

2. Henry W. Hoffman to Abraham Lincoln, 10 November 1864, Lincoln Papers.

3. Mary Hawley Diary, entry for 10 [November] 1864, New-York Historical Society.

4. Philadelphia *Inquirer*, November 17, 1864, quoted in Neely, *The Union Divided*, 171. A major impetus for the new political order arose directly out of the most serious factional battle in the Republican Party—in New York, where by the end of 1864 the more radical Greeley faction appeared to be gaining strength at the expense of the supporters of Seward and Weed. Weed had toyed with co-operation with moderate Democrats throughout the war in order to gain leverage against the radicals and the reasons for making such an alliance permanent appeared to be multiplying. See John H. Cox and LaWanda Cox, *Politics, Principle and Prejudice, 1865–1866: Dilemma of Reconstruction America* (New York, 1963), 31–49.

5. George E. Baker, *The Works of William H. Seward*, 5 vols. (Boston: Houghton, Mifflin, 1884), 5: 513–14.

6. Seward quoted in Cox, *Politics, Principle and Prejudice*, 33–38.

7. *Congressional Globe*, 38th Cong., 2d sess., 171 (January 9, 1865), quoted by Cox, *Politics, Principle and Prejudice*, 40. New York *Herald*, January 15 and February 15, 1865, quoted in Cox, *Politics, Principle and Prejudice*, 41, 43.

8. *Harper's Weekly*, February 25, 1865.

9. Edward Everett to Charles Francis Adams, December 18, 1864, Everett Papers, Massachusetts Historical Society.

10. *New York Times*, November 10, 1864. Bell's greatest strength had been in the Border States. He won a majority of the popular vote in Tennessee, Kentucky, and Virginia (with great strength in the counties that seceded to form West Virginia), and nearly won Missouri. In these states, Lincoln's poll share in 1864 must have come largely from former Constitutional Unionists, although they were clearly divided. In 1864 Lincoln won 27,786 votes in Kentucky, for example, a state in which he had only polled 1, 364 (less than one percent of the votes cast) in 1860.

11. Lincoln received 84 percent of the vote in the city of Baltimore.

12. See Paul Kleppner, *Third Electoral System*, 85; Robert Cook, *Baptism of Fire: The Republican Party in Iowa, 1838–1878* (Ames: Iowa State University Press, 1994).

13. John W. Forney to Abraham Lincoln, October 24, 1864, Abraham Lincoln Papers, Library of Congress. Lincoln's correspondence is scattered with patronage requests that indicate the broad base of the Union Party. See, for example, Forney to Lincoln, September 24, and October 18, 1864; Isaac N. Arnold to Lincoln, October 24, 1864; 'New York Democratic Party' to Lincoln, October 28, 1864. Letters from Republicans urging the President not to use patronage to dilute the composition of the party include E. Bentley to Lincoln, October 31, 1864; James W. White to Lincoln, October 28, 1864; and Jeremiah Fenno to Lincoln, October 23, 1864, all in the Lincoln Papers.

14. *New-York Daily Tribune*, June 27, 1861; Springfield *Republican*, June 28, 1862.

15. Gerald Stanley, "Civil War Politics in California," *Southern California Quarterly* 64 (1982) 115–32; Christopher Dell, *Lincoln and the War Democrats: The Grand Erosion of Conservative Tradition* (Cranbury, N.J.: Greenwood Press, 1975), 109.

16. In a stimulating and insightful essay, Michael Holt has echoed the accusations of some radical Republicans that the Union Party was concerned largely to build a political organization in the South that would support Lincoln's re-election and displace the sectional Republican Party. Holt, "Abraham Lincoln and the Politics of Union," in his *Political Parties and American Political Development from the Age of Jackson to the Age of Lincoln* (Baton Rouge: Louisiana State University Press, 1992), 323–53

17. This is a point made by Holt, "Abraham Lincoln and the Politics of Union" and David H. Donald, *The Politics of Reconstruction, 1863–1867* (Baton Rouge: Louisiana State University Press, 1965).

18. In no state where the military vote was separately tabulated can it be said to have been the decisive factor. But neither Connecticut nor New York counted soldiers' ballots separately—instead, supposedly sealed ballots were sent to each soldier's home ward—and it was in these two states that the military vote might well have tipped the balance in Lincoln's favor. In New York, the Union Party victory in the state as a whole was only 6,750. Since more than 70,000 soldiers cast absentee ballots, the military vote, assuming it to have been as biased in the Union Party's favor elsewhere must have made the difference, even allowing for the possibility that not all these votes reached town officials in time. *Tribune Almanac for 1865*, 48; *New York Times*, November 9, 1864. In Connecticut, 2,898 absentee soldier ballots were received, of which around 2,400 reached town officials in time to be counted. Lincoln's state-wide majority was only 2,406. See Samuel T. McSeveney, "Re-electing Lincoln: The Union Party Campaign and the Military Vote in Connecticut," *Civil War History* 32 (1986): 151–152; T. Harry Williams, "Voters in Blue," *Mississippi Valley Historical Review* 31 (1944): 187–204.

19. Naturally enough soldiers tended to be young—as were Republican voters in the 1860 election. Soldiers were also more likely to come from Anglo–Saxon rather than ethnic Irish or German backgrounds than was the population as a whole.

20. On this subject see Joseph Allen Frank, *With Ballot and Bayonet: The Political Socialization of Civil War Soldiers* (Athens: University of Georgia Press, 1999); T. Harry Williams, "Voters in Blue," *Mississippi Valley Historical Review* 31 (1944): 187–204.

21. On the function of parties in American history see John H. Aldrich, *Why Parties? The Origin and Transformation of Political Parties in America* (Chicago: University of Chicago Press, 1995).

22. Neely, *Divided Union*; Long, *Jewel of Liberty*, 261–75.

23. On the idea of party in eighteenth- and nineteenth-century England see Frank O'Gorman, *The Emergence of the British Two-Party System 1760–1832* (London: Edward Arnold, 1982); and O'Gorman, *Voters, Patrons, and Parties: The Unreformed Electoral System of Hanoverian England, 1734–1832* (New York: Oxford University Press, 1989), 317–83. O'Gorman argues that the later Hanoverian and early Victorian electorate, is best described as "partisan, participatory and popular" rather than deferential (*Voters, Patrons, and Parties*, 393.) For a similar argument see John A. Phillips, *The Great Reform Bill in the Boroughs: English Electoral Behaviour, 1818–1841* (New York: Oxford University Press, 1992) and *Electoral Behaviour in Unreformed England: Plumpers, Splitters and Straights* (Princeton, N.J.: Princeton University Press, 1982). A nuanced study of the meaning of party at the local level between the 1832 and the 1867 Reform Acts is provided by T. J. Nossiter, *Influence, Opinion and Political Idioms in Reformed England: Case Studies from the North East, 1832–1874* (Brighton: Harvester Press, 1975) and on the development of grass-roots party organization and the role of partisanship in structuring voting behavior after 1867 see the classic study by H. J. Hanham: *Elections and Party Management: Politics in the time of Disraeli and Gladstone* (Brighton: Harvester Press, 1978). A much more skeptical account of the significance of partisanship is provided by James Vernon, *Politics and the People: A Study in English Political Culture c. 1815–1867* (Cambridge, UK: Cambridge University Press, 1993).

24. Eric McKitrick, "Party Politics and the Union and Confederate War Efforts" in William Nisbet Chambers and Walter Dean Burnham, eds., *The American Party Systems: Stages of Political Development* (New York: Oxford University Press, 1967), 117–51.

25. Joel H. Silbey, *A Respectable Minority: The Democratic Party in the Civil War Era, 1860–1868* (New York: W.W. Norton, 1977). One of the ways in which McKitrick's thesis was helpful was that it integrated Civil War politics into an emerging synthesis by which American political history was divided into a series of successive "party systems." On the "party system" theory see William Nisbet Chambers and Walter Dean Burnham, eds., *The American Party Systems: Stages of Political Development* (New York: Oxford University Press, 1967); Paul Kleppner et al., *The Evolution of American Electoral Systems* (Westport, Conn.: Greenwood Press, 1981); Richard L. McCormick, "The Realignment Synthesis in American History," *Journal of Interdisciplinary History* 13 (Summer 1982): 85–105. For a refreshingly skepical revision of a critical element of the party system thesis see David Mayhew, *Electoral Realignments: A Critique of an American Genre* (New Haven, Conn.; Yale University Press, 2002).

26. See Peter J. Parish, "Conflict by Consent," *The North and the Nation in the Era of the Civil War*, Adam I. P. Smith and Susan-Mary Grant, eds. (New York: Fordham University Press, 2003), 149–70.

27. See for example, Gary Gallagher, *The Confederate War* (Cambridge, Mass.: Harvard University Press, 1997); and George C. Rable, *The Confederate Republic: A Revolution Against Politics* (Chapel Hill: University of North Carolina Press, 1994).

28. Rable, *Confederate Republic*, 277–98.

29. McKitrick concedes this point in "Party Politics and the Union and Confederate War Efforts," 120.

30. Mark E. Neely, *The Divided Union: Party Conflict in the Civil War North* (Cambridge, Mass.: Harvard University Press, 2002).

31. On this point see Carwardine, *Lincoln*, 257–67.

32. George W. Tillotson to Elizabeth Tillotson, November 21, 1863, Tillotson Correspondence, Gilder Lehrman Collection.

33. The same point can be made about Neely, *The Union Divided*.

34. *Cleveland Plain Dealer*, September 12, 1864.

35. For reports of state party platforms see *Boston Post*, September 9, 1864; New York *World*, September 18, 20, 1864.

36. See William Blair, "We are coming Father Abraham—eventually: the problem of Northern nationalism in the Pennsylvania recruiting drives of 1862" in Joan E. Cashin, ed., *The War Was You and Me: Civilians in the American Civil War* (Princeton, N.J.: Princeton University Press, 2002), 183–208.

37. This point is made persuasively by Joel Silbey, *A Respectable Minority*, 164.

38. McKitrick, "Party Politics and the Union and Confederate War Efforts," 141.

39. Lincoln to James C. Conkling, August 26, 1863, Basler, ed., *Collected Works of Abraham Lincoln*, 6:406.

40. *New York Times*, April 24, 1863.

41. "What educated men had to organize against was the political party," writes Michael E. McGerr in his influential study of the changing style of political mobilization in the late nineteenth century: *The Decline of Popular Politics: The American North, 1865–1928* (New York: Oxford University Press, 1986), 53. On Gilded Age anti-partyism, efforts to restrict the franchise and the debates about campaigning strategies and voting procedures see Peter Argersinger, "The Value of the Vote: Political Representation in the Gilded Age," *Journal of American History* 76 (June 1989): 59–90; Argersinger, "New Perspectives on Election Fraud in the Gilded Age," *Political Science Quarterly* 100 (Winter 1985–1986): 669–87; John Buenke, "The Politics of Resistance: The Rural-Based Yankee Republican Machines of Connecticut and Rhode Island," *New England Quarterly* 47 (June 1974): 212–37; Alexander Keyssar, *The Right to Vote: The Contested History of Democracy in the United States* (New York: Basic, 2000), 117–71.

42. W. E. Baker, "A Plan by which political parties in a republic may be legally empowered to select candidates for office," in Union League of Philadelphia, *Essays on Political Organization* (Philadelphia, 1868), 7–8.

43. Charles G. Came, "Legal Nominations," in Union League of Philadelphia, *Essays on Political Organization*, 23.

44. C. Goepp, "Legal Organization of the People," in Union League of Philadelphia, *Essays on Political Organization*, 76–77.

Bibliography

MANUSCRIPT COLLECTIONS

New York State Library, Albany
Edwin D. Morgan Papers (microfilm edition)

Boston Public Library
New England Loyal Publication Society Manuscripts

Massachusetts Historical Society
Adams Family Papers
John A. Andrew Papers
Henry W. Bellows Papers
Richard Henry Dana Papers
Edward Everett Papers
Winthrop Family Papers

Buffalo and Erie County Historical Society,
Millard Fillmore Papers (microfilm edition)

Watkinson Library, Trinity College, Hartford, Connecticut
Sydney Stanley Papers

Houghton Library, Harvard University, Cambridge, Massachusetts
Charles Sumner Papers

The Arthur and Elizabeth Schlesinger Library on the History of Women in America, Radcliffe College, Cambridge, Massachusetts
Anna E. Dickinson Letters

Ohio Historical Society, Columbus, Ohio
Thomas Ewing Papers, Archives-Library Division (microfilm edition)

Gilder Lehrman Collection, New-York Historical Society
John Jones Collection
Kelley Correspondence
Maitland Papers
Pearce Papers
George May Powell Papers
Tillotson Correspondence

New Hampshire Historical Society, Concord, New Hampshire
Nathan Kilbourn Abbott Diaries
William E. Chandler Papers
George C. Fogg Papers

Connecticut Historical Society Library, Hartford, Connecticut
James G. Batterson Papers
William Buckingham Correspondence
S. H. Norton Letters
Gideon Welles Papers

Historical Society of Dauphin County, Harrisburg Pennsylvannia
Simon Cameron Papers (microfilm edition)

Norlands Living History Center, Washburn Norlands Library, Livermore Falls, Maine
Israel Washburn Jr. Papers and Elihu B. Washburne Papers, Washburn Collection
    (microfilm edition)

Butler Library, Columbia University, New York, New York
August Belmont Papers
John A. Dix Papers
Hanibal Hamlin Papers (microfilm edition)

New York Public Library, New York, New York
Horace Greeley Papers
Thomas Kinsella Papers
Henry J. Raymond Papers
Theodore Tilton Papers
Samuel J. Tilden Papers

New-York Historical Society, New York, New York
Mary Hawley Diary
Papers of the Loyal League of Union Citizens
Poll Book, Montgomery County
John A. Stevens Papers
David M. Turnure Journals

Princeton University Library, Princeton, New Jersey
Francis P. Blair Papers

University of Rochester Library, Rochester, New York
William H. Seward Papers (microfilm edition)
Thurlow Weed Papers

Illinois State Historical Library, Springfield, Illinois
Orville Hickman Browning Papers
David Davis Family Papers
Augustus Beardsley Frey Letters
O. M. Hatch Papers

Henry Horner Lincoln Collection of pamphlets, prints and broadsides
Leonard Swett Collection
Lyman Trumbull Papers
Elihu B. Washburne Papers
Horace White Papers
Richard Yates Papers

Manuscripts Division, Library of Congress, Washington, D.C.
Jeremiah S. Black Papers Library of Congress (microfilm edition)
James G. Blaine Papers, Library of Congress (microfilm edition)
Blair Family Papers, Library of Congress (microfilm edition)
Benjamin F. Butler Papers
Simon Cameron Papers (microfilm edition)
Zachariah Chandler Papers (microfilm edition)
Salmon P. Chase Papers
Anna E. Dickinson Papers (microfilm edition)
James R. Doolittle Papers
Thomas Ewing Papers (microfilm edition)
William Pitt Fessenden Papers
John W. Forney Papers
Horace Greeley Papers
Joseph Holt Papers
Andrew Johnson Papers (microfilm edition)
Abraham Lincoln Papers (microfilm edition)
George B. McClellan Papers (microfilm edition)
Hugh McCulloch Papers
John G. Nicolay Papers
Reid Family Papers [Whitelaw Reid]
John Sherman Papers (microfilm edition)
Edwin M. Stanton Papers (microfilm edition)
Alfred Whittal Stern Collection of Lincolniana
Lyman Trumbull Papers (microfilm edition)
Benjamin F. Wade Papers
Gideon Welles Papers

CONTEMPORARY DOCUMENTS

Songs

Anon., "The Sword and the Red, White and Blue." New York: H. De Marsan, 1861. *American Songs and Ballads*, Series 4, Volume 4, Library of Congress.
Campaign Songs. [Democratic] Campaign document no. 19. New York, 1864.
Dadmun, J. W. *Union League melodies. A collection of patriotic hymns and tunes, original and selected adapted to Union League meetings, army and navy, and social gatherings generally*. Boston, 1864. New York Public Library.
Dale, William P. "A Good Time Coming" in *The Young Men's Republican Vocalist*. New York: A. Morris, 1860.
Drew, Thomas, "The Fine Old Fossil Bachelor," in *The Campaign of 1856. Fremont Songs for the People. Original and Selected*. Boston: John P. Jewett and Co., 1856.

Enarc [pseud.], "Lines to a copperhead." (n.p., n.d.), *American Song Sheets*, Series 1, Volume 5, Rare Book and Special Collections Division, Library of Congress.

Facts for men who do their own thinking. Washington, 1864. Alfred Whital Stern Collection, Library of Congress.

Foster, Stephen C. "That's what's the matter!" New York: H. De Marsan, [n. d.]

The Free Soil Minstrel. New York: Martyn and Ely, [1848].

James P. Giffing, *Songs for the People, or Tippecanoe Melodies,* New York, [1840].

The Lincoln and Johnson Union Campaign Songster for the use of clubs. Containing the most popular songs. Philadelphia, 1864.

The Log Cabin Songbook: A Collection of Popular and Patriotic Songs. New York: The Log Cabin Office, [1840].

National Clay Minstrel and Frelinghuysen Melodist. Philadelphia: George Hood, [1844].

Potts, William D. *Campaign songs for Christian patriots and true Democrats, accompanied with notes.* New York, 1864.

The President Lincoln Campaign Songster. New York, 1864.

Price, T. T., "The true Jersey blue," n.p., [1861]. *Civil War Song Sheets,* Series 1, Volume 3, Rare Book and Special Collections Division, Library of Congress.

Putnam, G. P. *Patriotic songs: a collection by G. P. Putnam.* New York, 1864.

George F. Root, *Just Before the Battle Mother,* Chicago: Root & Cady, 1864.

Tippecanoe Song Book: A Collection of Log Cabin and Patriotic Melodies. Philadelphia: Marshall, Williams and Butler, [1840].

Printed Broadsides

Crittenden, John J. *Strong Appeal to the Reason of the Country. Thursday, September 13, 1860.* Collection of Broadsides. Houghton Library, Harvard University.

Evans, Estwick. *To Reverdy Johnson.* Washington, 1864. [Broadside enclosed in Evans to Abraham Lincoln, November 1, 1864; Abraham Lincoln Papers. Library of Congress.]

National Conference Committee of the Union Lincoln Association of New York. *To the loyal citizens of the United States.* New York, 1864. [Broadside: Collection of Broadsides: Houghton Library, Harvard University.]

National Union Association of Ohio. *To the citizens of Ohio.* n.p., n.d. [Broadside: Alfred Whital Stern Collection. Library of Congress.]

National Union Committee for the West. *Lincoln and Johnson: address of the National Union Committee for the West, October 24, 1864.* St. Louis, Missouri, 1864. [Broadside: Collection of Broadsides, Houghton Library, Harvard University.]

National Union Committee. *The presidential election appeal of the National Union Committee to the People of the United States.* [New York, 1864.] [Broadside: Collection of Broadsides, Houghton Library, Harvard University.]

National Union Executive Committee. *How shall soldiers vote?* New York, 1864. [Broadside: Collection of Broadsides, Houghton Library, Harvard University.]

———. *How shall we end the rebellion? Shall we coax it or crush it?* New York, 1864. [Broadside: Henry Horner Lincoln Collection, Illinois State Historical Society.]

———. *How the war commenced, and how near it is ended.* New York, 1864. [Broadside: Collection of Broadsides, Houghton Library, Harvard University.]

————. *Who shall be vice-president?: Shall he be a loyal or a disloyal man?* New York, [1864]. [Broadside: Collection of Broadsides, Houghton Library, Harvard University].

New England Loyal Publication Society Broadsides Collection, Boston Public Library.

————. Collection of Broadsides, Houghton Library, Harvard University.

New York State Central Committee [of the Union party]. *How shall soldiers vote?* [New York, 1864]. [Broadside: Collection of broadsides, Houghton Library, Harvard University.]

President Lincoln and General Grant on peace and war. Interview with the President. Mr. Lincoln's view of Democratic strategy. N.p., n.d. [Broadside: Collection of Broadsides, Houghton Library, Harvard University].

Rally Round the Old Flag!, Broadside (1862) in the Collection of Broadsides, Houghton Library, Harvard University

Slavery and the next president. n.p., n.d. [Broadside: enclosed in the Abraham Lincoln Papers, Library of Congress, October 25, 1864].

Smith, Gerrit. *To the rank and file of the Democratic party.* n.p., 1864. [Alfred Whital Stern Collection, Library of Congress].

Stand by the President! Sustain the Government! [broadside published by the Republican County Committee, Worcester, Massachusetts, October 25, 1862] Collection of Pamphlets and Broadsides, Houghton Library, Harvard University.

The Real Chicago Platform, as expounded by the Democratic orators at Chicago. Philadelphia, 1864. [Broadside: Collection of Broadsides, Houghton Library, Harvard University.]

The true issues: what leading Democrats and conservatives say. n.p., n.d. [Broadside: Collection of Broadsides, Houghton Library, Harvard University.]

To Unconditional Union Voters, San Francisco, September, 1864., Collection of Broadsides, Houghton Library, Harvard University.

Unconditional Union State Central Committee of Maryland. *Let us close our ranks! Sound once more the battle cry along the whole line! Address of the Unconditional Union State Central Committee of the People of Maryland.* [Baltimore, 1864]. [Broadside: Collection of broadsides, Houghton Library, Harvard University.]

Union Congressional Committee. *A traitor's peace.* n.p., n.d. [Broadside: Collection of Broadsides, Houghton Library, Harvard University.]

————. *The cost of a rebel peace: plain words for working-men.* Washington, 1864. [Broadside: Collection of broadsides, Houghton Library, Harvard University.]

Union Democratic Association of Cincinnati. *The Union, it must be preserved.* Cincinnati, 1864. [Broadside: Collection of Broadsides, Houghton Library, Harvard University.]

Why the South hopes for Lincoln's reelection. n.p., n.d. [Broadside: Illinois State Historical Library.]

Pamphlets, Tracts, Reprinted Speeches, and Sermons

A Democratic peace offered for the acceptance of Pennsylvania voters. Philadelphia, 1864.

A Workingman's reasons for the re-election of Abraham Lincoln. [Philadelphia,1864]. [New York Public Library.]

Address of the Democratic League to the 'Loyal Leagues' and loyal men throughout the land. New York, 1864.

Address of the Workingmen's United Political Association of the City and County of New York, [New York], n.d.

American destiny, what shall it be, Republican or Cossack? An argument addressed to the people of the late Union, North and South. New York, 1864.

Anderson, Charles. *The cause of the war: who brought it on, and for what purpose? Speech of Col. Charles Anderson, late of Texas, now of U. S. volunteers.* Loyal Publication Society, pamphlet no. 17. New York, 1864.

Apsey, William S. (Rev.). *Causes for national thanksgiving. A discourse delivered at the first Baptist Church, Bennington, November 24, 1864.* n.p., n.d.

Arnold, Isaac N. *Reconstruction: liberty the corner-stone, and Lincoln the architect. Speech of Hon. Isaac N. Arnold, of Illinois. Delivered in the House of Representatives, March 19, 1864.* Washington, 1864.

Barnett, T. J. *Abraham Lincoln, The People's Candidate,* n.p. Union State Central Committee, 1864.

Beecher, Henry Ward. *Freedom and War.* 2nd ed. Freeport, New York, 1971.

Bellows, Henry W. *The State and the Nation-Sacred to Christian Citizens. A Sermon, etc.* New York: James Miller, 1861.

———. *The War to End only when the Rebellion ceases.* New York: A. D. F. Randolph, [1863.]

———. *Unconditional Loyalty.* New York, 1863.

Bishop, Joel Prentiss. *Secession and slavery, or the effect of secession on the relation of the United States to the seceded states and to slavery therein; considered as a question of constitutional law.* Boston, 1864.

Blaine, James G. *Letter of acceptance.* n.p., [1864]. [Broadside: Alfred Whital Stern Collection, Library of Congress.]

Bristed, Charles Astor. *The Cowards' Convention.* Loyal Publication Society, pamphlet no. 68. New York, 1864.

Brooks, James. *Speech of Hon. James Brooks, of New York, on the President's message, in the House of Representatives, December, 1864.* n.p., n.d.

Brough, John. *The defenders of the country and its enemies. The Chicago platform dissected. Speech of Governor John Brough, delivered at Circleville, Ohio, September 3, 1864.* Cincinnati, Ohio, 1864.

Campbell, John. *Unionists versus Traitors. The Political Parties of Philadelphia; or the nominees that ought to be elected in 1861.* Philadelphia, n.p., 1861

Central Union Club of Brooklyn. *Campaign Document no. 1 of the Central Union Club of Brooklyn.* New York, 1864.

Chandler, William E. *The soldier's right to vote. Who opposes it? Who favors it? Or the record of the McClellan Copperheads against allowing the soldier who fights the right to vote while fighting.* Union Congressional Committee. Washington, 1864.

Coddington, David S. *The crisis and the man. Address of David S. Coddington, on the presidential crisis, delivered before the Union War Democracy, at the Cooper Institute, New York, November 1, 1864.* New York, 1864.

Coffin, N. W. et al. *A vigorous prosecution of the war the only guaranty of an honorable peace!* Boston, 1864.

Comstock, George F. *'Let us reason together' by George F. Comstock of Syracuse, late Chief Justice of the Court of Appeals.* New York, 1864.

———. *Speech of Judge Geo. F. Comstock delivered at the Brooklyn Academy of Music.* New York, 1864.

Constitution and By-Laws of the Union League of Loyal Men of the 19th Ward, Brooklyn. New York, 1863.

Cook, William A. *Opinions and practice of the founders of the Republic, in relation to arbitrary arrests, imprisonment of Tories . . . or the administration of Abraham Lincoln sustained by the sages and heroes of the Revolution.* Washington, 1864.

Corruptions and frauds of Lincoln's administration. [Democratic] Campaign document no. 14. New York, 1864.

Cox, Samuel S. *Miscegenation or Amalgamation. Fate of the Freedmen. Speech of Samuel S. Cox of Ohio delivered in the House of Representatives, February 17, 1864.* Washington, 1864.

Curtis, George Ticknor. *Hon. George Ticknor Curtis on constitutional liberty.* Democratic campaign document no. 7. New York, 1864.

————. *Address of Hon. George Ticknor Curtis at Philadelphia, September 30, 1864.* New York, 1864.

Curtis, George William. *The President. Why he should be re-elected.* New York, 1864.

Defrees, John D. *The war commenced by the rebels—Copperheads of the North their allies. Speech of John D. Defrees in Washington D.C., Monday evening, August 1, 1864.* Washington, 1864.

Democratic League. *The real motives of the rebellion. The slaveholders' conspiracy, depicted by Southern loyalists in its treason against democratic principles, as well as against the National Union. Showing a contest of slavery and nobility versus free government.* n.p., n.d.

Democratic National Committee. *The Democratic platform: General McClellan's letter of acceptance.* Campaign document No. 1. New York, 1864.

Democratic National Committee. *The life and services of General George B. McClellan.* Campaign document no. 4. New York, 1864.

Dewey, Orville. *A Talk with the Camp.* New York, 1863.

Doolittle, James R. *The Rebels and not the Republican party destroyed slavery. Speech of Hon. J. R. Doolittle of Wisconsin, delivered in the senate of the United States, February 9, 1864.* Washington, 1864.

Drake, Charles D. *Speech of Hon. Charles D. Drake. Delivered before the National Union Association of Cincinnati, October 1, 1864.* n.p., 1864.

Edge, Frederick Milne. *Whom do the English Tories want elected to the Presidency?* Loyal Publication Society, pamphlet no. 69. New York, 1864.

Ellis, George E. *The Nation's ballot and its decision: A discourse delivered in Austin Street Church, Cambridgeport and in Harvard Church, Charlestown on Sunday, November 13, 1864, being the Sunday following the Presidential election.* Boston, 1864.

Emancipation and its results. Papers of the Society for the Diffusion of Political Knowledge no. 6. New York, 1864.

Emancipation Is Peace. New York: Loyal Publication Society, 1863.

Everett, Edward. *Address delivered in Faneuil Hall, October 19, 1864: 'The Duty of Supporting the Government in the Present Crisis of Affairs.'* New England Loyal Publication Society, pamphlet no. 237. Boston, 1864.

Ewer, F. C. (Rev.) *A Rector's reply to sundry requests and demands for a political sermon; preached in Christ Church, Fifth Avenue, New York, by Rev. F. C. Ewer, on the morning of the sixteenth Sunday after Trinity 1864; and repeated by request on the evening of the subsequent Sunday. A Protest against political preaching.* New York, 1864.

Fay, Caleb T. *Address, delivered before the Union League of America, No 1. Thursday evening, February 18th, 1864, in San Francisco*. San Francisco, 1864.

Forney, John W. *Eulogy upon Stephen A. Douglas, Delivered at the Smithsonian Institute, Washington, July 3, 1861*. Philadelphia, 1861.

Gallatin, James. *Address by Hon. James Gallatin, before the Democratic Union Association, October 18, 1864: 'George McClellan as a patriot, a warrior, and a statesman.'* New York, 1864.

Hamilton, John C. *Coercion completed, or treason triumphant. Remarks by John Church Hamilton, September 24, 1864*. Loyal Publication Society, pamphlet no. 66. [New York, 1864.]

Handlin, W. W. *American politics. A moral and political work, treating of the causes of the Civil War, the nature of government and the necessities of reform*. New Orleans, 1864.

Harlan, James. *The Constitution upheld and maintained. Speech of James Harlan of the United States Senate*. [Washington, 1864.]

Hear Hon. Geo. H. Pendleton. New York, 1864.

Hiatt, James. *The Test of Loyalty*. Indianapolis: Merrill and Smith, 1864.

Hitchcock, R. D. (Rev.) *Thanksgiving for victories. Discourse by Rev. R. D. Hitchcock*. New York, 1864.

Holt, Joseph. *Report of the Judge Advocate General on the 'Order of American Knights' or 'Sons of Liberty.' A Western conspiracy in aid of the Southern rebellion*. Washington, 1864.

Hopkins, John D. *Bible view of slavery*. Papers of the Society for the Diffusion of Political Knowledge no. 8. New York, 1864.

How Shall Soldiers Vote? The New York State Central Committee of "The Boys in Blue," Rooms 16 and 17, Astor House, New York, 1864.

Hunt, James. *The negroes place in nature: a paper read before the London Anthropological Society*. New York, 1864.

Illinois Republican Union State Central Committee. *To the voters of Illinois: Address of the Republican Union State Central committee*. n.p. [1864]. [Broadside: Henry Horner Lincoln Collection, Illinois State Historical Library.]

Immense Meeting in Favor of the Union (Philadelphia, [1863]), Houghton Library, Harvard University.

Installation ceremony, for the use of subordinate councils of the Union League of America in Illinois. By authority of the State Grand Council , [Springfield: Union League of America, 1863]. Illinois State Historical Library

Johnson, A. B. *The approaching presidential election (respectfully inscribed to the Chicago convention.) Utica, August 18, 1864*. Utica, 1864.

Johnson, Reverdy. *Speech of Hon Reverdy Johnson, of Maryland, delivered before the Brooklyn McClellan Central Association, October 21, 1864*. New York, 1864.

Jones, Charles. *A hopeful view of national affairs. A thanksgiving sermon preached at the Sailors Snug harbor, Staten Island, September 11, 1864 by Charles Jones, Chaplain*. New York, 1864.

Jones, William D. *Mirror of Modern Democracy: A History of the Democratic Party from its Organization in 1825 to its Last Great Achievement, the Rebellion of 1861*. New York, 1864.

Kelley, William D. *Replies of the Hon. William D. Kelley to George Northrop esq. In the joint debate in the fourth congressional district*. Philadelphia, 1864.

————. *Reply of William D. Kelley to George Northrop, esq. In West Philadelphia Hall, Thursday evening, October 6, 1864.* n.p., n.d. [Broadside: enclosed in Kelley to Abraham Lincoln, October 21, 1864, Abraham, Lincoln Papers, Library of Congress.]

Kirkland, Charles P. *The destiny of our country: an address delivered before the 'Association of Alumni' of Hamilton College, New York, July 20, 1864.* New York, 1864.

Laboulaye, Edouard M. *Upon whom rests the guilt of this war? Separation: war without end.* Loyal Publication Society. New York, 1863.

Lieber, Francis *Manual of Political Ethics.* 2 vols., Boston: C. C. Little and J. Brown, 1838–1839.

————. *Lincoln or McClellan?* Loyal Publication Society, pamphlet no. 67. New York, 1864.

————. *No Party Now But All For Our Country.* New York, 1863.

Lincoln's treatment of Gen. Grant. Mr. Lincoln's treatment of Gen. McClellan. Democratic campaign document no. 12. New York, 1864.

Lord, Charles E. *Slavery, secession and the constitution. An appeal to our country's loyalty.* Boston, 1864.

Loring, George B. *Another life long Democrat testifies to the truth! A patriotic letter from Dr. George B. Loring of Salem, Massachusetts. Support of the administration the only path to peace, unity, national prosperity. The elevation of McClellan a national calamity!!* n.p., n.d. [Alfred Whital Stern Collection, Library of Congress.]

Lowell, James Russell. *The president's policy.* Union league pamphlet no. 71. Philadelphia, 1864.

Loyal Publication Society [pamphlet no. 56]. *The assertions of a secessionist. From the speech of A. H. Stevens of Georgia. November 14, 1860.* New York, 1864. [Illinois State Historical Library.]

Loyal Publication Society [pamphlet no. 64]. *Letters of loyal soldiers* (4 parts). New York, 1864.

———— [pamphlet no. 65]. *The submissionists and their record: the dodges of Mr. Pendleton, Chicago candidate for vice-president.* New York, 1864.

————. *The echoes from the army. What our soldiers say about the copperheads.* New York, 1863.

Manhattan Union Club. *Address to the Young Men of New York.* [New York, 1864]. [New York Public Library.]

Mansfield, Edward D. *The issues and duties of the day.* Cincinnati, 1864.

Marble, Manton. *Freedom of the press wantonly violated. Letter of Mr. Marble to President Lincoln.* Papers of the Society for the Diffusion of Political Knowledge, no. 22. New York, 1864.

McClellan, George B. *Complete report on the organization and campaigns of the Army of the Potomac, by Major-General George B. McClellan.* Democratic campaign document no. 3. New York, 1864.

————. *West Point oration of Gen. George B. McClellan.* Democratic campaign document no. 4?. New York, 1864.

McKaye, James. *The mastership and its fruits: emancipated slave face to face with his old master. (A supplemental report to Edwin B. Stanton, Secretary of War, by James McKaye, special commissioner.)* [New York, 1864.]

Miscegenation indorsed by the Republican party. Democratic Party Campaign document no. 11. New York, 1864.

Moorhead, Hon. J. K. *'The perpetuity of the Union': speech delivered in the House of Representatives, March 26, 1864*. Washington, 1864.

Morse, Samuel et al. *The Constitution. Addresses of Prof. Morse, Mr. George Ticknor Curtis, and Mr. S. J. Tilden at the organization*. Papers of the Society for the Diffusion of Political Knowledge no. 1. New York, 1864.

Morse, Samuel F. B. *An argument on the ethical position of slavery on the social system, and its relation to the politics of the day*. Papers of the Society for the Diffusion of Political Knowledge no. 1. New York, 1863.

Mr. Lincoln's arbitrary arrests. The acts which the Baltimore platform approves. Democratic Party Campaign document no. 13. New York, 1864.

Murdock, William David Clark. *An address to the Democratic party on the present crisis and the next presidential election*. Washington, 1864.

Narrative of sufferings of US prisoners of war in the hands of rebel authorities. Loyal Publication Society, pamphlet no. 76. New York, 1864.

National Union Committee. *Pretexts of the rebels and their sympathisers refuted by the logic of facts. Rebellion against free government, as well as against the National Union, resulting from the conspiracy of the Slaveholding aristocracy; illustrated in the speech of the Hon. Lorenzo Sherwood, delivered before the Unionists of the city of Brooklyn, September, 1864 . . .* New York, 1864.

Nelson J. Waterbury, *Documents Relative to the Withdrawal of Nelson J. Waterbury from the Canvass in the Eighth Congressional District, New York, November 1862*. New York: Baptist & Taylor, 1862.

Only authentic life of Abraham Lincoln alias 'Old Abe': a son of the west. n.p., n.d. [Illinois State Historical Library.]

Parker, Joel. *Speech of Governor Joel Parker, at Freehold, NJ, Aug 20, 1864. Subject: Our national troubles—their causes and the remedy*. [Democratic] Campaign document no. 6. New York, 1864.

Patriotism. New York: Loyal Publication Society, 1863.

Payne, A. *Remarks at Central Falls, Rhode Island, November 1, 1864*. Providence, [1864].

Perham, Sidney. *The slaveholders' rebellion and modern democracy. Speech of Hon. Sidney Perham of Maine, in the House of Representatives, May 3, 1864*. Washington, 1864.

Perry, Aaron F. *Speech of Aaron F. Perry, esq. Delivered before the National Union Association, at Mozart Hall, Cincinnati, September 20, 1864*. Cincinnati, 1864.

Pierrepont, Edwards. *Speech of Edwards Pierrepont, delivered at the Convention and mass meeting of the democracy opposed to the Chicago platform, held at the Cooper Institute, New York, November 1, 1864*. New York, 1864.

Political Conservative circular; from an 'old-line Webster Whig' of forty years voting experience in support of constitutional freedom and sound conservative principles, with reasons for opposition to the re-election of Abraham Lincoln, for his gross violations of both spirit and provisions of the same. Boston, 1864.

Pomeroy, Samuel S. *Speech by Hon. S. C. Pomeroy, on the platform and party of the future, and national freedom secured by an amended constitution. Delivered in the senate of the United States, March 10, 1864*. Washington, 1864.

Powell, George May. *'Facts and figures for the hour.' Speech of George May Powell, of Wisconsin*. Washington, 1864.

Raymond, Henry J. *History of the administration of President Lincoln: including his speeches, letters and addresses, proclamations and messages. With a preliminary sketch of his life*. New York, 1864. [New York Public Library].

————. *The life of Abraham Lincoln of Illinois.* Chicago, 1864.

————. *The life of Abraham Lincoln, by Henry J. Raymond and of Andrew Johnson by John Savage.* Union Congressional Committee. New York, 1864.

Republican opinions about Lincoln. [Democratic] Campaign document no. 18. New York, 1864.

Sangamon Tribune, *An argument against the abolition of the Constitution of the United States.* Springfield, Illinois, 1864.

Schenck, Robert C. *No compromise with treason. Remarks of Mr. Schenck of Ohio in reply to Mr. Fernando Wood in the debate on the resolution to expel Mr. Long. Delivered in the House of Representatives, April 11, 1864.* [Washington, 1864].

Schurz, Carl. *'For the great empire of liberty, forward!' Speech of Maj.-General Carl Schurz delivered at Concert Hall, Philadelphia, on Friday, September 16, 1864.* New York, 1864.

Seward, William Henry. *Issues of the conflict: terms of peace: remarks of the Hon. William H. Seward, on the occasion of the fall of Atlanta, at Auburn, Saturday, Sept. 3, 1864.* New York, 1864.

Seymour, Horatio. *Speech of Governor Seymour at Philadelphia.* [Democratic] Campaign document no. 21. New York, 1864.

Seymour, Truman. *The condition of the South and the duty of the North. As set forth in a letter from Gen. T. Seymour, lately returned from 'under fire' at Charleston.* New York, 1864.

Shall the North vote for a disunion peace? Chicago Tribune Campaign document no. 1. Chicago, 1864.

Sights and notes by a looker on in Vienna. Dedicated to the Union army! Washington, 1864.

Smith, Gerrit. *Gerrit Smith to his neighbours.* [Peterboro, New York, 1864].

————. *Letter on Lincoln's nomination and acceptance.* Loyal Publication Society, pamphlet no. 63. New York, 1864.

————. *Letter to Hon. D. C. Littlejohn from Gerrit Smith, on the country.* [Peterboro, New York, 1864].

Smith, John [pseud.] *Speech of John Smith esq. Not delivered at Smithville, Sept. 15, 1864.* New York, 1864.

Spear, Samuel T. (Rev.) *Our Country and its Cause. A discourse preached October 2nd, 1864, in the South Presbyterian Church, of Brooklyn.* New York, 1864.

Spear, Samuel T. (Rev.) *The Duty of the Hour.* New York, 1863.

Speeches delivered at the Republican Union festival, in commemoration of the birth of Washington. New York: Putnam, 1862.

Stanbery, Henry. *The ballot and the bullet: How to save the nation. Address of Henry Stanbery, esq. Delivered in Newport, Ky. Saturday evening, Sept. 17, 1864.* Cincinnati, 1864.

Stebbins, Horatio. *The president, the people and the war: a thanksgiving discourse by Horatio Stebbins, minister of the first Unitarian Society in San Francisco.* San Francisco, 1864.

Stevens, John A. *Sherman vs. Hood. 'A low tart inclined to be very sweet'—something for Douglas Democrats to remember—an appeal to history—where Governor Seymour got this lesson—on the Chicago surrender.* Loyal Publication Society, pamphlet no. 61. New York, 1864.

————. *The submissionists and their record.* Loyal Publication Society, pamphlet no. 65. New York, 1864.

Stillé, Charles J. *How a free people conduct a long war.* Philadelphia, 1862.

Stowe, Harriet Beecher. *Abraham Lincoln.* n.p., n.d. [Reprinted from *Littell's Living Age* no. 1027 (Feb 6, 1864)].

Sumner, Charles. *Slavery and the rebellion, one and inseparable: speech of Hon. Charles Sumner, before the Young Men's Republican Union, at Cooper Institute, New York, on the afternoon of Nov 5, 1864.* Boston, 1864.

———. *Universal emancipation, without compensation: speech of Hon. Charles Sumner, on the proposed amendment to the Constitution, abolishing slavery throughout the United States in the Senate of the United States, April 8, 1864.* Union Congressional Committee. Washington, 1864.

Swinton, William. *A few plain words with the rank and file of the Union armies.* Union Congressional Committee. Washington, 1864.

———. *The 'Times' review of McClellan: his military career reviewed and exposed.* New York, 1864.

———. *The war for the Union: the first, second, third and fourth years of the war.* Loyal Publication Society, pamphlet no. 62. [New York, 1864].

Ten Eyck, John C. *Reconstruction in the states: speech of Hon. John C. Ten Eyck, of New Jersey. Delivered in the senate of the United States, May 6, 1864.* Union Congressional Committee. Washington, 1864.

Thayer, M. Russell. *Reconstruction of the rebel states: speech of Hon. M. R. Thayer delivered in the House of Representatives, April 20, 1864.* Union Congressional Committee. Washington, 1864.

The Death of Slavery, Letter from Peter Cooper to Governor Seymour. New York: Loyal Publication Society, 1863.

The Democratic Anti-Abolition State Rights Association of the City of New York. New York, 1863.

The Democratic party the soldier's friend. Legislation that speaks for itself. n.p., n.d. [Library of Congress.]

The Democratic Platform for 50 years. The immortal Kentucky and Virginia resolutions of 1798, with the history and application to the present to the present canvass. Chicago, 1864. [Illinois State Historical Library.]

The Democratic Times. n.p., n.d.

The Lincoln catechism wherein the eccentricities and beauties of despotism are fully set forth. New York, 1864.

The loyalists' ammunition. Philadelphia, 1863.

The loyalty for the times: a voice from Kentucky. April 1864. n.p., n.d.

The next presidency. The Chicago convention. Shall the people or 'the politicians' decide the issues? By one of the Democrats of Jackson's day. n.p., [1864]. [Illinois State Historical Library.]

The next presidential election. n.p., n.d.

The only alternative: a tract for the times, by a plain man. Philadelphia, 1864.

The positions of Abraham Lincoln and George B. McClellan on the Union. To unconditional Union voters. n.p., n.d.

The President's usurpations. The President's ultimatum to the propositions of the Confederate commissioners asking for peace. n.p., n.d. [Illinois State Historical Library.]

The Sumter Anniversary, 1863. Opinions of Loyalists Concerning the Great Question of the Times. New York, 1863.

Thompson, Joseph P. *Peace through victory; a thanksgiving sermon, preached in Broadway tabernacle church, New York, on Sabbath, September 11, 1864.* Loyal Publication Society. New York, 1864.

———. *Revolution against free government not a right but a crime: an address by Joseph P. Thompson delivered before the Union league club and published at their request.* New York, 1864.

Throop, Montgomery H. *The future: a political essay by Montgomery H. Throop.* New York, 1864.

Train, George Francis. *George Francis Train in Chicago: letter from a member of the convention.* n.p., n.d.

———. *Great Speech on the withdrawal of McClellan and the impeachment of Lincoln.* New York, 1864. [Illinois State Historical Society.]

Turpie, David. *Speech of Mr. Turpie.* Papers of the Society for the Diffusion of Political Knowledge no. 2. New York, 1863.

Union Congressional Committee. *Biographical sketch of Andrew Johnson of Tennessee, together with his speech at Nashville, June 10, 1864, and his letter accepting the nomination as vice-president of the United States, tendered by the National Union Convention held at Baltimore on the 7th and 8th of June, 1864.* Washington, 1864.

———. *Copperhead conspiracy in the north-west. An exposé of the treasonous order of the sons of 'Sons of Liberty.'* Washington, 1864.

———. *Peace to be enduring must be conquered.* New York, 1864.

———. *Political dialogues. Soldiers on their right to vote, and the men they should support.* Washington, 1864.

———. *Shall we have an armistice?* Washington, 1864.

———. *The Chicago copperhead convention (August 29, 1864): the treasonable and revolutionary utterances of the men who composed it, extracts from all the notable speeches delivered in and out of the National 'Democratic' convention.* Washington, 1864.

———. *The great surrender to the rebels in arms: the armistice: 'immediate efforts to be made for a cessation of hostilities': peace and disunion platform of the Chicago Copperhead convention.* Washington, [1864].

———. *The military and naval situation, and the glorious achievement of our soldiers and sailors.* Washington, 1864.

———. *The opinions of Abraham Lincoln, upon slavery and its issues: indicated by his speeches, letters, messages and proclamations.* Washington, 1864.

———. *The votes of the copperheads in the Congress of the United States.* [Washington, 1864].

Union League of America Executive Committee. *To the loyal citizens of the United States.* Washington, 1864.

Union League of Philadelphia, *Essays on Political Organization.* Philadelphia, 1868.

———. *A savory dish for loyal men.* Philadelphia, 1863.

———. *Abraham Lincoln.* Philadelphia, 1864.

———. *Address by the Union league of Philadelphia to the Citizens of Pennsylvania in Favor of the Re-election of Abraham Lincoln.* Philadelphia, 1864.

———. *The boot on the other leg, or loyalty above party.* Philadelphia, 1863.

———. *The will of the people.* [Philadelphia, 1864].

Union party state central committee of Pennsylvania. *Address of the Union State central committee to the people of Pennsylvania and the platforms of the two organizations for 1865.* Philadelphia, 1865.

Upham, Nathaniel. *Rebellion—slavery—peace. An address on the subject of rebellion, slavery and peace, delivered at Concord, New Hampshire, March 2, 1864.* Concord, NH, 1864.

Vallandigham, Clement L. *Speeches, arguments, and letters of Clement L. Vallandigham.* New York: J. Walter, 1864.

Voorhees, Daniel W. *Speech of D. W. Voorhees of Indiana, delivered in the House of Representatives, March 9, 1864.* Washington, 1864.

Voters' catechism. Plain questions and answers for the campaign. New York, 1864.

Wade, Benjamin F. *Facts for the people: Ben Wade on McClellan: and Gens. Hooker and Heinzelman's testimony: a crushing review of little Mac's military career.* Cincinnati, 1864.

Wakeman, Abram. *'Union' on dis-union principles! The Chicago platform, McClellan's letter of acceptance, and Pendleton's Hasking letter, reviewed and exposed. Speech...at Greenfield, Connecticut, Nov. 3, 1864.* New York, 1864. [Illinois State Historical Library.]

Walbridge, Hiram. *Speech of Gen. Hiram Walbridge, delivered before the convention of the War Democracy at Cooper Institute, New York, Tuesday, November 1, 1864.* New York, 1864. [Illinois State Historical Library.]

Walker, Robert J. *Letter of Hon. R. J. Walker in favor of the re-election of Abraham Lincoln.* New York, 1864.

War Democratic State Committee of New York. *Country Before Party: The Voice of the Loyal Democrats.* New York, 1864.

———. *Speech of Hon. Edwards Pierrepont, delivered at the convention and mass meeting of the Democracy opposed to the Chicago Convention, held at the Cooper Institute, New York, November 1, 1864 .* New York, 1864.

Wayland, Francis. *No failure for the North.* New York, 1864.

Wells, David Ames. *Our burden and our strength, or, a comprehensive and popular examination of the debt and resources of our country, present and prospective, by David A. Wells.* Troy, New York, 1864.

Whiting, William. *Military Government of Hostile Territory in time of war.* Boston, 1864.

———. *The return of rebellious states to the Union. A letter from Hon. Wm. Whiting to the Union League of Philadelphia.* Philadelphia, 1864.

Wilkes, George. *McClellan: 'who he is and what he has done' and Little Mac: 'from Ball's Bluff to Antietam.' Both in one. Revised by the author. By an old-line Democrat.* New York, 1864. [Illinois State Historical Library.]

Wilkinson, Joseph H. *Views on the war, the administration and the people, with special remarks on McClellan's campaign. By a soldier, three years in the Army of the Potomac.* Manchester, NH, 1864.

Williams, I. T. *The issues of the canvass. Speech of I. T. Williams.* n.p., n.d.

Wilson, James F. *A free Constitution: speech of Hon. James F. Wilson, of Iowa, delivered in the House of Representatives, March 19, 1864.* Washington, 1864.

Wilson, Thomas L. *A brief history of the cruelties and atrocities of the rebellion. Complied from the most authentic sources, by Thomas L. Wilson.* [Washington, 1864.]

Winthrop, Robert C. *Great Speech of Hon. Robert C. Winthrop, at New London, Conn., October 18. 'The Principles and interests of the Republican party against the Union. The election of McClellan the only hope for Union and peace.* [Democratic] Campaign document no. 23: New York, 1864.

————. *Speech of Hon. Robert C. Winthrop, at the great ratification meeting in union Square, New York, Sept. 17, 1864.* [Democratic] Campaign document no. 9. New York, 1864.

Wright, Charles. *Our political practice. The usurpations of vice through the popular negligence.* 3 vols. Boston, 1864–1865.

Wright, J. S. *Citizenship, sovereignty.* Chicago, 1864.

Young Men's Republican Union. *Our third campaign.* New York, 1864. [Broadside: Collection of broadsides, New York Public Library.]

Young, Harrison Perry. Indestructibility of the American Union. A lecture, by Harrison Perry Young, delivered before the Parker fraternity, in Templar's Hall, Boston, Mass. Boston, 1864.

OFFICIAL PROCEEDINGS

Appleton's annual cyclopaedia and register of important events. Embracing political, military, and ecclesiastical affairs; public documents; biography, statistics, commerce, finance, literature, science, agriculture, and mechanical industry. New York, 1865.

Chronicle of the Union League of Philadelphia, 1862 to 1902. Philadelphia, 1902.

Congressional Globe, 37th Cong., 1st sess..

————. 2d sess.

————. 3rd sess.

Congressional Globe, 38th Cong., 1st sess.

————. 2d sess.

Congressional Serial Set, Serial no. 1199 (38th Cong., 1st sess.), House of Representatives Misc Doc. 16: Thomas L. Price vs. Joseph W. McClurg, 5th Congressional District of Missouri; Doc. 17: Charles W. Carrigan vs. M. Russell Thayer, 5th Congressional District of Pennsylvania; Doc. 20: James H. Birch vs. Austin A. King, 6th Congressional District of Missouri; Doc. 26: John Kline vs. Leonard Myers, 3rd Congressional District of Pennsylvania; Doc. 27: J. B. S. Todd vs. William Jayne, delegate from Territory of Dakota.

————, Serial no. 1200 (38th Cong., 1st sess.), House of Representatives Misc. Doc. 36: John McHenry Jr., vs. George H. Yeaman, 2d Congressional District of Kentucky; Doc. 43: James Lindsay vs. John G. Scott, 3rd Congressional District of Missouri.

————, Serial no. 1269 (39th Cong., 1st sess.), House of Representatives Misc Doc. 7: Wm. E. Dodge vs. James Brooks, 8th Congressional District of New York.

————, Serial no. 1270 (39th Cong., 1st Sess.), House of Representatives Misc. Doc. 8: Chas. Follett vs. Columbus Delanao, 13th Congressional District of Ohio; Doc. 9: Smith Fuller vs John L. Dawson, 21st Congressional District of Pennsylvania; Doc. 10: Aug. C. Baldwin vs. Rowland E. Trowbridge, 5th Congressional District of Michigan; Doc. 11: Henry D. Washburn vs. Daniel W. Voorhees, 7th Congressional District of Indiana.

————, Serial no. 1271 (39th Cong., 1st sess.) House of Representatives Misc. Doc. 93: S. H. Boyd vs. John R. Kelso: 4th Congressional District of Missouri; Doc. 117: Wm. H. Koontz vs. Alexander H. Coffroth, 16th Congressional District of Pennsylvania.

————, Serial no. 1198 (38th Cong., 1st sess.), House of Representatives Misc. Doc 12: Lewis McKenzie vs. B. M. Kitchen, 7th Congressional District of Virginia;

Doc. 13: John P. Bruce vs. Benjamin F. Loan, 7th Congressional District of Missouri; Doc. 14: Hon. John S. Sleeper vs. Alexander H. Rice, 3rd Congressional District of Massachusetts; Doc. 15: Samuel Knox vs. Frnacis P. Blair. Jr., 1st Congressional District of Missouri.

Dubin, Michael J. *United States Congressional Elections, 1788–1997 : The Official Results of the Elections of the 1st Through 105th Congresses.* Jefferson, N.C.: McFarland, 1998.

John L. Moore, Jon P. Preimesberger, David R. Tarr, eds., *Congressional Quarterly Guide to US Elections* (Washington DC: CQ Press, 2001.

Loyal Publication Society. *Proceedings at the first anniversary meeting of the Loyal Publication Society.* New York, 1864.

Loyal Publication Society. *Proceedings at the second anniversary meeting of the Loyal Publication Society. February 11, 1865, with the annual reports, prepared by order of the society, by the secretary.* New York, 1865.

Loyal Publication Society. *Who is Responsible for this War? Who Accountable for its Horrors and Desolation?* n.p., [1864]. [Broadside: Collection of broadsides, Houghton Library, Harvard University.]

Murphy, D. F. *Proceedings of the National Union Convention, Baltimore, June, 1864* [reported by D. F. Murphy, of the official corps of reporters for the US senate.] New York, 1864.

Porter, Kirk H. and Donald B. Johnson, eds., *National Party Platforms, 1840–1956.* Urbana: University of Illinois Press, 1956.

Proceedings of the Convention of the Loyal Leagues Held at Mechanics Hall, Utica, Tuesday, 26 May, 1863. New York, 1863.

Proceedings of the first three Republican national conventions of 1856, 1860 and 1864: including proceedings of the antecedent national convention held at Pittsburg, in February, 1856, as reported by Horace Greeley. Minneapolis, Minn.: C.W. Johnson, 1893.

Proceedings of the National Convention, Union League of America, held at Cleveland, May 20 and 21, 1863. Washington, 1863.

Proceedings of the Union League of America, June 6, 1864. Washington, 1864.

Richardson, James D. ed. *Messages and Papers of the Presidents.* 20 vols., New York: Bureau of National Literature, 1917.

The Tribune Almanac and Political Register for 1860. New York, 1861.

The Tribune Almanac and Political Register for 1861. New York, 1862.

The Tribune Almanac and Political Register for 1862. New York, 1863.

The Tribune Almanac and Political Register for 1863. New York, 1864.

The Tribune Almanac and Political Register for 1864. New York, 1865.

The Tribune Almanac and Political Register for 1865. New York, 1866.

Union League of Philadelphia. *First annual report of the Board of Directors of the Union League of Philadelphia, December 14, 1863.* Philadelphia, 1863.

———. *Second annual report of the Board of Directors of the Union League of Philadelphia. December 12, 1864.* Philadelphia, 1864.

US War Department. *The war of the rebellion: a compilation of the official records of the Union and Confederate armies.* 128 vols. Washington, 1880–1901.

DIARIES, LETTERS, AND MEMOIRS

Adams, Charles Francis, Jr. *Individuality in Politics: A Lecture Delivered in Steinway Hall, New York, Wednesday Evening, April 21, 1880.* New York: Independent Republican Association, 1880.

————. *A cycle of Adams letters, 1861–1865.* Worthington Chauncey Ford, ed. 2 vols., London, 1921.

Baker, George E. *The works of William H. Seward.* 5 vols. Boston, 1853–1884.

Basler, Roy P., Marion Dolores Platt, and Lloyd A. Dunlap, eds. *The Collected Works of Abraham Lincoln.* 8 vols. New Brunswick, New Jersey: Rutgers University Press, 1953–1955.

Bates, David Homer. *Lincoln in the Telegraph Office: Recollections of the United States Military Telegraph Corps During the Civil War.* 2nd ed. Lincoln, Nebraska, 1995.

Bates, Edward. *The diary of Edward Bates, 1859–1866.* Howard K. Beale (ed.) Annual Report of the American Historical Association, 1930, vol. IV. Washington, 1933.

Bellows, Henry W. *Historical sketch of the Union League Club of New York, its organisation and work, 1863–1879.* New York: G. P. Putnam's Sons, 1879.

Belmont, August. *A Few Letters and Speeches of the Late Civil War.* New York: privately printed, 1870.

Benton, Joel, ed. *Greeley on Lincoln, with Mr. Greeley's letters to Charles A. Dana and a lady friend.* New York, 1893.

Bigelow, John G. *Retrospectives of an active life.* 5 vols. New York, 1910–1913.

Bigelow, John G. ed, *Letters and Literary Memorials of Samuel J. Tilden.* 2 vols. New York, 1908.

Black, Chauncy F. *Essays and speeches of Jeremiah S. Black.* New York, 1895.

Blaine, James G. *Twenty years of Congress: from Lincoln to Garfield: with a review of the events which led to the political revolution of 1860.* 2 vols. Norwich, Conn., 1884.

Blassingame, John W. ed. *The Frederick Douglass Papers.* New Haven, 1971.

Boutwell, George S. *Reminiscences of sixty years in public affairs.* 2 vols. New York, 1902.

————. *Speeches and papers relating to the rebellion.* Boston, 1867.

————. *Why I am a Republican. A history of the Republican party . . . With biographical sketches of the Republican candidates.* Hartford, Conn., 1884.

Brooks, Noah. "Lincoln's Re-election," *The Century Magazine* XLIX (April 1895): 865–72.

————. *Washington D.C. in Lincoln's time: A memoir of the Civil War era by the newspaper man who knew Lincoln best.* Herbert Mitang, ed. Athens: University of Georgia Press, 1989.

Brown, George R. (ed.). *Reminiscences of Senator William M. Stewart of Nevada.* New York, 1908.

Browne, Francis Fisher. *The Everyday Life of Abraham Lincoln.* 2nd ed. Lincoln, Nebraska, 1995.

Browning, Orville Hickman. *The Diary of Orville Hickman Browning,* edited by Theodore Calvin Pease and James G. Randall. 2 vols. Springfield, Ill.: Illinois State Historical Library, 1925–1933.

Brownson, Orestes A. *The American republic: its Constitution, tendencies and destiny.* Boston, 1865.

Bryant, William Cullen. *The letters of William Cullen Bryant.* William Cullen Bryant III and Thomas G. Voss (eds), 5 vols. New York, 1984.

Burn, James D. *Three years among the working-classes of the United States during the war.* London, 1865.

Butler, Benjamin F. *Autobiography and personal reminiscences of Major-General Benjamin F. Butler.* Boston, 1892.

Carpenter, F. B. *The inner life of Abraham Lincoln: six months on the White House.* 2nd ed. Lincoln, Nebraska, 1995. [originally published as *Six months at the White House with Abraham Lincoln,* New York, 1866.]

Chase, Salmon P. *Diary and Correspondence.* 2 vols. Annual Report of the American Historical Association, 1902. Washington, DC, 1903.

Cheney, Mary Bushell. ed. *The life and letters of Horace Bushnell,* New York, 1905.

Child, Lydia Maria. *Letters of Lydia Maria Child.* John G. Whittier, ed. Boston: Houghton, Mifflin, 1882.

Church, Charles A. *History of the Republican party in Illinois 1854–1912, with a review of the aggressions of the Slave-power.* Rockfort, Illinois, 1912.

Congdon, Charles T. *Reminiscences of a journalist.* Boston: J. R. Osgood, 1880.

Cox ,Samuel S. *Eight years in Congress, from 1857–1865. Memoir and speeches. By Samuel S. Cox.* New York, D. Appleton and Company, 1865.

———. *Union—Disunion—Reunion. Three decades of federal legislation, 1855–1885.* Providence, R.I., 1885.

Dana, Charles A. *Recollections of the Civil War: with the leaders at Washington and in the field in the sixties.* New York, 1913.

Dana, Richard Henry Jr. *An address upon the life and services of Edward Everett: delivered before the municipal authorities and citizens of Cambridge, February 22, 1865.* Cambridge, Mass., 1865.

———. *Speeches in stirring times, and letters to a son.* Edited by Richard Henry Dana III, Boston: Houghton Mifflin, 1910.

Dennett, Tyler, ed. *Lincoln and the Civil War in the diaries and letters of John Hay.* New York, 1939, repr. 1988.

Daniel S. Dickinson, ed., *Speeches, Correspondence etc., of the late Daniel S. Dickinson of New York,* ed. John R. Dickinson. 2 vols. New York: Putnam, 1867.

Donald, David H. *Inside Lincoln's Cabinet: The Civil War Diaries of Salmon P. Chase.* New York, 1954.

Fehrenbacher, Don E. and Virginia Fehrenbacher. *Recollected Words of Abraham Lincoln.* Stanford University Press, 1996.

Fillmore, Millard. *Millard Fillmore papers.* Frank H. Severence, ed., 2 vols. Buffalo, New York, 1907.

Foner, Philip S. *The life and writings of Frederick Douglass.* 5 vols. New York, 1950.

Forbes, John Murray. *Letters and recollections of John Murray Forbes.* Sarah Forbes Hughes, ed., 2 vols. Boston, 1899.

Forney, John W. *Anecdotes of public men.* New York, 1873–1881.

Freidel, Frank B. *Union pamphlets of the Civil War, 1861–1865.* 2 vols. Cambridge, Mass., 1967.

Giddings, Joshua R. *History of the rebellion.* New York, 1864.

Gilmore, James R. *Personal recollections of Abraham Lincoln and the Civil War.* Boston, 1898.

Grimke, Frederick *The Nature and Tendency of Free Institutions.* Cincinatti: H. W. Derby, 1848. Reprint, John William Ward, ed., Cambridge, Mass.: Harvard University Press, 1968.

Greeley, Horace. *Recollections of a busy life.* New York, 1868.

Gurowski, Adam von. *Diary.* 3 vols. Washington, 1862–1866.

Handy, Robert T. *A History of Union Theological Seminary in New York.* New York: Columbia University Press, 1987.

Haven, Gilbert. *National sermons.* Boston, 1869.

Hay, John. *Letters of John Hay and extracts from his diary*. 3 vols. Washington, DC, 1908.

Hazelwell, C.C. "The twentieth presidential election," *Atlantic Monthly* 14 (1864): 633–41.

Higginson, Thomas Wentworth ed. *Harvard Memorial Biographies*. 2 vols: Cambridge, Mass.: Harvard University Press, 1867.

Hoar, George Frisbie. *Autobiography of seventy years*. 2 vols. New York, 1903.

Ide, George B. *Battle echoes, or lessons from the war*. Boston, 1866.

Installation ceremony, for the use of subordinate councils of the Union League of America in Illinois. By authority of the State Grand Council. Springfield, 1863. [Illinois State Historical Library.]

Johnson, Andrew. *The papers of Andrew Johnson*. Larry P. Graf and Ralph W. Haskins, eds., 14 vols. Nashville, Tennessee, 1967.

Julian, George W. *Political recollections, 1840–72*. Chicago, 1884.

———. *Speeches on political questions*. New York, 1872.

LaRocca, Charles J. ed. *This Regiment of Heroes: A Compilation of Primary Materials Pertaining to the 124th New York State Volunteers*. Montgomery, N.Y., 1991.

Lathrop, George Parsons. *History of the Union League of Philadelphia from its origin and foundation to the year 1882*. Philadelphia, 1884.

Lee, Elizabeth Blair. *Wartime Washington: The Civil War Letters of Elizabeth Blair Lee*. Virginia Jeans Laas, ed. Urbana, Ill., 1991.

Locke, David Ross. *Civil War letters of Petroleum V. Nasby*. 2nd ed. Columbus, Ohio, 1962.

———. *The Nasby Papers. By Petroleum V. Nasby, 'paster uv sed church in charg.'* New York, 1912 edition.

The Loyal National League [of New York]. New York, [1864].

Lusk, D. W. *Politics and politicians: a succinct history of the politics of Illinois from 1856 to 1882 with anecdotes from 1809 to 1856*. Springfield, Ill., 1884.

McClure, Alexander K. *Lincoln and men of war-times: some personal recollections of war and politics during the Lincoln administration*. Philadelphia, 1892 edition.

———. *Old time notes of Pennsylvania: a connected and chronological record of the commercial, industrial and educational advancement of Pennsylvania, and the inner history of all political movements since the adoption of the constitution of 1838*. 2 vols. Library ed. Philadelphia: John C. Winston, 1905.

———. *Recollections of half a century*. Salem, Mass., 1902.

McCulloch, Hugh. *Men and measures of half a century*. New York, 1900.

McLoughlin, William G., ed. *The American Evangelicals, 1800–1900: an anthology*. New York, 1968.

Moore, Frank (ed.). *The rebellion record: a diary of American events, with documents, narratives, illustrative incidents, poetry, etc.* 12 vols. 1861–1868.

Moore, Frank. *The Civil War in song and story*. New York, 1889 edition.

Nevins, Allan and Thomas, Milton H. eds. *The Diary of George Templeton Strong*. 4 vols. New York: Macmillan, 1952. Vol. III: *The Civil War, 1860–1865*.

New England Loyal Publication Society, *Report of the executive committee of the New England Loyal Publication Society, May 1, 1865*. Boston, 1865.

Nicolay, John G. and John Hay. *Abraham Lincoln: A History*. 10 vols. New York: Century, 1890.

Norton, Charles Elliot. *Letters of Charles Elliot Norton*. Sarah Norton and M. A. de Wolfe Howe (eds.), 2 vols. Boston, 1913.

Perkins, Howard Cecil. *Northern Editorials on Secession.* 2 vols. New York: D. Appleton–Century, 1942.

Phillips, Wendell. *Speeches, lectures and letters.* Boston, 1864.

Pierce, Edward L. *Memoir and letters of Charles Sumner.* 4 vols. Boston, 1877–93.

Poore, Benjamin Perley. *Perley's reminiscences of sixty years in the national metropolis.* Philadelphia, 1886.

Ruchames, Louis, ed. *The letters of William Lloyd Garrison.* 4 vols. Cambridge, Mass. 1976.

Schurz, Carl. *Speeches, correspondence and political papers of Carl Schurz,* 'selected and edited by Frederic Bancroft on behalf of the Carl Schurz Memorial Committee.' New York, 1913.

———. *Abraham Lincoln: an essay.* New York, 1891.

Sears, Stephen B. ed. *The Civil War Papers of George B. McClellan.* New York: Ticknor & Fields, 1989.

Seward, Frederick W. *Seward at Washington as Senator and secretary of state.* 2 vols. New York, 1891.

Sherman, John. *Recollections of forty years in the House, senate, and cabinet.* 2 vols. Chicago, 1895.

Silber, Nina and Mary Beth Sievens, eds. *Yankee Correspondence: Civil War letters between New England soldiers and the home front.* Charlottesville: University of Virginia Press, 1996.

Smith, William Ernest. *The Francis Preston Blair Family in Politics.* 2 vols. New York: Macmillan, 1933.

Stevens, Thaddeus. *The selected letters of Thaddeus Stevens.* Beverly Wilson Palmer (ed.), 2 vols. Pittsburgh, 1997.

Stoddard, William O. *Abraham Lincoln and Andrew Johnson.* New York, 1888.

———. *Inside the White House in war time.* New York, 1890.

Sumner, Charles. *The works of Charles Sumner.* 15 vols. Boston, 1870–1873.

———. *The selected letters of Charles Sumner.* Beverly Wilson Palmer ed., 2 vols. Boston, 1990.

The Sumter anniversary, 1863. Opinions of loyalists concerning the great question of the times. New York, 1863.

Van Buren, Martin. *Inquiry into the origin and course of Political Parties in the United States.* New York: Hurd and Houghton, 1867

Wallis, Severn Teackle *The Writings of Severn Teackle Wallis.* 4 vols. Baltimore: John Murphy, 1896.

Weed, Thurlow. *Autobiography of Thurlow Weed.* Harriet A. Weed (ed.), Boston, 1883.

———. *Memoir of Thurlow Weed.* Boston, 1884.

Welles, Gideon. *Civil War and Reconstruction: essays.* Albert Morrell (ed.), New York, 1959.

———. *Diary of Gideon Welles, Secretary of the Navy under Lincoln and Johnson.* 3 vols. Boston and New York, 1911.

———. *Lincoln and Seward Remarks upon the memorial address of Chas. Francis Adams, on the late William H. Seward, with incidents and comments illustrative of the measures and policy of the administration of Abraham Lincoln. And views as to the relative positions of the late President and secretary of state.* New York, Sheldon & Company, 1874.

Wormeley, Katherine Prescott. *The United States Sanitary Commission: A Sketch of its Purposes and its Work.* Boston: Little, Brown, 1863.

White, Andrew D. *Autobiography.* 2 vols. New York: Century, 1905.

Wilson, John. *Memories of a Labour Leader: The Autobiography of John Wilson.* London: T. F. Unwin, 1910.

Winthrop, Robert C. *Addresses and speeches on various occasions.* 4 vols. Boston, 1867.

Winthrop, Robert C., Jr. *A memoir of Robert C. Winthrop: prepared for the Massachusetts Historical Society.* Boston: Little, Brown, 1897.

NEWSPAPERS

Microfilm copies of the following newspapers were consulted in the Government Documents Department, Lamont Library, Harvard University; the Boston Public Library; the New Hampshire State Historical Society Library, Concord, New Hampshire; Princeton University Library; the Illinois State Historical Library, Springfield; the Chicago Historical Society; the Library of Congress, Washington DC; and the British Library Newspaper Library at Collindale.

Albany (New York) *Evening Journal*
Albany (NY) *Atlas and Argus*
Boston Daily Evening Transcript
Boston Daily Advertiser
Boston *Post*
Boston *Courier*
Boston *Evening Transcript*
Brooklyn Daily Eagle
The Campaign for the Union (Boston)
Christian Watchman and Reflector (Boston)
Burlington (Vermont) *Sentinel*
Chicago *Tribune*
Chicago *Times*
Cincinnati Daily Enquirer
Cincinnati *Daily Gazette*
Christian Advocate and Journal (New York)
Cincinnati *Western Christian Advocate*
Cleveland *Plain Dealer*
Columbus *Crisis*
Concord (New Hampshire) *Monitor*
Dover (New Hampshire) *Enquirer*
Detroit *Free Press*
Frankfort (Kentucky) *Commonwealth*
Pennsylvania Daily Telegraph (Harrisburg)
Connecticut Courant (Hartford)
Indianapolis *Gazette*
Indianapolis *State Sentinel*
Indianapolis *Daily Journal*
Louisville *Journal*

New Haven *Register*
Louisville *Daily Courier*
Manchester (New Hampshire) *Democrat and Republican*
Christian Advocate and Journal (New York)
Frank Leslie's Illustrated Newspaper (New York)
Harper's Weekly (New York)
Independent (New York)
New-York Daily Tribune
New York Herald
New York Times
New York World
New York *Evening Post*
Philadelphia *Inquirer*
Philadelphia *Press*
Philadelphia *Public Ledger and Daily Transcript*
Philadelphia *Union League Gazette*
Pittsburgh Gazette
Portland (Maine) *Daily Press*
Providence (Rhode Island) *Post*
Daily Illinois State Register (Springfield)
Illinois State Journal (Springfield)
Springfield (Massachusetts) *Republican*
St. Louis (Missouri) *Democrat*
Washington *North American and United States Gazette*
Daily National Intelligencer (Washington, D.C.)
Worcester (Massachusetts) *Palladium*
(Philadelphia) *North American Inquirer*

SECONDARY SOURCES

Books

Abbot, Richard H. *The Republican Party and the South, 1855–1877: The First Southern Strategy*. Chapel Hill: University of North Carolina Press, 1986.
———. *Cotton and Capital: Boston Businessmen and Antislavery Reform, 1854–1868*. Amherst: Massachusetts University Press, 1991.
Aldrich, John H. *Why Parties? The Origin and Development of Party Politics in America*. Chicago: University of Chicago Press, 1995.
Altschuler, Glenn C. and Stuart M. Blumin, *Rude Republic: Americans and Their Politics in the Nineteenth Century*. Princeton, N.J.: Princeton University Press, 2000.
Anbinder, Tyler. *Nativism and Slavery: The Northern Know Nothings and the Politics of the 1850's*. New York: Oxford University Press. 1992
———. *Five Points the 19th-Century New York City Neighborhood that Invented Tap Dance, Stole Elections, and Became the World's Most Notorious Slum*. New York: Free Press, 2001.
Ashworth, John. *"Agrarians" and "Aristocrats": Party Political Ideology in the United States, 1837–1846*. London: Royal Historical Society, 1983.

Baker, Jean H. *Affairs of Party: The Political Culture of Northern Democrats in the Mid-Nineteenth Century.* Ithaca, N.Y.: Cornell University Press, 1983.

———. *The Politics of Continuity: Maryland Political Parties from 1858 to 1870.* Baltimore: Johns Hopkins University Press, 1973.

Baum, Dale. *The Civil War Party System: The Case of Massachusetts, 1848–1876.* Chapel Hill: University of North Carolina Press, 1984.

Baxter, Maurice. *Orville Hickman Browning: Lincoln's Friend and Critic.* Bloomington: University of Indiana Press, 1957.

Beckert, Sven. *Monied Metropolis: New York City and the Consolidation of the American Bourgeoisie, 1850–1896.* New York: Cambridge University Press, 2001.

Belz, Herman. *Abraham Lincoln, Constitutionalism, and Equal Rights in the Civil War Era.* New York: Fordham University Press, 1998.

———. *A New Birth of Freedom: The Republican Party and Freedmen's Rights 1861–1866.* Westport, Conn.: Greenwood Press, 1976.

———. *Reconstructing the Union: Theory and Policy during the Civil War.* Ithica, N.Y.: Cornell University Press, 1969.

Benedict, Michael Les. *A Compromise of Principle: Congressional Republicans and Reconstruction, 1863–1869.* New York: W. W. Norton, 1974.

Bensel, Richard Franklin. *Yankee Leviathan: The Origins of Central State Authority in America, 1859–1877.* New York: Cambridge University Press, 1990.

———. *The American Ballot Box in the Mid Nineteenth Century.* New York: Cambridge University Press, 2004.

Benson, Lee. *The Concept of Jacksonian Democracy: New York as a Test Case* Princeton, N. J.: Princeton University Press, 1967.

Benton, Josiah H. *Voting in the Field: A Forgotten Chapter of the Civil War.* Boston: Plimpton Press, 1915.

Bernstein, Iver. *The New York City Draft Riots, Their Significance for American Society and Politics in the Age of the Civil War.* New York: Oxford University Press, 1990.

Bilotta, James D. *Race and the Rise of the Republican Party, 1848–1865.* New York: V. P. Long, 1992.

Blue, Frederick. *Salmon P. Chase: A Life in Politics.* Kent, Ohio: Kent State University Press, 1987.

Bourke, Paul and DeBats, Donald. *Washington County: Politics and Community in Antebellum America.* Baltimore: Johns Hopkins University Press, 1995.

Bremner, Robert H. *The Public Good: Philanthropy and Welfare in the Civil War Era.* New York: Knopf, 1980.

Bridges, Amy. *A City in the Republic: Antebellum New York and the Origins of Machine Politics.* New York: Cambridge University Press, 1984.

Brown, W. Burlie. *The People's Choice: The Presidential Image in the Campaign Biography.* Baton Rouge: Louisiana State University Press, 1960.

Brummer, Sidney D. *Political History of New York State During the Period of the Civil War.* New York: Columbia University Press, 1911.

Burnham, Walter Dean. *Critical Elections and the Mainsprings of American Politics.* New York: W. W. Norton, 1970.

Campbell, Angus and Philip E. Converse, eds. *The Human Meaning of Social Change.* New York: Russell Sage Foundation, 1972.

Carman, Harry James and Luthin, Reinhard. *Lincoln and the Patronage.* New York: Columbia University Press, 1943.

Carwardine, Richard J. *Evangelicals and Politics in Antebellum America*. New Haven, Conn.: Yale University Press, 1993.

———. *Lincoln*. London: Pearson Education, 2003.

Cashin, Joan E. ed., *The War Was You and Me: Civilians in the American Civil War*. Princeton, N.J.: Princeton University Press, 2002.

Chambers, William Nisbet, and Walter Dean Burnham, eds. *The American Party Systems: Stages of Political Development*. New York: Oxford University Press, 1967.

Chase, James S. *The Emergence of the Presidential Nominating Convention, 1789–1832*. Urbana: University of Illinois Press, 1973.

Clark, Olynthus B. *The Politics of Iowa during the Civil War and Reconstruction*. Iowa City, Iowa: Clio Press, 1911.

Clinton, Catherine and Nina Silber, eds. *Divided Houses: Gender and the Civil War*. New York: Oxford University Press, 1992.

Clubb, Jerome M., Flanigan, William H., and Zingale, Nancy H. *Partisan Realignment: Voters, Parties and Government in American History*. Beverly Hills, Calif.: Sage Publications, 1980.

Cook, Robert. *Baptism of Fire: the Republican Party in Iowa, 1838–1878*. Ames: University of Iowa Press, 1994.

Cooper, William J., Jr. and James M McPherson, eds. *Writing the Civil War*. Columbia: University of South Carolina Press, 1998.

Cooper, William J., Michael F. Holt, and John McCardell eds, *A Master's Due: Essays in Honor of David Herbert Donald*. Baton Rouge: Louisiana State University Press, 1985.

Cox, Lawanda and John H. *Politics, Principle and Prejudice, 1865–1866: Dilemma of Reconstruction America*. New York: Free Press, 1963.

Cox, Lawanda. *Lincoln and Black Freedom: A Study in Presidential Leadership*. Columbia: University of South Carolina Press, 1981.

Crofts, Daniel W. *Reluctant Confederates: Upper South Unionists in the Secession Crisis*. Chapel Hill: University of North Carolina Press, 1989.

Current, Richard N. *Lincoln and the First Shot*. Philadelphia: Lippincott, 1963.

Davis, William C. *Breckinridge: Statesman, Soldier, Symbol*. Baton Rouge: Louisiana State University Press, 1974.

———. *Lincoln's Men: How President Lincoln became a Father to an Army and a Nation*. New York: Free Press, 1999.

Dell, Christopher. *Lincoln and the War Democrats: The Grand Erosion of Conservative Tradition*. Cranbury, N.J.: Farleigh Dickinson University Press, 1975.

Donald, David H. *Lincoln's Herndon*. New York, A.A. Knopf, 1948.

———. *Lincoln Reconsidered: Essays on the Civil War Era*. New York, 1956 (1972 ed.).

———. *Charles Sumner and the Coming of the Civil War*. New York: Knopf, 1960.

———. *Charles Sumner and the Rights of Man*. New York: Knopf, 1970.

———. *The Politics of Reconstruction, 1863–1867*. Baton Rouge: Louisiana State University Press, 1965.

———. *"We Are Lincoln Men": Abraham Lincoln and His Friends*. New York: Simon & Schuster, 2003.

Dusinberre, William. *Civil War Issues in Philadelphia 1856–1865*. Philadelphia: University of Pennsylvania Press, 1965.

Duverger, Maurice, *Political Parties: Their Organization and Activity in the Modern State*. Trans. Barbara North and Robert North. New York: Science Editions, 1963.

Ethington, Phillip J. *The Public City: The Political Construction of Urban Life in San Francisco, 1850–1900.* New York: Cambridge University Press, 1994.

Fehrenbacher, Don E., and Virginia Fehrenbacher, eds. *Recollected Words of Abraham Lincoln.* Palo Alto, Calif.: Stanford University Press, 1996.

Fermer, Douglas. *James Gordon Bennett and the New York Herald: A Study of Editorial Opinion during the Civil War Era, 1854–1867.* London: Royal Historical Society, 1986.

Fellman, Michael. *Inside War: The Guerrilla Conflict in Missouri during the American Civil War.* New York: Oxford University Press, 1989.

Field, Phyllis F. *The Politics of Race in New York: The Struggle for Black Suffrage in the Civil War Era.* Ithaca, N.Y.: Cornell University Press, 1982.

Fields, Barbara J. *Slavery and Freedom on the Middle Ground: Maryland During the Nineteenth Century.* New Haven, Conn.: Yale University press, 1985.

Fiorina, Morris P. *Retrospective Voting in American National Elections.* New Haven, Conn.: Yale University Press, 1981.

Foner, Eric. *Free Soil, Free Labor, Free Men: The Ideology of the Republican Party Before the Civil War.* New York: Oxford University Press, 1970.

———. *Politics and Ideology in the Age of the Civil War.* New York: Oxford University Press, 1980.

Formisano, Ronald P. *The Birth of Mass Political Parties: Michigan, 1827–1861.* Princeton, N. J.: Princeton University Press, 1971.

———. *The Transformation of Political Culture: Massachusetts Parties, 1790s–1840s.* New York: Oxford University Press, 1983.

Formisano, Ronald P. and Constance K. Burns, eds. *Boston, 1700–1980: The Evolution of Urban Politics.* Westport, Conn: Greenwood Press, 1984.

Förster, Stig and Jörg Nagler, *On the Road to Total War: The American Civil War and the German Wars of Unification, 1861–1871.* New York: Cambridge University Press, 1997.

Frank, Joseph Allan. *With Ballot and Bayonet: The Political Socialization of Civil War Soldiers.* Athens: University of Georgia Press, 1998.

Fredrickson, George M. *The Inner Civil War: Northern Intellectuals and the Crisis of the Union.* New York: Harper & Row, 1965.

Freidel, Frank. *Francis Lieber: Nineteenth Century Liberal.* Baton Rouge: Louisiana State University Press, 1947.

Gallagher, Gary. *The Confederate War.* Cambridge, Mass.: Harvard University Press. 1997.

Gallman, Matthew J. *Mastering Wartime: A Social History of Philadelphia during the Civil War.* New York: Cambridge, 1990.

Gambill, Edward L. *Conservative Ordeal: Northern Democrats and Reconstruction.* Ames: Iowa State University Press, 1981.

Geary, James W. *'We Need Men': The Union Draft in the Civil War.* Dekalb: Northern Illinois University Press, 1991.

Geertz, Clifford. *Interpretations of Culture: Selected Essays.* New York: Basic Books, 1973.

Gienapp, William E. *The Origins of the Republican Party, 1862–1856.* New York, 1987.

———. *Abraham Lincoln and Civil War America: A Biography.* New York: Oxford University Press, 2002.

Gillette, William. *Jersey Blue: Civil War Politics in New Jersey, 1854–1865.* New Brunswick, N. J.: Rutgers University Press, 1995.

Grant, Susan-Mary. *North Over South: Northern Nationalism and American Identity in the Antebellum Era.* Lawrence: University of Kansas Press, 2000.

Green, Michael S. *Freedom, Union and Power: The Ideology of the Republican Party in the Civil War.* New York: Fordham University Press, 2004.

Grimsley, Mark. *The Hard Hand of War: Union Military Policy Toward Southern Civilians, 1861–1865.* New York: Cambridge University Press, 1995.

Guelzo, Allen C. *Abraham Lincoln: Redeemer President.* Grand Rapids, Mich.: Eardmans, 1999.

Hall, Peter Dobkin. *The Organization of American Culture, 1700–1900: Private Institutions, Elites and the Origins of American Nationality.* New York: New York University Press, 1982.

Hanham, H. J. *Elections and Party Management in the Time of Disraeli and Gladstone.* London, 1959.

Hansen, Steven. *The Making of the Third Party System: Voters and Parties in Illinois 1850–1876.* Ann Arbor: University of Michigan Press, 1980.

Harper, Robert S. *Lincoln and the Press.* New York: McGraw-Hill, 1958.

Harris, William C. *With Charity for All: Lincoln and the Reconstruction of the Union.* Lexington: University of Kentucky Press, 1997.

Heale, Michael J. *The Presidential Quest: Candidates and Images in American Political Culture: 1787–1852.* New York: Longman, 1982.

Hendrick, Burton J. *Lincoln's War Cabinet.* Boston: Little, Brown, 1946.

Henig, Gerald S. *Henry Winter Davis: Antebellum and Civil War Congressman from Maryland.* New York: Twayne, 1973.

Hess, Earl J. *Liberty, Virtue and Progress: Northerners and Their War for the Union.* New York: New York University Press, 1988.

Hesseltine, William B. *Lincoln and the War Governors.* New York: Knopf, 1955.

Hofstadter, Richard. *The Idea of a Party System: The Rise of Legitimate Opposition in the United States, 1780–1840.* Berkeley: University of California Press, 1969.

———. *The Paranoid Style in American Politics and Other Essays.* New York: Knopf, 1965.

Holt, Michael F. *The Political Crisis of the 1850s.* New York: Wiley, 1978.

———. *Political Parties and American Political Development from the Age of Jackson to the Age of Lincoln.* Baton Rouge: Louisiana State University Press, 1992.

———. *The Rise and Fall of the American Whig Party: Jacksonian Politics and the Onset of the Civil War.* New York: Oxford University Press, 1999

Howard, Victor B. *Religion and the Radical Republican Movement, 1860–1870.* Lexington: University of Kentucky Press, 1990.

Howe, Daniel Walker. *The Unitarian Conscience: Harvard Moral Philosophy, 1805–1861.* Cambridge, Mass.: Harvard University Press, 1970.

———, ed. *The American Whigs: An Anthology.* New York: Wiley, 1973.

———. *The Political Culture of the American Whigs.* Chicago: University of Chicago Press, 1979.

Hunt, H. Draper. *Hannibal Hamlin of Maine: Lincoln's First Vice President.* Syracuse, N.Y.: Syracuse University Press, 1969.

Hyman, Harold M. *Era of the Oath: Northern Loyalty Tests during the Civil War and Reconstruction.* Philadelphia: Pennsylvania University Press, 1954.

———. *A More Perfect Union: The Impact of the Civil War and Reconstruction on the Constitution.* New York: Alfred A. Knopf, 1973.

————, ed., *The Radical Republicans and Reconstruction, 1861–1870*. Indianapolis: Bobbs-Merrill, 1967.

Jaffa, Harry V. *A New Birth of Freedom: Abraham Lincoln and the Coming of the Civil War*. Banham, Md.: Bowman and Littlefield, 2000.

Jacobs, Meg, William J. Novak, and Julien E. Zelizer, eds. *The Democratic Experiment: New Directions in American Political History*. Princeton, N. J.: Princeton University Press, 2003.

Johannsen, Robert W. *Stephen A. Douglas*. New York: Oxford University Press, 1973.

Katz, Irving. *August Belmont: A Political Biography*. New York: Columbia University Press, 1968.

Kelley, Robert. *The Transatlantic Persuasion: The Liberal-Democratic Mind in the Age of Gladstone*. New York: Alfred A. Knopf, 1969.

Ketcham, Ralph. *Presidents above Party: the First American Presidency, 1789–1829*. Chapel Hill: University of North Carolina Press, 1984.

Keyssar, Alexander. *The Right to Vote: The Contested History of Democracy in the United States*. New York: Basic Books, 2000.

Klement, Frank L. *The Copperheads in the Middle West*. Chicago: University of Chicago Press, 1960.

————. *The Limits of Dissent: Clement L. Vallandigham and the Civil War*. Lexington: University of Kentucky Press, 1970.

————. *Dark Lanterns: Secret Political Societies, Conspiracies and Treason Trials in the Civil War*. Baton Rouge: Louisiana University Press, 1984.

Kleppner, Paul. *The Third Electoral System, 1853–1892: Parties, Voters and Political Cultures*. Chapel Hill: University of North Carolina Press, 1979.

————, ed. *The Evolution of American Electoral Systems*. Westport, Conn.: Greenwood Press, 1981.

Knupfer, Peter. *The Union As It Is: Constitutional Unionism and Sectional Compromise, 1787–1861*. Chapel Hill: University of North Carolina Press, 1991.

Kruman, Marc. *Parties and Politics in North Carolina, 1836–1865*. Baton Rouge, Louisiana State University Press, 1983.

Lane, J. Robert. *A Political History of Connecticut During the Civil War*. Washington, D.C.: Catholic University of America Press, Washington, 1941

Lawson, Melinda. *Patriot Fires: Forging a New American Nationalism in the Civil War North*. Lawrence: University of Kansas Press, 2002.

Leonard, Gerald. *The Invention of Party Politics: Federalism, Popular Sovereignty and Constitutional Development in Jacksonian Illinois*. Chapel Hill: University of North Carolina Press, 2003.

Lindsey, David. *"Sunset" Cox: Irrepressible Democrat*. Detroit: Wayne State University Press, 1959.

Long, David E. *The Jewel of Liberty: Abraham Lincoln's Re-election and the End of Slavery*. Mechanicsburg, Pa.: Stackpole, 1994.

Maizlish, Stephen E. and John J. Kushuma, eds. *Essays on American Antebellum Politics, 1840–1860*. College Station: Texas A&M University Press, 1982.

Maxwell, William Q. *Lincoln's Fifth Wheel: The Sanitary Commission*. New York: Longmans, Green, 1956.

Mayhew, David. *Electoral Realignments: A Critique of an American Genre*. New Haven: Yale University Press, 2002.

McCormick, Richard L. *The Party Period and Public Policy: American Politics from the Age of Jackson to the Progressive Era.* New York: Oxford University Press, 1986.

McGerr, Michael E. *The Decline of Popular Politics: The American North, 1865–1920.* New York: Oxford University Press, 1986.

McJimsey, George. *Genteel Partisan: Manton Marble, 1834–1917.* Ames: University of Iowa Press, 1971.

McKay, Ernest A. *The Civil War and New York City.* Syracuse, N.Y.: University of Syracuse Press, 1990.

McPherson, James M. *Battle Cry of Freedom: The Civil War Era.* New York: Oxford University Press, 1988.

———. *Abraham Lincoln and the Second American Revolution.* New York: Oxford University Press, 1990.

———. *The Struggle for Equality: Abolitionists and the Negro in the Civil War and Reconstruction.* Princeton, N.J.: Princeton University Press, 1964.

———., ed. *'We Cannot Escape History': Lincoln and the Last Best Hope of Earth.* Urbana: Illinois University Press, 1995.

———. *For Cause and Comrades: Why Men Fought in the Civil War.* New York: Oxford University Press, 1997.

McPherson, James M. and William J. Cooper, Jr., eds. *Writing the Civil War: The Quest to Understand.* Columbia: University of South Carolina Press, 1998.

Mitchell, Stewart. *Horatio Seymour of New York.* Cambridge, Mass.: Harvard University Press, 1938.

Montgomery, David. *Beyond Equality: Labor and the Radical Republicans, 1862–1872.* New York: Knopf, 1967.

Moorhead, James H. *American Apocalypse: Yankee Protestants and the American Civil War, 1860–1869.* New Haven, Conn.: Yale University Press, 1978.

Mott, Frank Luther. *American Journalism: A History of Newspapers in the United States through 250 Years, 1690 to 1940.* New York: Macmillan, 1947.

Mushkat, Jerome. *The Reconstruction of the New York Democracy, 1861–1874.* Rutherford, N.J.: Farleigh Dickinson University Press, 1981.

———. *Fernando Wood: A Political Biography.* Kent, Ohio: Kent State University Press, 1990.

Neely, Mark E. *The Fate of Liberty: Abraham Lincoln and Civil Liberties.* New York: Oxford University Press, 1991.

———. *The Divided Union: Party Conflict in the Civil War North.* Cambridge, Mass.: Harvard University Press, 2002

Nelson, Larry E. *Bullets, Ballots, and Rhetoric: Confederate Policy for the United States Presidential Contest of 1864.* Tuscaloosa: University of Alabama Press, 1976.

Nevins, Allan. *Frémont: Pathmarker of the West.* New York: Longmans, 1955.

Newman, Simon P. *Parades and the Politics of the Street: Festive Culture in the Early American Republic.* Philadelphia: University of Pennsylvania Press, 1997.

Nichols, Roy F. *The Invention of the American Political Parties: A Study in Political Improvisation.* New York: Free Press, 1967.

Nicolay, John and John Hay, *Abraham Lincoln: A History*, 10 vols. New York: Century Co., 1890.

Niven, John. *Connecticut for the Union: The Role of the State in the Civil War.* New Haven, Conn.: Yale University Press, 1965.

———. *Gideon Welles: Lincoln's Secretary of the Navy.* New York: Oxford University Press, 1973.

——. *Salmon P. Chase: A Biography*. New York: Oxford University Press, 1995.

North, S. N. D. *History and Present Conditions of the Newspaper and Periodical Press of the United States*. Washington: General Printing Office, 1880.

Nossiter, T. J. *Influence, Opinion and Political Idioms in Reformed England: Case Studies From the North East, 1832–1874*. Brighton: Harvester Press, 1975.

O'Connor, Thomas H. *Lords of the Loom: The Cotton Whigs and the Coming of the Civil War*. New York: Scribner, 1968.

——. *Civil War Boston: Home front and Battlefield*. Boston: Northeastern University Press, 1997.

O'Gorman, Frank. *The Emergence of the British Two-Party System 1760–1832*. London: Edward Arnold, 1982.

——. *Voters, Patrons, and Parties: The Unreformed Electoral System of Hanoverian England, 1734–1832*. Oxford: Oxford University Press, 1989.

Paludan, Phillip Shaw. *'A People's Contest': The Union and Civil War, 1861–1865*. New York: Harper & Row, 1988.

——. *The Presidency of Abraham Lincoln*. Lawrence: University of Kansas Press, 1994.

Parish, Peter J. *The American Civil War*. London: Eyre Methuen, 1975.

——. *The North and the Nation in the Era of the Civil War*. Adam I. P. Smith and Susan-Mary Grant, eds. New York: Fordham University Press, 2003.

Parrish, William E. *Frank Blair: Lincoln's Conservative*. Columbia: University of Missouri Press, 1998.

——. *Turbulent Partnership: Missouri and the Union, 1861–1865*. Columbia: University of Missouri Press, 1963.

Pearson, Henry G. *The Life of John A. Andrew, Governor of Massachusetts, 1861–1865*, 2 vols. Boston: Houghton Mifflin, 1904.

Phillips, John A. *Electoral Behaviour in Unreformed England: Plumpers, Splitters and Straights*. Princeton, N. J.: Princeton University Press, 1982.

——. *The Great Reform Bill in the Boroughs: English Electoral Behaviour:, 1818–1841*. Oxford: Oxford University Press, 1992.

Porter, George H. *Ohio Politics during the Civil War Period*. New York: Columbia University Press, 1911.

Potter, David M. *Lincoln and His Party in the Secession Crisis*. New Haven, Conn.: Yale University Press, 1942.

Rable, George C. *The Confederate Republic: A Revolution Against Politics*. Chapel Hill: University of North Carolina Press, 1994.

Rakove, Jack N. *Original Meanings: Politics and Ideas in the Making of the Constitution*. New York: Knopf, 1996.

Randall, James G. *Lincoln the President*. 4 vols., completed and edited by Richard N. Current. New York: Dodd Mead, 1945–1955.

Rash, Nancy. *The Paintings and Politics of George Caleb Bingham*. New Haven, Conn.: Yale University Press, 1991.

Ratcliffe, Donald J. *Party Spirit in a Frontier Republic: Democratic Politics in Ohio, 1793–1821*. Columbus: Ohio State University Press, 1998.

——. *The Politics of Long Division: The Birth of the Second Party System in Ohio, 1818–1828*. Columbus: Ohio State University Press, 2000.

Rawley, James A. *Edwin D. Morgan, 1811–1883*. New York, 1955.

——. *The Politics of Union: Northern Politics during the Civil War*. Hinsdale, Ill.: Dryden Press, 1974.

Renda, Lex. *Running on the Record: Civil War Politics in New Hampshire.* Charlottesville: University of Virginia Press, 1997.

Richards, Leonard. *'Gentlemen of Property and Standing': Anti-Abolition Mobs in Jacksonian America.* New York, 1970.

Richardson, Heather Cox. *The Greatest Nation of the Earth: Republican Economic Policies during the Civil War.* Cambridge, Mass.: Harvard University Press, 1997.

Rose, Anne C. *Victorian American and the Civil War.* New York: Cambridge University Press, 1992.

Ryan, Mary P. *Civic Wars: Democracy and Public Life in the American City during the Nineteenth Century.* Berkeley: University of California Press, 1997.

Shafer, Byron E. and Anthony J. Badger, eds. *Contesting Democracy: Substance and Structure in American Political History, 1775–2000.* Lawrence: University of Kansas Press, 2001.

Schattschneider, E. E. *Party Government.* New York: Rinehart, 1942.

Schlesinger, Arthur M. Jr., ed. *History of American Presidential Elections, 1789–1968.* New York: Chelsea House, 1971.

Schudson, Michael. *Discovering the News: A Social History of American Newspapers.* New York: Basic Books, 1978.

———. *The Good Citizen: A History of American Civic Life.* New York: Martin Kessler Books, 1998.

Sears, Stephen W. *George B. McClellan: The Young Napoleon.* New York: Ticknor & Fields, 1988.

Shade, William G. *Banks or No Banks: The Money Issue in Western Politics, 1832–1865.* Detroit: Wayne State University Press, 1972.

Shade, William L. *Social Change and the Electoral Process.* Gainsville: University of Florida Press, 1973.

Shankman, Arnold M. *The Pennsylvania Antiwar Movement, 1861–1865.* Rutherford, N.J.: Fairleigh Dickinson University Press, 1980.

Silbey, Joel H. *A Respectable Minority: The Democratic Party in the Civil War Era, 1860–1868.* New York: Norton, 1977.

———. *The Partisan Imperative: The Dynamics of American Politics before the Civil War.* New York: Oxford University Press, 1985.

———. *The American Political Nation, 1838–1893.* Palo Alto, Calif.: Stanford University Press, 1991.

Silbey, Joel H., Allan G. Bogue, and William H. Flanigan, eds. *The History of American Electoral Behavior.* Princeton, N. J.: Princeton University Press, 1978.

Silvestro, Clement M. *Rally Round the Flag: The Union League in the Civil War, Clarence M. Burton Memorial lecture 1966.* Lansing, Mich.: Historical Society of Michigan, 1966.

Simpson, Brooks D. *Let Us Have Peace: Ulysses S. Grant and the Politics of War and Reconstruction, 1861–1868.* Chapel Hill: University of North Carolina Press, 1991.

Skowronek, Stephen. *Building a New American State: The Expansion of National Administrative Capacities, 1877–1920.* New York: Cambridge University Press, 1982

Smith, Culver Haygood. *The Press, Politics, and Patronage: The American Government's Use of Newspapers, 1789–1875.* Athens: University of Georgia Press, 1977.

Smith, Edward Conrad. *The Borderland in the Civil War.* New York: Macmillan, 1927.

Smith, Kimberly K. *Dominion of Voice: Riot, Reason, and Romance in Antebellum Politics.* Lawrence: University of Kansas Press, 1999.

Stampp, Kenneth M. *And the War Came: The North and the Secession Crisis.* Baton Rouge: Louisiana State University Press, 1950.

———. *Indiana Politics during the Civil War.* Indianapolis: Indiana Historical Bureau, 1949.

Summers, Mark Wahlgren. *The Plundering Generation: Corruption and the Crisis of the Union, 1849–1861.* New York: Oxford University Press, 1987.

Taylor, John M. *William Henry Seward: Lincoln's Right Hand Man.* New York: Harper Collins, 1991.

Thomas, John L., ed. *Abraham Lincoln and the American Political Tradition.* Amherst: University of Massachusetts Press, 1986.

Thorndike, S. Lothrop. *A Brief Sketch of the History of the Union Club of Boston.* Boston: Union Club, 1893.

Thornton, J. Mills. *Politics and Power in a Slave Society: Alabama, 1800–1860.* Baton Rouge: Louisiana State University Press, 1978.

Townsend, Reginald. *Mother of Clubs: Being the History of the First Hundred Years of the Union Club of the City of New York.* New York: W. E. Rudge, 1936.

Travers, Len. *Celebrating the Fourth: Independence Day and the Rites of Nationalism in the Early Republic.* Amherst: University of Massachusetts Press, 1997.

Trefouse, Hans L. *Ben Butler: The South Called Him Beast!* New York: Twayne Publishers, 1957.

———. *Benjamin Franklin Wade: Radical Republican from Ohio.* New York: Twayne Publishers, 1963.

———. *Carl Schurz: A Biography.* Knoxville: University of Tennessee Press, 1982.

Tunnell, Ted. *Crucible of Reconstruction: War, Radicalism, and Race in Louisiana,* Baton Rouge: Louisiana State University Press, 1984.

Van Deusen, Glyndon G. *William Henry Seward.* New York: Oxford University Press, 1967.

———. *Thurlow Weed: Wizard of the Lobby.* New York: DaCapo Press, 1969.

Vernon, James. *Politics and the People: A Study in English Political Culture, c1815–1867.* Cambridge UK: Cambridge University Press, 1993.

Voegeli, V. Jaques. *Free but Not Equal: The Midwest and the Negro during the Civil War.* Chicago: University of Chicago Press, 1967.

Vorenberg, Michael. *Final Freedom: The Civil War, the Abolition of Slavery and the Thirteenth Amendment.* New York: Cambridge University Press, 2001.

Voss-Hubbard, Mark. *Beyond Party: Cultures of Antipartisanship in Northern Politics before the Civil War.* Baltimore: Johns Hopkins University Press, 2002.

Waldstreicher, David. *In the Midst of Perpetual Fetes: The Making of American Nationalism, 1776–1820.* Chapel Hill: University of North Carolina Press, 1997.

Wang, Xi. *The Trial of Democracy: Black Suffrage and Northern Republicans, 1860–1910.* Athens: University of Georgia Press, 1997.

Waugh, John C. *Reelecting Lincoln: The Battle for the Presidency in 1864.* New York: Crown, 1998.

Whiteman, Maxwell. *Gentlemen in Crisis: The First Century of the Union League of Philadelphia, 1862–1962.* Philadelphia: Union League, 1975.

Wiebe, Robert H. *The Opening of American Society: From the Adoption of the Constitution to the Eve of Disunion.* New York: Knopf, 1984.

Wiebe, Robert H. *The Search for Order, 1877–1920*. New York: New York: Hill and Wang, 1967.

———. *Self-Rule: A Cultural History of American Democracy*. Chicago: University of Chicago Press, 1995.

Williams, Frank J., Pederson, William D., and Marsala, Vincent J. *Abraham Lincoln: Sources and Style of Leadership*. Westport, Conn.: Greenwood Press, 1994.

Williams, T. Harry. *Lincoln and the Radicals*. Madison: University of Wisconsin Press, 1941.

Wilson, Major. *Space, Time and Freedom*. Westport, Conn.: Greenwood Press, 1974.

Wright, Conrad. *The Liberal Christians: Essays on American Unitarian History*. Boston: Beacon Press, 1970.

Wood, Forest G. *Black Scare: The Racist Response to Emancipation and Reconstruction*. Berkeley: University of California Press, 1968.

Wood, Gordon S. *The Creation of the American Republic, 1776–1787*. Chapel Hill: University of North Carolina Press, 1969.

Wubben, Hubert W. *Civil War Iowa and the Copperhead Movement*. Ames: Iowa State University Press, 1980.

Zornow, William F. *Lincoln and the Party Divided*. Norman: University of Oklahoma Press, 1954.

Journal Articles

Abzug, Robert H. "The Copperheads: Historical Approaches to Civil War Dissent in the Midwest." *Indiana Magazine of History* 66 (1970): 40–55.

Alexander, Thomas B. "Persistent Whiggery in the Confederate South, 1860–1877." *Journal of Southern History*, 27 (1961): 305–29.

Altschuler, Glenn C. and Stuart M. Blumin. "Limits of Political Engagement in Antebellum America: A New Look at the Golden Age of Participatory Democracy." *Journal of American History* 84 (1997): 855–85.

Anbinder, Tyler G. "Fernando Wood and New York City's Secession from the Union: A Political Reappraisal." *New York History* 68 (1987): 67–92.

Appleby, Joyce. "Republicanism and Ideology." *American Quarterly*, 37:4 (Fall 1985): 461–73.

Argersinger, Peter. "New Pespectives on Election Fraud in the Gilded Age." *Political Science Quarterly* 100 (Winter 1985–1986): 669–87.

———. "The Value of the Vote: Political Representation in the Gilded Age." *Journal of American History* 76 (June 1989): 59–90.

Avillo, Phillips, Jr. "Ballots for the Faithful: The Oath and the Emergence of Slave State Republican Congressmen, 1861–1867," *Civil War History* 22 (1976): 164–74.

Baker, Jean H. "A Loyal Opposition: Northern Democrats and the Thirty-Seventh Congress." *Civil War History* 25 (1979): 139–55.

———. "Politics, Paradigms, and Public Culture." *Journal of American History* 84 (December 1997): 894–99.

Banning, Lance. "Jeffersonian Ideology Revisited: Liberal and Classical Ideas in the New American Republic." *William and Mary Quarterly* 43 (Jan. 1986): 3–19.

Carwardine, Richard J. "Lincoln, Evangelical Religion and American Political Culture in the Era of the Civil War." *Journal of the Abraham Lincoln Association* 18 (1997): 27–55.

Crofts, Daniel W. "The Union Party of 1861 and the Secession Crisis." *Perspectives in American History* 11 (1977–1978): 325–76.

Curry, Leonard. "Congressional Democrats 1861–1863." *Civil War History* 12 (1966): 213–29.

Demos, John. "George Caleb Bingham: The Artist as Social Historian." *American Quarterly* 17 (Summer 1965): 218–28.

Dennett, Tyler. "Lincoln and the Campaign of 1864." *Abraham Lincoln Association Papers for 1935*: 31–58.

Dunning, William A. "The Second Birth of the Republican Party." *American Historical Review* 16 (1910): 56–63.

Fehrenbacher, Don E. "The Making of a Myth: Lincoln and the Vice-Presidential Nomination in 1864." *Civil War History* 41 (December 1995): 273–90.

Fladeland, Betty L. "Compensated Emancipation: A Rejected Altenative." *Journal of Southern History* 42 (May 1976): 169–86.

Foner, Eric, "The Meaning of Freedom in the Age of Emancipation." *Journal of American History* 81 (September 1994): 435–60.

Formisano, Ronald P. "Political Character, Antipartyism and the Second Party System." *American Quarterly* 21:4 (Winter, 1969): 683–709.

———. "The "Party Period" Revisited." *Journal of American History* 86 (June 1999): 93–120.

Freeman, Joanne B. "The Culture of Politics: The Politics of Culture." *The Journal of Policy History* 16 (2004): 137–43.

Freidel, Frank. "The Loyal Publication Society: A Pro-Union Propaganda Agency." *Mississippi Valley Historical Review* 26 (1939): 359–76.

Gendzel, Glen. "Political Culture: Genealogy of a Concept." *Journal of Interdisciplinary History* 37 (1997): 225–50.

Gerteis, Louis S. "Salmon P. Chase, Radicalism and the Politics of Emancipation, 1861–1864." *Journal of American History* 60 (June 1973): 42–62.

Gienapp, William E. "Nativism and the Creation of a Republican Majority in the North before the Civil War." *Journal of American History* 72 (1985): 529–59.

Hanna, William. "The Boston Draft Riot." *Civil War History* 36 (1990): 260–75.

Harris, William C. "Conservative Unionists and the Presidential Election of 1864." *Civil War History* 37 (1992): 298–318.

Hays, Samuel. "Society and Politics: Politics and Society." *Journal of Interdisciplinary History* 15 (Winter 1985).

Holt, Michael F. "A Moving Target: President Lincoln Confronts a Two-Party System Still in the Making." Paper delivered to the Abraham Lincoln Association Symposium, 2004.

———. "The Primacy of Party Reasserted." *Journal of American History* 86 (June 1999): 151–57.

Howe, Daniel Walker. "The Evangelical Movement and Political Culture in the North During the Second Party System." *The Journal of American History* 77:4 (1991): 1216–39.

Johannsen, Robert W. "The Douglas Democracy and the Crisis of Disunion." *Civil War History* 9 (1963): 229–47.

Kaplan, Sidney. "The Miscegination Issue in the Election of 1864." *Journal of Negro History* 34 (1949): 274–343.

Klement, Frank L. "Midwestern Opposition to Lincoln's Emancipation Policy." *Journal of Negro History* 49 (1946): 169–83.

Kruman, Marc W. "The Second American Party System and the Transformation of Revolutionary Republicanism." *Journal of the Early Republic* 12 (Winter 1992): 509–37.

Mayo, Edward L. "Republicanism, Antipartyism, and Jacksonian Party Politics: A View from the Nation's Capital." *American Quarterly* 31:1 (Spring, 1979): 3–20.

McCormick, Richard L. "The Realignment Synthesis in American History." *Journal of Interdisciplinary History* 13 (Summer 1982): 85–105.

McSeveney, Samuel T. "Re-electing Lincoln: The Union Party Campaign and the Military Vote in Connecticut." *Civil War History* 32 (1986): 139–58.

O'Gorman, Frank. "The Social Meaning of Elections." *Past and Present* 135 (1992): 79–115.

Rogers, Daniel T. "Republicanism: Career of a Concept." *Journal of American History* 79:1 (June 1992): 11–38.

Sears, Stephen W. "McClellan and the Peace Plank of 1864: A Reappraisal." *Civil War History* 36 (1990): 57–64.

Shalhope, Robert E. "Republicanism and Early American Historiography." *William and Mary Quarterly* 39 (April 1982), 334–56.

———. "Toward a Republican Synthesis: The Emergence of an Understanding of Republicanism in American Historiography." *William and Mary Quarterly* 29 (Jan. 1972): 49–80.

Shankman, Arnold. "Soldier votes and Clement L. Vallandigham in the 1863 Ohio Gubernatorial Election," *Ohio History* 82 (1973): 88–104.

Smith, George Winston "The National War Committee of the Citizens of New York." *New York History* 28 (October, 1947): 440–57.

———. "Broadsides for Freedom: Civil War Propaganda in New England." *The New England Quarterly* (September 1948): 291–313.

———. "Union Propaganda in the American Civil War." *Social Studies* 35 (1943): 26–32.

Stampp, Kenneth M. "The Milligan Case and the Election of 1864 in Indiana." *Mississippi Valley Historical Review* 31 (June 1944): 41–58.

Stanley, Gerald. "Civil War Politics in California." *Southern California Quarterly* 64 (1982): 115–32.

Trefouse, Hans L. "Zachariah Chandler and the Withdrawal of Fremont in 1864: New Answer to an Old Riddle." *Lincoln Herald* 70 (1968): 181–88.

Van Riper, Paul and Sutherland, Keith A. "The Northern Civil Service: 1861–1865." *Civil War History* 11 (1965): 351–69.

Voss-Hubbard, Mark. "The 'Third Party Tradition' Reconsidered: Third Parties and American Public Life, 1830–1900." *Journal of American History* 86 (June 1999): 121–50.

Wallace, Michael. "Changing Concepts of Party in the United States: New York, 1815–1828." *American Historical Review* 74 (1968): 453–91.

White, Jonathan W. "Citizens and Soldiers: Party Competition and the Debate in Pennsylvania over Permitting Soldiers to Vote, 1861–64." *American Nineteenth Century History* 5.2 (Summer 2004): 47–70.

Williams, T. Harry. "Voters in Blue." *Mississippi Valley Historical Review* 31 (1944): 187–204.

Wilson, Major "Republicanism and the Idea of Party in the Jacksonian Period." *Journal of the Early Republic* 8 (Winter 1988).

Winther, Oscar. "Soldier Voting in the Election of 1864." *New York History* 25 (1944): 440–58.

Young, James Harvey. "Anna Elizabeth Dickinson and the Civil War: For and Against Lincoln." *Mississippi Valley Historical Review* 31 (June 1944): 59–80.

Unpublished Dissertations

Nelson, Russell K. "The Early Life and Congressional Career of Elihu B. Washburne." PhD diss., University of North Dakota, 1953.